Natural Law and Human Dignity

Studies in Contemporary German Social Thought
Thomas McCarthy, General Editor

Theodor W. Adorno, *Against Epistemology: A Metacritique*

Theodor W. Adorno, *Prisms*

Karl-Otto Apel, *Understanding and Explanation: A Transcendental-Pragmatic Perspective*

Richard J. Bernstein, editor, *Habermas and Modernity*

Ernst Bloch, *Natural Law and Human Dignity*

Hans Blumenberg, *The Legitimacy of the Modern Age*

Hans Blumenberg, *Work on Myth*

Helmut Dubiel, *Theory and Politics: Studies in the Development of Critical Theory*

John Forester, editor, *Critical Theory and Public Life*

Hans-Georg Gadamer, *Philosophical Apprenticeships*

Hans-Georg Gadamer, *Reason in the Age of Science*

Jürgen Habermas, *Philosophical-Political Profiles*

Jürgen Habermas, editor, *Observations on "The Spiritual Situation of the Age"*

Hans Joas, *G. H. Mead: A Contemporary Re-examination of His Thought*

Reinhart Koselleck, *Futures Past: On the Semantics of Historical Time*

Claus Offe, *Contradictions of the Welfare State*

Claus Offe, *Disorganized Capitalism: Contemporary Transformations of Work and Politics*

Helmut Peukert, *Science, Action, and Fundamental Theology: Toward a Theology of Communicative Action*

Joachim Ritter, *Hegel and the French Revolution: Essays on the* Philosophy of Right

Alfred Schmidt, *History and Structure: An Essay on Hegelian-Marxist and Structuralist Theories of History*

Carl Schmitt, *Political Theology: Four Chapters on the Concept of Sovereignty*

Carl Schmitt, *The Crisis of Parliamentary Democracy*

Michael Theunissen, *The Other: Studies in the Social Ontology of Husserl, Heidegger, Sartre, and Buber*

Natural Law and Human Dignity

Ernst Bloch
translated by Dennis J. Schmidt

The MIT Press, Cambridge, Massachusetts, and London, England

This translation © 1986 by The Massachusetts Institute of Technology. Originally published as *Naturrecht und menschliche Würde*, © 1961 by Suhrkamp Verlag, Frankfurt, Federal Republic of Germany.

This book was set in Baskerville by The MIT Press Computergraphics Department and was printed and bound by The Murray Printing Co. in the United States of America.

Library of Congress Cataloging-in-Publication Data

Bloch, Ernst, 1885–1977.
Natural law and human dignity.

(Studies in contemporary German social thought)
Translation of: Naturrecht und menschliche Würde.
Includes index.
1. Natural law. 2. Law—Philosophy. I. Title. II. Series.
K474.B56N3713 1986   171'.2   85-18167
ISBN 0-262-02221-4

Contents

Translator's Introduction: In the Spirit of Bloch
Dennis J. Schmidt

The question of law and the cause of rights has, for the most part, been absent from the agenda of social revolution. This lacuna, while troubling to many, seems inexorable: The conceptual frame that called and accounted for change was largely resistant to the static demands of law and rights. Consequently, any effort to wed the demands of law and rights to the agenda of social revolution would require a fundamental rethinking of the structure of political thought in order to reconcile otherwise antagonistic intentions. In short, any such effort would have to first undercut the prevailing outlines and foundations that have traditionally guided political philosophy. The intention of this book is precisely such a radical restructuring of our understanding of the social world. Taking the idea of natural law as his guiding thought, Bloch's intention is to show how revolution and right, rather than being antagonistic demands, are functionally and fundamentally interconnected.

To those already acquainted with Ernst Bloch's work such a sweeping and synthetic effort comes as no surprise. Indeed such refunctioning of concepts and reformulation of structures is the trademark of Bloch's work. But since Bloch has yet to gain the wide recognition and influence in the English-speaking world that he has long enjoyed on the Continent, some remarks about Bloch and his general philosophical project may help the reader in approaching this original and often difficult book.

Heritages

Bloch was born to Jewish parents on July 8, 1885. In a brief auto-biographical sketch he remarks on some of the juxtapositions and contradictions that impressed him as a child growing up in Ludwig-shafen, and that later surfaced as issues in his work:

Not incidentally and not without lasting effect, I was born in an industrial city in the southern, Bavarian, region of Germany. When I was born Ludwigshafen had some thirty thousand inhabitants and the city itself was just forty years old. Ugly, it wore the naked, pitiless face of late capitalism; the starving, ragged, exploited proletariat there enjoyed nothing of the so-called spiritual life.

On the other side of the Rhine there is the ancient imperial city of Mannheim, which is still famous today for its magnificent theater.

The difference between the two cities is that Mannheim had the largest theater in Germany, while Ludwigshafen had the largest factory, namely, I. G. Farben. . . . This conjunction of so many historical forces in one place led to provocations that [I] noticed early in life.[1]

Bloch's frequent allusions to the dissonances of living in sight of both the ugliest aspects of late capitalism and the magnificent spires of medieval cathedrals, of living in the "presence of noncontemporaneity," reflect a set of conflicts that haunted him throughout his life. Indeed, Bloch's lengthy career, though encyclopedic in scope, can be understood as a sustained and passionate effort to understand and overcome the inequities and injustices he found symbolized in such contradictions. The question announced in the first words of this book, "What is justice? What is right?," though answered through a rethinking of some of the most abstract texts in the Western tradition, has nothing abstract about it for Bloch: "We cannot avoid this question; it always demands our attention; it forces itself upon us and points out a path for us." One often senses that here an ancient question, though answered in new ways, is asked by one who had known and witnessed new forms of ancient injustices. Habermas's remark that the circumstances of Bloch's life and the external history of his books reflect the same point as the internal history of those books—"the odyssey of a mind from the spirit of exodus"[2]—is quite true. One ought not forget Bloch's experience of exile from 1933 to 1949 because the laws of his country sought to strip him of his dignity, if not his life. Remembering this, one can well understand the hopes that accompanied his return to East Germany, where he saw a chance to reconstruct society and the idea of the state on the basis of a "rectified" past. His decision to seek asylum in West Germany during the building of the Berlin Wall (carrying the manuscript of *Natural Law and Human Dignity* with him) was yet another move in a long personal odyssey. Significantly his inaugural lecture at the University of Tübingen was entitled "Can Hope Be Disappointed?" His answer was that it can, for failure and loss belong to the true essence of hope just as much as success and gain. This book was composed in East Germany during the period of Bloch's efforts to understand the failures of the Marxist tradition (in which he still placed his hope). It was published in West Germany when Bloch was seventy-six years old and is clearly the product of a lengthy personal and philosophical odyssey. Such is the sensibility that drives the search for what Bloch called the orthopedia of the upright carriage.

Bloch's career first flowered with the publication of *Spirit of Utopia* in 1923 and lasted until the publication of *Experimentum Mundi* two years before his death in 1977. Thus, his intellectual development covered not only the entry into modernism but the postwar critique of modernity and the assertions of "postmodernism" as well. Throughout he always seemed to be at the center of European intellectual developments, thanks to his own work and his friendships (with Brecht, Lukács, Benjamin, Weill, and Adorno), as well as the attention drawn to him by his masterful oratorical style. Yet the intellectual heritage of this distinctively twentieth-century thinker is deeply rooted in the Western tradition.

Bloch's intellectual temperament was shaped by a number of currents that ushered in the twentieth century. His studies with the philosopher and sociologist Georg Simmel proved an early influence. Simmel was a leading representative of *Lebensphilosophie* (also associated with the names Dilthey and Bergson), and though Bloch was disturbed by Simmel's lack of system, he did find here further ways in which his own efforts to concretize philosophy could be realized.[3] When Bloch met Lukács in one of Simmel's seminars, he found Lukács's efforts to develop the metaphysics of a dialectic of life and form congenial to his own purposes, and so it is not surprising that the friendship that formed between them left a lasting reciprocal philosophical mark. It was during this period (1908–1911) that Bloch began to develop a systematic metaphysics that did not reify and objectify the lived content of concrete experience, but was able to preserve the inherent future-oriented openness and "darkness" of all real experience.

Two further elements made essential contributions to the shape of Bloch's thought: messianic mysticism and twentieth-century expressionism. Both of these movements offered means by which Bloch could move away from the languages and ideologies of traditional metaphysics. Messianism understood the open-ended, future-oriented dimension of the present, while expressionism sought to preserve the disparities, contradictions, and discontinuities inherent in the present as the nexus of conflicting historical currents. Neither expressionism nor messianism shaped Bloch's philosophical intentions, but he found in each elements of something required for their fulfillment, namely, a philosophical style and methodology that would not distort those intentions. Both of these movements appeared to Bloch as a means of developing a form of expression which armored his own position against any erosion into formulas and closure and which resisted easy co-optation of his intentions.[4] They also make reading Bloch a difficult and intimidating matter. Most of the peculiarities of Bloch's prose and presentation—which Adorno aptly described as "great Bloch music"— can only be understood as reflections of Bloch's concept of the logic of expressionism.[5] The style of argumentation here and the texture of the text are shaped not only by conceptual principles but by rhetorical principles as well.

The philosophical position at which Bloch arrives is original and, consequently, quite difficult to enter into. One difficulty is that though Bloch belonged to specific traditions (even apparently competing traditions), he found no predecessor or single tradition adequate to his intentions. Like his contemporary, Martin Heidegger, with whom (against expectation) he shares some essential traits (such as the stress each places upon the future, the development of a nonmetaphysical literary style, and the effort to overcome the tradition of metaphysics via a reappraisal of its unthought contents), Bloch presents controversial and idiosyncratic readings of his predecessors that are guided, not by a sort of philosophical bookkeeping that simply wants to set the record of the past straight, but by an effort to retrieve the "unclaimed heritages" and unfulfilled forward-looking promises of the past. By looking at the intentions of his predecessors, Bloch is able to retrieve something living even from those whose achievements speak against his own purposes. He thus manages to be an insider where his apparent position is that of an outsider; and yet he remains an outsider even among his natural allies.

Even with respect to Marx and Marxism, where his deepest affinities lie, Bloch ultimately remains a renegade. Generally speaking, however, two characteristics might be said to qualify him as a Marxist. First, he consistently endorsed the young Marx's vision of the task of philosophy as promoting a "humanized nature and naturalized humanity"; and second, he held that the proper socialistic adjustment of determinate economic and social relations and the forces of production is a precondition for "the kingdom of freedom."[6] In short, Bloch shares Marx's intentions and basic methodological assumptions; but Bloch goes further, arguing that Marx's own economic analyses were inadequate to their full task. While not denying that the abolition of hunger and alienation, the "economic priority," is the prerequisite for emancipation, Bloch speaks equally of another prerequisite, "the other, transcendental hunger," the "humanistic primacy," which is the hidden unfulfilled demand announced in Marx's vision of society. This is what Habermas meant when he made the ambiguous comment apropos of Bloch that hunger is "the elemental energy of hope."[7] In large measure this book is Bloch's most direct attempt to outline the requirements that these mutual demands place upon society. Beginning with the assumption that "human dignity is not possible without the cause of human rights, which is beyond all forms of contracts and contractors," and that "liberation and dignity are not automatically born of the same act; rather they refer to each other reciprocally — with economic *priority* we find humanistic *primacy*," Bloch arrives at a framework of norms and rights that the true socialist society need realize (see esp. chapter 18). Such a society is marked by a solidarity in which dignity and happiness are not purchased at the price of the suffering or degradation of another.

Clearly such assumptions and such a project place Bloch at the margins of the Marxist tradition, in which sustained efforts to establish a system of rights and ethics, of moral and legal norms, have all too often been absent. Whereas others cite Marx's claim that "our ground is not the ground of right but of revolution" to show that the demands of right and of revolution are mutually exclusive, Bloch contends that Marxism must inherit some of the wealth of a natural law purged of bourgeois illusions, and even finds an implicit natural law in Marx himself, one that stands behind Marx's celebrated call "to overthrow all relations in which man is a degraded, enslaved, abandoned, or despised being." Bloch is aware that such a wedding of traditions requires a creative revision of their contents, but he also sees that without such a marriage between the traditions of social utopias and of natural law no full realization of the content of the unalienated society is possible. Thus Bloch asserts that "happiness and dignity, the concerns emphasized on the one hand by social utopias and on the other by doctrines of natural law, [which] for so long marched separately . . . [must] be recognized as functionally related and practically surmounted. . . . Both belong to the noble power of the anticipation of something 'better' than that which has 'become' . . . both issue from the empire of hope. . . . [This is the task of socialism] insofar as it simultaneously seeks to come to grips with the person and the collective, and to the extent that—far from the normalized masses of men, near to unalienated solidarity—it seeks to contain the one within the other." Though Bloch's Marxist heritage runs deep, it is ultimately only on the basis of his own "open system" that he is able to attempt such a reconciliation of the intentional fields of the social utopian and natural law traditions.

The Ontology of the Not-Yet

In order to satisfy his own intentions Bloch must provide the conceptual frame for both revolution and right, openness and norms. The radicality of his historical sense and the extent to which he is willing to go to preserve that sense is the hallmark of this conceptual frame that Bloch describes as an ontology of the not-yet. The present text does not develop or explicitly defend this ontology; but since it does surface in some of the key categories of this book ("novum," "rights forward," "not-yet," "preappearance," "hope"), and since many of the paths taken in the book are based upon such systematic concerns, some of the basic features of this ontology must be outlined.

Asked to provide some interpretive guidelines for navigating the labyrinth of his system, Bloch answered, "S is not yet P." This answer, which provides a clear link to Adorno's critique of identity thinking, is Bloch's way of explaining his concept of dialectic, for here he introduces the operative concept, the not-yet, that would be his means of avoiding any possible closure of the dialectic. Like Hegel, Bloch contends that reality is a process and that thought, if it is not to distort its object, must recognize the ontological priority of becoming. It is therefore not the static or finished self-identity of concepts, but their dynamic relativity to other concepts that lets them be meaningful or intelligible. Like Heidegger, Bloch argues that the real is never exhausted by the immediacy of the present, but is always infected by possibility. Heidegger's remark that "higher than actuality stands possibility"[8] could serve equally well as a motto for Bloch (though its concrete meaning would be quite different). The dialectic of contradictions and the radical incipience of the present and history are the fundamental traits of the real; it is the task of thought to become the living expression of this process. Thus, "actual thought never runs in straight lines, like a thought which is fixed, cut and dried, in which nothing expands or changes and which is therefore incapable of doing justice to transformation. Thought moves in triangles. These triangles which consist of contradiction, unity, new contradiction, new unity, and so on do not need to be schematically traced out each time. That would be incompatible with the free agility of thought. Indeed, the triangle is not the only possible form . . . and they do not all have to refer to the same point of unity."[9]

Bloch argues that the dialectic of history that spins every present into being can only be understood as the workings of both presence and absence, having and not having. This, of course, means that every present is necessarily incomplete, and Bloch contends that such incompletion is reflected in dreams, in refusals of every variety, in homesickness, and in language in the future tense. Measured in this way, the essential characteristic of the present is the incompletion and restlessness that mark it. The name Bloch gives to this forward-pressing urge latent in every moment is hope. Thus, hope is the principle by which Bloch intends to preserve the dialectic while simultaneously undercutting the empire-building tendencies of the Hegelian dialectic of Spirit. Unlike Spirit, the parousia of which leads to a reading of history as a universal theodicy, hope as a systematic principle discloses the truth of history as a multiversum of open possibilities. The appropriateness of the quotation from Tacitus with which this book concludes is clear: "Socordium eorum irridere licet qui praesenti potentia aevi temporis memoriam extinqui posse credunt," "One can only laugh at the narrowness of spirit of those who believe that the power of the present can extinguish the memory of future times." Bloch's historical sense is so strong that he can only consider as laughable any effort to interpret the present in the present tense or to move the object of thought out of the future. There is no room for the finality of closure or stasis in this ontology of the perpetual renewal of the not-yet.

For Bloch, the logos of history is best described as a *logos spermatikos*, since the true unifying thread of historical process is the suggestiveness, fertility, and forward-moving character of that process. The philosopher who believes that the best way to address the future and to understand the presence of the present is to speak of the unclaimed promises of the past, that is, the philosopher who has a genuine historical sense, needs to resist the urge to regard the past as finished or the present as a privileged position in history. Categories such as "Front," "preappearance," and "novum," future-directed concepts that open rather than solidify the lines of the past, are the result of his efforts to avoid any diminution of the historicity that thought must express. These categories of the principle of hope, and its hermeneutic, provide the underpinning of Bloch's effort to develop a systematic metaphysics that does not conflict with his intention of outlining the social framework of solidarity and plurality, of the society that "boasts of setting up the *facultas agendi* of finite unalienated man in the *norma agendi* of finite unalienated society." It is to the end of such a society that Bloch addresses the tradition of natural law, asking whether or not there are elements of this tradition that are unclaimed, yet necessary, revolutionary heritages. Bloch is aware that if hope is not to be restricted and rendered powerless, it must find a real place in history and praxis.

Natural Law

The term *natural law* in the title of this book refers to a wide variety of theories attempting to outline a moral basis of law and justice. Although doctrines of natural law exhibit a remarkable diversity of content (a characteristic Bloch frequently notes), a few basic shared features can be isolated. Generally, natural law is understood in opposition to "positive, existing, law," which, from the Marxist perspective as enacted, expresses the interests of the ruling class in a class society. Hobbes's remark in *Leviathan* that "no law can be unjust" is a fundamental credo of legal positivism, which answers the question of justice in conventional rather than moral terms. Unlike doctrines of natural law, positive law theories hold that no element of law preexists an act of the state. Consequently, the test of the validity of the law is not moral but procedural. Unlike positive law, which varies according to time and place, natural law is based upon invariant fundamental principles that provide norms for justice. Since the Sophists sharpened the distinction between man-made (*thesis*) and natural (*physis*) laws, the fundamental presupposition of all natural law has been that there is an essential unity between what is right and what is the highest expression of nature. All natural law theories hold that there is some natural standard independent of and above the positivity of existing conditions that provides the normative basis and free space for any legitimate critique of existing conditions. The metaphysical models for these normative principles have ranged from physical nature, to God, to reason, to human nature (naturally, each change in the metaphysical model entails a change in the determination of the content of such laws), and the nature of our cognitive approach to these principles varies as well. In every case, though, natural law theories have represented this principle as universal and immutable (cf. chapter 21).

With the rise of individualism in the seventeenth and eighteenth centuries a hitherto subterranean current in the tradition of natural law surfaced in full force, shifting the discussion of law to a discussion of the natural rights of the individual. It is during this period, and out of this shift in the tradition, that the revolutionary ideals of the French Revolution appear. It is out of this modification of the tradition that we find the development of Kant's concerns with autonomy and enlightenment as "man's release from his self-imposed tutelage" and Hegel's critique of all forms of positivity. The tricolor of the liberty, equality, and fraternity of the individual conceived as *citoyen* thus became the prevailing theme that Hegel and his successors had to confront as the inheritance of this tradition. It is at this point that we find the postulates of "inalienable" rights and the normative ideals of the just society.

Given such traits and the emphasis on the individual and the eternal, Bloch's largely sympathetic reading of the tradition of natural law comes as a surprise. Certainly his own systematic concerns, his efforts to preserve the openness of historical process, and his acceptance of the truth of the Marxist analysis, which argues for the priority of the social in questions of political philosophy and which discloses previous claims to right as having emerged from the grounds of a distorted bourgeois ideology, all speak for a critical rejection rather than a rehabilitation of any doctrine of natural law. Even those post-Hegelian theories of natural law that make an effort to confront history and to avoid the problems arising from the static character of such a doctrine (for example, Stammler's "natural law with a variable content") would seem antithetical to Bloch's concerns. Nevertheless, as he points out in the chapter on Hegel, since natural law exists only to the extent that the real is not restricted to the present, the basic presupposition of the doctrine of natural law does not violate a historical sensibility that begins with the assertion that "that which is cannot be true."

More importantly, Bloch considers the recognition of the human right to "walk upright" essential to the program of a socialist society and the humanity of its living praxis. For Bloch, every revolution, whether consciously or not, involves the preappearance, the hope, of this natural right. It is the pride of walking upright, the human dignity intended in natural law, which is the insurgent element in all revolution. For Bloch, Marxism must actively inherit and reform such anticipations of what is right and just if it is to legitimate its critique of existing conditions and its need to justify the right to resist exploitation and assaults upon human dignity. In a reformed inheritance from natural law, one purged of bourgeois fictions, Marxism can find the normative framework of the classless society, and once this happens it will be discovered that the classless society has long been the true basis of the intentions of natural law. Conversely, the discovery is made that the basic force of radical natural law in its resistance to the state is the realm of freedom that is the classless society. Thus his fondness for Marx's remark that "it will one day be shown that the world has long possessed a dream of something of which it only needs to become conscious in order to really possess." Bloch uses these reflections on the history and doctrine of natural law to argue that one component of this dream, hitherto largely neglected by the Marxist tradition, is suggested by the anticipation of dignity in natural law theories (see chapters 19–20). Thus, "that to which [doctrines of natural law] referred can never be a matter of indifference." It is to this end that Bloch asks how traditional natural law can be positively assessed from a Marxist perspective, and how such a tradition can be reformulated so that Marxism can overcome the dual threats of legal positivism and anarchy.

The attempt to preserve the best of the traditions of revolution and right without collapsing one into the other runs many risks, and these lay down a number of requirements. The model of the principles of nature cannot have anything about it that usurps the place of novelty and the openness of history. Rather than being modeled after a sense of nature that is calculable and mathematically ordered (an assumption crucial to capitalism, where a premium is placed upon the quantifiability of exchange and the predictability of the future), Bloch must develop a model of nature as elastic and able to preserve the place of novelty.

Nature no longer stands in contrast to time, but is regarded as being in process; there is no assumption of the opposition of nature and history at work here, but there is a recognition, similar to that in Schelling, of their essential identity. At issue in this book is the concept of nature as a model for law and what is right, but elsewhere Bloch has developed a philosophy of nature that does not shy away from explicitly linking transformations in relations between man, society, and history to transformations in nature and in man's relation to nature.[10] Clearly Bloch's intentions and their requisites fall outside the domain of natural law understood in any traditional sense. Indeed there is ample reason to say that even if one stretches the concept of natural law far enough to include the sense of law and justice outlined here, it still remains a natural law that can only be regarded as an affront to the very tradition whose name it adopts. Not that Bloch wants to wear any traditional masks. The philosophical and political shock waves of this book move in two directions: both left and right.

The book first raises the question of justice by means of an expressionistic account of a conflict of wills. In the background of this analysis are clearly echoes of Hegel's analysis of the dialectic of recognition that takes place in the master-slave relation; but for Bloch it is the inconclusiveness and dissatisfactions of this relation, not its inversion and sublation, that is the issue. What one finds from this point forward is a dialectical series of immanent critiques of the classic legal philosophers. These critiques yield a complex and highly original reading of this tradition, for in them Bloch places the postulates of natural law under the optics of the perspective and hermeneutic of hope in order to look for any residue of rights that could serve the ends of true socialism, that is, a socialism with democracy and without arbitrariness. Those rights that remain as a revolutionary heritage provide the outline of the orthopedia of the upright carriage.

Extracting such human rights and purging them of traditional class fictions is no simple matter, for as Bloch points out, even at its high point in the tricolor of freedom, equality, and fraternity, the revolutionary inheritance of natural law is accompanied by aporias and illusions. Understandably, then, one of the core chapters of this book is dedicated to exposing the illusions inherent in the bourgeois concept of natural right. Here Bloch gives perhaps his clearest account of those assumptions that hinder rather than advance the cause of overcoming the lingering antinomy of revolution and right. Chief among this mu-

seum of antiquated judicial postulates we find the notion of the inalienability of rights, the idea that property belongs to human rights,
all previous forms of according and securing rights, the view that
human beings have a static nature that lets them be fundamentally
in accord on matters of right, and the prejudice in favor of an ahistorical
thought that sits in judgment of history.

In short, Bloch finds it necessary to abandon most of the real characteristic content of traditional natural law theories; but he does not
abandon the humanistic ideals and intentions of the revolutionary
bourgeoisie. Classical natural law theories, lacking any genuine sense
of history, and conceiving human nature as composed of static properties, have been their own worst enemy, since in their efforts to
rescue human dignity they have reified that which was to be invigorated:
the forward-pressing, not-yet-determined nature of the human being.
Bloch does not seek to improve such traditional theories by substituting
an improved determination of the content and nature of the human
being and of social relations. It is not the proletarian or capitalist, the
slave or the master, who is the first determination of the center here.
It is, rather, the human being conceived as the unfinished being of
the future for whom the question of justice matters. Any law the locus
of which lies in a primordial past or eternal present victimizes and
alienates the not-yet-determined nature of the real, forward-living,
human being. Radical natural law is not a conservation of past or
present static natures, but an emancipation into the openness of the
future as the place of human hope and worth. Radical natural law
can only be founded upon a view of human nature that is not yet
closed and "determined to its end." Only here, says Bloch, can one
find a true home in solidarity. Such a natural law does not domesticate,
but rather liberates the human being at its center, and this is the
revolutionary accent in it. Such a natural law is determined, not "from
above," from the vantage point of what seems finished, but "from
below," from what is unfinished. It is then easy to see how such a
natural law complements the critical insight that the standpoint of the
victims of any society ought to always provide the starting point for
the critique of that society.

There is thus some legitimacy to the argument that Bloch does not
present a doctrine of natural law. Bloch's Marxism and his systematic
concerns with preserving history do not allow any room for such a
doctrine understood in any traditional sense. But what this argument

fails to recognize is Bloch's own contention that the traditional self-understanding of natural law theories has failed to grasp its own intentions, and that the claims and real achievements found in this tradition do not measure up to the unclaimed promises inherent in it. Essential to Bloch's efforts in this text is the recognition of the gaps and contradictions between the humanistic intentions of natural law and their distorted unhistorical realization. The rehabilitation of natural law begins with its intentions, not its achievements. In this way, the naive conception of natural law, which fancies itself exempt from material and historical conditions, can be rectified by a Marxist perspective. By not retreating from history and the goal of the nonantagonistic, classless society, Bloch is able to reclaim the promises of human dignity found in the intentions of natural law.

By advancing a normative basis for the socialist society, Bloch is in a position to reply to a problem by which many contemporary Marxists find themselves confronted, namely, how to identify and critique the distortions of ideology without claiming the epistemological privilege of being exempt from such distortions.[11] Those Marxists who no longer feel that the proletarian consciousness no longer provides a sufficient basis for the critique of existing social conditions require some sort of normative standpoint for their critique. This question of the legitimating grounds of critique, which is one of the dominant concerns of contemporary critical theory, could perhaps find the outlines of an answer in Bloch's efforts to uncover the normative framework of the true socialist society.

Bloch does not address such questions here. Instead his overarching concern is to reflect upon the role of natural law in history and to consider the possibility of rescuing natural law from its neglect of history. But this does not mean that Bloch is writing a history, revisionist or otherwise, of natural law; to read this book with such an expectation would only lead to disappointment. There is no narrative of natural law here; too many of the rules of both narrative and natural law are violated for that. One does, nevertheless, find thoughtful reflections upon the dreams and means of the abolition of poverty, degradation, and the state, and the installation of freedom and dignity. In short, one finds a reappraisal and rethinking of the fundamental concerns and principles of political philosophy.

The discussions cover much ground. Indeed it is difficult to think of a significant contributor to this tradition who does not make an appearance in this analysis. But it is not to produce a tour de force that Bloch ranges so widely; rather, it is the urge to illuminate and crystallize what has hitherto been concealed within this tradition that shapes the route of Bloch's reflections. His presentation begins somewhat tentatively, but mounts in force until, at the junctures represented by Kant, Hegel, and Marx, Bloch begins to unfold the socialist inheritance of natural law. The result is not a blueprint of improved socialist rights. He makes no effort to prescribe the laws and rights of the classless or the class society. That would be self-defeating, since a description of such rights can only be made in terms of the not-yet-achieved rights of preserving the open, forward-moving place and possibilities of the human being. Bloch is quite clear and unhesitant when called upon to point out what is illusory among the past conceptions of right and law, but only a few positive suggestions are found.

To reconstruct such a list would be possible. One need simply begin with the chapter on the tricolor and move forward, finding suggestions for the content of right under terms like *solidarity, struggle, dignity, the end of exploitation, equality that does not equalize, fraternity that goes beyond fraternization,* and *the polis without* politeia. In other words, one can find here a theory of law and right, and though it does not bear many of the traditional trademarks of such a theory, it is not on that account merely abstract and distant from the reality of its theme. One might argue that Bloch's theory of natural law, however far from the mainstream of both such theories and their Marxist critiques, is closer to the reality of the issue than the mainstream is. The discussion is never distant from the reality and concreteness of alienation, degradation, and suffering. The eye sensitive to the contradictions embodied in existing conditions, a sensitivity that impressed Bloch as a child in Ludwigshafen, is always at work here. Not surprisingly, Bloch finds previous natural law theorists too often lacking in this essential sensitivity, or worse, manifesting hypocrisy ("the tribute of vice to virtue"). Only Christian Thomasius, who "was justly uncomfortable in his sleepy and servile surroundings," is singled out as possessing the sensitivity and honest eye that exemplify the vision and attitude of uprightness. Thus, the lengthy appendix to this book, which is an essay on Thomasius written shortly after Bloch's return to East Germany from the United States, begins by saying that in Thomasius we encounter "an honorable spirit, one who is both honorable and spirited, and who speaks of

progress [making] himself unavoidable in the long run." The special
attention Bloch gives Thomasius is only an external indication of a
real inner kinship between them.

The flavor of Bloch's remarks on Thomasius and many of the circumstances of their lives invite a comparison of them on a number
of points. One shared concern might especially help illuminate one
of Bloch's chief, but unspoken, concerns in this book. As Bloch frequently points out, Thomasius was among the first jurists to speak
out against the witch trials and torture ("madness with method"). Later
he makes a tacit link between himself and Thomasius when he says:
"The last witch was not burned in Germany in 1775 in Kempten;
rather, thousands of similar victims, called Jews by the Nazis, went
along with so many others, even in 1945, into the gas chambers and
crematoria of Auschwitz and Meidanek. Something genuinely diabolic
has reappeared, and its consequences are not limited to Germany."
In this and other such passages one detects both the ambiguity and
the pathos and urgency of Bloch's turn to the tradition of natural law.
Fascism, in both the brutal and audacious form of the Nazis and the
"metapolitical phenomenon" of closure,[12] is never far from Bloch's
questioning of the natural law tradition. The legalized illegalities of
fascism provide at once the constant reminders of the dangers of law
and revolution (Bloch analyzed fascism as a distorted revolution)[13] as
well as the need for both law and revolution. Since Horkheimer and
Adorno's *Dialectic of Enlightenment* had revealed the way in which fascism
was able to turn the Enlightenment tradition into its own, that tradition
and indeed philosophy itself were rendered suspect. But recognizing
the truth of their intentions, Bloch refuses to consign such suspect and
tainted traditions to oblivion. This is the sense of his agreement with
Hölderlin's remark that the place of rescue and hope grows where
there is danger. But for Bloch, the risks in returning to a disgraced
tradition to look for the unclaimed promises and residue of truth are
necessary for the thinker whose intent is to walk the long and difficult
path of humanity out of degradation and servitude. He reminds us
that if the unalienated society of solidarity is to be realized, then the
priority of the economic question does not abolish the primacy of the
humanistic question. That is why the referent of natural law—human
dignity—cannot be forgotten; it belongs to the true intentional field
of socialism: "Only when he has none can it be said that man lives

from bread alone. When he has his daily bread, then the red dream of something else and more begins."[14]

Reading Bloch

A number of factors make reading Bloch difficult, but there are special problems for the reader accustomed to Anglo-Saxon discussions of natural law. Because most of these problems are by-products of the originality of Bloch's systematic and intentional concerns, it is worth addressing them briefly.

Bloch refers to many figures and texts not widely known among Anglo-Saxon readers. And even when he approaches otherwise familiar territory, Bloch's typology of the terrain and the details of his analyses are highly unusual. Thus Bachofen receives more attention than Kant and Fichte combined. A glance at the table of contents will confirm that the contours of what Bloch finds significant are in no way the traditional contours of this tradition. The new landscape found here is one of the more provocative features of the text, jarring our own expectations and prejudices, and revitalizing the past in characteristic Blochian fashion. Though Bloch's own unwillingness to inhabit any single tradition, along with his willingness to draw from the best of any number of traditions, will perhaps be initially confusing, it is also the source of the freshness of his analyses. By redefining what has been thought, Bloch changes our present self-understanding of what remains problematic and thus to be thought. This is the enduring timeliness of this book about an untimely tradition.

English-speaking readers accustomed to the distinction between rights and laws might be disturbed by the way in which the German word *recht* conflates both "right" and "law." Ultimately, the only criterion for the distinction when translating into English is context, and occasionally the context is not clear or it demands that both senses of the word come through (as is the case with the word *Naturrecht* in the title). This is a linguistic problem that is not unique to Bloch but does compound the problem of access for the English-speaking reader, who might have to struggle to restrain the advantage of making a distinction, and work to gain the other advantage of hearing unity in its stead.[15] Furthermore, Bloch often plays with the duality of meaning in the German word, and this occasionally allows him to make some connections and conceptual moves that might otherwise puzzle the reader.

Any reader of Bloch, whether German-speaking or not, soon discovers the peculiarities of Bloch's prose. As already mentioned, Bloch insisted that the style of the presentation of his open system should not conflict with the content and intent of that system, and so he sought a prose style that expressed all of the ambiguities, openness, and suggestiveness characteristic of his position. It is on this point that Bloch found the languages and syntaxes of expressionism and the cabala helpful, for in these Bloch found the means of avoiding the language of abstraction and reflection while mirroring the expressiveness and elasticity of his themes. Frequently episodic and staccato, such prose reflects the disjointed and fragmented quality of experience and of possibilities left dormant. Adorno is quite right when he says that in the final analysis Bloch's thought must be understood in its relation to expressionism, but he is wrong when he suggests that this structural feature of Bloch's thought has rendered it outdated. Bloch's prose is no more outdated than James Joyce's could ever be. Like Joyce, Bloch regards the matter of his prose as of fundamental importance; indeed, as George Steiner has noted, there are passages in Bloch that find some measure of coherence only by force of literary style, and so it can be said that "his books belong as much to the history of rhetoric as they do that of philosophic or polemic argument."[16] The metaphors, semantic structure, and punctuated style are all part of the texture, the subject, and the substance of the text. Insofar as it is possible, I have tried to retain these elements in this translation, but there are limits to any translation, and special limits to translating Bloch. Bloch's German is legendary for its imagistic power, its pregnancy, and its density. In the end, these struggles with his style have their special reward, for there is no doubt that reading Bloch enlarges and stretches one's understanding of the flexibility and reciprocity of the relationship between language and thought.

Bloch remarks that Christian Thomasius's inventive style of speaking introduced a warmth and vitality into the language and thought of the philosophy of his time. For Bloch, language is not a secondary matter, nor does it belong to the superstructure. Rather, the "living colors" of language provide the fabric and unity of any culture and any thought. His comment on Thomasius applies equally well to his own contributions: "Since then, Minerva has not forgotten to speak German, and to speak it with a special vigor."

Bloch's method of citation is unhappily quite casual and irregular; frequently the reference information which he does provide is inadequate for locating the given passage. Furthermore, when dealing with texts written in languages other than German, Bloch occasionally seems to have used a German translation. Given the large number of quotations from so many different authors and texts, it proved impossible to remedy the problems with the footnote style of the original German text. This means that the translations of quotations in the text are usually my own, though there are a few exceptions (especially in the cases of Hegel and Marx) where I have been able to identify and use the standard translations.

Two brief sections of this text, pages 174–180 and 276–280, have previously appeared in English[17], and I have profited by being able to use them to corroborate and correct my own translation when editing it.

Although I must bear full responsibility for this translation, I would like to acknowledge my indebtedness to my colleagues Thomas Nenon and Anthony Preus, who offered advice and assistance at various stages in the preparation of this translation. Most especially, I thank my wife, Lisa Fegley-Schmidt, for her insightful criticisms, labor, and support at every stage on the way.

Notes

1. Ernst Bloch, *Tagträume vom aufrechten Gang*, ed. A. Münster (Frankfurt, Suhrkamp, 1977), p. 21.

2. Jürgen Habermas, *Philosophical-Political Profiles*, trans. Frederick Lawrence (Cambridge: MIT Press, 1983), p. 60.

3. See Wayne Hudson, *The Marxist Philosophy of Ernst Bloch* (London: Macmillan Press, 1982), pp. 4–19, and Habermas, "Ernst Bloch: A Marxist Schelling," in *Profiles*.

4. A sustained argument to this effect apears in A. Münster, *Utopie: Messianismus und Apokalypse im Frühwerk von Ernst Bloch* (Frankfurt: Suhrkamp, 1982), and Eberhard Simons, *Das expressive Denken Ernst Bloch* (Freiburg: Alber Verlag, 1983).

5. T. Adorno, "Grosse Blochmusik," *Neue deutsche Heft*, no. 69, April 1960.

Translator's Introduction

6. For a detailed discussion of Bloch's relation to Marx and Marxism see Hudson, *Marxist Philosophy*, and Gerard Raulet, *Humanisation de la Nature, Naturalisation de L'Homme* (Paris: Klincksieck, 1982).

7. Habermas, *Profiles*, p. 60.

8. Martin Heidegger, *Being and Time*, trans. J. Macquarrie and E. Robinson (New York: Harper & Row, 1962), p. 63.

9. E. Bloch, "The Dialectical Method," trans. J. Lamb, *Man and World*, vol. 16, no. 4, 1983, p. 284.

10. See Ernst Bloch, *Das Materialismusproblem, seine Geschichte und Substanz* (Frankfurt: Suhrkamp, 1972), and Anton F. Christen, *Ernst Blochs Metaphysik der Materie* (Bonn: Bouvier Verlag, 1979).

11. See S. K. White, "The Normative Basis of Critical Theory," *Polity*, Fall 1983.

12. Cf. E. Nolte, *Three Faces of Fascism* (New York: New American Library, 1969), pp. 537–543.

13. E. Bloch, *Erbschaft dieser Zeit* (Frankfurt: Suhrkamp, 1962), pp. 126–145.

14. Ibid., pp. 404–405.

15. Translators of English philosophical texts into German face the reverse problem; cf. H. Reiner, "Was heisst und wie ubersetz man *right* und *wrong* als Grundbegriffe der Moral ins Deutsche?", *Archiv fur Rechts- und Sozialphilosophie*, Bd. 67/2 (1978).

16. G. Steiner, "Forward Dreams," *Times Literary Supplement*, October 3, 1975, p. 1128.

17. Pages 174–180, "*L'homme* and *citoyen* in Marx," have appeared as "Man and Citizen in Marx," in *On Karl Marx*, trans. John Maxwell (New York: Herder and Herder, 1971), pp. 46–53; pp. 276–280, "The Nationalized God and the Right to Community," have appeared under the same title in *Man on His Own: Essays in the Philosophy of Religion*, trans. E. B. Ashton (New York: Herder and Herder, 1970), pp. 142–146.

Author's Preface

What is justice? What is right? We cannot avoid this question; it always demands our attention; it forces itself upon us and points out a path for us. One school of thought that has taken up this question in principle and not just on occasion is characterized by its attachment to the idea of natural law. No matter what position one took with respect to this idea of natural law, whether critical or undecided, and no matter how abstract it often was, what it referred to could never be a matter of indifference. Where everything has been alienated, inalienable rights stand out in sharp relief. Yet because these rights had no real, enduring place for themselves, this provided little comfort for the obedient subject.

"No one must be compelled"—although this principle of natural law is quite false in everyday affairs, it gave the impression of being all the more true by being so uncommon, and by being the expression of a natural disposition and claim. In the nineteenth century this revolutionary disposition was opposed first by that school of thought attached to the view that law is a product of history, and then by the judicial positivism that this view restored as being more modern and more conveniently suited to the time, that is, as being empirical. But both of these rejections of natural law were too vehement to appear as detached and balanced as they pretended to be. The rising middle class often only idealized itself in its natural law, but once it had established its power, it cunningly protected itself with an antinatural law, clearly for its own profit and often out of cynicism. The idea of any sort of judicial standard was dismissed, the old attempts to elaborate one were looked upon as laughable, or at least as suspect; this dismissal was carried out in such a wholesale fashion that it had the appearance of objectivity. Nevertheless, even those fictions in the old natural law that were easily seen through (such as the social contract, which was posited as prehistorical) only rendered the idea of natural law suspect in the eyes of those who already had a strong inclination to consider existing positive law as above suspicion. In any event, the rejection of natural law did not last long, for with the growth of social contradictions it became necessary for injustice itself to don the cloak of natural law. At first, with neo-Kantianism, something like genuine law was attached to the letter of the law, but this patchwork did not prove viable for very long. Thus, fascism entered the picture all the more energetically: For economic leaders it invented the primordial right of the mighty, and for victims another right, the bloody right of one born a slave. A sort of clerical natural law took root once again, this time soothed with more ointment; and wherever possible its demeanor was not explosive but in accord with the doctrine of social harmony. Capital and labor join forces in an ostensible *lex aeterna* of property, one arranged in a hierarchy and with a corporate order ordained by God and conforming to nature.

So much for such residues of our times, since judicial positivism no longer suffices, and since these residues no longer reside wherever justice rules. But beyond these residues there is only so much liberal memory—that which speaks of liberty and gladly invokes fraternity, but less so equality—which for the bourgeois can mean little more than a Sunday, a special room that is seldom used, an apology. What is more surprising and quite irregular is that socialistically, where *expressis verbis* the real human being is at the center as the person to be liberated and satisfied, that here the rejection of natural law is still largely in vogue. To this end the often abstract, purely generic character of the eternally static old doctrines of natural law was strongly emphasized; this was done for negative reasons, though of course there were other reasons. And yet it is precisely at this point that one of the most decisive themes of humanism comes into play. To this humanism there belongs the question of the *genuine* intentions of the old natural law, to it there belongs the task of a socialistic heritage in these formally liberal, but not merely liberal, *human rights.* The establishment of honesty and uprightness against a well-padded, rechristened, and retrogressive subordination is a postulate of natural law that is found nowhere else. The exasperation that Kant felt was not only a moral exasperation when he said that he refused to consider it an insignificant matter that man was treated as insignificant by his rulers "in that they treat him as a beast of burden, or as a mere instrument of their own intentions, or in that they array men against each other in order to resolve their own quarrels." And Marx is not merely giving economic advice when he teaches us "to overthrow all relations in which man is a degraded, enslaved, abandoned, or despised being." It is therefore quite understandable that this being that is always set aside or reduced to a merely "sociological" subject continues to command our attention. It does not belong on the scrap heap; what is outdated is not natural law itself but what it attacks. The simple critical saying "A thousand years of injustice still do not make an hour of justice" and the constructive definition "Enlightenment is man's release from his self-imposed tutelage" both retain their value, for neither has its worth in that which natural law once attacked. This means that human dignity is not possible without economic liberation, and this liberation is not possible without the cause of human rights, which is beyond all forms of contracts and contractors. Liberation and dignity are not automatically born of the same act; rather they refer to each other reciprocally—with economic *priority* we find humanistic *primacy*. There can be no true installation of human rights without the end of exploitation, no true end of exploitation without the installation of human rights. There is a bit of Beethoven in them, ripping up the dedication of *Eroica* when Napoleon became emperor. The fundamental characteristic of natural law, especially classical natural law, is its resoluteness: It boasts of setting up the *facultas agendi* of finite unalienated man in the *norma agendi* of finite unalienated society.

To this end, many competent men who have emphasized what is important are referred to here. We are concerned with a peculiar heritage; its best remains in abeyance and is still to be appended. What is past does not return, especially not in an out-of-date way; but it can be taken at its word. It is just as urgent *suo modo* to raise the problem of a heritage of classical natural law as it was to speak of the heritage of social utopias. Social utopias and natural law had mutually complementary concerns within the same human space; they marched separately but, sadly, did not strike together. Although they were in accord on the decisive issue, a more humane society, there nevertheless arose important differences between the doctrines of social utopia and natural law. Those differences can be formulated as follows. Social utopian thought directed its efforts toward human happiness, natural law was directed toward human dignity. Social utopias depicted relations in which *toil* and *burden* ceased, natural law constructed relations in which *degradation* and *insult* ceased. Unlike most dreams of happiness, the anticipations of dignity are predominantly sober; we have many dramatic examples of this in the figures of such representatives of natural law as Odoardo Galotti, Verrina, and even Oranien.

Genuine natural law, which posits the free will in accord with reason, was the first to reclaim the justice that can only be obtained by struggle; it did not understand justice as something that descends from above and prescribes to each his share, distributing or retaliating, but rather as an active justice of below, one that would make justice itself unnecessary. Natural law never coincided with a mere sense of justice, but (in the Stoics, and clearly in Rousseau's "good nature") it easily found for itself an ancient place of security and its measure: maternal law. It is from this point, from these grounds that are almost forgotten, that it set itself, warm and full, against arbitrariness and artificiality. Its essential point, however, was the manly attempt at emancipation into the free space it sought to construct. This is most concisely expressed in Schiller's treatise *On the Sublime*; it is a plan the perspective of which can be heard even in an old language: "The will is the generic character of mankind, and reason itself is only its eternal rule. For this reason, there is no greater indignity for man than to suffer violence, because violence cancels him. One who commits violence does nothing less than contest humanity; one who cowardly suffers violence throws away his humanity." It is high time that we finally came to see how the differences between the intentions of happiness, which belonged to previous social utopias, and of dignity, which belonged to previous theories of natural law, are functionally connected and surmounted. This much is certain: There is just as little human dignity without the end of misery as there is happiness without the end of all old and new forms of subjugation. It is precisely at this point that the best contributions of the Enlightenment enter the picture in a way that does not permit them to be pushed aside again. This book is offered as a historical and, more importantly, thoughtful contribution to what is right and just and yet still outstanding: the problem of the upright carriage. It is a treatise of a peculiar sort, one that begins with the responsibility of questioning and demanding and that does not end with classical theories of natural law.

Natural Law and Human Dignity

1

Overly Used

You feel it. You believe that you have a sense of what is right. But it is precisely this word that changes so often. From the beginning many things merge.

You sense that something is not right. If matters were otherwise, then you would have a sense of well-being. Or you cannot make another person's circumstances right. If things were different, then the other would be satisfied with his circumstances, and the situation would be a comfortable one. But it could also be said that such people are not what they should be. In this case, one must look to the finger that does the pointing. For here again, what is meant is that they do not fit in, that they are not sufficiently wealthy or respected. Conversely, it could be said that the other is not acting right. Were he to comport himself more respectably, then he would be what he should be: a proper man. We could continue with such wordplay for some time, because too much is called right in everyday parlance. And yet one always means by this word something that is good when it is present. That which is as it should be is thus right. But it is often said of many things, especially when viewed from the vantage point of up high, that matters are right when such is not the case. The little man always notices that something is out of whack. As always the greater man leads the way.

2

It Is a Third Who Decides

No one lives because he wills to live. Yet from the moment one is alive one must will it. One must persevere in order to make something of oneself. Not only in the sense that one works. Many of those who do not work do well, often even especially well. They pocket the products of others. But then the one tries to recover the bounty from the other. They are never really certain to whom it belongs.

Eventually a dispute arises and the spoils are fought over. Two desires, two wills to possess the same thing, confront each other. Divergent claims upon the same issue are usually irreconcilable. A quarrel ensues, and one of the wills can now lodge a complaint against the other. Insofar as a third is present, one who has been given the power to decide impartially, the dispute can be smoothed over. One party wins its suit, the other, rejected or penalized, does not. In this way the civil dispute remains a more or less private matter; nevertheless, it always encroaches upon the territory of public law and can always be resolved by it. If public law is seriously violated by a deed that is more criminal than civil, then it is not a fine that pays the law, but the body. But who or what is this third who sets himself up as impartial, or is set up as such by others? And who and what directs the judge? A feeling, one which is a matter of intimacy to the one who judges, is the deciding factor, but often an unjust one. This feeling might even be impartial and disinterested, and yet, is this how justice is to be measured? What measures and adjusts the measure itself and illuminates it in a way which lets it serve equally well as a measure of those fluid, even slippery, legal cases? These questions have always been asked; they were never taken as self-evident, especially not by the little people who are in a subordinate position where dealings are more rigorous and from which one cannot run away. Once a judgment is rendered, one must bow down to it. Then the tolerable life begins again, until the next time.

3

The So-Called Sense of Justice

One who has lost does not want to admit it. To be sure, occasionally the plaintiff or defendant knew beforehand that his cause was unjust. But since no judicial outcome is certain, one takes a chance. One never knows what role chance will play, and with cleverness the direction of the trial can be steered. But even the run-of-the-mill scoundrel believes that the judgment was unjust after he has lost his case. Such a feeling is even stronger when one was convinced of one's self and of one's cause from the outset. One feels violated, inwardly one holds one's claims to be just. If this feeling simply arose because the case was lost, then the resulting dissatisfaction would be as understandable as it would be tedious. Yet it is precisely in those who are not crooks, but who are merely economically weaker and surpassed by others in matters of power, that we find an ancient, almost proverbial, mistrust of the courts. That is why they live in the shadows and are accustomed to expecting no good to come their way. Even justice is not constructed for them, but against them. The dog who deserves the bone does not get it.

It would seem to be easy to find out what would be right in this case: namely, that the dog finally gets the bone and more of the same. Occasionally the master who refused the dog and for a change must hand over the bone beats his breast and then believes, *nolens volens*, that he hears the voice of outraged justice. In such cases a very confused feeling dwells in the heart, the so-called sense of justice. Even in one and the same person this sense of justice often reveals itself as composed of the most diverse feelings and emotions. Initially, it is a very unclear feeling; but from the petit-bourgeois vantage point, being clear is not at all important. There are even some theorists who want to find something so strange as a juridical instinct in animals, that is, a legal instinct in the sense of vengeance and retaliation. Thus there are those who claim that when higher animals are not faced with the question of their immediate defense, the response is postponed to a later, more favorable moment. There is even an Oriental fable about an elephant who waited many days before spraying water over a tailor who had tormented the elephant with needles. And of course there is the alleged communal sense, a species of insectlike justice that some believe they find in bees and ants. But none of this goes very far toward explaining the sense of justice found in human beings; to be sure, this human feeling has shown itself, as a juridical sense, to be individualistic. If it does go to the door and out onto the street, it does so simply in order to look for its due in the state. But when it really seeks justice, that is, when it represents the causes of the oppressed and does not content itself with its own egotistical faultfindings, then the human sense of justice cannot be traced back to animal mores. When we speak of the human sense of justice, it should not be a beehive that comes to mind, but that primordial *human* age before the division of labor, where "mine" and "yours" had not yet appeared. Then the sense of justice of one who felt and was guided by the "mine" would not be so fine-tuned to its own demands, and not so deaf toward the "yours" of the next person, as is usually the case. One can see how that which the Nazis had the audacity to call the people and its good sense, far removed from this distant golden age, revolves around the crudest and shabbiest prejudices of the new middle class. The deeds of this blood were simply bloody deeds, the voices of these natures were simply the voices of murderers. The Nazis appealed to a sense of justice; the mob court had done the same thing for a long time. When the white power holders and Babbits of the Southern states in America began to feel the urge toward justice, blacks began to shudder, and with good reason. There was never a proletariat whose affairs were in good hands when left to the judicial class instincts of a jury of petits bourgeois. But even in harmless cases, when the soul of the people does not seethe as much, the sense of justice, as hollow and shortsighted, does not correspond to the ends to which one who is oppressed might relate. This sense of justice is easily accessible to those who are dissatisfied, not with the actual economic conditions, but only with the place they occupy within those conditions. Thus when the value of money began to fall, even the revaluation of the currency was able to be justified by a natural feeling. And the scales of the heart seem to be especially natural when they condemn unnatural love among men (though curiously enough not among women). The woodpile with the witch upon it fit in quite well with a sense of justice popular at the time but not at all with that of those few who wanted to extinguish the flames. According to natural law it is impossible to mix the mildew in, even when one wants to; that is true even for higher lights. Thus Jhering believed that he was acting almost entirely according to the principles of natural law when he suggested that one who lost a trial be penalized by a fine. On the other hand he took great pains to emphasize that, after a long trial, an accuser should not obtain more from the defendant than was due him from the beginning.

Things begin to change as soon as this sense of justice begins to reflect upon itself. Soon it becomes sufficiently penetrating to pose the problem of innate rights and to distinguish these from an injustice that has been instituted by articles of law. For example, that a piece of property is used and abandoned and one who is needy may take possession of it; in this matter the sense of justice does not go completely astray. And it strays even less in the judgment that a property owner who destroys coffee, wheat, or cotton in order to keep prices high must himself be destroyed as a property owner. But even in order to hold on to *such* a sense of justice a concept must be supplied for it. This requirement is not only limited to magistrates or, if the occasion arises, to jurors, that is, to the decisions of the court and their individual cases. It has been said that it is easy to tell whether or not the facts of a case and its judicial consequence are in precise accord, and that it is quite easy to see whether a judicial decision is artificial or even random. An example of the administration of justice that is artificial, or of justice that is incomprehensible to the people, can be seen in the decision that was rendered in 1820 by the demagogue judge in Hoffmanns's *Master Flea*: We have the perpetrator, that is the main thing; the deed we will find out soon. The people never ceased shaking their heads, especially in times of oppression; from the repressed fury of the people there arose various legends of the simple judge, the judge of good sense, and finally, without need of Brecht's *The Chalk Circle*, of such assessors, magistrates, jurors. Of course for the friends of the people, a sense of justice in itself, even one that is democratic, only has value as a signal and nothing more. Even as a pure and direct sentiment, it is too vague, too easily reworked, too susceptible to cliché; it needs a shrewd ally. Even if good sense is given a good ear for listening, it must always be an ear that is capable of self-critique and assessment. The ear is better still when it becomes sensitive and hostile to the causes of interested laws and their commercial ethics. Then, in the place of injustice and the partial justice of the state (for the rich and poor alike), that order which makes visible the real sense of justice can come into view. One has to step back and remove oneself from one's customs, so that one can better serve one's understanding. Bias begins when one brings along what is only one's own. But to avoid bias a very strong will is required, one that brings the sense of justice to a point in order to really penetrate with it.

4

The First Opponents of Institutions

It is not surprising that those who are isolated are the first to revolt. It must be this way because groups tend to stay together for a long time. Custom is a strong cement, one that binds tenaciously, and often even paralyzes. Habits, mores, and laws tend to be one for a long time, and this state of affairs helps to keep the slaves in line. All the more so as long as poverty and oppression were themselves not enough to stir up a revolt against the hereditary whip. Apathetically, the slave let himself grow accustomed to the whip; but it did not take long until from among those who had been battered and bruised some stood up to speak and hurl insults. The first opponents of habits and traditions were always solitary individuals, lone wolves, or even those among the masters who defended their special circumstances; they frequently rose to the fight before those who were subjugated did. Thus it is easier to speak of a Cain than of the troops of Corah; resentful slaves banded together only after a long waiting period. Historically, the individual who rejects tradition and the existing articles of law is first taken note of when he enters the picture in a sensational way while still preserving the dignity of his social status. He did not appear on the scene as a revolutionary with Peloponnesian slaves rallied behind him, but as a refined man, impertinent and full of spirit even in the midst of cultivated, emancipated *jeunesse dorée* itself. Among such gilded youth of Athens, which dissipated its revenues quite freely, there was an ignorance of the ancient discipline of the warrior class, which was still found in Sparta, and an ignorance of the old taboos of the priest class, which was still found in the Near East. The Sophists represented this Athens, and they did so in such a way that they not only set the arbitrary opinion of the individual against traditions, but for the first time posited *physis* as a natural concept of value. They introduced a byword that was not reserved for the sons of commerce; for the first time "to reason" meant also "to criticize." The savage and arbitrary was still intertwined with the universal and constant in the sophistical use of *physis*; the same was true of lawlessness and of the demand of equal rights for all. The unity of *physis* as a concept of value resides solely in its opposition to traditional institutions, to the law, to *nomos*. The law, said Hippias, tyrannizes man, it compels him to do much that is physically repugnant to him. In this connection the savage and the arbitrary were exaggerated in the efforts to slander the Sophists: Parents were permitted to marry their children, justice is enjoyment or advantage, for the powerful everything is permitted. But because for the Sophists all things are by nature equal, one finds in the Sophists only philanthropic laws. Lycophron called aristocracy an imaginary superiority, and Alcidamas pointed out that the opposition between slaves and freemen is unknown in nature. Hippias explained why it is that all people are related by nature as fellow citizens and why their separation (including the separation that follows from the unequal distribution of property) was violently introduced by law. And of course Pythagoras already taught that the origin of the law was to be found in an *hathroizesthai*, a "self-gathering"; accordingly the state must offer its services to all people. But why and to what end do men gather together? The explanations for this remain hesitant and confused, because this Athenian enlightenment was not mandated by a new class. Only this much is certain: that nature, which simultaneously stands for the right of the mightier and the equality of all, enters the picture in opposition to tradition, that is to say, in opposition to normalized good behavior that has been reduced to breeding and mores. In opposition to this, the Sophists introduced the figure of the subject, of the naturally free and cunning individual.

Such positions were absolutely progressive and so could not be reduced to silence. The excitement that was born of this impulse, despite occasional astonishing excesses, was continued in the sharp distinctions that were drawn between two attitudes: on the one hand, of private frugality, and on the other hand, of private desires. Any institution that contradicted either one of these intentions was judged to be unhealthy and thus unnatural. In this way, the Cynics and the Hedonists introduced compatible concepts of natural law, although the ends toward which they were directed differed. The byword of the Cynics was frugality and the charm of the simple life. When Antisthenes posited this as being in conformity with nature, the battle of the Sophists against tradition became a battle against the artificial developments in tradition. The wise person only recognizes what animal nature unyieldingly demands; he disdains that which is considered desirable or worth pursuing only as a result of human invention.

Among these are legal relationships such as family, nation, and civic duty; they are not innate in any person, not even humanity itself is innate. The life of the dog is the right life: without property, without marriage, without shame, unconcerned in deed and behavior. Beyond this recommendation for licentiousness, the Cynics offered simplicity as the criterion of natural law. This criterion has not disappeared from movements that are inspired by a disgust of abundance and excess, whether the movement is revolutionary and within undeveloped economy, or is an artificial one prompted by an upper class that is surfeited or is beginning to fall. In this way, the upper class could praise the dog's life to the poor, because they had nothing else to offer them. And yet they always took it badly when the labor leaders were not satisfied by having to live in a barrel.

That is why the hedonistic attitude, that of pleasure—as always private pleasure—is less prone to misunderstanding than the attitude of the Cynic. Aristippus considered pleasure alone to be the supreme good, and he measured the value of every institution, as a complex that is not only artificial but ascetic as well, according to whether or not this good remains undisturbed. In contrast to Antisthenes and Diogenes, Aristippus led a life of luxury, and it was upon this life, one of parasitic scrounging or of inheriting wealth, that he founded natural law; yet he said of wealth that for him it was the same as with shoes, one cannot use it when it is too large. Thus, even property was posited exclusively in relation to consumption, in relation to a delight in pleasure that was intrinsically without limits although full of external considerations. For the gilded youth, pleasure is taken for granted, but as is well known, pleasure is not so taken for granted by the poor and the oppressed even though pleasure was always an impulse in revolutionary movements toward happiness. In this way, the Hedonists, with the natural law of being happy, furnished a criterion that, for the exploiters who were compelled to make life unhappy, was a much less convenient criterion than frugality was. Society had to make its position clear; was it to be guided more by the chicken in the pot or by a tranquil simplicity and moderation? It is not surprising that the rulers of the state have almost always been angered by the simple demand that the state provide the space for pleasure. This universal right to pleasure appeared more difficult to fulfill than the right to some meager dwelling. Preaching the universal right to pleasure without hypocrisy is an awkward business so long as there are rich and poor.

5

On the Natural Law of Epicurus and the Stoics

None of this had any corrosive effect upon the status quo; such a view merely wants to be left in peace. It was even demonstrated how one could live wisely and amiably with law. So in a way that was much less uncertain than that of the Sophists, Epicurean reflections were directed toward founding a law outside institutions and statutes of the status quo. This law is the law of pleasure, reappropriated from Aristippus, but coldly considered and completely devoid of celebration. This worked very well, for here the statutes and institutions were immediately tested against the obvious evidence of the senses. Epicurus posited the right to undisturbed, tranquil pleasure as the condition that is best for mankind and worthy of its dignity, and as the first right (from a chronological point of view). In this way he deprived the origin of the state of the holy status that had traditionally been accorded it. The Athenians banished their kings, but Epicurus banished the polis as that which had turned out to be a burden for the private life; that is, he made the polis into a union merely in light of the goals fixed by convention. By making an astonishing transition to the issue of private right, he was the first to teach that the state was formed by a *contract* that was concluded by free and equal individuals. The occasion for this contract, *syntheke*, is quite sober, namely, the will not to harm one another. Its goal is the beneficial, that is, the *sympheron*, the utility of every participant, the tranquillity of each with every other. Since this agreement takes place among equals, every trace of a contract of subjugation is absent; since it presupposes an equality of interests, it is more of an agreement (in the judicial sense) than a contract. The arrangement that creates the state is at most a contract of unification with mutual utility as the sole basis for those obligations that carry the force of natural law. But even natural law itself, which appears in a utilitarian manner as the right to individual security, does not imply any sort of consecration (as it later will), or any solemn relation to an "eternal nature." When the Sophists set *physis* against *nomos*, nature against human law, they adopted the concept of *physis* in the sense that the Ionian philosophers had already developed and determined: namely, that which endures throughout change, is the same amid the diversity of things. Thus *physis* was defined as the constant value in the changes of human institutions and laws; yet, in doing this the Sophists did not posit the content of this constant or essential element as something particularly lofty or solemn. Epicurus himself does not recognize anything at all that would be valid "by nature" for all people without distinction between peoples and times, and that, therefore, would have been originally valid before time. His natural law is formed completely in time, through laws that are made and produced by contracts that are themselves made, even if they are made according to the criterion of utility. The validity of his natural law only extends as far as the power and interests of the people who posit law for their security. Yet nevertheless, this modest form of natural law—apart from the first conception of the social contact that it contains—proved to be rich in consequences. This form of natural law contains the liberal "night watchman state" in miniature, and significantly, it does not make natural law richer, but rather more meager than positive law; in fact, it defines natural law in an essentially negative way. Law is law only to the extent that it prevents mutual injury and harm; this is the sole constituent of its worth and is the tribunal that judges the worth of all law.

Of course, that the desires and life of the slave could also be taken into consideration when securing such guarantees is not even a possibility in this society of slave owners with its Epicurean garden for the elite. The Epicurean right to pleasure needed calloused hands to sustain it by providing something to eat; that is why this elegant and tranquil pleasure had an interest in leaving slaves out of the contract. Slaves are not people, but things of which one takes possession; they do not even have the power to submit or subjugate themselves to another, and they certainly do not have the power to conclude a contract of association. This natural right to peacefulness remained valid only for those who were free and equal, and that, in the final analysis, in praxis, meant that it was valid only for an elite group of sages. Others may simply have to suffer their laws or their whip, for there is no *physis* that, with substantial universality, could be raised up against this "injustice." The sage never considered it worth his while to insert himself into the confusion of a fight for his own peacefulness, and the effort to fight for the peacefulness of others was regarded as even less worthwhile. The gain of a political minimum did not appear worth any political ambition; this minimum was already acquired by the Epicurean insofar as he remained as far removed as possible from the positive state. Writing in opposition to the Epicurean Colotes, Plutarch depicted this attitude in the following manner: "For Epicurus there exists neither tyrannicide, nor heroes, nor legislators, nor advisers to the king, nor leaders of the people, nor martyrs for justice." Nothing is said here of the audacity of the Epicurean conception of the world that remains shamelessly worldly: But something is said about nature and natures that stay all too private. These are the limits; Epicurean law lies down in the field at the point where injustice is to be fought. Political indifference is the price it pays for the premature insight that the state which would be best is the one which exists the least.

Other sages did appear, sages who did not merely aspire to the pleasurable life whether for themselves alone or in association with a few friends who regarded themselves as an elite abbey of hedonistic friends of the arts. The Stoics fought for such a private life, although with their definition of the wise one they would make themselves its victims. This school also sought tranquillity above all else; yet unlike the Epicureans, they did not do so out of a reflective prudence, but out of an imperturbability that had come to be unquestioned. And importantly, from this point forward, happiness ceased to be the more or less pioneering honor of the sage, as it was for Epicurus; happiness was no longer a ticket to the dignified life. Rather, happiness should follow as a consequence of this dignified life: For the Stoics happiness was not a sensible, palpable happiness, but something stronger — the pride of being human. From the time of the Stoics dignity was detached from happiness; the difference between their paths was that on one there was a willingness to enter into a struggle. Passion continued, stoically, to flow into severity, for it was still the head held high that was, in the end, considered worthy. Only thus did the person who was not docile, the person who held himself upright, who from the outset related to natural right, become indisputably visible. Of course it is true that for the Stoics, for whom the social mandate was still unclear, the sage and his pride appeared to be able to blossom everywhere. There was nothing plebeian, and in most cases nothing especially aristocratic in this imperturbability; because it was essentially formal it seemed able to blossom in any class. The slave Epictetus was a Stoic, and so was the emperor Marcus Aurelius; and in ataraxia indifference was compatible with inflexibility, Philistinism with iron. A pride that was universally formal set an all-encompassing attitude of kinship upon the autonomous individual. The affirmation of this kinship suppressed, or at least mitigated, the private side of life. Natural law became universal, international, even cosmic law. The Sophists had set *physis* in opposition to *nomos*; the Stoics had restricted this opposition to that of *physis* and *thesis* and thereby opened the space for the most remarkable expansion of the concept of *nomos*. *Nomos* was equated with the law of the universe, with the inviolable *ananke* [necessity] named in Democritus's philosophy of nature: *Physis* was no longer in opposition to *nomos*, but a synonym for it; *physis* became the first *nomos*, which was universally grounded. In this way the first lasting, although troublesome, relation between the concepts of nature and law was achieved; for the first time we find natural law as a *pathos*. For the Sophists, and even for Epicurus, there was nothing particularly lofty or moving about *physis*; it was more essential, but not more sacred, than the demythologized state. Unlike the Sophists and Epicurus, the Stoics did not reappropriate the Ionian concept of *physis* merely as the incarnation of what endures, as the essential in all appearances; rather, for Stoicism *physis* also names that which is holy, and even divine. An extremely anthropocentric, yet divinely sublime, nature governed by necessity was held over positive society and became the sole criterion of valid *nomos*: *lex naturae* [the law of nature], *to physei dikaion*, is *lex divina* [the law of god]. More clearly than anywhere else, one finds at the base of this natural law the appeal to a golden age and the reference to the legend of a golden age that has been preserved. One finds mythological reminiscences of the primitive commune, of an age without private property, states, or war, an age governed by the unwritten *nomos*. The contents of this unwritten law, as it resurfaced in Stoic natural law, were the innate *equality* of all people (the abolition of a difference in worth between slaves and masters, barbarians and Greeks), and the *unity* of all people as members of an international community, that is, the rational empire of love. Stoicism is enormously democratic here: Its natural law is uniquely philanthropic, its state is a brotherhood. The task of politics is intimately bound to the task of universal humanity, which must be based upon the rational essence of human nature and the rule that results from it. This rule is intrinsically just as much the overcoming of slavish passions as it is extrinsically the overcoming of interests that are egotistical, localized, or national; this accorded well with the death of the polis, and the expansion of the Hellenistic, then Roman, horizon. Euripides had already said: "Just as the eagle can fly through the air everywhere, so too is every nation a fatherland for the nobleman." The economy of the polis became too narrow. The Greek law of the community similarly became too restricted; a universal law, common to all Greeks, had already begun to develop before the time of Alexander (parallel to the Roman *jus gentium*). From this there arose an extremely broad, and so extremely universal, theory of law as a theory of rights. This theory of law, which arose politically out of the contemporary world, descended upon the world as the ideology of the Alexandrian Empire, then as the ideology of imperial Rome, and finally as that of the beginning of the Christian ecumenism. In any case, the extension of this law, as *orthos logos* [right reason], was wide both above and below. Chrysippus already spoke of the common rational universe as a state, and Posidonius formulated the central dogma of Stoicism when he described the world as "the commonwealth of the gods and men and that which results to this end"; an enormous mother nature appears for the sake of just laws and the laws of justice.

Two pillars support the true Stoic *doctrine* of natural law: the concept of common notions, *koinai ennoiai*, and the postulate of a life in harmony with nature, *homologoumenos te physei zen*. These common ideas are, thanks to the nature of our thought, able to be deduced from experience by everyone. They not only provide the basis for the essential consensus of all people, the *consensus gentium* spoken of in the later theories of natural law (Cicero, Grotius), but they also contain the most certain truth insofar as they can be deduced with natural necessity. These common ideas even make natural law evident to every person who abandons himself to them; their *orthos logos* points continually to the truth of being orderly and upright. But this truth is only expressed to the extent that the rational nature of men is in harmony with the *substance of nature* and is maintained in this harmony. Judicial truth, as with any truth, appears as "an idea that seizes thought," *phantasia kataleptike*, that is, as an idea wherein the mind conceives its object just as unyieldingly as the object grips the mind (so that the mind is in accord with its object). The highest criterion of the true life, of true justice, and of true knowledge is on this account a cosmomorphic one: participation in the reason of the universe. This reason was continually

praised by the Stoics as a guideline for action: The world in its totality
is the supreme judge, supreme wisdom itself. The world supplies the
model of autarky, for "it contains everything that it needs"; it posits
the canon of ataraxia, for "with supreme beatitude and wisdom, it
traverses infinite time in infinite periods, in constant concern, in the
most just and perfect domination" (Dion, I, 42). It provides the basis
for ecumenism, for the world knows nothing that is not embraced by
it and the law of its reason: All-encompassing necessity, bound to
reason and finality, does not tolerate any localized interruption or any
limits. The law of reason is itself Zeus; the equality of *lex naturae* and
lex divina thus remains immanent in the world: The cosmomorphe
did not require a transcendental legislator or obedience to commandments that are not written in, and contained by, the living law
of the universe. Of course, in this way a certain dissonance in the
Stoic hymn to nature became apparent in its monism. Since the time
of the Sophists, the privateness of this notion of natural law did not
fit in so well or so simply with the all-gathering, cosmic law. Even
the pride of this privateness, namely, the victory over the passions
and irrational affects, was incompatible with this universal optimism
of the universal world, for the affect presupposed an irrationality in
the individual that did not have a place in the universe. To reconcile
this a new concept of the *homologoumenos te physei zen* was formed.
Chrysippus had already emphasized that people had to live not only
according to universal human nature but also according to a specific
human nature. This restriction did, of course, have a place within the
Stoic system, since its monism was not inarticulate: All individual
"natures"—plants, animals, people—were particular forms of the universal logos. Included in the idea of a universal world economy was
a specific deployment of the special excellence of the individual forms,
one that was particularly well suited to establish and reinforce the
significance of the individual human being and the specific nature of
man within the context of everything. Nevertheless, there arose a
break *in concreto* within this conception of the world, which supported
on the one side the independence of sages and on the other side the
urge toward a universal necessity. This break also revealed itself politically: While some Stoics defended the republic, others were able
to defend the monarchy. On the one hand they defended the idea of
a masculine inflexibility; on the other hand they spoke of the need
to submit to an earthly Zeus—in the hope, of course, that he would
be in accord with the universal Zeus, that is, with the rational, universal

government of the universe. But none of these dissonances in the Stoic position was sufficient to obscure its clear point: Stoicism had taught equal rights for all on the basis of the unity of the human race. The contact with the ancient prophets of Israel, who were the first to lay claim to an analogous position, was a singular event full of consequence. The unity of the human race, the natural right to peace, formal democracy, mutual aid—through the Stoics, all of these principles came to be the beginnings of a more or less definite concept.

6

Stoic Doctrines and Roman Law

One who lives by the pen seldom finds it necessary to turn to the sword. In this world well-placed people usually tend to preach wine and drink water—the contrary seldom occurs. This was usually the attitude of the Stoics; for the most part they remained in the realm of the universal with their law and their love. There was no dissatisfied class standing behind the sages, and these sages, though themselves often poor and dependent, remained out of touch with uncultured poverty. Culture elevated one out of the lower class, and the lower class had no use for culture. Spartacus did not understand the Stoic theory of natural law; Epictetus, the slave, understood more but would have condemned the rebellion as lacking ataraxia. Once again we find limits: While Epicurean law spoke against injustice, this was nevertheless couched in a disinterestedness that inclined it to run from the fight; similarly, the Stoics either took refuge in interiority or in the universal perfection of the world. Nothing is really changed when one claims that the way slaves were treated was modified by the Stoic theory of natural law, or that organizations that aided the poor and other charities were begun. Such impulses of generosity, which usually only had to do with slaves, did not begin because of someone preaching universal equality and brotherhood. Much of the Stoic theory of natural law sounds like a disclaimer, and what was disclaimed was taken as seriously as twentieth-century Freemasonry and the brotherhood of all classes. Seneca, the rich courtesan, never drew any conclusions from this idea of brotherhood, not even with regard to his relations with Epictetus, who was a slave. Fraternity was found only in his writings (as well as in those of the gentle and placid Epictetus) and it was sufficient to find it there. It is true that a few of the other Stoics were supposed to have distinguished themselves by their denunciations and conspiracies. Plutarch reports in his *Lives* that Cleomenes, the Spartan king who introduced a sort of military commune (with the abolition of debts and the division of real estate), was said to have been raised by a student of Zeno named Sphairus. Plutarch added that it was Sphairus who inspired the young king to make risky decisions, "for the fiery natures of the Stoics easily led to audacity." And it has been shown that Tiberius Gracchus, who was of a patrician family, came to adopt the plebeian, revolutionary line through the intermediary of natural law. His teacher was the Stoic Gaius Blossius from Cumae, a man who therefore did more than Socrates to seduce youth. But such Stoics were exceptions, there are only a few such well-known mentors; the best-known, Seneca, had Nero as a student. Of course even in Epicurus, the Stoic reserve was only related to the act of wisdom, *qui habet bonam pacem et sedet post fornacem*; it was not concerned with the enormously wide *lex humana* of the most extended of all schools. Theoretically, the Stoic doctrine said that all were free from the time of birth, that all were equal on the basis of their rational human nature, and they even spoke of a cosmic fraternity in a way that almost evokes Schiller. Man appears as a being of dignity; Marcus Aurelius believed that everything was contained in the formula *to anthropou poiein*, that the human lot is to care, that it is human to act. It is from this point that the pathos of human dignity appeared in the specific form that was characteristic of natural law; this development was due to the Stoics. This requirement disappeared until the times of the classical theories of natural law, when the social mission that had been absent became clearer. But first, Stoicism was to exert an astonishing legal and political influence upon Roman law.

It was astonishing because nothing could be more innately sober than Roman law. Nothing was further from the language of fraternity, nothing more practically (indeed almost exclusively) related to the protection of property. Roman law was centered on the law of indebtedness; it is the creditor, not the sage, and certainly not the poor person who is protected legally. Only property, as the limitless *dominum of an individual*, is a self-evident concept; not property, but its limitations (for reasons of neighborly coexistence and general well-being) need to be justified. Roman law has nothing in common with the law of the golden age, the Stoic law of declamation. The sources of the law here were thoroughly empirical: They arose from common praxis of the legally protected interests. At the base of Roman law, there was the common law, the original local law of Rome, which was first called *jus quiritum* and later called *jus civile*. Above this law there gradually arose a more flexible law of the courts, one that took many of its principles from the peoples who lived in the region. The legal sources of this *jus honorarium* and this *jus gentium* were found in the edict that the praetor and town councilor posted at the start of each administrative year in which they announced the principles according to which they intended to pass judgment. But in order to preserve continuity of edicts, the new praetor or councilor stayed as close as possible to the edicts of his predecessors, improvements or innovation were only made on individual points, and there was certainly nothing at work here that was borrowed from the principles of speculative reason or natural law theories. In the end, the law of the court, or *jus gentium*, developed into the imperial law of the empire: The sources of the law were the decrees of the emperor and the expert opinions of jurists, which were signed with the *jus respondendi*; the last canon of law was given by the collected works of Justinian. The entry of Stoicism into Roman law obviously did not happen because of a philanthropic, or even speculative, interest. Its entry was mediated by the snobbishness of the Roman upper class, and especially by the need to formulate the court law with a logic and homogeneity that would guarantee the unity of the system. Roman jurists were introduced to Stoic theories of natural law beginning about 150 B.C. Their first encounter was through Panaetius, one of the most important of the middle Stoics, who had been welcomed in Rome as a guest of the young Scipio. The law of the court adopted the art of precise definition, the logic of classification (*genus proximum* and *species*); abstractions secured a place for themselves (for example, in the law of liens it was no longer necessary to put up tangible property as it was when the law of liens was read literally). But above all, the "trial according to definitions," which was customary in the law of the courts, required a sophisticated set of definitions, whereas the older law of the people (*jus civile*), which worked according to "legislative action," did not have such a need. The difference is this: The judicial procedure of the *law of the people* was related to the universal law, which was established by a plebiscite, *actio* was *legis actio*; the judicial procedure of the *law of the courts*, on the other hand, was defined by a formula given by the praetor that replaced the awkward *legis actio*. This formula was more flexible and better suited to the multiplicity of legal relations that extended beyond the agrarian community. None of these sophisticated definitions had anything to do with natural law; they simply were the descendants of Greek logic (in particular the idea of a logical formula, which the Stoics were the first to develop). A semblance of natural law only became necessary with the expansion of the already extensive empire within which the law of the courts (as *jus gentium*) was in effect. Of course, the *jus gentium* itself (which was radically different from the later law of the people in the sense developed by Grotius), even in its complicated forms, was not shaped by natural law; it is rather the product of economic and political relations that extended beyond the barriers of local law. The *jus gentium* is an international commercial law that simultaneously established the praxis of international relations. Thus the Hellenistic Age had already substituted a universal legal assistance for the old contractual assistance that was set up between Greek states (the *dike apo symbolon*). Nevertheless, in Greece and even more so in Rome this situation had the effect of pushing thought toward a consideration of universal legal norms; there was even the move toward an idea of law that all nations had in common. The laws of Rome and the laws of foreign lands had to be gathered together in a third law that was common to both — "jus gentium omni humano generi commune est" (*Inst.*, I, 2, 2). To this end the Stoic doctrine of natural law presented itself as the desired ideological aid: The Stoic concept of *lex universalis* was placed alongside the *utilitas*. Cicero wrote a philosophical treatise on this form of positive law and thereby handed down the Stoic theory of natural law to succeeding generations. He even turned the legally awkward creations of Stoic natural law into something so polished and versatile that when it was necessary they bowed before the sovereigns of the seventeenth century. In his own way Cicero completed what Panaetius had only begun: He transformed universality, which had been a reflex of the Alexandrian Empire, into the legal ideology of imperial Rome. All positive law was to be traced back to the universal, to the human, to the divine to the extent that such a move is possible. The basic principles upon which Cicero made the judgment whether or not a law was in accord with natural law were the *koinai ennoiai*, the *orthos logos*, and the *homologoumenos te physei zen*; of course, almost all of these basic concepts were made into more conciliatory commonplaces in Latin "translation." The *koinai ennoiai* cease being ideas that are necessarily bound up with the essence of human being. They become *innatae notiones*, and innate ideas become an exclusively psychological phenomenon. The *orthos logos*, wherein natural necessity follows the pathway of justice, becomes the *recta ratio* of good sense, though of course as a common sense that has become the supreme source of law. The edict of the praetor was thus rationalized technically and philosophically — it must be thinkable by all reasonable beings, that is, it must be found in the evidence of the protection of property and contracts. "Quibus enim ratio natura data est, isdam etiam recta ratio data est, ergo et lex, quae est recta ratio in iubendo et vetando" (*De leg.*, I, 33): Where there is intelligence there is to be found law, and the law, as *recta ratio*, should be inflexible, a stranger to privilege, and something general. In this regard the requirements of the *homologoumenos te physei zen* were only utilized for the ordering of the framework of the *recta ratio*, the pathway of the law. Cicero formulated the Stoic requirement in a completely cosmomorphic way when he said: "Ipse autem homo ortus est ad mundum contemplandum et imitandum" (*De nat. deor.*, II, 37). But for Cicero the world is a unique network of utility and uses; that is, natural elements, like all phenomena of nature, are ordered by providence for the satisfaction of the needs of people. Consequently, even the paths of law follow this visible teleology: The realm of things is subordinated to the uses of people, and is bound up with the realm of persons. The law of things is linked with the laws of obligation, family, and inheritance according to the structure of this world; even the jurisprudence of possession, of property, and of servitude (*servitutes*) had a stake in a universal teleology of the utility in the world. In this way the content of the positively posited law could be made to coincide with the supposed, or even authentic, natural law of the Stoics (and the formalities in their natural law lent support to this effort). Papinian said of the law of the court that it was essentially "juris civilis adjuvandi vel supplendi vel corrigendi causa," but in Rome even natural law had very few other functions. There remained as an element of positive law a sort of vent for the *just strictum*, a special sort of instrument, whose effect was especially noble, namely, the so-called practical sense. As such it even appeared explicitly in concepts such as *bona fides* or *justa causa*, and especially so in a special virtue of the judge: *aequitas*. But at first even *aequitas* signified more a logical technique than an adjustment according to the principles of natural law, let alone a rejection of positive law in the name of natural law. *Aequitas* is fairness primarily because it permitted the freest application of judicial reason to law in instances of special and exceptional cases. Only in an improper or secondary sense is *aequitas* fairness in the sense of an appreciation of humanity, or of an intelligence that is full of insight. Furthermore, Roman law sparkled with an abundance of *paroemias* (adages) that were pronounced as if they were valid across space and time. For instance, "Volenti non fit injuria," or "Nemo potest secum contrahere," or "Nemo plus juris transferre potest quam ipse habet" (an even older adage would have said "Manus manum lavat"). Even these principles are primarily a logical formulation of judicial technique, not deductions from a *lex divina* and *lex naturae*. Yet, on the whole, from the time of Cicero Stoic natural law at least remained as a decoration in Roman jurisprudence. Indeed, in the works of Gaius, Papinian, and Julius Paulus, and in the articles of law of the corpus juris, it was even present as a sort of basis even if it was a basis that was rarely appealed to in making positive determinations. "From the beginning all men are born free" ("Ab initio omnes homines liberi nascebantur," *Inst.*, I, 2, 2). This sentence would not sound so bad if it were applied to slaves, and a poor debtor would gladly turn back to this beginning. "The universal judicial precepts read as follows: Live honestly, do not harm others, and give to each his own" ("Juris praecepta sunt haec: honeste vivere, alterum non laedere, suum cuique tribuere," *Inst.*, I, 1, 3). The *suum cuique* in this sentence points to a certain dubious tendency to defend privilege, or at least the patriarchal order, but if this sentence had been taken seriously, with the *alterum non laedere*, it would have had the effect of doing away with the entire Latin military state. But even more surprising is the definition and acceptance of natural law by Ulpian in the first book of his *Institutiones*: "Natural law is that which nature has taught all living beings; for this law is not solely the possession of the human race, but is common to all living beings that live on the land, are born in the seas, indeed it belongs even to birds" ("Jus naturae est, quod natura omnia animalia docuit; nam jus istud non humani generis proprium[!], sed omnium animalium, quae in terra, quae in mari nascuntur, avium quoque commune est"). This sentence is a model of reduction by extension; for insofar as natural law is extended to all living beings it loses the human sparkle and pride. And how far removed this definition is from the one that Cicero gives in the first book of his *De legibus*: "Omnium, quae in hominum doctorum disputatione versantur, nihil est praestabilius, quam plane intelligi nos ad justitiam esse natos, neque opinione, sed natura substitutum esse jus." In Ulpian one finds not only the disappearance of Cicero's rhetorical ring (which is no loss) but also a zoological expansion that usurps the human realm. Later reactionaries (as for instance F. L. Stahl in his conservative, Christian-inspired philosophy of right) always remarked that this broad definition of natural law by Ulpian had the effect of doing away with natural law: *quod licet bovi, non licet homini*. Nevertheless, birds were not the most repulsive example; they were always highly symbolic as beings that were not bound by any barriers. This is an ancient revolutionary image: to be as free as a bird in the sky. Yet Ulpian deduces nothing humbling or exalting from his definition; he simply draws the natural right of the union of the sexes, of marriage, procreation, and education ("Hinc descendit maris atque feminae conjuctio, quam matrimonium appellamus, hinc liberorum procreatio, hinc educatio"). Ulpian adds that even wild animals are to be judged according to the knowledge of these laws, for they are the commandments of "mother nature," and indeed among these laws one finds the right to defend oneself (*vim vi compellere*). Bachofen contends that Ulpian, who came from Tyre (the Phoenicians were an ancient hereditary and matriarchal culture), defended the ideas of the primitive maternal law, which had been drawn from the animal nature of man, more than he did the ideas contained in the Stoic doctrine of natural law. Precisely in its application to marriage, procreation, and education "the Ulpianian form of natural law shows itself to be the law of Aphrodite, which permeates matter and results in its fecundity." According to Bachofen it is not accidental "that Ulpian most clearly and prominently defines the physical natural law, and that he does so most clearly in the sense of the ancient maternal religions" (*Maternal Law*, 1861, p. 66). However that might be, Ulpian no more drew upon the consequences of a recollected feminine law than he did so with respect to an original freedom or the inviolability of one's fellow man. He did not even do so in those issues that presented the possibility of such a move, as for example the issue of extramarital relations; the strictly patriarchal constitution of the family forbids such a move from the outset. Nevertheless, the basis, or the fiction of a basis, which is in accord with the principles of natural law, is not lacking: The Stoics made frequent recourse to a golden age, even to the "ideal" of the *communis possessio*. The more social conditions decayed, the less profitable the Latin-based economy became, the more desperate the condition of the urban lumpen proletariat became, and the more criminal the mercenaries who, along with their emperor, were the sole representatives of the state became, the more seductive became the power of innate right, which did not have to be acquired, and of the fraternal order dreamt of by the Stoics. The Roman Empire still put more hope in the coming of this order—or at least it outfitted itself with words to such effect—than it feared the threat of the barbarians outside of the empire. On the basis of these considerations most church theologians were able to come to terms with (although rather badly) the existing state after Christianity had made its "confession." With the end of the persecution of Christians, the baptized state became further removed from the "barbarian law of the scythe." Around A.D. 300, Lactantius, the "Christian Cicero," paved the way for the assimilation of the church with the state even with respect to the incipient Christian doctrine of natural law. This merger was made with confidence, since Lactantius recognized virtually everything involved in the Stoic theory of natural law, which, since Cicero, was deeply impregnated by the public law of Rome. Indeed Lactantius accomplished this assimilation with the help of the Stoic equivalence of *lex naturae* and *lex divina*: In his magnum opus, which is aptly entitled *Institutiones divinae*, Lactantius employs this equivalence as a means of interpreting the Stoic theory of natural law through the biblical Ten Commandments and vice versa. This relation between the Stoics and the Decalogue was maintained up to, and even beyond, the time of Thomas Aquinas, for with it came the advantage that the state was no longer measured against an "absolute original law" (the golden age of paradise), but against a "relative natural law" (the iron age of the state of sin and of its commandments). In this way Lactantius forms the connecting link between the Stoic and the medieval theories of natural law, just as Cicero formed the link between the Stoics and Roman jurisprudence. But this time, in a class society, the principle of "justice" (*suum cuique tribuere*) could more easily protect its image.

7

The Relative Natural Law of Thomas Aquinas and of the Reformation

It now became a question of sharing power with newly arisen masters. Power had completely transformed itself; it was no longer something static, but now rested upon the field and serf. Even the medieval city with its patriarchal social system did not laud itself as a cold administration, but as a sort of enlarged family life. The church found it easier to fit into this organic order than did the cold reason of the Roman state. But then the church became a fully developed power in its own right, and it fought with the emperor over its share of the products of exploitation and over the extent of its domination, but it did not quarrel about the right to exploit or dominate. The higher clergy had already given themselves this right; thus, in principle one could not criticize it. This means that as a power the church could not tolerate the Decalogue, let alone the original Christian commandment of radical love. Lengthy and convoluted trains of thought were needed in order to formulate a precise and yet elastic theory of natural law. The church fathers prepared the groundwork for this, but it is not until Thomas Aquinas that the medieval form of natural law is codified. The relation that the Stoics had established between *lex naturae* and *lex divina* remained in force, as did the equivalence, which Lactantius had introduced, between *lex naturae* and the Decalogue. Natural law was revealed anew in the Decalogue: It was revealed to a fallen humanity and was modified accordingly. It presupposed a sinful, no-longer-just Adam; it is the natural law of a state of sin and therefore a relativized natural law. In the golden age, which is called the original state or Paradise, freedom and the absence of violence were alive (even if there was no undifferentiated equality); in it there was the law of *communis possessio*. But these original laws were lost in the attenuated or relative natural law, which is what was left after the Fall; thus Adam's sin justified the church's fall into sin, that is, its fall from the original Christian communism to the rules of the world. Indeed, relative natural law fell far behind the Stoic position: It even sanctioned slavery, and above all it endorsed authority and its sword. The effect of Adam's fall was that natural law took on a new form; it became the retribution and remedy for sin, a form legitimated by the Fall itself. Since the Fall, humanity, which God had created as perfected, needed courts and, from a moral-theological viewpoint, grace. In this way the worst *embarrassment* of natural law, namely, oppression, was founded upon natural law itself as something that had been relativized. Yet early on the difference between Western and Eastern churches became apparent: The Oriental church only occasionally conceived of law and the state as a remedy against sin. Neither Byzantium nor the czarist church knew any relative natural law: Property was tolerated, but not defended as a divine institution; family law and public law have no priority over monasticism and the commune of the cloister. The ancient Stoics and their vague world state had a greater influence upon the Oriental church fathers than did the Roman Stoics and their strong connection to the law of the Roman Empire. Special emphasis was placed upon the distance that Christ professed from law, and upon his refusal to take the role of judge (Luke 12:13–15)—this was retained and ideologized. The practical consequence of all of this was that in Byzantium and then in czarist Russia there was absolutely no tension between the church orthodoxy and the state. In ancient Russia, as in the West, left-wing opposition inspired by the Gospel was limited to sects, but even right-wing opposition, like that found between the German emperor and the pope (and later in the Jesuits), was completely lacking in Russia. For this to happen another element was lacking: the integration of law and state in a divine plan such as that found in the West and brought to fruition by Thomas. Only here is relative natural law to be found: To be sure, the state was held to be (as in the Orient) a consequence of Original Sin, but in the West the state also functioned as the order of the state of sin and so was justified as an authority. *Poena et remedium peccati*— these were its prerogatives. The critique of positive law was only founded in the fact that the state had to exercise this prerogative under the leadership of the church and could not overstep the limits. Besides, the state not only stood for *poena* but also for a *remedium peccati*, and to the extent that human nature was not completely corrupted by the Fall, but only weakened by it, to this extent the state contained a *bonum naturae* as its goal. This goal is the rational goal of general well-being and security, and it is the supreme compendium of relative natural law, the Decalogue, that guarantees it and furnishes norms for it. The commandments of the Decalogue are not given as the legal grounds for the justice of punishment (of transgressions), but as a remedy (by the observance of the commandments). In equating the Decalogue with relative natural law Thomas almost posited the Decalogue as a technical, rational canon of positive law; all this was done in the spirit of a preevangelical patriarchalism. It is a patriarchalism that is so rational, so civil, that it has no intention of imposing norms upon the peasant-master relation or upon any aspect of feudalism. Rather, with a striking one-sidedness Thomas related it almost exclusively to the medieval city with its division of labor and its corporate structure, with its transparent proportions of labor and income, with its semblance of social assistance for everyone, and with its supposedly Christian pacifism (as opposed to the spirit of chivalry). In this way, relative natural law in Thomas came to be impregnated with the content of values of the middle class; and for the most part these remained the ideals that facilitated the compromise between the world and Christ. But it was not as if this compromise could only be attained through a relativization of natural law as some sort of slackening or washing-out of absolute natural law through the Fall. Such a compromise could also be reached through an outbidding, namely, through rivaling the absolute natural law as it occurred in the original state of Paradise, which is spoken of in the Gospel. The law of the Decalogue is related to the rational goals internal to the world; the *nova lex* of the Gospel, on the other hand, is related to the supernatural goal of grace. Thus an otherworldly goal appears, which guarantees the supremacy of the church in the face of the relative natural law of the political order, and which even substituted a heavenly law for the absolute natural law of earthly paradise. The absolute natural law of Paradise is a mere *lex divina* of Creation; the Gospel, on the other hand, gives the *lex divina* of Redemption. The Gospel abandons the work of six days en masse and perfects nature as supernatural until it is rendered incomprehensible. This loving union of blessed spirits in God, which is portrayed in Dante's *Paradiso* according to Thomistic concepts, no longer had anything in common with the *libertas* and *communis possessio* of the earthly paradise. It is not so much the loss of absolute natural law that Christ restored as it is the loss of the mystical perfection of grace. One can see how deeply natural law has sunk once one recognizes how far the perfection of grace (of the pious), which is attained by virtue of the new God-man established by Christ, surpasses the original condition of Adam. "Vita aeterna est quoddam bonum excedens proportionem naturae creatae," and the proportion of right in the original condition as well. Of course Thomas never set up a formal opposition between the Gospel and natural law, or between the Gospel and the relative natural law of the Decalogue. For this unmediated dualism did not mesh well with the supremacy of the church over the temporal worldly order: Supremacy implies a relation. Thus, the Decalogue and the Gospel were integrated as "embryo and seed," and this was accomplished under the form Thomas had perfected: the form of sequential mediation and architectonic hierarchy. The same logos governs the world and manifests itself according to the mode of appearance proper to different phenomena and domains ("qui operatur in unoquoque secundum ejus proprietatem"). *Lex divina* and *lex naturae* are not identical as they were in the world-immanent theology of the Stoics. Rather *lex divina* and *lex naturae* are divided into the beyond and the here, but the beyond is related to the here by means of a series of harmoniously graduated passages. These are the passages of heavenly participation and transformation: "Et talis participatio legis aeternae in rationali natura lex naturalis dicitur" (*Summa theologiae*, II, 1, quest. 91). Justice is the canonical form of this participation, for justice is the supreme earthly virtue (just as love is the supreme heavenly virtue) and thus is the criterion of positive law. It was divine justice—a principle not alien to the Stoics, but not essential to them either—that brought about an accord with the Old Testament. Justice is a principle of graduation: In giving to each his due—whether that be a requital in the form of punishment or reward, or distributive according to merit—it expressed a graduation, namely, that architectonic hierarchy which Thomism had erected as the mediation between earth and heaven, heaven and earth. Thus the dualism between a *lex divina* of nature and a *lex divina* of the supernatural was attenuated even in the sphere that was peculiar to justice, that is, in the sphere of law. The Decalogue remained contained in the legislation of Christ, which returned to the Decalogue as its own embryo. Similarly, the imitation of Christ implied the natural law of the original condition, as is demonstrated by the communism of love found in primitive Christianity. Amid all of this attempt to outbid natural law Thomas never burned the bridges to *lex imperfecta*—"gratia naturam non tollit, sed perficit." But however much the church hypostatized the Gospel as something related to the purely otherworldly goal of grace, it was never fully able to eliminate the world from its proximate norms and hopes.

All of this happened when the fox was permitted to guard the chicken coop; that is, when the squire became the judge and the lord of the manor became all-powerful, and there was no possibility that natural law or something else could intervene. Luther absolved authority from any external critique; he regarded the state as a thoroughly legitimate constraint. In this way he delivered the entire church doctrine of the state as the instrument of the repression of sin to the reactionaries. Luther's natural law is absolutely inconceivable when one takes it as something antipapal like his theology. His real adversary is the *natural law of sects*, and the social-revolutionary desire to recover the original condition. To be sure, the supremacy of the church must also be set aside, for the bourgeois, monarchical-authoritarian state needed room; nevertheless, Luther's position meshed so well with the definition of the state given by Thomas (*poena et remedium peccati*) that Luther adopted it. But matters were different with the Anabaptist doctrine of natural law, with the ultimately revolutionary ray of light of an unrestricted original condition. The Anabaptists erased the distinction between a natural law of the state of sin (which could only be the ideology of a class state) and an absolute natural law. They only recognized an absolute natural law without compromise, without the profit that the Fall had thrown to the ruling class, and above all without the division between natural law and the Gospel. The natural laws of the original condition and the laws of Christ are identical here; since the fourteenth century this is the conviction common to all Christian sects despite whatever other differences they might have with respect to attitudes and doctrines. There is no natural law in the state of sin, and therefore the authority of God's grace does not exist; for the radical Anabaptist this authority is not a remedy, but "the feast of profiteers, thieves, and plunderers." "That is why," said Thomas Münzer in his *Explicit Denunciation of False Beliefs* (in complete opposition to the political theology of Luther), "it is necessary to overthrow violent, insolent, unbelieving men, because they obstruct the holy Christian belief in the throne and in the world; once this is done belief will arise with all of the truth of its origin." But for the ideal of the sects this origin was deformed by authority itself, more so by temporal authority than by the spiritual; only an existence without property, without state, and without coercive law permitted the expansion of Christian piety with its true grief and authentic grace. In short, the sects regarded the so-called natural law of the state of sin only as the law of the devil. The radicalism of the sects projected the *lex Christi* into the middle of the world, not simply alongside the world in some mere internality, and not over the world into some beyond. This is the background against which Luther's perverted natural law arose—it arose as a reply to the ideal of original purity of the "Lord of All." The essential point in Luther's conception of natural law is that it views its subjects only as criminals and as in a mortal state of sin, and as a consequence it represents the state exclusively as a force of reprisal and deduces it as the natural law of the antidevil. The stronger the state, the better it is; the more barbarous, the closer it is to God. Thus, in his work *Whether Warriors Can Also Be in a State of Grace*, Luther explained that the Greeks and Romans never knew the true natural law, whereas this law was better maintained by Persians, Tatars, and other such peoples. In this way there appeared a natural law of oppression, of the omnipotence of a despotic state, one that was no longer constrained by an oblique regard for the original state and the Gospel. Even the Ten Commandments and the guarantees of rights that flow from them are invalidated; Luther said that the Ten Commandments were nothing more than a "Jewish Saxon Mirror," and as such they carry no obligatory force for Christians; at best they serve to inculcate a fear of sin. It is true that the Decalogue was also omitted by the sects, but only in order to take seriously the whole of natural law or the Gospel of the original state; they were not concerned with a partial natural law, that is, the natural law of the sinful state that, according to Thomas, was contained in the Decalogue. Luther, on the other hand, reduced the importance of the Decalogue in order to avoid having any moral remnants in his special natural law—that is, the natural law of the state penitentiary that God imposed as punishment. All the more reason that the Gospel as a pure, personal morality of intention is separated from the reprisals of the state or the antidevil. Christian freedom is never carnal and the will is never worldly, with the single, very significant exception of the nonresistance of evil. When it comes to peasants and serfs, Luther has no trouble applying the "empire of God" and its law, namely, infinite patience; here natural law and the Gospel seem perfectly compatible to Luther: "Suffering, suffering, the cross, the cross, is the Christian law and none other." All other messages of good news for those who are exploited and oppressed, humiliated and offended, disappear into inwardness, and there they remain as invisible as possible. On the one hand, Luther's natural law is a reflection of the absolutism of the state that was making inroads in his time (in the "naturalism" of Machiavelli and, later, Hobbes); on the other hand (and this is its principal point), the natural law of Luther is the apotheosis of force for the sake of force, of authority for the sake of authority. Whereas for the Stoics and, as will be seen later, for the natural law theorists of the Enlightenment nothing was more difficult than the deduction of penal law, for Luther it was the easiest step to take. Conversely Luther's natural law as a *jus divinae irae* [the earthly law of God] obstructed every slippage toward human rights, especially to the paradisiacal *libertas et communis possessio*. In its place, justice, this mythical-demoniacal ideal of law, was isolated and absolutized until it became the highest terror. The mythical-demoniacal correlate of this ideal came along in the bargain: guilt and original guilt, the thoroughly damnable fundamental guilt of all human existence. But what is completely lacking here is the luminous category of right, of the natural right that man poses to himself and demands of himself: not as the "right to be punished," but as the natural right to an original freedom, equality, and quality of life such as the Stoics had formulated in a manner that was at least halfway adequate. Calvin was the first to return to more familiar paths, for the simple reason that with him the tension with the Anabaptists disappeared. But above all this worldly-wise jurist lived in the West, in the midst of a progressive bourgeoisie that had begun to have some influence upon the state. Consequently, that which one commonly called Christian moved out of the tranquillity of the sanctum in order to insert itself into the temporal world order, where it could actively shape the world in conformity with the commandments of God. But for Calvin all of this was already laid out in the Decalogue, as well as in the entire history of ancient Israel. Even then, he said, the state existed, and it showed itself in the warnings that the prophets could direct against bad kings. The state was not only a means of compulsion against the consequences of the Fall. It contained the order of the goodness of God, and had to be administered to his honor; that is, it had to be administered in accord with the Decalogue, which is not the "Jewish Saxon Mirror," but the "perpetual and infallible rules of all justice." In place of the dualism found in Luther's reactionary separation of the authoritarian state from Christianity (of the Decalogue of the just God, and the Gospel of the loving God), Calvin substituted the attempt to unite the Decalogue and the Gospel. Calvin explained that there is no tension between the divine law of the Old and New Testaments; the Decalogue must be understood in a Christian manner, while the Sermon on the Mount must be understood in light of the old God of war and law. Not only must it be understood in this spirit, but above all—in accordance with the framework of a more developed Western economy—it must be understood in opposition to Luther's progressively perverted natural law. It must be understood in a way that understood trade and barter; that is, as speaking of diligence, methodologically rationalized work, and the multiplication of goods. In this way Calvin opened the door in theology for the development that had already begun capitalistically; frugality, modesty, and reprobation of pleasure all demanded a type of person who did not have to wait until the *citoyen* became a bourgeois in order to come into being. From the outset he was set up as a "steward of God," or so the Puritans regarded this type; after some initial hesitations, the business of money was Christianized. In this regard everything that admitted of, or included, the law of Moses or the natural law of the state of sin, such as punitive violence, war, religious pride, the wrath of prophets, or fanatic piety, came to be highly regarded in Calvinism. It was no longer reducible to the natural law in the state of mere sin, but was related to the order of that benevolent God who had his faithful predestined subjects and was a sort of capitalistic hero. In this way Calvin mitigated the tension with the Gospel, which was necessary if the theologians of the formation of capital were to show how the rich could enter the gates of heaven. Of the ideal of radical love that was given in the Sermon on the Mount only the demand of a largehearted charity remained, and even this demand was imposed in a richer and more meaningfully concrete way in the Old Testament. Unlike Luther, Calvin interpreted natural law so completely in terms of the Old Testament and the equation of the Decalogue with the *lex divina* that for him the Sermon on the Mount was no longer a source of embarrassment, nor did he have any need to resort to the sort of double entry bookkeeping found in Luther. As such, Calvin's assimilation of the Sermon on the Mount to Moses and the prophets, to David and the Psalms, became an anti-Luther showpiece (and, from the viewpoint of the history of dogmas, anti-Paul, anti-Augustine, and especially anti-Marcion); but even at this point absolute natural law is completely abandoned. In his book, which bore the rather telling title *Against the Anabaptists*, and in letters and instructions Calvin demanded (with the utmost seriousness) that a rapprochement with the Decalogue (on account of "the immutability of God") be pushed up to the point of identity; in this case that means pushed to the point of abandoning the *lex Christi*. Jesus added nothing and changed nothing of the *lex Mosis*, as the natural law of the state of sin; in the Sermon on the Mount he simply paid heed to uniquely Pharisaic misinterpretations. The sermon simply emphasized that the same acts of relative natural law be carried out without personal hatred or passion. As he did with the Gospel, Calvin attenuated, and even suppressed, the contrast here with the original condition of Paradise (the golden age of the Stoics). The ideal of natural law in incipient capitalistic society tolerated the *communis possessio* even less than it did the ideal of radical love; and thus the original condition was not taken into consideration at all. There is never discussion of the transformation of the original equality of goods into private property; from the outset private property seemed to be a primal creation of God. God, in the natural law of sin as in the original condition and in the Gospel, is the supreme proprietor; for Calvin, communism is practical as well as theological nonsense. Such are the purely capitalistic traits in Calvin's natural law: There was an interdiction placed upon the Gospel for the benefit of the affairs of a rising middle class. To this extent, Calvin is as far removed as possible from the ideal of the sects, at least from the ideal of the radical sects that declined in capitalism and never (as the Quakers did) contributed much to it methodologically.

But Calvin also knew of natural law according to the paths that had been traced in it by Stoicism; he did not know the *communis possessio*, but he did know the *libertas* of the individual. He only saw the ideology of the incipient capitalist in this *libertas*, but all the same it formed a point of resistance against the omnipotence of the state. This is the source of the celebrated theory of the right of the lower magistrates to resistance and reform as soon as the highest power degenerates into "tyranny." Here *tyranny* means that the high powers oppose themselves to, and permanently move away from, the natural law that has been set down in the Decalogue. The ancient history of Israel was rich in sermons that opposed godless tyrants (as opposed to the peace that Paul concluded with the higher authorities); the prevalence of the Old over the New Testament tipped the scales favorably to the side of the opposition. Although no trace of the later doctrine of the social contract was to be found in Calvin (nor was it to be found in his clever disciple Bèze), there were already to be found the beginnings of the sovereignty of the people, the right to revolt, and constitutional bonds (here the term *people* largely coincides with classes, that is, with class rights). Saint Bartholomew kindled a substantial quantity of resistance literature; and it is these lessons that eventually cost Charles I of England his head. In the end, in later Calvinism even the demands of freedom of conscience and worship (as the natural right that, with corresponding reinterpretations, had been deduced from the Decalogue) prepared the way for latter-day human rights; even here we find a theological root of later, purely rationalistic theories of natural law (of human rights). Yet even in Calvinism the right to resist was extremely restricted; it was only permitted of "legal professionals" and "lower magistrates," and as long as authority was in any regard tolerable, that authority was recognized as ordained by God. The so-called reformers never supplied a radical justification for tyrannicide; it was Jesuits such as Bellarmine and Mariana who did so. Moreover, they are the first in whom we find the rudiments of a radically asserted, even decapitated, doctrine of the social contract. The interests of the church inclined it to retreat from the Thomistic definition of the state as a divine institution for the repression of sins. Rather, even if the state is a divine remedy against sins, it is nevertheless entwined in sinfulness itself. This is all the more reason for the state to actively turn against the church once it has liberated itself from its leadership: Once this happens the state is no longer held to be the repressor of sin, but its nature becomes that of sinfulness itself and it is viewed as the work of the devil. Of course, even Thomas endorses the right of resistance in the face of bad or godless princes; but this right was so restricted that it was practically inapplicable. According to it both the individual and the masses were forbidden to take action against the tyrant under every and any circumstance; such action is only permitted to the *autoritas publica* in concert with recourse to the pope. This is the extent of the right to resistance in Thomas; it is an especially relativized right in an already relativized theory of natural law; it tolerated extreme injustice because the church could still count on the state as the ground floor of its hierarchy. This harmony between the state and church changed with the arrival of the Protestant state and when the Counter-Reformation could not grant authority to the *lex divina* of oppression. There was yet another, completely different source for such a reservation (or whatever one wants to call it): the ancient tension between the pope and the emperor, especially in the later Middle Ages and in the interdict. But during the Counter-Reformation this tension burns hotter than ever before. It was extremely useful for a papacy that wanted to latch onto its newfound popularity. Accordingly even the Jesuits Bellarmine and Mariana taught (toward the end of the sixteenth century) that the prince received his power solely from the people, who have the natural right to retract their mandate and so depose the tyrant. In doing this Mariana (*De rege et regis institutione*, 1598) defended even individual action as propaganda sanctified by the deed. He permitted insurrection not only for the people, but when such a gathering was not possible ("si publici conventus facultas erit subtlata"), every private individual was called upon to assassinate the tyrant; for even though the citizens had lost the possibility of assembling, they had not therefore also lost their right or will to do away with the tyrant. Moreover, authority here is (unlike in Calvin) vulnerable in the strictest sense. The state is a fabrication of men, completely from below; its origin is in the social contract; its only natural law was to serve the church. It arose with this function, was sanctioned by it, and disappeared with it. In this way the temporal natural law was negated, or rather made thoroughly dependent upon the *lex divina* that the church possessed. But by the same token a basis for the new rationalistic natural law was made known: the social contract. Paradoxically, to this extent it was precisely the Jesuits who initiated a detheologization of natural law: The natural law of a real enlightenment could put tyrannicide as well as the social contract to good use.

8

The Ideal According to Relative Natural Law: Justice from Above

Each of those men we have considered up to now took what he taught seriously. But hardly any of them seriously practiced what they preached once it went against tradition. No wealthy thinker put himself in the unnatural position of giving up his money simply because there was no money in the golden age. No Sophist, and hardly any Stoics, freed his slaves simply because slavery contradicted natural law. The idea that all are born free lay at the basis of Roman law, but the structure of the Roman world was another matter. The *Digests* cite a passage from Ulpian that explains why all men are free and equal according to natural law, in order in the next sentence to develop slavery as an article of civil law. As we have seen, the ancient natural law preached by the bohemians or philanthropists of the landed class did not erode anything, nor did it prove to be a nuisance to the existing order. Epicurus was the first to speak of the state as a contract, which, because it is a contract, can be terminated. This was extremely important, but it was never developed. One needed money or the Stoic virtue of pilgrimage in order to escape the state (society); Spartacus never knew or had anything of the kind. The doctrine of the original freedom of men did not have the right to freedom even as a theoretical consequence. Medieval theological theories of natural law did just as little, or even less, to damage the judicial order of their time; despite all the tensions between them, church and state were entangled together in a conspiracy. This understanding between the worldly and the spiritual Caesar was economically necessary; the universalistic tendency of the High Middle Ages enlarged the riches of Henry IV and then Innocent III. Nevertheless, the doctrine that best placed the Fall at the service of the authorities and relativized natural law is a surprising doctrine. Even the pathos of justice, which Thomas emphasized more strongly than Stoic theorists of natural law, did not in any way exacerbate the tension between the *justum* and the positive law. Quite the contrary, it becomes clear at this point that justice, which presented itself as a category of natural law, more clearly expressed the advantage of the ruling class than it expressed the rejection of a "fair law" that had been misused or deformed by power. Practically, the demand of justice was as good as satisfied (even when it was the object of the state) once the law was administered without bias and without exception; justice was the synonym for the observance of legality. But just as the Sophists turned *physis* against *nomos*, and the Stoics set *physis* and *nomos* together against *thesis* (as in the articles of law), so this was a movement against tradition in the law and, to this extent, a movement from below. Chrysippus regarded all existing laws as defective, even when his school gave no thought to reversing this situation. Only a sage with the strength and power of a Hercules would be able to reorganize the world philosophically; nevertheless, a Hercules was always imagined, even if not a Prometheus. But that justice wherein Thomas saw the norm of natural law, more concretely of relative natural law, did not involve any movement from below, but rather a gift from above; it clearly denoted a protective, patriarchal spirit. It is not thought in the same way as the subjective "justice" of Adam before the Fall, that is, as the completely different *rectitudo* or integrity of human nature and its absolute natural law in the original state. As objective justice it stems from the time after the Fall, that is, from the relative natural law of the Atonement, and amends for the Fall; in any case it flows from up high. The attribute of the justice of God was especially important in the Old Testament; and, in fact, this significantly distinguishes the God the Father, Yahweh, who does not spare even his own people, from creaturelike pagan gods even when they appeared as guardians of contracts. Yahweh is the God who "punishes the children for the sins of the father" (Exod. 34:7), and even if Maimonides pointed out that this vengeance "was only valid for the sin of idolatry" (*Guide for the Perplexed*, I, chap. 54), the Scriptures universally say of God the Father that "all of his ways are the ways of justice" (Deut. 33:4). About A.D. 120 Marcion, the great heretic of the church (or father of the heretical church), demonstrated an unmistakably antipatriarchal attitude when he disputed the pathos of justice in God. Marcion did not merely describe Yahweh as an evil creator, as did the majority of the Gnostics of his time; although he certainly is that too, the God of the Old Testament is the imperfect creator of this imperfect world, but he is not simply evil. Instead of the flat antithesis of good and evil, of night and light (which reappeared later in Manichaeism as a significant relapse behind Marcion), Marcion spoke of the justice that is in evil; in place of the simple antithesis of night and light he set that of justice and love. Yahweh, the jealous, irascible God who measures, the God of the law, is thoroughly just. He is the strict embodiment of that justice which rewards evil with evil, good with good; he has both in his arsenal and distributes each as the Lord of the measure. But as creator and father to the world, he is alien to the God whom Jesus, and Jesus alone, announced: This God is not law, but love, not the scales of justice, but *gratia gratis data*. According to Marcion, it is this alien God, and he alone, who is the father of Christ; he appears as the Savior of mankind, as the one who lifted mankind out of the paternal home of the world, out of the *aequinoctium* of guilt and sin, of service and servitude. That is the extent of this remark about the patriarchal, indeed even despotic, character of justice; this remark, despite all of the attendant mythology, is instructive. In every particular epoch, at least in nonrevolutionary times, justice remains (in the overwhelmingly dominant static periods of history) a justice from above. This meant that nothing in the existing standards of law was fundamentally altered in these times; these standards were and remain the primordial measure of the dominant relations to the extent that these are able to be measured and weighed statically. From the viewpoint of its compensatory nature, justice does not act as critique, but as a critical apology of positive legislation. Despite the various equivocations with its homonym, subjective and moral quality, justice only belongs in inauthentic natural law, namely, in the relative natural law of the compensatory repression of the sins of deeds. Authentic social revolution was not satisfied with "a fair wage," which only partially restored surpluses, and in the same way genuine natural law did not simply speak of the balance of "the just application" of the laws or the equality of "just laws," but made use of categories that were not as stable as those that brought about balance and equality.

That is why justice is not a category that thought, justifiably dissatisfied, could consider its own. Justice supposes an authority that dispenses charitably and that appeals to its conscience as impartial. But the golden age to which Greek natural law referred is explicitly glorified by Stoicism as a period without authority. No Themis, Dike, or Nemesis reigned at that time; according to Homer and Hesiod, Themis is nothing but the goddess of custom and deliberation, of the customary law that perpetuates itself. The idea of portraying her with scales and a sword, as in the painting by Raphael, is without question a later astrological idea that did not occur in antiquity. The idea of a Themis rationalized and monopolized by a ruling class was unknown in ancient natural law. Justice, as a category, certainly did appear in Stoic natural law (particularly in Chrysippus), but it stayed at the borders of that law to the extent that it was democratic. It is not accidental that justice occupied a key position for those philosophers who, although they are counted among the greatest of antiquity, have written not about natural law but of patriarchal, lordly law. Plato and Aristotle made out of justice that which Stoicism never made out of nature, namely, the genius of domination. Plato posits his just state of virtue in explicit opposition to the cynical state of nature, and the *politeia* of Aristotle knew of no model of the state other than that given positively by tradition. Plato taught that justice was already in the soul as a dominant and regulative element; it is the virtue of the whole and it watches to see that all interior faculties, desire as well as courage and reason, fulfill their task without overstepping it. Plato introduces the book about the state with discussions concerning this harmony, with attempts to define its concept; in any case, it is in the state, and not in the individual, that justice is most recognizable. Just as in the virtue of the household, which determines places, prescribes portions, and puts the table in order, all other virtues are subordinated to the justice of the state in a way that is clearly administrative in character. Justice in the state means "that no one should do several things at a time, but that each—young and old, boy, woman, slave, craftsman, ruler and ruled—does only their appropriate tasks"; it controls the *to ta autou prattein* as the constant fulfillment of the duties that the state gives to each person (*Republic*, IV, 10). Aristotle is less authoritarian, but he also elevates justice to the principle of political virtue. Justice is the basis of communal life, of a communal life where all classes are in equilibrium. Theoretically speaking, the fifth book of the *Nicomachean Ethics*, which is dedicated exclusively to justice, did not require the harmony of Thomas, which is tenable only in a relative natural law. Aristotle posited and reflected a judicial order in which the common good of the collective was the result of a situation where the different social classes only recognized the influence and advantages that corresponded exactly to their importance for the political totality. "Justice is accordingly something proportional" (*Nic. Eth.*, V, 6), and it is this proportion "that produces and preserves happiness and its components in the political community" (V, 3). Furthermore, Aristotle is the first (and here he is followed by Thomas) to distinguish between communicative and distributive justice. The first form of justice is related to contracts and to the equalization of the disturbances that were produced by a violation of the law; whereas the latter form is concerned with the apportionment of social advantages and honors as a function of the worthiness of the recipient. Indeed because (since Pythagoras) justice has been thought without hesitation as proportionality par excellence (expressed by the square number), a proportionality in which a given quantity is multiplied by itself, it is no surprise that we find that *dikaiosyne* in Aristotle is further mathematized in its dual form: Communicative justice works arithmetically, distributive justice works according to a geometrical proportion. The rule for arithmetic justice runs as follows: One who has too much will have enough taken away so that both parties have equal amounts (this is only valid for penal law and the law of liens). The rule of geometrical justice runs thus: Just as the worthiness of A is related to that of B, so too does that which A contains of honors and advantages relate to that which B contains (thus one finds a highly differentiated equality). Ultimately, the proportion for distributive justice infringes upon that given for communicative justice, which means that Aristotle is able to sanction differentiations between the justice of classes and estates; he is opposed to a uniform law of retribution. "If, for example, a person of public authority strikes someone, he may not be struck in return; but if someone strikes such a person he must not only be struck but punished as well" (*Nic. Eth.*, V, 8). That is justice; equity (*epikia*), though it is "a corrective of justice," does not, in the sense of a natural law, lie outside or beyond justice. Equity is simply "a corrective of the law in places where it is deficient on account of its general formulation" (V, 14); it is not something distinct from justice (as is usually the case in the Roman tradition).

Enough said about Aristotle; it soon becomes clear that Aristotle does not explode the patriarchal habitus of justice, but rather supplies it with a cold (with respect to action) government. Of course, there is in Aristotle the justice of the individual and the justice of relations between individuals. But there too it is a virtue that is not concerned with emotions or intentions (such as generosity or noble sentiments), but with a virtue of external action: The individual can act unjustly without already being unjust; this means that justice and injustice can be objectively decided upon. At bottom, *dikaiosyne* has its model in that impartiality out of which springs its superiority and its power to "grant justice or to each his share." This is why the Scholastics were able to combine Aristotle's concept of justice quite easily with that of the Old Testament despite all of the differences in their respective doctrines of retribution. The purely ideal justice of Yahweh did not in any sense legitimate a justice differentiated by class: In the courtroom no one should receive special respects; rather one should listen to the little person just as to the great and avoid no person; for the tribunal of justice is God's (5 Mos. 1:17). Such clear procedures do not only stem from the ancient Israeli peasant democracy and from the primitive recollection of equality in the time of the gentes; rather they first stem from a patriarchal conception of God that has been pushed to such a high point that the standards of social levels disappear before his majesty. But the condition of the recipient of distributive justice and the measure of his ration do not disappear. The connection between Aristotle and the Old Testament was brilliantly drawn by Maimonides, who passed on to Thomas the synthesis between *dikaiosyne* and *zedeq* (the concept of justice in the Old Testament). Maimonides thus gave the most concise definition of the justice of a graduated patriarchy from the point of view of the *Nicomachean Ethics* as well as from the Bible: "Justice consists in granting his right to everyone who has a right, and in giving to each living being that which he should receive according to his rights" (*Guide for the Perplexed*, III, chap. 53). This then is the way in which Thomas introduces justice into natural law via the Old Testament and Aristotle; he thus establishes a relative natural law that does not destroy positive law, but on the contrary receives and ideally completes it. Nevertheless, in the ancient tradition natural law had little to do with justice; at least it never played a leading role. Here on the other hand justice becomes an ideal; it occupies the highest place among the natural virtues, and orients all of the administrations of the state in accordance with the relative natural law of the state as *poena et remedium peccati*. In the economy justice demands *pretium justum*, that is, a price that corresponds to the "objective value" of the goods plus the charges for reproduction incurred by the merchant; it implies of course the continuation of a standard of living differentiated by social class. It calls for a social differentiation founded upon a natural inequality—one already present in Paradise and therefore with all the more reason to be found in the state of sin—and it is legitimated by the division of labor, from the lumberjack to the prince. Justice, as the form of the "participatio legis aeternae in rationali natura," normalizes the relation of each social order with respect to the general goal of temporal prosperity: celestial salvation (it is only in the highest law, canon law, the law of the Christian corpus, that all social differences disappear). Temporal authority, with its relative natural law, in its efforts to maintain order and civil peace, is completely dominated by the ideal of justice as both commutative and distributive; in other words, it is incumbent upon this authority to take pains that each is able to participate in the *bonum commune* according to his social condition, and that all of the judicial actions respect a strict correspondence between the services rendered and services received, between the damage and the penalty. The value attached to each social condition and the good conscience that accompanies it have been perfected: "And to this extent distributive justice gives to each that which corresponds to his degree of importance [*principalitas*] in the community" (*Summa theologiae*, II, 2, quest. 61). This is justice in the sense of the *suum cuique*, a hierarchical and class justice, where the triumph of the patriarchical principle is magnified by the social architecture. It is the same justice that—from the point of view of the principle of form—is visible in the strictly weighed proportions of the Scholastic systems, where an object begins to be known as soon as the value of its place in the hierarchy of the other forms of existence is established. "Just as God, because he created the world, placed everything in the place that corresponded to it and produced such a universal articulation that the world appeared as a harmonious unity, so too the founders of a state must assign to each member of the collective their corresponding place . . . and must order everything in such a way that there arises an intrinsically articulated organic political unity" (Thomas, *De regimine principum*, chap. 13)—*Justitia fundamentum regnorum*. This was certainly the cornerstone of the natural law of the Middle Ages, of the natural law of the ideology of an organic-hierarchical society. The plastic arts of the Middle Ages paid homage to justice in the allegories of *Justitia*, which first appears here with a sword and a scale, with the *suum cuique* of the scale that judges but also distributes. The elegant corner capital of the doge's palace symbolizes justice as the foundation of the house: Aristotle is hidden in the scrollwork, above which there appears a pictorial relief of the judgment of Solomon. No governmental building was ever obliged to choose the Sermon on the Mount or the golden age as the allegory for its cornerstone. It is, on the other hand, characteristic of the natural law of the modern age that the pathos of justice diminishes before that of freedom and equality. God retreats as both patriarch and the supreme judge; man ceases to be nothing more than an object of justice. The word *justice* remains, but its supremacy in natural law disappears, and above all, the undeniable moment of condescension and acquiescence, inherent in the severity that the word confers upon itself, disappears. And so does its appearance of impartiality (saturated with false consciousness), its worn-out equivocation with moderation as the moral attitude (wisely understood from above), and its Areopagus of remuneration and dispensation. The Enlightenment, despite Tellheim and after him Kohlhaus, robbed the pathos of justice of its role as the primordial standard and measure; and if Tell, as a defender of natural law, calls Gessler to account, it is not due to any deficiency of justice. Rousseau defines *justice* simply as "the love of man derived from the love of oneself" (*Emile*, IV); yet love of oneself (*amour de soi*) is the innocent self-love of the state of nature and is distinguished from self-esteem (*amour propre*) as a selfishness born of property and the division of classes. The love of mankind and its companion, justice, both of which stem from the love of oneself, are no longer divided between the strong and the weak, between those who distribute and those who receive: This justice is no longer hierarchical and consequently no longer a justice. Without doubt, the form of justice from above that has been valid hitherto, as the way in which the formal legality of above was maintained, still offers relative protection in social relations that have become barbaric or dominated by state totalitarianism; this is of course the reason that Nazi jurists wanted to eliminate it in all of its forms. Thus, the fascist jurist J. Binder, after first having explained that "for the individual the claim to justice can only mean that he finds himself in accord with a positive law" (*Philosophy of Right*, 1925, p. 389), later "finds no place in the authoritarian state" for justice (*Foundations of the Philosophy of Right*, 1935, p. 163). But this absolute elimination of right does not obscure the simultaneously palliative role played by the *suum cuique* in the fascism that is completely devoid of justice and constructed upon reactionary law: We find the same situation in the dreams of corporate societies, in the defenses of a legitimate monarchy, in efficacious slogans and devices of the Prussian crown and the sort of state that it represents. Thus, the founder of the conservative party, F. L. Stahl, begins the first page of his *Philosophy of Right* with the suspicious proclamation: "The philosophy of right is the science of that which is just. . . . There is no more holy belief of mankind than that there is a justice and that we have a knowledge of it, even if it is only a limited knowledge." But in the three volumes that follow we find only the Middle Ages dressed up; we find an adapted relative natural law. Here we only find Original Sin, reprisal confined to the state, the caste principle, and public authority divinely invested; justice logically leads to a species of eternal government together with the neo-Thomist reconstructions that lament the passing of the corporate state. Thus the relative natural law that descends from above ended some four centuries ago. Now there begins the struggle for subjective, public rights, conceived not only as a judicial discipline but also as the bourgeois-progressive content of natural law itself.

9

Althaus, Hobbes, Grotius: Rationalized Natural Law and the New Edifice of the Law

From this point forward the search for justice has a force behind it. It no longer appears, as it did for the ancients, as the reflection of people of a good will. Nor did it appear as the art, handed down by the ancient Adam, of sanctifying the oppressions and constraints of the corporate system: The new sense of justice arose out of the contradiction between new economic forces and the old rigidified forms of doing business. This new sense could be detected judicially first in the Huguenot resistance against persecution, a persecution that left its mark upon the body. It was still a civilized, moral resistance, but one with more than enough reasons to oppose the existing state. With the beginning of the economic ascension of the bourgeoisie, productive capital entered into conflict with the old landowners and with a society that was still feudal. From the seventeenth century onward, commerce and manufacture created the grande bourgeoisie, who submitted to the fading guilds and undermined the feudal state. Subjectively, the freedom of conscience presented itself as the watchword of the beginning of individual enterprise, and the classical doctrine of the social contract began to take on a new acuity with Saint Bartholomew. The most significant person of the Calvinist resistance was Althaus (*Politica*, 1610), for with him a new tone appeared in the citizenry. He was one of the first to teach that power must be returned to the people as soon as it was no longer being exercised to their advantage. From the outset he distinguished between the social contract and the contract of domination, and he conferred upon the people the glory that had hitherto been reserved for the crown; Althaus is the first to give credence to the concept of the people as sovereign. It is of course true, as Gierke has demonstrated, that the postulation of the sovereignty of the people can be traced back to the late Middle Ages. It appears rather abruptly and suddenly in the nominalist Marsilius of Padua (*Defensor pacis*, 1325); it is also found in Nicholas of Cusa. But it was the bourgeois faction of the Huguenots that lent the first driving force to the doctrine of natural law as the law of the people, a law with a different sort of sovereign, one without any crown whatsoever. After such an un-equivocal beginning, no one could suspect that the modern form of natural law would once again benefit the prince, or at least the gov-ernmental power in general. Nevertheless, this transformation, which did take place, was funded by Machiavelli, and perhaps by Luther as well, but its master was Hobbes.

In Hobbes, the English Revolution produced the most profound thinker of the new form of natural law and, simultaneously, the harsh-est, most acid-tongued critic of its democratic content. Even if his fidelity to the king was never unambiguous (Hobbes made peace with Cromwell), his fidelity to his dictatorship was never in doubt. But it is precisely this fidelity that, in full accord with natural law, stripped the statesman of all consecration, and more: It denounced him as the last of the wolves. Texts such as *De cive* (1642), and even the least royalistic and thoroughly anticlerical *Leviathan* (1651), laud the state, *de jure naturae*, as being monstrous. This transformation was made possible by a profoundly pessimistic conception of human nature prior to and outside its socialization. If every person is evil by nature, that is, if every person is the enemy and obstacle of the other whom he is inclined to harm, then the state contract can never be a social contract; from this premise of the hatred of men, Hobbes emphasizes anew the contracts of submission and of domination. In the state of nature man is *homini lupus*; that is his sole freedom, and self-preservation demands that man abolish it. In order to bring about security, indi-viduals must abdicate their power and their rights (in the original, state power and right coincide) in favor of an individual who is the only one in the state that is formed who preserves the power of the wolf found in the original state. This unique individual is the sovereign, who still possesses (but only by restraint) the privilege of the ancient right of the stronger. Even more, following the abdication of all of the others, the sovereign is the people, and outside of him there are only subordinates whose duty is unconditional obedience with respect to every command of the authorities (with the sole exception that they cannot be constrained to commit suicide). Naturally, Hobbes, like the revolutionary theoreticians of international contract, deduces the philosophical content of law from a single principle—here it is the principle of self-preservation, which seeks security and peace—and he does so in a manner that is totally constructivist and demonstrative.

But the initial principle that is radically pessimistic (or better, extremely naturalistic) reintroduces oppression into the deduction of the ancient theory of the state, this time directed against the "homo homini lupus, bellum omnium contra omnes." Furthermore, it fits seamlessly into the plan of the antifeudal absolutism of that time—"autoritas, non veritas facit legem" (Leviathan, chap. 19). With this Hobbes secularizes the doctrine of the primacy of the will of God over the reason of God, which Duns Scotus had established in the preabsolutist period. Around 1300 Scotus taught that the good is not good because God willed and commanded it, because God could just as well have ordained murder, thievery, and adultery in the commandments and then not murdering, not stealing, and not committing adultery would be sins (Op. Oxoniense, dist. 37). In short, the good would not have been able to be a preordained idea in accord with the absolute will, but simply a bonum ex institutione in accordance with God's unlimited power of issuing decrees. Duns Scotus's successor, Ockham, even drew from this primacy of the will the conclusion that in Bethlehem God could have taken the form of a piece of wood, of a rock, of an ass (instead of a human form)—"autoritas de potentia absoluta, non intellectus facit incarnationem" (Centrilogium theologicum., concl. 6). The political theology of Hobbes is thus formed as a pure "decisionism"—but of course he does so in the midst of the developing classical natural law itself and even for the sake of it. Hobbes obviously possesses a purely bourgeois ideology and his convoluted natural law is at its service; but one must not forget that despite Salböl and Olymp, the absolutism of the seventeenth century possesses a thoroughly bourgeois function and is closely and complexly entangled in the economy of the state, that is, with the mercantile system. Absolutism, otherwise called the dictatorship of the national state, which is incarnated in it, broke the local, feudal, economic order in the interest of the grande bourgeoisie; the exercise of absolutism, as it occurs in Hobbes, does not contradict the antifeudal tendency of classical natural law. To be sure, the purity of nature is absent in the Hobbesian conception of the original condition ("homo homini lupus, bellum omnium contra omnes"), and consequently it lacks the tendency to try to reproduce it and the sacred character of its guiding standards. The Hobbesian theory of natural law is by no means an anti–natural law in the classical sense, as propounded by Carl Schmitt and other prostitutes of the absolutism that became mortal in the form of National Socialism. In Hobbes, the obvious Byzantinism is so sardonic, so lacking respect, so seditious even, that faced with the absolutist beast, which is the only thing to remain intact from the precivilized wolfage, everything that is consecrated by the grace of God (including the father of the fatherland) is shattered as never before. This happens despite the *submission* that is inserted into the social contract; indeed in the end it is even because of this decisive clause. In the end, even the beast that is dressed up in finery does not contain its own absolute "decisionism," because it is tied, if not to ideas of right, at least to the content of the will of those who have abdicated in its favor their right to power. This content of the will was security and peace, as the abolition of the "bellum omnium contra omnes"; consequently, Hobbes said (*De cive*, 13, 2) that the laws of the state cannot conflict with their function, which is to guarantee security and peace. If bestiality was the first determination of nature, then for this very reason security and peace are the second or apodictic and irrefutable principle upon which positive law depends. This is how convoluted Hobbes's theory of natural law becomes, and how unusual his absolutism is, with its Mephistophelean reflections and with its connections to the classical tradition of liberalism at decisive points. Yet the authentic form of natural law is broken here: The social contract confirms the sovereign but at the price that he must remain a wolf among men, all of whom are equally without rights.

Such an unusual detour to the path of equal rights for all does not detain us long. It was too closely tied to the situation in England, and did not relate itself to anything either before or afterward. The feudal Magna Carta, which had restricted the royal power, entered into bourgeois-parliamentary order. Hobbes was unintelligible on the Continent because he presupposed too much that was English. Natural law became authentic once again when the social contract was separated from the contract of domination in the way that Althaus had already outlined. That is what happened with Grotius, the theoretician of a law that did not seem to rest upon the power of the state and that should be able to be justified simply by means of pure reason. Grotius dedicated his efforts to the right of the people, and this forms his fundamental a priori construction of natural law in *De jure belli et pacis* (1625), which Hobbes had before him and which remained a standard up to Rousseau. Grotius made his starting point a more optimistic one: It was not the *drive for self-preservation* motivated by the *fear* of one's neighbor, but the social drive, *appetitus socialis*, that led to the social contract. In this way connections are made to Stoicism (and even to Aristotle, the first to have taught that man is a social being per se). For Grotius all that was necessary was that he progress from this established point with a rigorous logic, and then no one could doubt the truth of his results without doing violence to his starting point. The conformity of a juridical proposition with the natural law is induced a posteriori by Grotius; namely, by comparison and double-checking of the universal validity of this juridical proposition in all peoples and all epochs. But for him this method is uncertain; like any inductive method it is not apodictic, and consequently its results have nothing obligatory about them. That which could not be doubted is only the construction of the valid juridical contents from an established starting principle that defines the creation of a law in general; in this case, from the principle of sociability. With the same logic, but starting with the principle of self-preservation (of egoism), Hobbes deduced the state of oppression; his contemporaries nonetheless continued to accept the proof of the rational method of natural law. That which entered into mathematics only much later, namely, the transformation of the complete structure through the change of axiomatic presuppositions, had already entered into the construction of natural law and thus made possible systems so different as those of Hobbes and Grotius. In any case, the following result comes from this principle of sociability: Injustice is that which conflicts with an ordered community of individual rational beings, and all that does not come under the rubric of injustice is just. That is a negative, extremely liberal definition of justice, one that latches onto a positive definition: Justice is all that belongs to the natural instinct of sociability (and only that), and all that is obviously conformable to communal satisfaction. The natural law is thus a *dictatum rectae rationis*, and *recta ratio* is agreement with the reasonable and universal human nature. "That which in various epochs and places was considered certain must be related to a universal cause [*ad causam universalem*]" (*De jure belli et pacis*, Proleg. par. 40). In Grotius's bourgeois ideal, recognition of property obviously belongs to the basic rights; the *natura socialis* did not go so far as to forget that it is speaking of the nature of the individual who is a rising capitalist. In this way, Grotius was the first to clearly separate human natural law as a creation of human reason from the theological context—the ancient relationship that united *jus naturae* and *lex divina* is broken. The law of reason, said Grotius, is valid even if—*per impossibile*—there were no God; the identification of natural law with the Decalogue, as well as with the Sermon on the Mount, is abandoned. It is true that Grotius destroys the relation with the Sermon on the Mount solely on account of its "superior sanctity," and in his commentary on the Bible, in his apologetics, Grotius remains fully and not indifferently on the terrain of Scripture. He only goes so far as to speak of the unification of the Catholic and Protestant churches, and of a Christianity common to all sects (*De veritate religionis christianae*, 1627). Despite this there remains the relation that his cosmopolitan natural law had to the tolerance, universality, and reason of "natural religion," that is, to a persisting religion that is common to all people of the earth, one existing before the division into sects. Despite its reach, the thought of Grotius, a representative of the corporate aristocracy, is in no way detached from the corporate system. In this regard, he remains behind Hobbes's position with its equality of the bourgeoisie (at the price of nullity). Grotius delivered natural law from theology, but was not himself delivered from the "gentleman," and as such he is not yet suitable for the democratic revolution. And he was even less suited for such a revolution in the form that he came to take in his disciples in bourgeois Germany, a country that was almost undeveloped in comparison with Holland. Out of the political weakness of the German bourgeoisie, men like Pufendorf, Christian von Wolff, and the inspiring Thomasius loom like the phoenixes of natural law. But the clarity of the deduction, which Pufendorf introduced and Wolff systematically continued, was not sufficient to set itself against the throne. The systems of natural law in Pufendorf and Christian von Wolff, in themselves already unique combinations of Hobbes and Grotius, serve principally to justify the constraints of the state in the name of natural law. Pufendorf (*De jure naturae et gentium*, 1672) takes from Hobbes the thesis according to which man is by nature an egoist and selfish, and from Grotius the idea that man is by nature sociable and aspires to found a society. Because nature itself cannot harmonize its two basic drives, harmony can only be introduced by constraint, by the power of the state; the state watches to see that the egoism of the individual exercises itself reasonably within the framework of the satisfaction of the needs of sociability. The state exists therefore *de jure naturae* because nature, which intends the harmony of its basic drives but cannot realize this, hands this task over to the state. The constraint of the state is deduced from the weakness of nature, and the content of the law of the state from the (early capitalistic) counterpoint of egoism and altruism. In this framework, the right to resistance, which Pufendorf includes (contrary to Hobbes), only relates to tangential matters, and the critique does not see the decrees of the baronial good will, but does see the weakness of the German empire (it is, Pufendorf contends, "not a monarchy, but a monstrosity"). In Christian von Wolff natural law sinks completely to the level of an apology for the state, for the state of mercantile prosperity, even the police state. Just as the "rational portion" of the Wolffian philosophy did not try to prove anything a priori that was not demonstrable a posteriori in the "empirical portion," so too did Wolffian natural law consider juridical relationships that are empirically given as the confirmation, after the fact, of its validity. Just as the givenness of the free fall had been deduced from the definition of movement, the givenness of enlightened despotism was deduced with an "equal rigor" from the definition of perfection. Wolff's constructive method therefore implied that all that was necessarily deduced from the concept should also be shown to empirically correspond to something in the phenomenal world, in other words, that it should be rationally verified. In spite of all this, dissonances resulted that even arose out of the definition of perfection, and this is what would usher in the only German natural law theorist of this age who deduced more than the existing state from bourgeois reason. Because nature is not an impulse and urge toward freedom and equality, the state is not the product of any *impulsus internus* but rather of the *impulsus externus* of fear and poverty. Thomasius, who genuinely restricted the power of the state, had such a doctrine (*Institutiones jur. div.*, 1688, III, chap. 6; *Fundamenta juris naturae et gentium*, 1705), one that says that objective law is restricted in the name of subjective law (at least in the domain of the freedom of belief and of conscience). To this end Thomasius defines the objective law that the state can demand as the *justum* that is the counterpart of the nondemandable laws of the *honestum* or *decorum*. In this way the right to resist the state and its church is restored to the religious individual. The significance of the freedom of belief can be measured in that in it we find the first germ of the illumination of the other human rights. But Thomasius also placed limits upon the interior of the sphere of the *justum* (on the external deductibility of demandability): He was the first jurist to oppose the witch trials, and the first lawyer to denounce torture. Grotius had liberated natural law from theology, but Thomasius was the first to find in natural law the courage and reason to protest against the stake and the rack as "divine judgment." His impartiality went so far as to assert the paradox (*De crimine bigamiae*, 1685) that only positive law, not natural law, forbids polygamy. But what is most interesting in all of this is the liberation that operates in natural law itself insofar as it is not only separated from theology, as in Grotius, but from morality as well. There are two results here. First, the definition that Kant adopts from Thomasius and his school is born here: Law is solely the external relationships of individuals. Second, there arises the separation of *law* from morality, which is equally the separation of *morality* from law; and this implies an emancipation of internal conviction. Morality thus became a synonym for an internal group of subjective laws, for the law to obey the duty dictated by conscience as that which cannot be demanded or compelled externally. Neither the police state nor the church state have the right to meddle in the *honestum*: For Thomasius this is the asylum of the freedom of conscience, a natural law of tolerance. It would be necessary to wait a century before the forces which would take over the defense of this asylum wake up in the offensive of human rights. And it is not until much later that the society, which is always in the future, appears that would not have the need of such an inner asylum, because there would no longer be reason to oppose the really good society of solidarity where being a citizen was a happiness (that which Socrates called the best).

10

Once Again: Rationalist Natural Law, Its Relation to Mathematical Construction and to Natural Religion

Man, in order to be free, must become a good businessman; that is the minimum price to be paid. But even a capitalist and his individual business were good and progressive when they first developed in contradiction to the feudal bonds that were finally broken. How much more valuable was the juridical movement toward individual freedom, which began simultaneously with the period of rising capitalism. It appeared in the form of classical and rational natural law, which sought to reconstruct laws on the basis of pure reason. The two mythical moments contained in medieval theories of natural law, the Fall and the divine legislator, fall by the wayside. With the disappearance of the Fall there also disappeared the compromise concept of relative natural law (in a state of sin), which adapted natural law to the authority that oppresses and dominates. With the disappearance of the divine legislator there evaporated the intangible consecration that had surrounded authority as authority invested by the grace of God. The feudal-theological crust cracked, and the ancient-modern elements of another natural law, which became visible in the late Middle Ages, were liberated. One is reminded of the Epicurean doctrine according to which the state comes into being through a contract. We are reminded of the Stoic doctrine according to which the juridical and governmental order was deduced from "human nature," which must be in harmony with the reason of the world. Both theories, separated in antiquity, are reunited in classical natural law and, fertilizing one another, become enormously powerful. Humanism transmitted them in a renewed form, but the Scholastics too helped to keep them alive. The late Scholastics, especially Ockham (*Disputatio inter clericum et militem*), Marsilius of Padua (*Defensor pacis*), and Nicholas of Cusa (*De concordantia catholica*) recognized the doctrine of contract, and positioned the state outside the theological hierarchy as an assembly of individuals exercising their will. The earlier Scholastics preserved the Stoic inheritance: the natural drive toward sociability (which subsequently became highly important with Grotius), and the pregovernmental state of nature of universal freedom and equality (clothed in the mythos of an original or paradisiacal state). That "human nature" would have a different appearance in classical natural law from that it had in the Stoics is self-evident; at bottom, it is the natural law of the incipient capitalist, not that of the sage. It is revolutionary and bourgeois, and engaged in the fight against feudal arbitrariness, suppression, and disorder. Classical natural law is the ideology of an individual economy and of the capitalist relationships of merchants, who require that everything should be calculable and who therefore replace the variegated rights of privilege found in the Middle Ages with the formal equality and universality of the laws. In this spirit, contract, the principal legal relation between those who own property, seems to constitute the obvious origin of the state as a simple association of goals that guarantee bourgeois security. With a grandiose fiction, the civil relation in its most modern form was retrospectively dated as coming from a primordial past: an authority instituted by general assembly, not God. From Althaus to Rousseau, the social contract unites all doctrines of classical natural law, despite the differing degrees of sharpness of the bourgeois class consciousness that is expressed in them. That which is decisively new in this manner of presenting the doctrine of the social contract is the accent placed upon the capacity to terminate the contract; this aspect is still lacking in Epicurus. It could only appear once a new class entered the picture, one that intended to destroy the power lines of the old system.

Four historically conditioned hypotheses are at the basis of this doctrine, which viewed itself as permanent. In the first place, we find the belief that *individuals* constitute and preserve social life. Entrepreneurs regard the state as theirs; the viewpoint that is characterized by private rights sustains their view, and this viewpoint cannot be violated except under the one condition that the individual consents to let this happen out of what he considers his own best interest. It was a juridical rather than a historical concept that led to the view that a just state could not be thought except as the product of the will of its members. Jurists are particularly fond of this sort of interpretation, which is given as soon as the question of contracts arises; it assumes that a will presides wherever something is agreed upon. Everything that the partners to an agreement ought to rationally foresee as the consequence of their agreement, whether or not they have really thought about it, is considered as their will as contractors. Similarly, the fictitious genesis of the state, including the assessment of that which later developed from it, speaks less the language of history than that of the contract: That which cannot have been rationally willed cannot have been willed at all.

In the second place, this doctrine rests upon the belief in the power of a logical *construction*, that is, the deduction of all valid definitions from a few principles, or even from a single principle. To the extent that the state was founded in a reflective manner, it must subsequently be able to defend itself before reason; indeed there is really nothing other than reason present in it. This is an essential trait of modern bourgeois thought since its inception: It knows only that which has been rationally produced, and it must be able to be reconstructed logically from its elements and foundations. The universal rationalistic demand of this age was for a genetic deduction from pure reason; here mathematics provided the model. If that alone is truly understood, and if the only given that is recognized as real before the forum of reason is one that can be deduced and constructed from its first principles, then the judicial and governmental forms can only legitimate themselves for thought when they can trace their first elements back to the juridical fundament of their foundation. Hobbes (*De corpore*, I, chap. 6) explicitly made Galileo's method his own and then applied it to the construction of the state: It is a "resolutive method" that describes the simplest determinant processes of movement, and it is a "compositive method" that furnishes a synthetic interpretation of given experience from a description of the concurrent action of its elements. Beginning with this finished totality of the state one goes back analytically to the drives and the rational goal that characterize the individual will that forms the state. This is done in order to reconstruct the state out of its constitutive elements according to a methodological purity, and, if necessary, in order to measure the empirical reality that is confused with this purity. Such a deduction from principles, a deduction without any gaps, is one of the principal traits that distinguish rational natural law from the analyses and fixed, but not homogeneous, juridical concepts that had become common in the Roman law that had been remolded by the glossators in Italy. The method of *continuo ratiocinationis filo deducere* confers upon natural law, along with mathematics, a prestige almost equal to that accorded the ideal of a demonstrative science. The Wolffian Baumgarten formulated this ideal in an especially concise manner: "Scientia est certa deductio ex certis" (*Philos. generalis*, 1769, par. 21). Kant's criticism was the first to abolish the cognitive value accorded to a synthetic construction a priori in the historical-material field—he did this without renouncing rational law himself.

In the third place, this was the time of the definitive triumph of the belief in a universality in which all determinations are homogeneous and constant: It was the belief in the leveling idea of a mechanical nature. This belief becomes an antifeudal ideology to the extent that it gets rid of everything that is arbitrary as well as every idea of a hierarchy of classes. By means of the Stoic concept of natural necessity, another pathos was adjoined to that of the perpetual equality of the concept of *physis*: This one was absolute conformity to the law. But the mathematical natural science of the modern period, with an entirely different *ananke*, completely discarded from nature that which was irregular and so could not be trusted. Whereas the Middle Ages seemed to have found in nature that which was irregular, the grotesque, wandering stars, and other exceptions, infractions without measure and number, there now stands a realm of especially certain laws that oppose every possible arbitrariness here below. This permitted mathematical construction a priori to attain a substratum that could not be expected outside the bourgeois ideology: The theory of numbers outlined by Pythagoras was combined with the theory of matter given by Democritus. At the same time natural law seemed to be a different one from that of the original state of the Middle Ages or of the future transfiguration. Even where the law of nature was not presented *more geometrico*, it looked like the cosmos of Newton: firm, continuous, immutable; indeed, from this point forward natural law, like nature, is considered something particularly eternal. And it is precisely this mechanical law that was set in opposition to feudal arbitrariness, to the artifices of despotism, to heterogeneous inequality—the universe itself is homogeneous.

In the fourth place, there is the lasting effect of the sentimental belief in a natural purity outside the human realm, in a *natura immaculata*. Nature not only had to radiate according to the law, but it must be like the morning, something without falsity, and with a fresh clean air. The original, predominantly pastoral desire becomes a fight against the narrow alleyways, narrow relationships, and rotten forms.

All this occurred long before Rousseau: The natural man had already appeared in the dry and sober Grotius as one who was fulfilled by the effort to achieve a peaceful and rational community—an idyllic creature in a natural paradise. This idea contrasted sharply with the "artificiality" of a homogeneous nature governed by law; indeed, in Rousseau Arcadia is already opposed to capitalistic artifice and reification. To be sure, conformity to the law remains an attribute of nature; in particular, the Spinozism that was accepted during the time of Rousseau was used to prove the perfection of nature. But the nature that is governed by law increasingly becomes the reservoir of attitudes that are critical of the age and set themselves above the law: The crystal of mathematical physics simultaneously appears as the rock of justice and a panacea of happiness. This last theme in particular underscores the fact that these hypotheses that were at the basis of the rationalistic natural law were not always entirely rational, or at least were exaggerated on this score; thus, its influence was stronger when the posterity of Rousseau exploded it.

That which hands down rules easily moves into the role of the mother or father. It is always venerated, and the more men feel related to it as a member of its family, the more confidence is placed in it. Nature had become such a family, such a tribe. Always present, it became the object of a cult, much like the cult of ancestors, which was thoroughly ahistorical. Understandably, the laws that nature seemed to teach did not remain limited to law in the strict sense of the word. They extended to art and religion as well, and from there provided further evidence for natural law. The juridical ideal of the seventeenth and, especially, eighteenth century lived in a symbiosis with a *jus naturale* in art and religion. Winckelmann's "noble simplicity and calm grandeur" point in the direction of a purity that is not only found in Phidias. Schiller's thesis that the poet either is nature or searches for nature clearly posits an aesthetic natural law; the "imitation of nature," with all of the questionableness and fitnesses of this theme, was a fundamental problem of the aesthetics of the Enlightenment. Schiller's thesis owes much to Kant's thought-provoking concept of genius in the *Critique of Judgment*: Genius is an intelligence that creates like nature; a work of art is perfected once it appears to be a product of nature without any intention. The economic-social basis of this opposition to the mere "work of men" is the same as that which occurs in natural law: The idea of a whole and a naive perfection is itself a protest against artificiality and divisiveness, and is intended to provide a path out of them. Consequently, the entire movement, at least in its popular form, landed in an aesthetic religion of nature. The bourgeois-revolutionary sense of nature, aimed at from all sides, finds a refuge here, as does the renunciation of transcendence. The baroque princes had begun to move their palaces down from the mountains to the plains, and so too with the palace of the supreme Lord and Master of the heavens. An ultimate norm, both internal and external, issued forth from the invisible subject, which was the most certain object of nature. This singular ideal was, of course, much older than rationalistic natural law. It was already evident *mutatis mutandis* in the Stoics and especially in Arabic Scholasticism (where almost all of the theologians were also doctors). Lessing's fable of the three rings surfaces here, as does the notion of the "natural light," which permits every person to come to the "pure" natural religion without revelation and without existing religions. This natural religion obviously is not a natural religion in the primitive, shaman, sense of the word, but rather is the universal religion common to all people by nature; and the content of this religion was, according to Averroës, morality. Just as the right of men is innate, so too is there an original belief that is common to all men. Just as the innate right has been obstructed by despots, so too was the natural religion separated into different competing factions by ecclesiastical interests and the ignorance of peoples. But as Toland, who was the leader of the English deists, said, wise people of all times have had the same religion, namely, the innate religion of the natural light. In Toland's *Pantheisticon* (1720) Jehovah, Jupiter, and Brahma disappear in that they join forces and unite into one; namely, they come together in the same lawgiver and creator of the world and, in the end, by abandoning the actors, in a "universal nature." It is this "universal nature" that is supposed to give the religion of nature not only its anthropological innateness but also its highest object: God becomes nature, deism becomes pantheism. Thus on the route to *natura immaculata* Spinoza surfaces once again as offering the most pronounced and distinct presentation of *Deus sive natura*; Spinoza's philosophy of right, which is value-free and stands outside normative natural law, was obviously left out of consideration here. Nevertheless, the characteristic feeling of a connection between the rationalism of nature in a political and in a religious sense is well captured by Lichtenberg's famous remark: "If the world continues to exist an innumerable number of years, then the universal religion would be a purified Spinozism. Left to itself reason does not lead anywhere else, and it is impossible that it could lead anywhere else." At the same time the Spinozistic figure of right, which had nothing revolutionary about it, points to an ultimate distinction between the hitherto common and compatible values of conformity to law and purity. Nature's conformity to law served the quiet needs of the bourgois calculus, while the pathos of the *natura immaculata* served an actively revolutionary antifeudal interest, as well as the rising anticapitalist interests. Lawfulness was the form taken by the content of the bourgeois mechanization; purity was the form of bourgeois protest against feudalism, but also against its own divisions and mechanisms. This distinction, which one can characterize as a distinction between the ideals of nature as calculable and as sentimental, appears quite clearly in one of the major books of this epoch, *The System of Nature* (1770) by Holbach and Diderot. Spinoza and Rousseau, who speak of a value-free conformity to law in nature and who deduce all true values from nature, significantly meet here in the contrast between the principal part of the book and its conclusion. The central portion of the book argues in a way that eliminates every anthropomorphism, every judgment of value in the consideration of the lawfulness of nature; it even makes statutes to this effect: Order and disorder are not in nature. The conclusion of the book, on the other hand, conceived by Diderot ("Abrégé du code de la nature"), posited nature and its code as the source and manual of that which is humanly just. In this hymn, nature intervenes and exhorts man to follow its laws, to enjoy the happiness that is accorded man, to serve virtue, to distrust vice, and not to hate those who are depraved but to have pity on them for they are unhappy. "Virtue, reason, truth, are all the daughters of nature": This is not said allegorically, but literally, in perfect accord with the sentimental natural law as well as with the pathos of purity belonging to natural religion. It is simultaneously the pathos of natural law and natural religion that animates Rutli's scene in Schiller:

If the oppressed can never find justice,
If the burden is unbearable — he reaches
Upward toward the heaven with courage consoled
And there he finds his eternal rights,
Which stand there inalienable
And inviolable like the stars themselves.

Thus mother nature surfaces once again and she should stand by her own not only to assist men but also to be a central support, a Demeter-Zeus who seemed to have been forgotten since the time of the Stoics; that is, since they had celebrated the reign of the perfection of the world, a juridical pantheism, and since the assimilation of justice and the cosmos. That is the background out of which the rationalistic natural law worked in a more or less overt manner; it is a background that is certainly not entirely rationalistic. The important exclamation in Rutli's scene—"No, the power of tyrants has a limit"—asserts and finds a limit as much in the personal will as in a nature that, despite mechanics, is a unity. Its most essential traits—morning freshness, virginity, the sublime—were attributed to the natural law of the still-revolutionary bourgeoisie.

11

Rousseau's Social Contract, the American Declaration of Independence, Human Rights

Nothing is more fortifying than the call to begin from the beginning. It is youthful as long as it is; to it there belongs a young and aspiring class. It is innocent of the bad things that have happened, for it has never had a real opportunity to be guilty. When this happens, justice has the effect of a morning; it opposes itself to that eternal sickness which was handed down before it. Beginning anew is freshness through and through; it is a first if it appears completely ahistorical, and if it seems to lead back to the beginning of history. The place where one believes one arrives is the place of "nonfalsified" nature, while nature and all that belongs to it corresponds exactly to the image that the bourgeois revolutionary wishes it to have. It carries the image of the pastoral mood, of the shepherd, of the simple and upright man; one can play with it even in the dark. The citizen regards himself as unspoiled, as a folk song; and the more arcane relationships are (without cosmetics, without incense), the more they are his own. This is how one regarded the people who had concluded the social contract, and the countryside that surrounded the contract. Rousseau is also a lyric poet, not only the jurist of the individual who makes the free resolution to begin anew among equals. In the framework of their groups each member can still embrace the standpoint of the whole, its masculine virtue, and the mutuality of aid that it offers. *The Social Contract* (1762) thus became the Bible of the Jacobins, or one might even say, in an anachronist image, that it became the Sermon on the Mount of a rejuvenated people. For the sake of the hymn to liberty, which here is an inalienable liberty, natural law prevails. It was a revolutionary act when Rousseau, going far beyond Grotius, completely erased the contract of domination from the social contract; there is nothing left of the original subjugation in Rousseau's social contract. *The absolute inalienability of the person* — that is the novum that Rousseau introduced into classical natural law. The problem of an ideal law was this: to find a form wherein *individual freedom* could not be abdicated ("to find a form of association that defends and protects the communal force of the person"). The solution Rousseau offers to this truly difficult problem is twofold: first, to point to the voluntariness with which the individual enters into the social contract; and second, to show the immediacy with which the individual relates to the ensemble of communality, and is therefore not alienated. The person does not hand himself over to any species of representation, or to any prince, any aristocratic body, or even to any parliament, but solely to the general will ("Each of us places his person in the community and all of our power under the supreme direction of the general will, and in return we receive each member as an indivisible part of the whole," *The Social Contract*, I, 6). In this way, Rousseau contends that the subject does not alienate his freedom, since it remains an equal part of the general will and since an equally large number of wills ally themselves to his will as the number to which he allies himself. Rousseau contends that by virtue of this "reciprocity" individual freedom remains as it always was: The will of all adjusts itself to the general will. But however this relates to the rescue of the person, it is true that for the first time natural law turns up *exclusively* as the natural law of the sovereignty of the people; it is the people, without distinction, who should be visible and who should decide. More precisely, in the words of that time, it is the third estate that appears, unrepresentable and unrestricted, to posit the government solely as the executive organ of the general will. The government only exists by its mandate; it is constantly subordinated to the sole legitimate sovereign: the people. The general will itself is therefore nothing other than the constant affirmation and validation of the principle of natural law with which Rousseau commenced: *individual freedom* in community. It is the freedom, not of wolves, but of men who are originally good, who were only brought to the *bellum omnium contra omnes* through the division of classes and its antinatural law. The social contract occurred solely as a means of protecting this freedom, and it can be terminated in the name of its defense. All human rights came from this freedom. It corresponded to the content of classes of the bourgeois revolution, so that even in Rousseau private property is counted among human rights (although, in the *Discourse*, which preceded *The Social Contract*, he had defined the creation of property as the source of all cultural evil). Despite this, Rousseau accorded property a legitimate place among human rights in his later writings, even in *Emile*. Among these rights, which according to the general will proclaimed a general equality, there was an equality that was only supposed to work "to hinder the excessive inequality of the faculties." On this point Rousseau finds himself in a position similar to that taken later by Robespierre, and consequently a position radically different from that of Babeuf or the egalitarian theoreticians of his age such as communists like Morelly (*Code de la nature*, 1755) and Malby, who retained Rousseau's conception of property as the source of all social evil and called for its abolition in the name of natural law. The ideological basis for Rousseau's position unquestionably lies in the principle of individual freedom and its omnipotent power, which penetrates the general will of the community. As the completer of the classical doctrine of natural law, Rousseau taught not only revolution but also constant control of its achievements by the people, and this was accomplished precisely by means of the inalienability of human rights—their most important quality. But of course, to the extent that private property was counted among the inalienable human rights, these same rights could be alienated in capitalism, in a much more radical power of alienation than despotism and class representation. For the masses little remains here of individual freedom, and of equality there remains nothing more than a general illusion. Still a sense of gratitude for the progressive intentions of rationalistic natural law compels the remark: Without its work we would not even have the *absence* of real freedom, and real equality could not even be established *expressis verbis*. The magical formula of abstract reason, of the deduction from principles, is dismissed, as are the bourgeois interests that this formula gave birth to and used. Concrete reason has come due, and with it comes a real historical content instead of the formal quasi democracy of widespread inequality. But Marxist reason is deeply obliged to rationalistic natural law not only on account of the theory of revolution but also on account of the declaration of human rights. But because property was counted among these rights and because equality was restricted to the political sphere, these rights were not properly declared and clarified.

In any event, they were declared and they pushed their way out of the closet into the fields. For the first time a people seized an idea and sought to make it real. The word *man* was the universal sign that rendered everything equal. Previously, death alone had this role; now it was life (to the extent that it did not bring death to the nobility). All this had a long period of preparation: The proposition that men are born free and equal can already be found in Roman law; now it should also be found in reality. The new formula, first proposed in June 1793, was freedom, equality, fraternity. Its birthplace was the Club of Cordeliers, a political society, which at first had Jacobin leanings with Danton and Desmoulins as its leaders. Despite its youth, this formula summed up the entire bourgeois revolution; indeed Engels even characterized it as the gentrified conception of primitive communism. Human rights are surprisingly not such a univocal product of the events or results of the French Revolution as they are the product of the formula of this tricolor. It was customary to trace the essential influence and formulation of human rights back to Rousseau, as found for example in the "Declaration of the Rights of Man and the Citizen" and in the French National Assembly of August 26, 1789. This manifest of the fundamental rights of man—liberty, property, security, and resistance to oppression—corresponds rather precisely to the final stage of classical natural law. But Jellinek (*The Declaration of Human Rights*, 1904) draws attention to Rousseau's notice of the American Declaration of Independence and to its influence upon French and other traditions. The laws of nature that were recorded in the Declaration of Independence (1776)—life, liberty, and the pursuit of happiness—have a precedent in the *freedom of religious conscience* that the American Roger Williams instituted when he founded Providence in 1636 for "the haven of all who are persecuted on account of their beliefs." The major article (VI) of the Constitution of New Hampshire defines the basic right as the right of a person to honor God "only according to the dictates of his own conscience and reason"—freedom of religion created the opening that led to the Bill of Rights. Even in Germany Thomasius's demands for tolerance were the first attempt at emancipation from an authoritarian state—with God at his side the bourgeois could take courage. On the basis of the American religious priorities, Jellinek concludes that the "Declaration of the Rights of Man" is, at bottom, a work of the Reformation, not of the revolution. Lafayette, who was commissioned to draft the "Declaration" and made an outline of it, was supposed to have brought this outline from the newly liberated states in America and to have had the Bill of Rights as its basis. The model of fundamental rights was supposedly, not Rousseau's *Social Contract*, which since the French Revolution had passed into constitutions all over Europe, but the Bill of Rights and the resulting tolerance sanctioned by the state (first found in Providence). The freedom of religion guaranteed by the state served as a catalyst for the purely juridical idea of establishing a set of universal human rights in the law, that is, through their insertion into the constitution. Only one point is correct about this interpretation: that between the right to a freedom of religious conscience, as a companion and inspiration of natural law since its St. Bartholomew's Night beginnings, and its final Rousseauvian form, there has existed a rapport and interaction—even in America with all its worldliness. This influence of Grotius and his successors was the first to give a civil law expression to the freedom of cults, a freedom that was not only religious. The framers of the American Declaration of Independence were well aware of the writings on natural law that the Grotius epigone, Locke, had produced. Similarly, the French Declaration recognized those definitions that Rousseau gave to liberty, to this fundamental right, which as the conscience of the other was not puritanically conceived, but thought in an ancient way as the *citoyen*. The Declaration of Human Rights should pave the way for the citizen and, in the end, not only the *citoyen*. Its formula is far vaster—liberty, equality, fraternity—and goes far beyond the revolutions that took place in America and France and the corruptions that followed from them. Nevertheless, classical natural law is still contained in the American Declaration of Independence, and despite many reformations, its predominance remains just as univocal as the storming of the Bastille. Liberty, equality, fraternity, do not have only a historical but also a progressive, normative weight each time a Bastille is taken. We will later see the applications of this tricolor banner, which could not have been raised above human rights without Rousseau's notion of the general will. *This was the high point of natural law, but the epoch in which it flourished was an illusion, for out of the* citoyen *there came the bourgeois; it was a foreshadowing, for the bourgeois was judged by the* citoyen. Still, all peoples only have and achieve the sort and degree of revolution that they are ready for on the basis of the human rights they have acquired and preserved. If, in the four ancient basic rights, a new meaning is given to property—that is, instead of freedom to attain it, it is defined as freedom from attaining it—then, and only then, do liberty and security come to life. And what of resistance to oppression? In the freshness of the revolution and its goals, the Fourteenth of July always infuses a new life and a human face, even after and without the Bastille. This light of 1789 persists everywhere: Like the Ninth Symphony, which is so close to the citizen, it cannot be taken back.

12

Kant's and Fichte's Natural Law without Nature: The A Priori Law of Reason

That which is strongly felt is never the occasion for much discussion. Moreover, if it is clearly accepted and desired, then it appears reasonable even without a concept. Such is the effect of individual freedom upon the French, for whom individual freedom itself did not need to be thought, unlike that which could be legitimately deduced from it. But the matter is different for the Germans; for them freedom was by no means self-evident by virtue of some impulse. In the external world it never cast a shadow, nor did it provide the premises for a political life. Always a thought, it could never be set to work empirically and that was its special excellence. This is demonstrated most clearly, and certainly in its purest form, in the way later German natural law theorists (especially Kant and Fichte) harkened back to Rousseau. Kant in particular remarkably attenuated important advances made by the prevailing theory of natural law—in the beginning at least. *The Metaphysical Elements of Law and Ethics* (1797) is a late work (Anselm Feuerbach even saw senility at work in it), but even earlier and more lively writings on the same topic—such as the important essay "On the Old Saw: That Might Be True in Theory, but Doesn't Work in Practice" (1793)—revert to a position before the eighteenth or even sixteenth (Althaus) century with respect to penal law and civil law. Kant endorses the idea of retributive punishment (an eye for an eye, a tooth for a tooth), and he denies the right of resistance even if it is against a satanic authority. The idea of the social contract—namely, that every legislator has to make his laws as if they could have arisen from the unified will of the people—applies only to "the judgment of the legislator, not the subject." This despite the fact that Kant's doctrine of law guarantees, in the same way as Rousseau's, that the people are the sole legislator and the prince merely the executor. And again, a few pages later, in complete contradiction to this, the prince is introduced as legislator and it is said that even emergency laws cannot be invoked against him. "Thus freedom of the pen" (and this only within the

constraints of the constitution under which one lives) "is the sole safeguard of the rights of the people." Still Kant showed "a strong sense
of enthusiasm" for the French Revolution (except those of its acts of
resistance in which it surpassed itself—such as the execution of the
king, the "crimen immortale, inexpiable"). Kant's theory of natural
law also kept a noticeable distance from enlightened absolutism, which
had been deduced *ex ratione* by the Wolffian school and, in fact, constituted a German form of Enlightenment. Yet Kant, who was a subject
of Friedrich II, did not deduce the Prussian state from the principles
of reason, and rejected the "natural model" of *patria potestas* as well:
"The greatest conceivable despotism is a government that is set up
upon the principle of benevolence toward the people (as that of a
father toward his children), that is, a paternal government, where the
subjects, as dependent children who cannot distinguish what is useful
or harmful for themselves, are compelled to behave passively and
await the judgment of the sovereign in order to see how they are to
be happy" (*Works*, Hartenstein, VI, p. 323). In this way, Kant completely
discards institutions such as feudal law and the constitution of churches
from the deduction of law, institutions that the corrupt "natural law"
of the Wolffian school still retained. Enlightenment does not tolerate
any sort of dictatorship for it is "man's release from his self-imposed
tutelage." But man and civil self-determination, as they are meant
here, do not represent any empirical reality. For Rousseau they remained outside every discussion; human nature simply must be freed
from historical deterioration and developed for the better. Nothing of
the sort is empirically given for Kant; no natural law of freedom is
taken for granted within the political misery of Germany. Neither
Grotius's urge toward sociability nor Rousseau's individual freedom
is posited and accepted as something that exists and lives; they are
only thought, concept, idea pure and simple, and only as such do they
provide the basis for a deduction of natural law. This, in turn, means
that in order to appear absolutely without remainder, rationalism
includes the principle of its own derivation in itself. All previous doctrines of natural law, no matter how rationally they proceeded, were
based upon a nonrational, empirically assembled element and drive;
only the consequences followed from them purely in accord with
reason. In his ethics and philosophy of right, Kant denies this empirical
drive as methodologically impure; in its place, he calls for a deduction
of the principle of deduction itself, that is, the founding of the deter-

mining ground of natural law in an a priori principle. But this principle is not individual freedom (with empirical happiness as the goal); rather it is exclusively restricted or general freedom as the principle of any possible human coexistence. "Justice is the limitation of the freedom of each person in such a way that it accords with that of everyone else, insofar as this is possible according to a universal law; and public law is the aggregate of the external laws that make possible such a thoroughgoing agreement" (*Works*, VI, p. 332). Elsewhere he makes the same point, this time with relation to what is abstract in the doctrine of justice, that is, the wooden iron of nonindividual freedom: "Justice is therefore the aggregate of those conditions under which the will of one person can be united with the will of another in accordance with a universal law of freedom" (*Works*, VII, p. 27). The primordial right is therefore not so much the freedom of the individual as a creature (caprice) as it is the thought of the most primordial and, at the same time, limited freedom; this a priori law of justice exists primarily as social contract. Thus the social contract itself becomes an idea, and because all empirical determinations have become meaningless, it becomes a regulative fiction. Not that it appears as it would in the first representatives of natural law, that is, as a kind of pure, prehistoric reality. To say that would be to misunderstand its function. Althaus had already held that it made no difference if the contract was entered into explicitly or implicitly; and as far as Hobbes and even Rousseau are concerned, they never had need of the critique that Hume, among others, raised with such energy: namely, that men were never asocial and that society is the product of an implicit agreement. But Kant, in his rejection of any empirical sanction of law whatsoever, removes the problem from any association with prehistory: It does not matter how the state actually came to be, though it is permissible and advantageous to treat it as if it were the product of a contract. Thus, in keeping with Kant's methodically pure rationalism, the social contract loses the characteristic of being a natural occurrence; it becomes instead a regulative idea. This only means that nothing can be decided and carried out in the state that could not be if the state had come into being as the result of a contract; this is the touchstone of legality, that is, the preservation of external, general freedom in conformity with the judicial idea of coexistence. All the more reason that this rationalism is imbued with particular definitions, with definitions of private, civil, and international law as that which follows from the principle of coexistence, the analysis of which sketches out their contours. The classical theory of natural law also proceeded according to analysis of a principle, but the abstract purity of Kant's theory surpasses the classical theory both in its initial principle and in the consequences that follow from it. The attempt is made to posit determinations of the content according to the purely formal principle of noncontradiction; thus according to natural law it would belong to the essence of property not to be without an owner, to the essence of a deposit not to be withheld, and so on. (Against this, Hegel posed the following question in his early work, *Natural Law* [1802]: "But where is the contradiction if there were no deposits?") But even the more important determinations of the condition of justice, such as the equality of all people, remain formal. This is quite compatible with the greatest possible economic inequality because such an inequality is a material one. People are only equal with one another in the eyes of civil law, "which as an expression of the general will can only be a law that is unrivaled and that can only concern the form of right, not the matter or the object upon which I have a right" (*Works*, VI, p. 324). The norms of the philosophy of right are, like those of ethics, without any content; for the way in which practical reason radically produces itself, without the slightest admixture of empirical elements, cannot determine the content of any *justum* or *bonum* even with the aid of the principle of noncontradiction. In his theoretical philosophy Kant persistently emphasized that the logical consistency of a proposition never constituted the proof of its empirical reality; in his philosophy of right and ethics this criterion loses its value with regard to content. The logical principle of noncontradiction, which makes a criterion of practical reason under the names *universality* and *necessity*, unifies the philosophy of right and ethics, but it does so at a price: Both become indifferent with respect to any content and therefore—and this is the same thing—both can tolerate any content. It is true that with this the "logic of the will" is differentiated on one point: Kant's concept of right refers to external action and not to an internal intention, as does his concept of morals. Consequently, the obligations of justice can be externally imposed, whereas the obligations of virtue on the other hand are posited by self-restraint, that is, by the internal legislation of the good will. Thus, legality and morality are completely separated, and the portion of intent (premeditation, *dolus*) that encroaches upon the obligations of justice is dispassionately set aside. Nevertheless, with respect to the obligatory character of the judicial law Kant's attitude, which was always hostile toward despotism, shows through: Only those laws that are passed for the purpose of maintaining external, general freedom can be justly enforced. Even the rigorously abstract separation between legality and morality is, in the final analysis, brought about in accordance with a priori principles of reason: Legality corresponds to the aggregate of external laws that secure the coexistence of the members of a commonwealth; morality, on the contrary, corresponds to the internal law that concerns the "intelligible character" of man as a "citizen of intelligible worlds." Yet the natural character of man (instinctual determination, caprice) is also abandoned within the framework of deducible legality. That is why, in the end, Kant does away with the concept of natural law itself: His philosophy of rights deals with original law purely as *rational law*. That which, since the Stoics and even since the Sophists, seemed to lend to the ideal of law its stability and content—nature as a category of social opposition—ceases to be synonymous with the juridical logos. This Greek heritage, which survived the transcendence of the Middle Ages, only disappeared with German idealism, when it disappeared uniformly. Nature as the measure, even as the measure of that which would be superior to nature, remains for Kant and his successors only in aesthetics and not in the philsophy of right. This Kantianism influenced the way in which all succeeding philosophers of right, even those who are completely different in intent and rank, approached the subject. It even unites antipodes such as Fries and Hegel. "The law of right," Fries said, "arises from our inner conscience; we do not learn it from nature, rather through this same law, as a law of freedom, we oppose the society of men to all of nature" (preface to *A Philosophical Theory of Law*, 1803). Hegel, who completely removed himself from this subaltern psychologism, nevertheless said: "The phrase *natural law*, which has been in use in the philosophy of right, contains the ambiguity that it may mean either law as something existing ready-made in nature, or law as governed by the nature of the subject, that is, as the concept's self-determination. . . . The truth of the matter is that law and all of its definitions and articles are founded in free personality alone, on a self-determination that is the contrary of determination by nature" (*Encyclopedia*, par. 502). Kant prevailed here against all of the data for an original, empirical state of humanity; the methodology of the idea was victorious, *ab ovo usque ad finem*. Henceforth, nature, not only in the Hobbesian sense but also in the Rousseauvian sense (the sense of nature that inspired confidence), is cut off from the rational law of the citizen. Nevertheless, all of the intentions that animated the concept of the citizen continued to have an effect, indeed one that was even stronger, in those who admired the French Revolution and in the philosophers of spontaneity. Thus the guiding principle was (*Works*, IV, p. 161): "Enlightenment is the release of man from his self-imposed tutelage." And thus, the judgment that was announced like a thunderclap in the conflict between the philosophic faculty and the judicial faculty (*Works*, VII, p. 403): "For the omnipotence of nature, or better for its highest cause, which is inaccessible to us, man is only a bagatelle. But that the rulers of his species take him as a bagatelle and treat him as such in that they treat him as a beast of burden, or as a mere instrument of their own intentions, or in that they array men against each other in order to resolve their own quarrels—that is no small matter, but is the reversal of the final purpose of creation itself." Despite the formalism of the exposition, the best postulates of the classical theories of natural law are preserved here, and they are even enriched with a rigor that Rousseau did not have. Thus, characteristically, it is through the absence and then the refusal of any empirical resource that the citizen is posited after formalization.

This continued and, of course, all of this happened more than ever in the head. If there were inconsistencies, remainders from the exterior world, they were to be purified by the renovating work of thought. Thus, Fichte began everything, even the original law, with a "think thy self," with free rational activity. As a simple presupposition he had the concept of self-consciousness, which posited the I and Thou, and their free, rational operation. Accordingly, nothing is given to reason as reason is given to itself: Thus the first sentence of the *Foundations of Natural Law* (1796) reads: "The character of rationality consists in this, that the subject who acts and the object of that action are one and the same; in saying this the domain of reason, as such, is exhausted" (*Works*, Medicus, II, p. 5). Here too the original right of man is characterized as a fiction insofar as man only has rights in a community with other men, but this fiction is necessarily posited with the initial concept of free, rational activity. "The original right is therefore the absolute right of the person only to be a cause in the sensible world and never to be an effect" (*Works*, II, p. 117); right thus relates to the individual will and original right to the self-determination of the individual will. For Fichte autonomy in general is only determinable through itself; the I and nothing outside of it is *causa sui*. Thus, not surprisingly, Fichte called his science of knowledge "inverse Spinozism," in which all that is outside or above receives its tenure from the positing subjectivity. Or, in other words, "from start to finish, my system is an analysis of the concept of freedom," and thus of the original practical right to freedom. Now, upon closer inspection this original right includes the freedom and the inviolability of the physical person and the established mastery in the sensible world, that is, property. Nevertheless, as in Kant, the original right must limit itself so that a coexistence of juridical persons may be possible; it is through this self-limitation that they recognize one another as free and rational beings. But the emphasis on the essence of individual freedom is not the same as it is in Kant: Freedom can only be limited by the freedom of all and solely in the name of freedom. That is the goal; and with this only those particular determinations of private, penal, and civil law that have been recognized as the means and *conditio sine qua non* to the goal are considered to be deducible. Fichte's doctrine of science (theoretical) had already determined that the ground of all being is to be found in the "ought," that is, in the purposive activity of consciousness. To this end theoretical categories were rendered mobile and labeled as such; it was to this end that they were developed and rendered dialectical as the "history of self-consciousness." But from the beginning the goal was practical reason, and in the sphere of law this end is precisely the complete self-determination of man as a juridical person. The state functions here solely as the liberal institution for security and subsistence; the social contract itself, this regulative idea, as the contract of property, of defense, and of association, is only a contract of interests, a regulative idea in connection with which the young Fichte, unlike Kant, defended the right to violently transform any political constitution that was not liberal. Justice is the product of its citizens; it is that upon which they freely agree in the same way as merchants agree upon their business transactions. Therefore, the state is indeed an institution dedicated to security, not for the purpose of an irresponsible and gregarious life, but for the purpose of personal freedom and its preservation. Since for Fichte the state can only be deduced as an institution to guarantee security for the maintenance of personal liberty, there appears for the first time the concept of the right of the citizens to make an economic claim upon the state, and thus of the obligation of the state to satisfy this demand (for the preservation of personal freedom). There is a right to work and to subsistence: "Everyone must be able to live from their work—this is the principle that has been established. . . . Since everyone has the responsibility of seeing to it that all can live from their work and of subsidizing one when he is not able to do so, they also necessarily have the right to control whether or not each person is working as much as is necessary for life, and they entrust this right of control to the branch of the state that is commissioned for commerce and social rights. . . . In a state that conforms to reason there can be neither poverty nor indolence" (Works, II, pp. 215f.). Fichte developed the details of this idea of the state—which suddenly ceased to be liberal—in one of his later works (The Closed Commercial State, 1801); despite its small-scale commercialism, which is not yet industrialized, the centralized socialism of this utopia comes remarkably close to the position of later Saint-Simonism. Nevertheless, Fichte's project does not in the least form a pure social utopia; it belongs at least, and in the end perhaps more so, to the juridical ideal of the state and is a construct of reason. But the backward relations of Germany at that time did not incline toward the basis of a social utopia (as in England and France); in addition, Fichte's project appeared explicitly as an "appendix to the doctrine of right." And the closed commercial state is presented as a supplement to the "judicial state" and to the end "of suppressing the anarchy of commerce in the same way that one suppresses political anarchy little by little, and of closing the commercial state as it is closed in its legislation and its judiciary" (Works, III, p. 483). In this way the state is thought, as it must be, to be a preamble of the rational state: It controls and organizes all of the branches of production, of agriculture, as well as of industry; as the highest corporate authority it apportions to each person his field of activity according to the needs of the market; it takes care of foreign commerce itself in order to allot to the citizen his work as well as the bounty of his work. Fichte, the political liberal, is by no means an economic liberal; he was never a defender of the free play of forces, or of the Manchester principle and of the prosperous harmony that followed from this free play of forces. However naive Fichte might have been in economic matters (though one need not attribute a love of manufacture to him), he never believed in a parallelogram of individual capitalistic forces: "To say that everything will come about of its own accord, that everyone will always find work and bread, and that this should be left to good luck, is unworthy of a constitution based upon justice" (*Works*, III, p. 477). Not that it would be completely worthy of the rational state itself to perpetually rest upon this complex of authoritative regulations; even from this point of view Fichte's closed commercial state cannot be described as an ideological state of manufacture. The original character of autonomy, the almost anarchistic impulse, in Fichte's construction of law reacts to every constraint as something alien and, in the end, abandons the attempt to improve the positively given "emergency state" within its own structure. For this reason, this state socialism must serve only as the means to the end of personal nonoppression and the development of all. In the 1793 essay "Call for the Freedom of Thought," the young Fichte compared the constitution of the state founded upon justice to a candle "that consumes itself as it illuminates, and that is extinguished when the day breaks." In the posthumously published *Doctrine of the State* (1813), the later Fichte once again constructively posited the decline of the state, and in its place prophesied the commune, the "realm of reason." In so doing Fichte gave an interesting twist to the abstract separation, which he took over from Kant, of compulsory legality and pure morality. To be sure, law ignores morality, but in return morality does away with law insofar as where there is complete morality, there is no law whatsoever that remains to constrain it. In the same way, the "realm of reason" abolishes the existing state that regiments, and is even the counterpoint of purely private interests. That which the state must necessarily leave to the individual sphere of freedom—morality, art, religion, science—in the "realm of reason" becomes a matter of a universal consciousness. Knowledge of the path that leads to this point is handed down not only by politicians but also by teachers and all educators through the doctrine of science insofar as here "every authority as such is negated that produced itself through the authority of the given." That is the same thing as the interiority of a theocracy completely without nature, or of the most extreme Christianity: "Thus the coercion of the actual state quietly withers away with time and without any violent opposition fades into its own vanity," to the ultimate end when "the entire species of humanity is enclosed in a single, internally united Christian state, which, following a common plan, will conquer nature and so enter into the higher sphere of another life" (*Works*, VI, pp. 624f.). This solution simultaneously fights against the state and the world; with it the natural law of German idealism achieves the *abolition of nature.*

From the beginning, Fichte had tended toward a position that was rigorously alien, indeed even hostile, with respect to nature; this tendency culminated in the empty, and significant, acosmism of the last period. At the same time we find a highly idealized transformation in the correspondence that natural law theories of the eighteenth century sought to open between natural law and a natural religion, which was thoroughly intoxicated by Being, drunk with the immanence of Being, and thus substituted the visible exuberance of nature for the invisible divinity. In Fichte, nature becomes the "sensibilized material of duty," but God, as pure activity, is so far superior to all material categories of substantiality that he is disengaged from the being of nature, indeed from all being. The substrateless activity, which first posits the sensuous existence of objects, cannot be mixed with existence. There is no being that is not sensuous, not nature, not world: "All being," Fichte wrote in the *Science of Knowledge* of 1797, "is, for the science of knowledge, necessarily sensuous being, for it derives its entire concept only from the form of sensibility." The highest being is consequently too good for this being of nature, and—in a peculiar reversal of the attack that was directed against him—Fichte labels as atheists all those who conceive of God as being, that is, God conceived as secularized and so stripped of divinity. Thus, it becomes clear that "rational right" could no longer correspond to "natural religion"; there does not correspond any *natura naturans* to this "rational right"; rather there corresponds only an *ordo ordinans*. In this way, the optimism of Being, which had accompanied the old theories of natural law, yields to a pure optimism of the goal (which is not bound to Being): autonomy in and for itself. If in this way natural law loses nature, which as pure being has nothing to add at this point, in return it loses the sought-after self-consciousness of that which must be or must not be according to justice. Fichte's extreme idealism abandoned natural law precisely at the point where it takes up its battle against artificiality. The abdication of "conformity to nature" as a standard in favor of a highly artificial horizon in the subject without an object corresponding to it had concealed an important position and impeded an alliance. Despite all of this Fichte appeared to be the inflexible one, something like a Cato of natural law, even if he recognized the "nature" of this law as being neither internal nor external. The law of freedom forfeits nothing but reason to this healthy equilibrium (in Goethe's sense), which characterizes the citizen, and certainly not—at least not here—its dignity as giving itself its own law.

13

On the Passion of Law within Positive Law (Kohlhaus and the Seriousness of Minos)

Something that has just been forgotten can suddenly appear to be of immeasurable significance. All that has been neglected concentrates itself in a lost memory. Thus there is likewise an empty passion for an existing law as soon as it is casually not respected on some not very significant issue. The passion would then become worthy of a better cause, or it even takes the place of a better cause. It is at this point that the contentious person is to be found: His legal claim has been neurotically reified in him, until it ends up becoming a fixed idea. He fights for this idea as if it were an idea of natural law. For the most part, he fights for this idea disinterestedly, economically speaking, and as the initial, private judicial interest becomes increasingly senseless, he fights all the more vehemently with an apparently objective consciousness of justice to lend validity to the idea. But this troublemaker is clearly neurotic and, besides suffering from a persecution complex, comes close to being a madman. But he is too miserly and troublesome to arouse the sort of sympathy that usually goes out to one who is abnormal or even one who is narrow-minded. Only once has such a troublemaker been presented as great and canonized in the way that he deserves: Michael Kohlhaus. Only for him did the letter of an existing law shine as if a divine law were inscribed in it. Only Kohlhaus insisted upon adhering to the letter of the law to the point of rebellion, as if natural law were to be found in it, as if these laws were the jewels of natural law. He furnished the material for the most powerful and most disconcerting didactic novel about one who, out of a sense of justice, is a stickler for the law. Kleist portrays his hero as becoming necessarily more and more terrible as a result of a loss that he could have easily learned to live with. He gave two well-nourished stallions to the squire of Tronka as a security, and a few weeks later he returned to find two sorry-looking mares in their place; to make matters worse, the squire's claim was illegal. The castle of Tronka, the thieves' den that afterward becomes the palace of feudal nepotism, where Kohlhaus was in each case denied his rights, is thoroughly unforgettable. By the time Kohlhaus takes his defense in his own hands, "his sense of justice, which was like a jeweler's scale," can no longer support the weight of this fundamental break of justice; Kohlhaus becomes chief of the brigands and an arsonist who kills in the name of justice. In his *Struggle for Justice* Jhering, who praises Kohlhaus as a martyr for justice, also pays special notice to another obstinate person, one far less dazzling who was ridiculed by his own poet: Shylock. This liberal jurist respects Shylock as one who followed the law (not only for his own private profit), while in his view Portia, the "wise Daniel," comes close to the level of the betrayal of justice that closed in around Kohlhaus. According to Jhering, it is "a miserable trick, a deplorable hairsplitting dodge, to refuse to permit a man, whom the judge has already granted the right to cut out a pound of flesh from the living body, to shed any of the blood that would flow from this flesh. A judge could just as well acknowledge the legitimate right of a servant to walk on the land, but forbid him to leave footprints on the grounds because this is not explicitly stipulated as permitted by the institution of servitude." Seen in this way, Shylock appears better in Jhering than he does in Shakespeare, where he appears as "the typical Jewish figure in the Middle Ages, the pariah of society who cries in vain for justice." And it is in this form that his cry resounded in the liberal royal theater, in spite of the grotesque immorality and vanity of his contract. Still, one cannot compare the shedding of blood to the leaving of footprints, nor can Shylock be put on the same plane as Kohlhaus, the martyr of justice. Shylock would have become a criminal as soon as he was granted his supposed right; that is, as soon as he was permitted to cut out a piece of flesh from wherever he wished (even from the heart). Kohlhaus, on the other hand, became a criminal precisely because his unambiguous right was not accorded to him. That is the difference between Shakespeare's comedy (despite all of its background seriousness) and Kleist's novel of rebellion (despite all of the pettiness of motive in the foreground). Thus, Kohlhaus only becomes a criminal because his sense of justice was offended, and he becomes an outlaw out of a passion for justice. The content of this passion is, of course, nothing other than a law that already exists. It is only a question of the definition of the usual right of lien, which the horse-trader knew but had hardly considered important before the onset of his mania. There is thus an absurd disproportion between the crimes, of such grand style, that he commits out of his conviction and the content of that conviction itself. From the standpoint of real rebellion, Kohlhaus renders the disproportion blasphemous; but it is just as impossible to overlook the smallness of the content. The incongruity between the tenacity of Kohlhaus and the provisions of the law, in whose name he risks himself, is significantly reduced. The responsibility for the preservation of the value of the goods that are handed over (a responsibility that, in Pufendorf and Wolff, is even derived from their view of natural law) then becomes a substitute for the abstract consciousness of justice that is associated with it. In the end, this is what is served by the atrocious, the comic-blasphemous excess, the action that is undertaken out of belligerence and blind fanaticism. Because the case at stake is insignificant in itself (for it is a consciousness of law always without content), it is impossible to think that there is any real resemblance between Kohlhaus and a Shylock. Kohlhaus belongs more to the lineage of Don Quixote, but with this difference—Kohlhaus does not fight for an ideal long gone, but for a positive law that has faded, remaining only as a dumb and stupid identity: Law must remain law. Quixote fights without any attachment to an existing order; his fight is romantic. Kohlhaus fights with an attachment to an existing article of the law; his fight is abstract. Quixote's chivalry has an immediate content in its gallant morals and valiant imagination and as a species of knightly Christianity; it is a content that continues to impress and fascinate even if it has faded a bit with time. Michael Kohlhaus's dream of justice has as its immediate content something that at the time was current in the entire network of pawnbrokers and is satisfied even today in paragraphs 1219–1221 of the Civil Laws: The principle that remains the substrate of the abstract consciousness of law is that contracts must be honored. Thus, the immediate content of the ideals of Don Quixote is considerably stronger than that of Kohlhaus, and yet Kohlhaus's ideal has a stronger effect. He is not the courageous fool, but rather the rebellious dogmatist of law in his own time. Indeed, one could say, with an exaggeration appropriate to both figures, that Don Quixote is a romantic knight who has arrived too late, whereas Michael Kohlhaus is paradoxically a Jacobin who has arrived prematurely. With respect to abstract rigor, antedating the sixteenth century, one could almost say that Kohlhaus is the Immanuel Kant of the doctrine of law in the form of a Don Quixote. He becomes this as a result of the abstract consciousness of law, and the bourgeois moral severity that is immediately applied in every case; of course, his madness is that, by chance, he has anchored this consciousness of justice in an indifferent positive principle of law that is not at all antifeudal. The historical Kohlhaus acted in the name of positive law as if it were natural law; if this offense against the law of liens did not lead to a revolutionary slogan, that is due to the nature of the horse-trader, as well as to the age (about 1540), when the spirit of revolution was exhausted. Violations of positive law have often started rebellions when the people have had enough and the pretext was appropriate. It was not the regulation that typified law in general, but the offense that represented all that was unjust, that is, unbearable oppression. In such cases, a Michael Kohlhaus is not blasphemous and his sense of justice does not lead him to set fire to a palace only to bring home to the squire the liabilities of a neglected responsibility.

It would be different if the given law were reinforced from above, particularly where there was a special pretext for oppression. There is no need to tamper with the law when one breaks it in such a way; all that is needed for the omnipresent class justice to become what it really can be and to be untouchable is that a law favorable to the ruling class be enforced more rigorously than other laws. But that is not the issue here; rather the issue is of an *art pour l'art* in jurisprudence even when it comes from above. The issue concerns not only a dogmatic, conceptual jurisprudence, not only pedantry and bureaucracy, but also ultimately a real, rigorous passion for positive law. Again, in the Kohlhausian sense, law must remain law, but now this thought and passion is pronounced by an inflexible judge or by those who say that a judge is too lenient. But even though this attitude is dictated by class interests, it can exceed those interests to the extent that it is out of step with the immediate advantage of the ruling interests. On the one hand, a deep, almost dialectical sigh comes from this point: *Summum jus summa injuria;* and on the other hand, from the same point comes the maxim that Kohlhaus remembers: *Fiat justitia, pereat mundus.* Of course, even this judicial excess from above, which is apparently quite impractical within the body of existing laws, has the indirect advantage for the ruling class that a passionate attachment to its legal order is fostered. If as Nietzsche said when divulging the secrets of the morals of rulers, all positive law is the attempt to eternalize the powers of the moment, then the fanaticism of this judicial *art pour l'art* can only be a means of aiding this eternalization. Severity always has an objective aspect, inflexibility the appearance of impartiality, at least when class justice does not appear too clearly as what it really is. The mythical model for such judicial seriousness is handed down from antiquity in the "eternal judge," especially when this judge can give free reign to his inflexibility by having delegated his function to *dii minores*; then his relentlessness is undisturbed by either mercy or love. The Greeks saw the incarnation of this inflexibility in the three judges of Hades: Minos, Aeacus, and Rhadamanthus; the seriousness of Minos has since become proverbial. Doubtless, this seriousness is captivating; it has all of the vengeance of the law of retribution on its side in its ostensible observation of a strict justice. Furthermore, seriousness has a more attractive demeanor than does gentleness; it appears more masculine, even more radical (in the most formal sense of the word). The passion for law, in the purest affective sense of the word as the passion of the law of retribution, has without a doubt found refuge in the intransigence of a harsh bearing; the so-called majesty of the law is at home here. Indeed, the severe judge is even greeted as an ally of the bourgeois natural law of the equality of all before the law. Certainly, the majesty of law—which means the nullity of all subjects before the royal court—was especially convenient for the absolute monarchy, which broke the power of the nobility by playing it against the bourgeois. In so doing, the rationale of the state coincided in a deceptive way with judicial radicalism, even when it was in the service of that which is precisely the contrary of judicial radicalism per se, namely, despotism. Thus, the ministerial decree of Friedrich Wilhelm I did not subject the chief culprit, the young crown prince, Friedrich, to the seriousness of Minos, but did subject his friend Katte to it. This seriousness had an even more powerful effect upon those of the time (and even Kant) in that "bonhomie" was absent from it: "His Royal Highness went through school and learned the proverb: *Fiat justitia et pereat mundus*. Thus, His Majesty wills that Katte should be put to death by the sword. When the military court makes the sentence known to Katte, it should be said to him that this makes His Majesty sad, but that it is better that he die than that justice should depart from the world." But the idolatry of justice had other ways of expressing itself for the Minos of Brandenburg: He commanded that a lawyer or any person who presented a written petition to the court "be immediately, and without pity, taken to the gallows and hanged, and that a dog should be hanged by his side" (Edict of 1739). This

Minos fits in quite well with such a *justitia* as *fundamentum regnorum*, and such a *regna* fits in quite profitably with the fetish that results from the unrestricted *fiat* of such *justitia*. Despite this, the maxim *fiat justitia, pereat mundus* contains, beyond this serious and instructive test of fetishism, such a strong expression of the unconditionedness of principles that even a philosopher who found no expression of principles in the reason of the state could make this maxim his guiding light.

Kant praised positive law, even when it was not categorical and was regulated without respect to the person, finding in it an example of the magnitude and "implacability" that otherwise was attributed to the law of reason (and most of all to morals). Intrinsically, Kant's philosophy of right was anything but a reification of judicial means, and it was even less an eternalizing of empirical principles of law; its principle was not the state but the coexistence of free individuals. Law was not imperious; it was absolutely not categorical, and as the aggregate of the pure *conditions* of free coexistence, it could not be so; nevertheless, the implacable character of these conditions, once they were posited, lent them a sacred aspect for Kant, one that he attributed, not to Being, but to the "ought." This consecration was made easier by the concept of justice as that which replaces the rationale of the state, or even coincided with it to the extent that the rationale of the state is patriarchal. As was to be seen, justice belonged to the unpredictable grandeurs of natural law; justice is certainly not indispensable for the natural law of the Enlightenment, nor is it central to Kant's philosophy of right. But it has a character that is so closely related to Kantian rigor that, in this point, a second natural law seems to emerge in the middle of positive law. Friedrich Wilhelm I becomes the legitimate *de jure philosophico* when Kant attacks the right of pardon, calling it one of the "most obscene" of all laws. The *fiat justitia, pereat mundus* is literally justified according to its exact wording: "For if legal justice perishes, then it is no longer worthwhile for men to live on the earth" (*Works*, VII, p. 150). At this point in his philosophy of right, Kant even calls penal law a categorical imperative, while according to Kant's own definition it could at best be the most rigorous of all hypothetical or conditional imperatives. To be sure, the rigor of Minos posits its quasi-rational law in the following definitive example: "Even if a civil society were to dissolve itself by common agreement of all its members (for example, if the people inhabiting an island decided to separate and disperse themselves around the world), the last murderer remaining in prison must first be executed, so that everyone will come to know what his actions are worth and so that the bloodguilt of those actions will not be fixed upon the people because they failed to insist on carrying out the punishment; for if they fail to do so, they may be regarded as accomplices in this public violation of legal justice" (*Works*, VII, p. 151). Such is the fury that this passion for law can stir up within the framework of questionable positive laws; the law of the gallows (which was denied by all of the natural law theoreticians of the Enlightenment), even though presented as a product of pure radicalism, can still appear as a passion *ex ratione*. Positive law that has been pushed to its own end tries to make up in intensity (implacability) what it lacks in quality (coexistence of free individuals). In this, something quite peculiar becomes apparent: The maxim *fiat justitia, pereat mundus* in its original sense is not so far removed from Kant's example, except to the extent that it is an expression of fanaticism, for the origin of this maxim is probably to be found in early Christianity (cf. Del Vecchio, *Justice*, 1950, p. 174), since there one could really believe in the disappearance of society as well as of the world. The antithesis is thus: "May Charis, grace (the better eon), appear, and this world disappear." To the extent that the effect of grace was conceived eschatologically, justice (in the early Christian, still-messianic, traditional sense of *olam ha tikkum*) was conceived as the effect of the coming of the future world of justice, while the *pereat mundus* later fades away to a sort of shoulder-shrugging subjunctive, far removed from its original mode as optative and postulate. What one finds in this maxim in its infancy is not a fanaticism for positive law, but a completely nonpositive, eschatological fanaticism, a fanaticism that does not accept the *pereat mundus* for the sake of its rigor, but accepts it in the name of an eschatological conception of law. Despite all of this, to the extent that the passion for the protection of law *e lege* opposes the existing world as bad, it partakes from afar of a completely different seriousness of a completely different Minos. Then even the most attractive judicial rigor appears in a framework of existing legal justice, but in such a way that legal justice is exhausted by being put to use for completely inverse purposes, not for the ultrasevere condemnation, but for annulling a lax, even criminally unjust judgment.

The most passionate advocate of positive law in this final sense of rigor was Zola; he was not a lawyer, but a poet, and his defense was an attack, an accusation, a *J'accuse* leveled against violations of justice.

Here, too, the intensity came from above, but not from the government and its policies, but from the principles that had once seemed to create these policies as an aspect of *raison humaine*. Actually, Zola's fanaticism employed positive law as if it were natural law; furthermore, he utilized the element of classical natural law theory that *nolens volens* had been recognized so that the republic could be reformed again. A Quixotelike effort, but one that for some decades did in fact have the effect of cleaning the surface and of concealing the background. And yet at this point one is struck by something else, that this goes beyond any irony of "eternal law." The force of Zola's conviction in bourgeois law is not only subjectively impressive but also objectively impressive in a way that does not happen with ideals that have passed their time or with those that were established in an irregular manner. Thus, a comparison between Zola and Quixote is without any basis; the contents of Zola's judicial fanaticism do not demonstrate the equivalent historical fixedness (and thereby the quality of being past its time) of Quixote's knightly ideals. The argument that bourgeois positive law is always worth more than an injustice without scruples is a false one; for the world of chivalry seemed to be better, more humane, than the world of shopkeepers of which Don Quixote ran afoul. The decisive argument is rather another argument for the objective content of Zola's fanaticism for justice: It is the weight that is given to the evidence, the pathos for "the discovery of judicial truth" in Zola's *J'accuse*. In fact one finds here moral, methodical elements, not of an "eternal law," but rather of a will to scientifically establish the facts that are to serve as instructions for locating justice. That no one who is innocent may be condemned, that one who is guilty and revealed as such must be struck down without any possible protection, that no important document may be based upon falsehoods, and that no document that may exonerate someone may be kept secret or only treated as a small matter: These "self-evident truths" are not historically transient or subject to fluctuations like stocks on the market, which rise and fall according to the military or governmental state of affairs. Their validity is certainly more or less frustrated by societies with a sense of justice that is corrupted by castes or by fascistically warped privileges; but even in the midst of such castes or on the highest level of gangsters black cannot be made to be white, and the execution of an innocent person is at least perpetrated with the consciousness of what it really is. The path that leads to the classless society will not be permitted to be distinguished from this image of the impartiality of the consciousness of law and the rigor of a legality that is not merely formally democratic. Revolutions overturn the old positive law, but if they remain revolutions they do not create a new injustice; thus, the *J'accuse* of genuine judicial fanaticism has always retained its validity in opposing the murder of an innocent person, and insofar as it does so it constitutes a remarkable substitute for resistance in the name of natural law. *Summum jus* in this final usage is, therefore, not always necessarily *summa injuria*. It should give one pause that it was not even this for Kohlhaus, and all the more so in the case of Friedrich Wilhelm I, who made frequent and tyrannical usage of the *fiat justitia*. The truly radical principle according to the orthodox sense of natural law (which here means rational law) is thus: *Fiat jus naturale, vivat mundus cum hominis dignitate*, "The world without arbitrariness, with human dignity."

14

Anselm Feuerbach, Savigny; The Fate of Rational Law in Schelling's Darker Nature

A sober thought, one that holds fast to the facts, can be arrived at any number of different ways. Such thought can be of the most honorable intentions and not want to take any step that is not verifiable at every moment. But it can also be born of a way of thinking that is less exhaustive, namely, adaptation to the given. To take things as they are is an obligation for the researcher, but by no means for one who acts and one who judges. Accommodation to the given is a bad positivism when it moves whichever way the wind blows or—as we say with an image that is absolutely pertinent here—when it takes a realistic view of the facts. In the transition from abstract natural law to historical positive law there were two attitudes in play: that of research and that of accommodation. With this transition (which occurred after the Thermidor) the middle class abandoned its constructive as well as its exacting essence: This even happened in places like Germany, where no revolution had taken place beyond a purely contemplative "participation" in the revolution. A participation that quite rapidly passed from a disengaged admiration to an abhorrence, and therefore led to a revision of that natural law the fruits of which were believed to have finally been witnessed. The German middle class discovered in itself a sense for what is in process; that is, it discovered a historical sense, and by expanding this sense to cover all that is given it increased its influence as well. In jurisprudence this is the path that leads from romanticism to positivism. The foundations of natural law faltered once bourgeois society itself ceased to be persuaded by its absolutely necessary and rationally deducible character. In his universal denial of innate ideas Hume attacked natural law: No universal principle is necessary and inevitable; rather they are all conventional. Kant, however, in his critique of synthetic a priori reason facilitated the historical positivistic solution in Germany, even though he himself stood in close proximity to rationalistic normative natural law. In his *Manual of Natural Law* (1799) the self-styled Kantian and professor of public law at Göttingen, Hugo, destroyed both the construction and the ideal of law. With the rejection of an *a priori construction* it only remained to investigate law as a historical formation that is susceptible to change, and is an expression of economic and social relations of needs and powers that are completely different in different times and places. But the rejection of the *ideal* immediately entailed a reactionary attitude of a posteriori cynicism. Among other things, Hugo demonstrates the justice of slavery by pointing out that it was considered just by many millions of cultivated people for many millennia (*Manual of Natural Law*, par. 141). Thus, the last trace of the Rousseauvian spirit disappeared with the abstract construction of that which was called justice (only Feuerbach held onto this Rousseauvian spirit at the time). This fight against construction was more successful when it was fought in terms of the *history of justice*, that is, in a domain where a sense of facts was permissible, and where the thoroughly ahistoric projection (which the eighteenth century established and used as its own standard) was abandoned. Here the rejection of natural law was fruitful: Hugo provided the foundations for the history of Roman law, Eichhorn did the same for the history of Germanic law, and Savigny provided a dogmatic of Roman law, which was illuminated by a rich historical documentation. All of this was viewed as a path back to the sources, which were regarded not only as literary sources but as those subterranean sources where there was a murmur of something profound. Thus, that which to this point was considered to be the contribution of reason sank to the level of the historical research of genuine facts. It was not cynicism that was hostile to reason at this point; rather it was the overflow of romanticism that was antagonistic to reason here. Savigny saw something magical in law; for him law originated out of "unconscious forces," and out of the "involuntary action of the spirit of the people." Far from excavating an economic root, Savigny, the romantic, even found in the Roman law a deep, unconscious generic character that was formed by clearly practical ends. Not only did he observe ancient judicial customs in their religious connections, which Bachofen later detailed, but he even found these connections in the dry edicts that the praetor posted anew each year, and he even regarded the later pandects as ancient magic. Thus the formation of law was mystified in such a way that the doctrine of the social contract looked like an economic and material concept. Above all, rational law was dismissed as thoroughly inessential, indeed even as ignoble, while law that had been transmitted through the ages was considered something honorable, as the product of the wisdom of the past traditions, language, and myths. On the other hand, any law taken from reason or corresponding to it was regarded as something vulgar, like "concrete literature" (to use a modern, but not completely anachronistic phrase). The abdication of conscious *ratio* took place so profoundly in Savigny that he restricted the power to create law to prehistoric times and he denied his epoch the capacity to legislate. A law cannot be formed artificially any more than a language can be, and it can no more be the product of the intellect than a popular song can be. Yet it was precisely this epoch that, under the ideological and systematic influence of natural law, succeeded in producing such efficient codifications as the General Civil Code of Russia (1794) and the Napoleonic Code (1804–1808); but the juridical romanticism of the historical school only glorified the customary development of law. According to the English model, which did not operate on the basis of principles—but with this difference that in all of its countless developments in a series of logically impenetrable precedents English praxis always remained based upon a democratic common sense—the judge was permitted to create a new law in the course of a trial when the case was not covered by precedent. Savigny, on the other hand, in opposing the project of a unified German private law contended that the development of law could only be the work of the "silent forces, and not of the caprice of a legislator." He did not stand upon the basis of relative reason, which appeared or could be endorsed as common sense; rather he stood upon the basis of that which had developed organically (without the Magna Charta). For Savigny this organic law is not the law of customs; rather it appears as cults among the forefathers, and it can only be revived in such a way; the pandects, this precarious patchwork, are "holy books" for Savigny (*On the Vocation of Our Time*). Even Hegel, who was certainly not eager for new laws but sought a codification of laws by reason, was compelled to remark against Savigny's historicism: "No greater insult could be offered to a civilized people or to its lawyers . . . than to deny them the ability to construct a legal system" (*Philosophy of Right*, par. 211). In this way the historical school of law arrived at a quite unique conclusion: *Ratio sui generis* did not remain forbidden to the extent that it did not take part in any creative judicial action. The abandonment of creativity in matters of law was favorable to a self-satisfied dogmatic jurisprudence. With this an inheritance from the construction of natural law entered the picture, though of course only as a formal element. The historical school of law inherited the program of an unbroken context of formal concepts of law from Hobbes and Grotius. In this way, nineteenth-century jurisprudence not only renovated and surpassed the conceptual clarity and acuity of Roman law but also, despite all of the *irratio* of judicial genesis, was led to a system of that which had resulted from this genesis. Savigny's *System of Contemporary Roman Law* (1840–1849) did not find its adherents in its myths, but rather in the (antiquarian) purity of its concepts; in this way the historical school of Romanists became great believers in technicalities and formalities. We have already noticed that when faced with a mythification that sees the hand of God in the pandects, the fiction of the social contract proposed by the old natural law looked like an economic and materialistic concept. The historical school of law made known countless facts and disclosed an enormous amount of material on the development of law; but it revealed the real history of law just as little as it had revealed natural law (which it never had as an ambition), for the real history of law is primarily related to economy. Savigny had a strong intuition for traditional relations, but for him traditional relations were celestial beings whose origin could never be legitimately accounted for by any profane history. Thus, an ahistorical natural law was replaced by a sort of secret history of law, but this organic and magical fiction was no less ahistorical than the law that was formed. Even the effort to destroy the a priori construction of law, a task that Hugo had already begun and that Savigny intended to use to make room for his cult of believers in organic law, did not turn out to be as radical as it appeared to be. The bourgeois foundation of natural law remained and, with this, the abstract system of calculation, which after Savigny was even more formalistic than before. The only thing that vanished was the revolutionary impulse, which was founded in "a priori reason," that is, in the consciousness of the postulates of the progressive bourgeois who measured and judged the given law. A completely empty construction was substituted for this consciousness of postulates; this construction did not judge the positive judicial facts, for it had less to do with them than the old, supposedly unworldly natural law had to do with the judicial facts of absolutism. Thus, to the extent that dogmatic jurisprudence abstracts from all content, it stands upon the basis of this content and its facticity. Dogmatic jurisprudence thus made peace with content, the peace of a double truth: here the practical life, there impractical law; here the greasy foundation of capital, there the soil of esoteric conceptuality. Thus, natural law never found any sort of rectification in the historical school; Grotius remains unrefuted and irrefutable from the point of view of Savigny and those who followed him. Thus it comes as no surprise that the antipode of Savigny, Paul Johann Anselm von Feuerbach, did not believe that rational law could be refuted by romanticism. Feuerbach stood just as much upon the basis of facts, but as a sort of mediating volcano. Feuerbach was similarly inclined toward historical research of laws, but because his epoch was supposed to be enlightened, he did not deny it the capacity to legislate according to rational law. In penal law, his specialty, Feuerbach encountered the most dreadful position of ancient jurisprudence; he did not believe that torture or the rack were sanctified by being characterized as traditional or by being mythologized. Feuerbach's wonderfully written *Presentation of Noteworthy Crimes* demonstrates a psychological, almost social, understanding for the victims of the laws. As the creator of the celebrated Penal Code for the State of Bavaria (1813), he introduced the viewpoint of the Enlightenment into penal law. His *Revision of the Principles and Basic Concepts of Penal Law* (1800) even today contains the best introduction to the principles of liberal penal law (the abolition of retributive justice). Here the penal code was not only the source of penalties but also their limitation; it served to protect not only the state from the criminal but also the criminal from the state—thanks to the precision of the penal regulations and the principle of *nulla poena sine lege*. The mythical character of punishment disappeared. It disappeared as a disgrace and a stigma, and reappeared as a security measure taken by the existing society. Punishment is no longer regarded as a moral reprisal or religious atonement; instead it is secularized (something that was never achieved by the classical theories of natural law). Feuerbach was not confused by the nebulous categories of the historical school, and he ignored customs, kinship, hereditary dynasties, and other supposed "qualities of the nature of the people." His *Anti-Hobbes* (1798) defined the limits of the power of the state and the right to resistance in a way that was rare for Germany. In doing this Feuerbach explained that the anarchy that was the result of such resistance, even passive resistance, was always more tolerable than despotism. The *Critique of Natural Law* (1796) even defined—with a boldness that still remains unprecedented and unused—law as the sum of rights, not of prohibitions. The claim to life, security, and liberty is not defined as a negative permission, as "exemptions from the sphere of domination," but as "juridicial faculties," as "positively sanctioned privileges"—the bourgeois is opposed to the citizen. In this way, Feuerbach separates morals from law; to the extent that law appears as a coercive force (in the service of public security), Feuerbach expels all pharisaism, and to the extent that law appears as a subjective privilege he frees it from the necessity of proving the moral dignity of those who are accorded this privilege. The state is no judge of morals, nor is it a protector of religion; morals, like religion, become a private matter. Indeed, Feuerbach is not even afraid, in the pathos of this authority, of giving the appearance that he has subordinated morals to law. Out of this there comes a remarkable and grandiose phrase: "Morality is the science of duties, natural law is the science of rights." In saying this, Feuerbach said more than he wanted to say; for in another passage he says that the juridical faculty must "follow from practical reason and exist for the purposes of practical reason (morals), in order to be ethically sanctioned and to be restricted." Nevertheless, in his later theory of natural law, Feuerbach outlined the positive juridical capacity, as the sphere of the individual, and did not let it be overwhelmed by the universality of Kantian moral precepts. It is remarkable that, in the later Feuerbach, the sphere of individuality that is to be preserved does not in the least coincide with the sphere of property. The comprehensive studies of comparative law that form his posthumous work, *Expositions and Ideas toward a Universal History of Legislation*, seemed to him to provide the proof that the pride of man did not always coincide with private property. His ethnological jurisprudence removed the shell of the bourgeois natural law from the core that Feuerbach had found so useful. Man was never solely "what existence gives to him while simultaneously making him the citizen of a collective." On the other hand, the concept of obligation, which lies at the basis of every contract, even the hypothetical social contract, "is one of those concepts that are developed with the most difficulty and latest among men." But it is ultimately in matters of private property and in marriage that comparative law topples the universally valid concepts of law; no a posteriori consensus exists here. In the methodological introduction to a late work, Feuerbach went so far as to say that abstract natural law is "a spiritual distillation of Roman law." With this critique he was thinking of the concern of natural law with the "sanctity of private property," and also with the forms of contracts in private law. Nevertheless, Feuerbach never ceased being a practitioner of liberal natural law, and "true judicial sense" (a sense that conformed completely to natural law) did not seem to him to be destroyed by the relativities of comparative law, but to be supported by them. It is precisely the widest form of empiricism, especially of all that which exists external to Roman law, that leads to a reaffirmation of this sense: "Ten lectures on the judicial constitution of the Persians and Chinese" are more beneficial "to the true judicial sense" than "one hundred lectures on the deplorable charlatanries to which the series of those who died intestate, from Augustine to Justinian, succumbed." In this way Feuerbach turned against "the prejudice that the European intellect should be considered world reason itself"; thus, China, which he viewed charitably, contained not less but more of the advantages of natural law (in the liberal sense this term retained in the eighteenth century) than Europe, which had abandoned it, in part organically, in part factically.

The philanthropic trait, which once was a bourgeois character trait, did not vanish immediately. 1789 echoed all the more loudly in the German mind the less it was found in German fists; and the domain of facts did not always receive the cynical attention of a Hugo. In the passion for subjective rights, Feuerbach found a philosophical companion in the young Schelling, who was later a friend of Savigny and the historical school. Schelling's early work, *A Deduction of Natural Law* (1795), agrees with Feuerbach's text with respect to Fichte's concepts of freedom; indeed, the text even indicates that Schelling had an a priori juridical spontaneity (*Works*, I, pp. 245ff.). Law is not an "ought," but rather a permission, a freedom; this is what the young Schelling proclaimed in a series of rigorous and concise aphorisms. The freedom of the individual will is only limited for its own sake: "I only stop opposing my freedom to the freedom of other moral beings so that, conversely, they will cease opposing their freedom to mine" (par. 46). Or again, this time more imperatively: "I impose the general will as law upon myself, so that my will may be the law for every other will" (par. 50). Or still again, and this time at the extreme point of individual juridical faculties as defined by natural law: "I have a right to all that by which I affirm the individuality of my will according to its form" (par. 68); and the form of the will, as individual and as general, is precisely freedom. Its material is morality, but this is the morality of self-determination (of the attempt "to become a being in itself"), and not the morality of the general duty of virtue: "Thus freedom is not dependent upon morality; rather morality is dependent upon freedom" (par. 35). Schelling thus shows that he is still working within a system of judicial capacities in an apriorism of rational law. This is the same philosopher who, through his historical sense, would later dissolve rational law even within philosophy itself. One could say that the historical school of law would have arisen only with difficulty, as it is presented by Savigny, if Schelling had not introduced romanticism into science, if he had not substituted organic and historical formation for rational construction. In the *System of Transcendental Idealism* (1800), Schelling had already said that law is "a purely natural order, which freedom has no more power over than it has over sensible nature. It is no wonder, therefore, that all attempts to transform it into a moral order" (that is, in conformity with rational law) "present themselves as detestable through their own perversity, and through that most dreadful kind of despotism" (that is, the French Revolution) "which is their immediate consequence" (*Works*, III, pp. 583ff.). In the *Lectures on the Methods of Academic Study* (1803), Schelling resolutely turns away from natural law; law and the state appear as necessary products, and no details such as security or freedom can be removed from them and put forth as primary in order "to distort their image for the masses." The bases of the historical school are found here: The production of law was rendered organic, existing law was removed from the critique of rational law, and the organic character of law was made into a sign of its correctness. The objective will—as the will of God, not of man—blossomed at the real and ideal intersection of the forms that developed, among which were judicial connections that were just as much ethical organisms as necessary products of a divine process. Just as the process of creation in nature necessarily produced its different types, species and diverse regions, so too it produces in the ethical world organisms such as family, state, and church. The critique of the contemporary state no longer takes place from the perspective of natural law, from the perspective of "the individual and the abstraction," but takes place solely according to the measure of "the identity of the universal and the particular." In the ancient republic unity and multiplicity, state and people, were one and the same; in modern monarchies they are divided; objectivity and subjectivity, public law and private law, have torn themselves loose from one another. Nevertheless, this did not mean that the tendency to strive for the supposed ancient unity was renewed as it was in the dreams of a polis that abounded in 1789. On the contrary, the unity that was lacking was formed by the church and given to the state: "The concept of the monarchy is thus essentially bound up with the concept of the church." But the state itself, as a necessary form of the world, has, in union with the church, no goal outside itself; it is an end in itself in its "grand and sublime institutions" and in "the beauty of public life"; it is therefore not there for the individual. There are no external goals for the state such as happiness or the satisfaction of social drives or the coexistence of free beings under the conditions of the greatest possible freedom— for the later Schelling all of that constitutes the false natural law of an isolated construct according to a relative end. In his *Methods of Academic Study*, Schelling said that true construction is, by nature, absolute: "It is not, for example, the construction of the state as such, but of the absolute organism in the form of the state. To construct this does not therefore mean that it is conceived as the condition of the possibility of anything that is external; when it is presented at first as the visible image of absolute life, it fulfills all ends from itself: just as nature does not exist so that there can be an equilibrium of matter, but that this equilibrium is only because nature is" (*Works*, V, p. 316). These are words that are self-contained in their generality; they speak of the autarky of the state, which imitates that of a work of art or of a beautiful animal; they speak of what is necessary "by nature," but this nature is no longer from the nature that is allied with individuals and their freedom and that is the patron of revolution and the future. Schelling's organic concept of nature became all the more energetic in moving from a concept of "growth" to one concerned with "the result of growth," that is, the past. The organic relation of particularities to the organism became the same as the arrangement, or at least the orientation, of the past and future in a "holy primordial time." As a mythologist, Schelling brought facts home to the historical school, facts that were to be found well before the time of Roman law; Bachofen's excavation of maternal law was hardly thinkable without Schelling, and certainly the pathos that accompanied this exhumation and the significance accorded it would have been impossible had it not been for Schelling's work. Schelling's text *On the Divinities of Samothrace* already contained the seeds of the discovery of a prehistoric world of the night, mother, and earth; in short, Bachofen's chthonic world of maternal law. The fragment that is entitled *Ages of the World* plunges nature itself into archaic times, and hurls us into the darkness of the beginning that surrounds us: "Nature is an abyss of the past, and once all that is contingent and the result of becoming is removed, this abyss is what is most ancient in it and what remains most profound even today" (*Works*, VIII, p. 243). In this way the concept of nature maintained its opposition to all that is merely contingent, all that is merely the result of becoming (here in the sense of the transitory); genuine natural law rarely lacked the relation to a happy primordial age or an archaic paradise. This primordial age was always conceived as a time of freedom (as the absence of constraint, of war, and of the state); but at best, Schelling accorded this age an innocence, because freedom itself was still dormant there. Supposedly, freedom was first awakened by the onset of history, though, of course, its roots go back into the "dark-evil baselessness of things," exterior to the "nature in God." Despite its philosophical depth, *Of Human Freedom* (1809), whose ideological connection with reactionary movements is unmistakable, makes freedom devilish, and ultimately nature too insofar as it appears as a separate realm of Being. According to the Schelling of 1809, freedom is a fall, it is a self-detachment from the being of the self; from out of this Luciferlike essence stems disunion and irregularity, sin, deformity, sickness, and death. From such freedom of nature one can deduce only injustice, whereas law and justice exist only by virtue of a return to unfreedom, into that unfreedom which resides in abandonment and love. This return is, however, not merely a return to a golden age or to the dormancy of freedom (the "time of indecision, where there was neither good nor evil"), rather this return is the reappropriation of the nature of freedom in the "universal Christian will." For this will, nature in its primordial depth, appears as "that which is the first, or Old, Testament since things are still outside the center and therefore under the law. Since he is related to God (after the last separation), man is the beginning of the new covenant through which he also accepts nature and makes it his own" (*Works*, VII, p. 411). Consequently, the individual as such (the crowning glory of the freedom of nature) only has the right of decline, that is, return, "from its divine nature." A concept of nature that is alternately dazzling and obscure deprived the old concept of nature of its optimistic and even panlogical basis. Schelling's own youthful text, which gives the Napoleonic command of judicial self-determination, is thus completely

abandoned: Savigny was victorious over Feuerbach, historical romanticism triumphed over the French Revolution. For this organic traditional speculation, there only remains the question of whether or
not the "epoch of blissful indecision" of which Schelling speaks (and
of which he speaks in ways different from those in which he speaks
of the later patriarchal-Christian diremption) can be distinguished, if
not by freedom, then at least by a childlike equality, even if not in
the romantic concept of nature, which almost against its will lends
itself to a Rousseauvian echo. Thus in *Philosophy and Religion* (1804),
Schelling asserts: "The sayings of all peoples in the myths of the golden
age preserved that state of unconscious happiness as well as the first
gentleness of the earth: As was natural, the second generation of the
human race eternalized these guardian spirits of their childhood, these
benefactors thanks to whom man, already guided by instinct, was
endowed with the première arts of life, and so was protected ahead
of time against the coming hardness of nature and thus acquired the
first rudiments of the sciences, arts, and legislation—these were eternalized in the image of lords and the gods with whom the human
race began its history and which continued in the traditions of the
most ancient peoples" (*Works*, VI, p. 59). But as Schelling later speculated
in the *Divinities of Samothrace*, this history does not begin with heroes
and gods, but with the protective forms of the night, with "oracles
that spring up out of the earth" and with goddesses. "For the teaching
of all peoples who reckoned time according to nights was that the
night is the most ancient in the whole nature of things. . . . For this
reason, Hestia was honored as the most ancient being and the ideas
of Ceres and Persephone, the oldest divinities, were mingled with
those of Hestia" (*Works*, VIII, p. 352). Schelling interpreted this primeval
time, which was defined by its femininity, only in the sense of a dark
longing, and therefore, to use another of Bachofen's phrases, in the
sense of "the epoch of the hetaerical swamp," which was prior to the
age of agriculture, of matriarchy, of Ceres. Nevertheless, the protective
night is situated as a new element of natural law prior to and external
to the patriarchal world: the original element of the womb that gives
birth, the protective mother. From this point of view, the organic
concept of nature had, despite everything else, made possible a view
of the contents of natural law. Even though this contradicted the will
of natural law just as the reaction set itself against the revolution, it
did permit the judicial conception of a canonic element of the golden

age: that of maternal law. In this way the discoveries of Bachofen split away from Savigny and Schelling. The dominant tenor is reactionary and with an unwanted portion that had its primary power in revolutionary history. In his inaugural lecture at Basel (1841), Bachofen declared: "Let us leave natural law and historical law in their opposition"—"let us leave the divinization of human reason and idolatry of self-made idols. Let us unswervingly follow the path that history has prescribed for us. To find peace, let us adhere to the ancient oracle, the oracle given to Aeneas: *Antiquam exquirite matrem.*" But the peace that contemplation won thereby was the restlessness of true natural law external to historical, all too historical, reason; it was the restlessness for the lost equality. *Antiquam exquirite matrem,* "Search for the primordial mother"—this oracle does not deny the natural law of the golden age, but rather clarifies, even if partially in an unholy mythological manner, a part of its content that was different, namely, a content archaically recollected.

15

Bachofen, Gaea-Themis, and Natural Law

A look backward to a life of another time can be cold. It does not need to dig up its treasures; it is consciously satisfied when it discovers bones. Dreams that saw in the savage a better person were necessary for novels about Indians, but not for a science that brought to light extinct animals and prehistoric tombs and had an interest in positively establishing what is and was, whether or not the discovery points to prehistoric seas of a mythical funerary cult. It is entirely possible to treat primitive, so-called natural, judicial relations as if no one had ever dealt with, or even sung about, natural law. Thus Lewis H. Morgan discovered the vestiges of a matriarchal constitution in Indian tribes; he did this as a species of Western man and not as a romantic, and he did this entirely independently of the mythologist Bachofen. *The League of the Iroquois* (1851), which was enlarged upon in a succeeding work, *Systems of Consanguinity and Affinity of Human Family* (1869), and the magnum opus *Ancient Society* (1877) presented matrilineal affiliations as the most ancient from the point of view of family law.

Blood relations were established by the mother's side; father and son were not considered relations. Outside the Iroquois, these unusual relations are especially clear among the Fiji Islanders, and in part among the blacks of Senegal and the Congo, and Guinea. In all of these cases it is the female line that counts. But even in the tribes of a higher level of culture, such as the Tuareg Berbers, the child inherits its social rank exclusively from its mother. Today it has been established that many peoples have passed through a stage of matriarchal law (even though more precise data are lacking for Indo-Germanic peoples), and that vestiges of this law are still conserved in most primitive people. Most of what the historian of law and mythologist Bachofen (to whom Engels referred in *The Origin of the Family*) discovered, or at least is believed to have discovered, is certainly far from being certain, and the consequences that he drew are the least agreed upon.

In Bachofen, the look backward toward the first, earliest, ages does not seek to be cold. On the contrary, he is much more impressed, even possessed, by the law that has long since disappeared, and he is intoxicated by the belief that it could have been embedded in earlier times. For the conservative Bachofen, man is a product of the land of his ancestors, a child of the mores of his native land; the family as a creation and domain of the woman is untouchable. The capitalist development that liberated men from the fixity of the domicile, took them from the land, and exploded inherited relationships is, in part, not taken into consideration and, in part, is denied in the name of a pathos of the mother that is completely foreign to an empirical ethnology. To this is added a sharp and unique criticism, from a conservative soul, an ambassador of an ancient, completely feminine world. The critique that emanates from the ancient world, warm and maternal, is not only romantic and opposed to enterprise but also, if we can speak against all logic, a romantic antifeudalism. Bachofen dedicated one of his last works, *Antiquarian Letters*, to Morgan, but his major work, *Maternal Law* (1861), is the oldest child of German romanticism. Bachofen dedicated this work to the memory of his mother, who represented an entirely personal image, and the title page bears an aphorism that reveals the hold the past exercised on Bachofen: *Materos aglaon eidos*, "the splendid image of mother." Bachofen not only studied these myths, he believed in them as well. To the degree that love animates this attachment to the mother, which transforms prehistory, there is engendered an equal degree of diligent obedience, lack of choice, and excess. Besides Herodotus, Bachofen uses sources from the Hellenistic epoch and from late antiquity without taking into account their centuries-long distance (or even more than just centuries) from the era of maternal law. Nor did he take into account the interpretation, already fabulous or allegorical, that authors such as Pausanias, Strabo, Plutarch, Proclus, and even the epic poet Nonnus have applied to the ancient period. To justify his claims Bachofen calls upon the relationships and the bonds that united a senile civilization in its infancy, and mentions most particularly the maintenance of traditional mysteries. But late antiquity was not so senile (it gives rather the impression of an exuberance and an extraordinary imagination); still, the Eleusis of Neoplatonism is not comparable with the Pelasger of the first inhabitants of Greece. Furthermore, the work of Bachofen includes an entire feminine and nocturnal nature that is a metamorphosis, an obscuring of Rousseau's revolutionary Arcadia by the restorative romantic. Thus Bachofen does not undertake any investigation to find the living residue of maternal law, as does the empirically minded Morgan (who has his

Iroquois just outside his door); instead, these distant matriarchal people are discovered exclusively in myths, and in place of the relationships of real life it is the exclusively religious reflexes that appear as the causes of the sexual constitution of groups and of their transformation. Despite these mystical traces or excesses, Engels underlined the pioneer spirit of Bachofen (*The Origin of the Family*, 1861 [1884 — tr.]), and especially admired the relevance of most of his intentions, whether it is a question of the passage from unruly sexual relations to monogamy, or whether it concerns "the new, but absolutely correct interpretation of the *Oresteia*." And once the activating influence of the superstructure representation upon the social substructure is no longer underestimated, the remarkable, often grandiose, enthusiasm with which Bachofen has grouped his discoveries around three basic ideas is no longer without effect. The first of these ideas is an "original hetaeristic stage" (the horde) with the "swamp" as the place of unruly sexual congress; it is a place where property was absent and equality reigned. Next, there is a "Demetrian middle stage" with the field and village as the place of property, marriage, family, sedentary peace, divinities of the land, and a matriarchy full of goodness and wisdom. Finally, there is an "Apollonian final stage" with the polis as the place of the celestial, Olympian gods of light, a patriarchy of rational justice. Those ideas are abstracted from an enormous stock of literary material produced by the ancient world, and it is through these ideas that this literature is interpreted with an (often) lightning clarity. Creuzer's book *Symbols and Myths of Ancient Peoples*, Schelling's archaeological-mystical work (itself indebted to Creuzer) *On the Divinities of Samothrace*, and of course Görres's *Cult of Ancestors* (with, it is true, quite a few ghosts and a simple faith in the investigation of myths) had already preceded the hermeneutic of Bachofen. The fascination exercised by the mother, by the archetype of the mother, manifested itself especially in the unreal importance that Bachofen confers to a real power, namely, the *domination* by the mother. If it is so certain that numerous peoples have gone through the matriarchal forms of family law, it is just as certain that this matrilineal affiliation coincides with this veneration of the woman, with all the chthonic symbols (earth, Isis), and does not coincide with a political *matriarchy*. Even when it is grouped, full of veneration, around those who give their blood, who have invented agriculture, who have prepared the food and made cloth, the tribe is directed by men even in agricultural societies, and not only in societies that are based upon the raising of animals and are governed by masculine laws. Masculine associations exist alongside the maternal law, but this does not in the least diminish "the man's scepter"; neither ethnology nor prehistorical studies confirmed the existence of a gynecocracy with the special, cultural dimensions that Bachofen attributed to it. Bachofen himself even made a chronological division: "Maternal law, inasmuch as it is one-sided maternal law, and inasmuch as it restricts itself to establishing the line of descent through the mother, is a *jus naturalis* and as old as the human race; the gynecocracy related to this maternal law, which gives a dominant role in the family and the state to the mother, is on the other hand of later origin. . . . It arises from the reaction of the woman to sexual relations that lack all rules, and from which she is the first to wish to be liberated" (*Maternal Law*, par. 7). It is a matter here of a seizure of power, which is quite surprising given its puritan motives and which is quite enigmatic as to the means of its realization: There has never been the political matriarchy that Bachofen points to, for the good reason that in the agricultural period, which is still characterized by maternal law and represents the only period in which a gynecocracy could have developed, we find evidence that there was already a division of labor between the sexes, and that the beginnings of a class society and the general relations of domination were already present. With this romantic centralization of the woman, history is eroticized, divided according to the difference between the sexes, and even into a political idolatry of the difference between the sexes. From this point of view the Trojan War literally looks like "it could be traced back to violation of the marriage bed"; it is presented as "a battle between the Aphroditic-hetaeristic principle and the hetaeric-bond principle" (Preface to *Maternal Law*). Even the slaughter at Actium becomes a battle between the hetaeristic principle of the queen, Cleopatra (the "last Oriental Candace who was completely Aphroditic-hetaeristic"), and Augustus, who was the resurrected Orestes with his sober, masculine law. At this level the Christian patrician Bachofen reveals himself as ultimately ambivalent; he cannot condemn Orestes, the murderer of such a mother, and he cannot only find justice on the side of the Furies. In this way the matriarchy is lauded as "poetry in history," which already reflected the glory of Apollo, Roman law is distinguished "in the higher purity of its paternal principle," and Christianity is absolutized as the religion of the father. On the one hand, then, we find in Bachofen the plea for a geometric law that falls to its knees before the mystery of the mother earth, and on the other hand the same Bachofen recognizes the superiority of the Apollonian-Christian spirit over the maternal Gaea-Materia with its domain that moves between the breast and the tomb. Bachofen's heart is with the matriarchy, his head is with the patriarchy; but it is doubtless the work of the heart that ultimately leads him to discover the matriarchy in a form that is more supportable than the political form, namely, in *the form of a religious cult*, a cult of the earth that is bound to agriculture. There was no political gynecocracy (Bachofen got that idea from fables written on this subject by the geographer Strabo). There was, however, a majestic myth of the underworld, of earthly divinities and their laws, and this was parallel to maternal law. Bachofen deduces the primeval "chthonic" law from the myth of the Eumenides (who only avenged matricide) and from the matriarchal habits of ancient mountain dwellers, especially the Lycians (the Lycians to whom he dedicated a special work were for him as the Iroquois were for Morgan). The cult of caves, of Hecate, of Isis, and of Demeter, sacred agrarian rites, and the symbolism of graves permitted Bachofen to bring to light the myth of the earth that is at the basis of (or at least frequently accompanies) maternal law. For Bachofen the important point is the discovery of the relation, even identity, between birth and death within the chthonic religion: All births return to the mother, the woman is the earth, the earth is the field, the field is the grave. Demeter in Greece, Ceres, even Bona Dea in ancient Rome, *terra mater* in general, is the plowed field that receives the seed and lets it germinate; *terra mater, magna mater*, is equally the graveyard into which the fruit falls once again, where it is protected. Bachofen has, if not discovered, then at least powerfully brought this polarity back to memory, and he posits it alongside polarities of return and compensation that belong to maternal law. This is not a fictional matriarchy; it is research into the profound mythology of the cult of the mother: *The gynecocracy is historically demonstrable and valid for religion, but not for politics.* In the religion of the earth and of the moon passion outweighs action, the left over the right, below over above, night over day, hell over heaven, the subterranean over the Olympian—in short, it is a world to which only a romantic could find access, a world of the left hand, in every respect a domain of *major honos laevarum partium* (to renew the expression that the greatest Roman jurist, Papinian, could bestow upon certain judicial atavisms). Even Bachofen is often lost in speculations here; these speculations are overwhelmingly the result of the characteristic excesses of an ideal type, or even of hypostases that flow from a point of view that is not entirely wrong, as in the case of the political matriarchy. Bachofen even intended to write a treatise "of natural science and nothing else" (notice the strangeness of this phrase); this science was to be founded upon the agrarian superstructure of the matriarchal law of the Demeter, Ceres, Bona Dea, and of mother Isis, and not upon demystified real nature. With Bachofen natural law, which had been dismissed as something rational, for the first time penetrates, as the hetaerist-Demetrian law, to the depths of the imagination. In one fell swoop the Philistine spirit of reaction was driven away and was thereby made all the more dangerous. But in an unanticipated way this drew attention to primitive communist peoples, along with numerous speculations that were more than pagan (which Bachofen himself later makes an object of mythology), and therefore it unearthed a myth of a wise Demetrian law and its gentle government.

In the first phase, where everything began, there reigned a certain frenzy. The look that Bachofen turns toward the past believes that it only sees sensual pleasures without parallel, brought together in the bosom of femininity. Human beings lived by gathering and hunting, "interchangeable without any rules," in other words in a hetaerist way; this image is given by the luxurious jungle of the swamp. In the horde of primeval eras, women were at everyone's service; moreover: as with woman, everything else was held in common, "there was no property." The law of this first phase is the *first natural law*, a pure *jus naturale* shared by animals and people alike. That most higher animals live monogamously, at least for long periods, and that the swamp can be an image but not a home does not disrupt Bachofen's conception of the hetaerist phase. It is "the law of Aphrodite that penetrates and fertilizes matter. It is Aphrodite who fills both sexes with the desire to procreate, who implants the urge to care for children, who seals the closest bond between mother and child, and who assures equality and liberty for all who are born. The same goddess hates all special property; thus the same law for all is traced back to the sea, to the riverbanks, to the air, and the *communis omnium possessio* is traced back to the *jus naturale*" (*Maternal Law*, par. 66). Just as ancient is the law of giving like for like, of responding to violence with violence.

The *jus talionis*, the "bloody feminine law of Nemesis," makes its first voluptuous and sinister appearance here. The swamp, which expels that which lives in it from its depths only to engulf it once again in an endless cycle of births and engulfings, is the background for the vengeance of blood. But human beings become sedentary, sink their plowshares into the earth, build walls, found families, and in this way the hetaerist age vanishes. With the beginning of the second phase Aphrodite is conquered by Demeter, who "embraces property and family in a *single* concept, in a *single* mystery, in a *single* law." Bachofen tries to bestow an economic basis of an almost physiocratic quality on this *second natural law*: "Marriage was conceived as an agrarian relation by the ancients, and the entire terminology of marriage law is derived from agrarian relations"; and therefore: "The law rests in the same primordial mother to whom goods owe their birth" (*Maternal Law*, para. 67, 68). But again, the principal point for Bachofen is that law is a part of the religion of the mother; it is deduced from the cult and primacy of the fecund body, the nourishing, caring, maternal love. The natural law of the Demetrian phase is anchored in this cult; yet this Demetrian natural law is so much like another, philosophical, natural law that Bachofen—and this is extremely interesting and important—almost speaks the language of the Stoics in this passage. As one sees finally in the next section, "mother" nature was always a powerful ingredient in different phases of natural law, one that was neglected till now. Historically it is through maternal law that this element was transmitted and brought back to natural law, often in an unconscious, or at least unreflected, way. This is why Bachofen can say that there is "a law that is independent of every human institution, one that participates in the divinity of nature itself and coincides with maternal *aequitas*" (*Maternal Law*, par. 66). This is no longer the law of Nemesis, but of Themis, of Gaea-Themis (of Isis in Egypt, of Bona Dea in ancient Rome); Gaea-Themis "nourishes her earthly children with milk, and divides all of the terrestrial goods among them with the utmost equity. . . . The mother becomes the expression of the supreme *justitia*, which divides everything among her children with an impartiality full of love" (par. 63). The preface to *Maternal Law* even arrives at the following formulation on the basis of the remarkable materialistic categories that Bachofen reads in the gynecocracy: "The gynecocratic existence is the *ordered naturalism*, its law of thought is the material law, its development is predominately physical." But the maternal *aequitas* does not lack the *jus talionis* that accompanied the hetaerist natural law; in fact, it is precisely because it is maternal that the natural life is a polarity, in other words, that it is an "attack and counterattack that never ceases." From this ceaseless attack-counterattack there arises the pitiless Eumenides, who make blood spill from those who spill blood from maternal relations, or even from the mother herself. We find here an astonishing hetaerist residue in the gentle matriarchy: "A double mode forms the movement of life as well as of the law, and this interplay of two forces, like the cycle of death and life in visible creation, never ceases; every injustice that is committed has as a consequence an injustice suffered, which in turn engenders a new and equal injustice. The same action that ought to establish the equilibrium, the *ison kai dikaion*, provokes a new disturbance in the *partium aequa libratio*" (*Maternal Law*, par. 64). Thus, for Bachofen, the numerous problems of commutative justice are even found in maternal natural law; its very cycle corresponds to the ineluctable cycle of a purely organic nature. This organic quality is shared by both the Demetrian and hetaerist worlds: "For both cultural phases the life of nature is the model and standard of the human condition; nature has taken the law into its bosom" (par. 68). Bachofen applies this image in order to lend to his romantic concept of natural law a special reality (in contrast to the abstraction of the Enlightenment). "The ancient *jus naturale* is not like that which one calls by that name today, namely, pure philosophical speculation. It is a historical event, a level of culture that is older than the purely governmental-positive law; it is an expression of the earliest religious ideas. It is a monument of conditions that humanity has experienced, and it is just as historical as maternal law, which itself is a part of it" (par. 66). As such, mother earth teaches both the obligation to care for children and that death is the *debitum naturae*. But this does not lessen the ultimate triumph of an equilibrium between organic matter and the gentle nonrationalistic spirit; in this interiority the maternal law represents "poetry in history." It represents the golden age, if not by the *communis possessio*, then by maternal-physical superabundance (milk and honey) and by *aequitas*. Bachofen integrates images into the maternal law that are blatantly feudal, images such as Homer's land of the Phoenicians, and wherever there is happiness the mother is present. For Bachofen the queen Arete and the princess Nausicaä surpass the king Alcinoüs in the land of the Phoenician, for Scheria, the Phoenician island, is precisely this island of Demeter. "It continually deserves the greatest attention that on Scheria the gynecocratic form of life appears as the basis of higher customs and of a life dedicated to peace, agriculture, and the practice of the arts (especially song and dance), which often accompany maternal peoples" (par. 134). At this point Bachofen emphasizes the symbol of natural law that Hesiod ascribed to the golden age: Themis-Dike, who, holding a handful of grain in the left hand, is enthroned in the nocturnal sky. Nature is of course just another word for the destiny that engenders and swallows; it is material that cannot be mastered and is without advance. Its sole dialectic is between life and death, death and life—this dialectic ultimately founds the *justitia* for those who have not committed any crimes. It is the basis of the *justitia* of death: Nature is Penelope, who always undoes that which she has woven, who eternally weaves the same from the new. But nature is also the native land; in the language of the religion of maternal law to die means to return home, and, as Bachofen states with great conviction, its law did not disappear in the postmatriarchal epoch. It survives and gives its warm warning; it is certainly not the law of the Eumenides, but rather the law of Antigone against Creon, the law of *unwritten piety* in opposition to the *jus strictum* of the rationale of the state. A warm harmony, which in the midst of the history of law of the romantic origin, unexpectedly reminds one of Rousseau's return to nature, of a natural law without artificiality.

With all this, the era that begins with the state, the era of paternalistic law, gradually comes to a close. The forms of relation of the *patriarchy*, violence and domination, are no longer presented as a form of "organic natural law." The value judgment Bachofen makes with respect to this new phase simultaneously demonstrates the thoroughgoing ambivalence of his romanticism, a romanticism that generally looked backward and is devoted to the "disorderly," but which is nevertheless bourgeois-humanistic. In the end, Bachofen even praises Apollo: "The determinant character of the human race consists in increasingly overcoming the law of matter, and elevating itself beyond this material side of its nature, by virtue of which it belongs to the remaining animal world, to a superior form of purely human existence" (*Maternal Law*, par. 66). Thus paternal law becomes ultimately the correct law, against every objection founded upon the seductions of the unruly hetaerae and especially the sanctified solicitude of the image of Demeter. But as was already pointed out, Bachofen—as a good Christian patrician and as enamoured of that other more luminous, more humane discipline that is associated with Apollo and Pallas Athena—turns his attention toward the masculine domain of the Greek polis and Augustinean statesmanship, even if they stay on the other shore. The "poetry in history" of other times no longer only appears as blood and its lineage, but also as sanguine: "The material law of the first times indicated the law of blood, the celestial law of light, the law of expiation. It is in vain that Clytemnestra invokes the blood relationship for in the eyes of Electra the spiritual law of the father is higher than that of material maternalism. In the person of Clytemnestra this maternalism is condemned to disappear, while in Electra a new day dawns, one that Apollo leads to a final victory through the intermediary of Orestes" (par. 31). The paternity of Greece and even of Rome only leaves behind the rubric of the *jus naturale*; some ruins (like that of aequitas) are projected "unexpectedly, just like the ruins of past ages, into a world where the order of the state was completely civil," and the inherited ruins were reconstructed and inserted into the rational, masculine law of antiquity. The *jus naturale* is integrated into the *jus civile*, which absorbs it; the law of the Grecian day, of the Roman state, is lifted above the instinctive community of the night. Of course not without recoil, not without the return of gynecocratic, even hetaerist times in the midst of the patriarchy: The law of men seems to have dissolved natural law entirely without ever having achieved it. According to Bachofen there remains a void, an absence, and into this flows a last force of the old nature: Dionysus. He becomes the god of women. Under his emblem the Maenads gather and a new hetaerist culture blossoms. The "fantastically bejeweled courtesans" of the Orient have a place here too: the royal odalisque, the polyandrous princess, Helen, Cleopatra. Out of the exotically shining first *jus naturale*, Bachofen writes the following doctrine of justification: "Helen is not decked out with all of the charms of Pandora in order to give herself to the exclusive possession of *one*." The Dionysian community itself, it is true, is no longer found in the judicial sign of the maternal breast, but of the phallus; for male domination is not weakened by orgies. Dionysus is the "phallic master of the luxurious life of nature," but of course without masculine brutality and domination. He is rather a sensuous and soft god who relaxes members, dismembers the polis, a god of intoxication and of antiform. As the god of intoxication he makes men effeminate; to this extent Dionysian forms of life carry with them a sort of womanly power. In this *enclave of feasting*, limited but not for that able to be overlooked (for it is indeed of vital import for antiquity), that which reigns is no longer the family-bound, maternal woman, the "pivot of existence," but the debauchery and delirium of Venusberg and of its attribute, the phallus. This is the beginning of the most refined of gynecocracies, one in which "the silent power of Aphroditism does not so much affirm itself in juridical forms as in the domination of all of existence" (Preface to *Maternal Law*). Bachofen goes well beyond ancient masculine law and its enclaves: The courtly love, the cult of the lady, and the worship of Mary, as they appeared in French chivalry about 1100, seemed to be a possible echo of a prehistoric hetaerist cult mixed with that of the Demetrian homage of the woman. Bachofen relates the cult of Mary to the power of the French queens and hazards the following hypothesis: "The high dignity, which the mysteries of the Dionysian cult bestow upon the woman, finds its last echoes here" (par. 151). Nevertheless, Bachofen not only relates the god of intoxication, Dionysus, to the erotic, but attaches him to political Aphroditism as well, namely, to the *jus naturale* of democracy. The original hetaerist epoch was to be distinguished by natural liberty and equality, even by the absence of property; Aphrodite "abhors all separate property." Bachofen sees the approaching return of these conditions, "the absence of all property, the absence of all special laws of every sort," and in the eyes of this reactionary, patrician, and churchly man they are "low and a vile return to primitive barbarism"; but the gynecocracy that is so full of contradictions vindicates them in the name of the refined god of the night, Dionysus. By a remarkable series of inferences Dionysus thus becomes, first, the god of erotic and aesthetic naturalism, and then the god of political naturalism: "This progress of the sensualization everywhere coincides with the dissolution of political organization and with the decay of the life of the state. In place of the richly articulated hierarchy one finds the affirmation of the law of democracy, of the indistinct masses, and of that freedom and equality which characterized natural life before the appearance of civil order, and which belong to the carnal aspect, the material side, of human nature" (Preface to *Maternal Law*). However despised every form of communism is for Bachofen, he predicts a return to it "on account of the cycle": "The end of the development of the state is equivalent to the beginning of human existence; that is, the original equality finally returns. The maternal, material principle opens and closes the cycle of human things" (*The Symbolism of Tombs*, 1859, pp. 237ff.). Thus, Dionysus leads back to something that looks like primitive barbarism to the patrician and Lutheran Bachofen; in vain, Bachofen gives it a grandiose and genuinely utopian title: *The Enigmatic God of the Developing World*. On this subject he has yet another prophesy, one that justifiably announces a final natural law. The patriarchy should not be abolished by this, but fulfilled; the condition of positive law is not the last condition for this antiquarian-minded mythologist. It is surprising that in a romantic who so decisively follows the path of tombs his mythology is so extremely historical that it turns into a cult of ancestors; accordingly, the past looks like profundity itself, and the future becomes an empty wind. But all of a sudden there falls into the crypt a shaft of lightning, almost illicitly, announcing the future that has not yet arrived; already in his early period Bachofen prepared a window for his store of antiquities. The historical method of observation involves him in "a presentation of the law of reason as posited as the final goal of the development, at the end of time, not the beginning, with which the work of history is crowned, and not the ornament of a prehistorical condition" (*Natural Law and Historical Law*, ed. 1927, p. 62). In an extremely general, yet unmistakable, way, a reminiscence of the medieval heretic and millennialist Joachim of Fiore enters the exposition of this conviction. "At the end of one whole juridical development there is a *jus naturale*, not the *jus naturale* of matter, but of spirit, a final law that, like the original law, was universal; like the original material-physical law, it is free of everything arbitrary; it is given in things, and is not invented by men, but recognized by men in the same way as the original physical law appeared as an immanent material order." As Aphroditian without arbitrariness and Demetrian without bondage, this final law becomes "the expression of a pure light that belongs to the good principle. . . . In the liberation from every material additive law becomes love, love is then the supreme law." This is not hetaerist love (which shares with Christian love at least the name), nor is it the maternal love (the "immobility of its physical basis" is abolished); it is, according to Bachofen, the virile love of the Sermon on the Mount that renounces retribution. "This doctrine realizes the highest justice; it is perfection itself in that it abolishes the concept of law and thus appears as the last and complete overcoming of materiality, as the resolution of all dissonance" (*Maternal Law*, par. 66). Whether or not property or special rights persist in this supreme law, which is nonlaw, is a question about which this spiritual prophecy, so far above material concerns, remains silent. If they do not persist, if all of the distinctions in fraternity were leveled, then even the difference with the infamous democracy is obscured. Nevertheless, the utopian light in antiquity is so faint that it cannot make any idealism of the future clear, let alone any realism of the future. Still less does it illuminate a materialism, which among materialisms does not represent itself by the swamp or physical materiality or ultimately by the *magna mater*, but neither does it refer to the productive forces, the economic conditions that are the content that move every social ensemble. And yet, something as astonishing as the three sorts of natural law—the hetaerist, the Demetrian, and even the final stage— could not be expected from the historical school of law to which, in the end, Bachofen belonged and which was on a campaign to annihilate natural law. Indeed, one could even say that *philosophical natural law, from the Sophists till Rousseau, maintains some connections with the maternal law (of the bond to Demeter) which Bachofen discovered.* If this was not done in the context of a direct recollection (transmitted by the conservation of organizations and feasts), then it was done in the continuing effect of a mythology of an underworld, which Bachofen disclosed and exaggerated. In paganism nature was the mother, in Christianity she was the sister of men; that is why she has something to say to the mythological juridical consciousness, which Bachofen had so largely revealed even in its secularized form. There is a mythological undercurrent in rational natural law: "Nature" was in fact often still Demeter, the "institution" still Apollo and Zeus. Thus, the essential being, which in Bachofen's sources was called *justissima tellus*, has an empire that extends well beyond the Demetrian images that are related to the agrarian stage. In this way images of the land on which one lived— in other ways enigmatic—could well have determined the value attached to "mother nature" along with its purely physical concept.

16

Confrontation: Gaea-Themis and Its Survival in the Collective Schools of Natural Law

> Wreathe the golden ear of corn into a crown,
> Intertwine in it the Cyon blueness!
> Joy should brighten every eye,
> For the Queen approaches,
> She who gave us the sweet homeland,
> She who blessed men as men.
> Our song should joyfully lift up
> The beneficent Mother of the World.
> —Schiller, "Eleusinian Festival"

> But you, Mother Earth, in the light pursue
> Your steady course. Your springtime as ever flowers,
> Melodious in their modulations,
> Seasons go by but leave you more living.
> —Hölderlin, "Peace"

It is very difficult to get the core out of the legendary husk. And yet it must be found, for the beautiful look and stare of the aesthete alone are not appropriate to the thing itself. But the core should never be removed in a straightforward manner; even a view that has a special angle must be knowledgeable; if not, it either destroys its treasure or takes no prize at all. Enlightenment ought not to rub up against what Lessing called the shams of enlightenment (*Aufkläricht*) and which Engels even called dregs of a sham enlightenment (*Abspülicht vom Aufkläricht*). Simple good sense installed in an undialectical fashion in fields and prairies, and ready only to accept something well known to it for a long time, cannot change its ways without being penalized. It becomes the *terrible simplificateur*. Thus it is necessary to wage war on two principal fronts in ideological and historical matters: against those who vulgarly reach below reality as well as against those who reach romantically and utopianly above reality. The omissions to which both are party become omissions in the dual sense of the word: Significant, or at least meaningful, portions of a rich reality are left out. The

Hellenistic satirist (and of course utopianist) Euhemerus was the first
to try to bring myths together into what was supposed to be a real
history: Zeus was once upon a time a real king and died in Crete,
Hephaestus was an erstwhile inventor, and so forth. The spell of the
myth was broken by such stories, but it was still not clear how such
a fog had been wrapped around such everyday, commonplace material
in the first place; a follower of Euhemerus took up the task of demystification once again, with a novel whose archaic figures are all
men from the time of the author and just as enlightened as him. The
romantic, on the other hand, often enshrouds legends in a fog, and
puts its husk in an ever-thicker image of antiquity. Eating and drinking,
the sobriety of daily affairs, considerations about the dealings of production and commerce, and all the real relations of life as they were
constituted in the workday of ancestors (no matter how animistic) are,
for the romantic, absent from prehistory. In their place he sees a
consciousness eternally pregnated by magic, and he often even goes
so far as to find this magic in the smallest details of everyday life.
Any old pot becomes the caldron of a Medea, every entertainment
of a Neolithic user of tools here vibrates with ceremonial customs and
mysteries, and every superstition excites profound feelings. All of this
was communicated in a language whose formation and shape are
made quite distant from the murmurs and whispers of the primeval
times by numerous visits to the library. Nevertheless, the romantic
mythologist, and especially the warmed-over epigone of recent times,
makes himself more archaic than a Druid as far as the scope of his
mythical excesses go. He hypostatizes ancient mythical hypotheses (or
at any rate those that are reported to him by philologists), and furthermore, he reifies them in a modern way, making them into a
mythological merchandise. He does not dig up the real historical terrain
upon which all movement of primary needs and their satisfaction takes
place, and above which all consecrations and clouds of the mythos
take place and change their ideological function. It is either this, or
one arrives at the point of affirming a completely massive body of
superstition as happens in Görres, the most extreme anti-Euhemerian,
where we find a superstition that no longer studies anything, but that
is happy with an obscurantist veneration of its object, which because
of its very massiveness is nothing but illusion. In ancient Egypt they
knelt down before the statue of Isis; in romanticism they founded a
quasi-naturalist, quasi-fantastic journal that carried her name. Despite

all of this, when the romantic mythologist, who reaches his high point
in the figure of Bachofen, devotes himself to myth, he touches it more
implicitly than any member of the Enlightenment, who hates and
banalizes myth. Bachofen, who was the most devoted of all mythol-
ogists, discovered maternal law by means of his attachment to his
mother and to the image of Demeter. But in this way he produces
something quite astonishing: despite the anti-Euhemerian elements,
which certainly are not absent in Bachofen, and thanks to the unification
of the mythologist and the historian of law in one person, instructive
traits of a good variety of Euhemerisms are present. Thus we find the
following announcement concerning the history of law: "In all the
myths that relate to our object of research, there is the remembrance
of events that had really been experienced by the human race" (*Maternal
Law*, par. 8). Of course, unreal mythical events are superimposed on
top of real events; indeed prehistory as such is conceived as a visible
expression of the history of myths that were believed in, just as the
history of myths is viewed as the substance of history both from its
cultic and its profane side: "The same mythical formation embraces
both cultural and historical facts; the two are not separate, but identical.
Oedipus and Orestes belong to religion and history simultaneously,
each by virtue of the other" (par. 81). But however grotesque this
identification might be, it does not exhaust itself in romanticism, but
intends to make prehistory visible along with its notoriously effective
religious consciousness, and in this way it leads to concrete maternal
law. It is quite telling that in his *Origin of the Family* (1884), Friedrich
Engels, who did not speak well of "the idiocies of primitive states"
(letter to Conrad Schmidt, 1890), refers to Bachofen's discovery of
maternal law (at a time when Bachofen was largely neglected) and
relates it to Morgan's ethnological discoveries. The original family is,
and remains, a family founded merely on consanguinity, that is, a
matriarchal family. This is found precisely in the unveiled agrarian-
Demeter myth, as a myth wherein the vanishing classless original
society reconstitutes itself once again ideologically and mythically,
ideologically and normatively. From this point the principal problem
that was largely neglected in previous research into natural law is this:
Is the remembrance of *maternal law contained* in the diverse forms of
philosophical *natural law*, and if so, to what extent? Insofar as Bachofen
tries to designate an explicit cult of the mother earth as the mythical
center of the classless society, and therefore of the end of the golden

age, Bachofen has driven directly to the heart of *the problem of recovering maternal law in natural law* (up to and including the forms of *bon sens*, or Bona Dea, which are so difficult to conceptualize, like those that in *jus strictum* represent equity or even the act of grace). It is not a question here of a zoological breed of pretended natural law, which Ulpian defined in a way completely devoid of content in his *Institutiones* as if he wanted to give a genuinely unruly background in opposition to Bachofen's "hetaerism": *Jus naturae non humani generis proprium, sed omnium animalium*. Rather it is more a question of that human government which Bachofen called matriarchalism and whose warmth (with the sole partial exception of Hobbes) sounds throughout the tenor of the entire philosophy of natural law (with its most Arcadian accents found in Rousseau). This principal voice in philosophical natural law is more ancient than its philosophical appearance, just as the worship of the earth and sun is older than the goddess of reason. It is assuredly a singular sort of natural law, one still tied to Gaea-Themis, yet one that subsequently let a rebellion take place within its own borders. In this regard, the rebellion of the chthonic law conserved by Antigone against the masculine law of Creon is the most perfect example. It is an example that is given in one of the greatest poetic creations, one where Sophocles lets a tragic collision occur between the ancient maternal law and the new law of the state and its lords. In this opposition, the prevalence of the voice of Antigone allows us to perceive natural law—despite its otherwise masculine dignity—in its proper *physis*.

That men are all born equal and have need of being protected should never be forgotten. The ancient element of ties to earth and blood maintains itself for a long time in the new law and does so in its most attractive aspect: the maternal breast, the protective and sheltering cave. That is why the right to sanctuary is preferably attached to feminine divinities, even when they belong to the Olympian circle. The fugitive was saved once he had penetrated the sacred region whether it be Hera's, or the Delphic, still quasi-chthonic Apollo. Rome did not recognize any regularized right to asylum; but, on the other hand, in the most ancient Roman times the emancipation of slaves took place at the altar of Feronia, who was a goddess related to mother earth (Bona Dea), if not identical to her. The divinities of chthonian myths thus form the basis for the warmest *jus naturale*, for the objects of *jus strictum*, and they form the basis for security and freedom. "I am not here to hate, but to love," said Sophocles' Antigone; a chorus in the same drama celebrates in an overtly chthonian manner those in the community who "venerate the laws of the depths of the earth and the law sworn of the ancient gods." Creon, the king, had ordered that the body of Polyneices, a rebel, should be left to be eaten by the birds; but Antigone, the sister of Polyneices, disobeys the law. She does not trust or obey the rationale of the state manifested in this order, and in the secret of the night, outside the walls, she buries him in the mother earth. She regards Creon's commandment as a violence and injustice, and opposes it with the ancient unwritten law of the relationship of blood. Sophocles' tragedy is constructed, not on the conflict of duties, which pose a political-ethical problem, but on the conflict of two laws. On the one side there is the Demetrian natural law, of which Antigone says: "It does not only live today or yesterday, it lives always." And on the other side there is the new, masculine law of Zeus, upon which Creon depends. Creon is violently misogynous: "So long as I live, no woman shall rule," but of Antigone he says, clearly evoking the relationship of brotherly love, the piety of the grave, and chthonism: "Let her beseech Hades, whom she serves." Antigone represents this same natural law of the relationship of blood, and therefore of the night and of the mother earth, who in Aeschylus' *Eumenides* unleashes the Furies against Orestes, the one who commits matricide. In *Antigone* the maternal domination of the world is warm and human; in the *Eumenides* it is dark and bloody (that is why it is Apollo and Athena, the gods of light, who rescue Orestes); but toward the end of *Antigone* Teiresias clearly expresses the law of the night: Creon, having taken a corpse away from the lower gods, is devoted to the Furies. But the decisive point represented by Antigone herself is the law of piety, which lives in her and is "nourished by the lower flames," and the fact that this law is protected against the law of the day. This content surfaces in an extremely energetic manner in the matriarchal myth to the extent that its natural law appears as soft and feminine and consequently oppositional. Opposition to "the artificial law in the name of nature" was, however, the sign of the real historical appearance of natural law; nevertheless, relations still pertain between the "humanity" of natural law and the "piety" of Antigone's law—and, in general, to all of the interruptions of the *jus factum*, of the *jus strictum*, within the perimeter of Bona Dea. It is quite understandable why Roman jurists were hostile to the old right to asylum, for it interrupted the execution of the dominant law. But as *natural law* matures it feels itself drawn all the more to *the invisible undercurrents of nature conceived as a woman*; for the Cynics it is even conceived as a bitch, whereas for the Hedonists it was symbolized by the joyful couple of Helen and Paris, who were immune to institutions. To be sure, this relation obviously exists only thinly, if at all, in the Epicurean conception of natural law, which does not in the least presuppose a golden age, let alone a line of a feminine nature. Wherever the sanction of the laws consists in hindering the greatest displeasure and in liberating the greatest pleasure, the pleasure principle itself can be continuous with a bacchanalian principle. But for Epicurus, pleasure is something subdued, considered, thoroughly undemonic, and lacking dark edges; it is Apollonian joy. This holds true despite the orgiastic calls of Epicurean sects, despite Horace's *porcus de grege Epicuri*. In any case, in Messenia and in Rome formal proscriptions against Epicureanism were to be found, while in Crete its followers were driven out by accusing them (borrowing a motif from Tacticus) of being "representatives of a feminine and shameful philosophy." However that might be, Lucretius begins his didactic Epicurean poem with an appeal to Venus, the "dispenser of life, abundance, and peace," and in Lucretius nature appears under the guise of a feminine divinity who exhorts her children to joy without fear and to practice the natural law of physical happiness. Despite all of this no trait was more alien to the Epicurean garden than Dionysiac stimuli; even Demeter does not yet arrange the relaxed community of that terrestrial garden. On the other hand, there exists an all the more remarkable alliance between the *natural law of the Stoics* and this rootedness, this manner of making nature the proper dwelling place of *the attitude of maternal law*. Enlightenment does not constitute a break here; on the contrary the Stoics accept all of the popular gods, the protective spirits and demons, the gods of prophecy, and thereby the feminine-subterranean gods. Certainly, the hetaerist traits are not present here, and, of course, Cleopatra cannot be compared with the ancient pride in virtue that is to be found in a Stoic—even to speak of such a comparison would be laughable. It is nevertheless true that there is no greater contrast than the exaltation of the Dionysian feast, which is nothing more than collective intoxication, and the ataraxia of the sage, individual pride and the mastery of all the *perturbationes animae*. Ataraxia, with its noticeably masculine character, is clearly an exception to the otherwise undeniable Demetrian influence upon Stoic natural law and, for a while at least, to the influence of patriarchal sources upon natural law. Thus we find the pathos of the free person in bourgeois neo-Stoic law, the virile pride in the face of royal throne, the power of dignity in the figures of hard, inflexible men who match the Stoic model: All of these forms of ataraxia stem from the Stoics, from an opposition that presupposes patriarchal authorities in order to deny them. And nevertheless, one finds here the strong effect of the archetype of the great mother, for the ataxaria of the person was regularly associated with her. The power of the dignity of the person is here finally built into the power of a generic concept of the *protector*, of a concept of Bona Dea with light enlarged to a universal dimension: It was called *humanitas*. In the person who does not bow down, it was the dignity of humanity that was being saved; but *humanitas* is given a pride and a firmness softer and milder than peace. All of this was assimilated *in a completely Demetrian way* according to the rule of life that is decisive for the Stoics: to live in harmony with nature. It is precisely from this hidden retreat that a voice comes forth to which one could not pretend to be deaf: the remembrance of Bona Dea, who cares for and protects the order of being that was called innate even when it was reflected. The Demetrian element even impregnated the Zeus of the Stoics, there too on the basis of ancient recollections (in early Attica Zeus was revered as a god of the fields and harvest, and even as a god of birth, with Dionysus born of his thigh and Athena born of his head, and at least as a god of vegetation and of storms). This "chthonic Zeus," who even had a temple at Corinth, permitted the addition of the traits of maternal government to his other heavenly traits; in the changing universe, wherein one seeks happiness and with which one seeks to harmonize, this Zeus could be identified as the god of a good destiny. For the Stoics, then, Zeus is not only the creator of the providential course of the universe but is also that course itself; thus, Seneca says, "The founder and guide of the universe has written the sentence of destiny, and he follows it as well, he always obeys it, he has only ordained it once." Zeus is certainly called logos, even the fertilizing logos, *logos spermatikos*, but in Stoic theology the definition of Zeus as a fire already brings Zeus into a matriarchal relationship. It attaches Zeus to the chthonic-volcanic fire to which Dionysus belonged as to the *flamma non ardens* of the heavenly light. The *cyclical* mythology, as Stoicism reappropriated it from Heraclitus and his Orphic heritage, also moves within the categories of maternal law. Marcus Aurelius celebrates the return of the individual and of the world in Zeus as "the disappearance into that which has engendered you"—an equality is established between the maternal breast and the grave and the rebirth, all of which turns the original fire into a sort of celestial Cybele when it takes the world back into itself and then releases it once again. Zeus, Phoenix of the world—who in Egypt was already feminine in the image of the sun, which unites its funerary ashes and own cradle—thus opposes the *logos spermatikos*. And the very masculine *hegemonikon* in Stoic sages does not change anything in this regard, no more than the very masculine hymn to Zeus does, which has been handed down by the Stoic Cleanthes and aptly called a "Hellenistic Our Father." But in Stoicism, where the father god has "an accord with nature," he is celebrated as possessing a majesty that is calm and enveloping, and clearly maternal. Thus his concern takes on characteristics of the Demetrian Bona Dea: The domination of the Stoic Zeus is not an external one, not a compulsion forced in from outside of the world in the way of some oppressor. Rather the law of the world, and thus the natural law of the Stoic Zeus, is conceived as the most internal law of the life of the world itself, the tie that sympathetically binds the parts of the world with a good-willed destiny and necessity: In the later Stoics, Zeus is the father conceived as *magna mater*. The world does not have its centers in the heavens, but on the earth: The earth, as Cleanthes said, is the "common hearth," and some Stoics even called the earth the *hegemonikon* of the cosmos, totally transforming Zeus from fire to earth, or even pneuma to earth. From this point of view it becomes clear wherein the analogy consists between the Stoic advice given in the philosophy of right "to live in harmony with nature" and the chthonic cosmomorphism of maternal law. At one point Bachofen wanted to recognize the feminine principle "in that harmony which the ancients designated predominantly as *gynaikeia*, in that religion in which the deepest need of the feminine soul, love, elevates itself to the consciousness of its accord with the fundamental law of the universe . . . and finally in that consistency and conservatism of all of existence to which the woman is predisposed by nature itself" (preface to *Maternal Law*). Significant definitions of this sort are to be found in the Stoics in the way that they counseled a harmony as well as in the way that they spoke of the object of this harmony. For the Stoic world, the body of Zeus is a pure harmony with itself; it is the autarky that after all the periodical fires rests in the perfect and complete return of the same in itself. Such are the relationships in Stoicism that the law of Zeus has to the *magna mater* as the dispenser of a sweet and relaxed natural law of an all-embracing "philanthropy" both below and above the thunder of Cronos. And the logos that protects her is the soul of the world, which animates everything as the pure spirit separated from the monarchy. This explains why the Stoic ideas of community and philanthropy, though abstract, succeeded in attaching themselves to the plebeian cult of this Bona Dea. If it is true that the idea of community in Stoicism is related to the law of life of the sage and finds its limits there, then it is just as true that the Stoic sage, by his own law of life, is tied to the life of the universal community: And here relations to the people emerge, relations that largely contradict the aristocratism of masculine law. We have already noted that Tiberius Gracchus was a Stoic, but the tribune of the people was assisted by a belief in Ceres, the protectress of the plebeians, in whose name bread was distributed to the poor and a battle was waged against the patricians. At Ceres' side one even sees a goddess appear, Bona Mens, the patroness of reason, who does not disappear in the face of Jupiter and who guards *aequitas*, the old virtue of the matriarchs, and consequently of Stoic natural law (despite the logos and Zeus).

To summarize, from the beginning Demeter was related to Stoicism much more than Aphrodite was related to Epicureanism, mitigating the harshness of the measured justice of the legislator. This is not contradicted by the historical alliance that Stoic natural law ultimately engaged in during the Middle Ages with the Ten Commandments, which were commandments of a strict patriarchalism. Despite this, Stoic natural law rested in memory as an immanent law of the world, prior to the heresies of tolerance. Demeter had, of course, left the game, Mary had become the queen of the heaven, and *the terrestrial globe and lunar disc were to be found at her feet*; and thus, despite the cult of the woman and of Mary, Demeter had no place in medieval natural law. Mary only seems to come into play in legends, but even there she does not appear as a legislator like Demeter or Isis; rather she seems to represent supreme Christian pity: Throughout the night Mary supports one who has been hanged so that he will be alive when cut loose in the morning. But this legend does not aim at any radical break in the concept of justice, but only at a sporadic and abrupt rupture, and so does not pretend to have a place in natural law. In the relative natural law of the Middle Ages we find a kind of *poena et remedium peccati* that was incontestably closer than any other to positive legislation. Until the Reformation it was almost exclusively in the movements of the sects in which one found a "preaching of Mary" that allied itself with the revolts against the law of the masters: The "pure and beautiful mother," the "door of pity," the "mistress of the kingdoms of heaven and earth," as Tauler called her, becomes the patron of the poor more easily than the resurrected Jesus with his heavenly glory. In this Rousseauism one can recognize a matriarchal concordance, which arises from the side of Demeter and could help in interpreting Rousseauism. Nature, as a social category, has clearly undergone such a transformation that only a very thin and general breath remains of the essence of the Bona Dea. And nevertheless, Rousseau's grand return to an earlier time, with the feeling that accompanied this return, breathes in thoroughly maternal images of nature, images of an Elysian feast. Thus, not only in *Emile* but also in *The Social Contract*, nature is transfigured as if she had been the protective nature found in *Nouvelle Héloïse*. Even the so-called religious naturalism, which attaches itself to Rousseau, gives him this confidence in nature as a mother and as a sort of protective retreat, which can only be understood as a positive feminization of pantheism. At the same time, *the traits of the ancient maternal law have remained recognizable in the many formations of philosophical natural law* insofar as nature conserves, or presents anew, the face of a *magna mater*. And when this relationship has become manifest, it also reveals a kind of unique government—"one in harmony with nature"—in the strictness of the dignity that differentiates classical natural law from social utopias as tales of happiness.

17

The Oath on the Styx, the Ambiguous Cosmos in Hegel's *Philosophy of Right*

Thought does not long for itself, although it searches. It calms itself as soon as it finds its object and grasps it, just as if this object were made for thought. The passion of thought is to comprehend and conceive that which is, that is, the real; for Hegel, correct thought even coincides with reality. It is true that being in general is greater than being that is now; for Hegel, the thinker of becoming, these two kinds of reality do not coincide in the least. If that were the case, if only that which is would be, if it did not have a becoming behind it, a being that was no longer, if it were always the same, then the vast Hegel would be the most narrow-minded yes-man of all times; he would not have any room for any sort of dream content, and least of all would he have any place for the content of natural law, since it exists only where the real is not restricted to the present. The young Hegel, however, had an especially clear view of the past stages of the real, of the forms before dawn, and of the law that has become ordinary today. Thus, Hegel fully recognized the spirit of natural law, though for him it only lived on the basis of the present reality, whose largest part is the past. Long before Bachofen, Hegel distinguished the "law of shadows" from the "law of the day," and though he did not find a maternal law to be the basis of all law, he did recognize an undeniably chthonic basis of law. It was not a golden age, but rather one that Hegel, a thoroughly patriarchal thinker and later philosopher of the Prussian state, spoke of with warmth and of which he took leave only with a sense of melancholy. It is in this age that the philosopher of the concept discovers the first form of the concept: the form of feeling, the elementary relation of blood, the relation of Antigone to her brother, the simple and unconscious purity of immutable natural custom. Thus Hegel was the first to point to the significance of *Antigone*. For the ancient world the Styx itself was the oath, not only its guardian, and the Styx was a goddess, the daughter of Ocean. The natural law of the oldest of the sages, the maternal natural law, lived with her; it is the river that crosses the stalactite grotto of shadowy interiority. Thus, in the *Phenomenology of Spirit* Hegel speaks chthonically (indeed one even hears genuine whispers from the primeval times): "Spirit which is manifest has the root of its power in the subterranean world; the certainty of the people, sure of itself and assuring itself, only has the truth of its oath, which binds all in one in the unconscious substance of everything, in the waters of forgetfulness" (*Works*, II, p. 356). It is obviously only a natural law of mythology, and Hegel, underlining the absence of consciousness in it, separates it from every possible reappropriation by later times. Neither the forms nor the content of this "all in one binding oath" have anything in common with Rousseauism, no matter how much Rousseau might have in common with Antigone's world of love. Nevertheless, that which resounded in both cases was the law of the heart, the same law about which Hegel speaks so badly in present reality, but about which he speaks approvingly in the past, in the root of the present. For him this root is and remains the nature of Antigone—an origin of law and a lasting opposition to the rationale of the state. Even the jurist Hegel gives "piety" this oppositional place: "For this reason, family piety is expounded in Sophocles' *Antigone*—one of the most sublime presentations of this virtue—as principally the law of woman, and as the law of a substantiality at once subjective and on the plane of feeling, the law of the inner life, a life that has not yet attained its full actualization; as the law of the ancient gods, the gods of the underworld; as an eternal law, and no one knows when it first appeared. It is first presented as a law opposed to public law, to the law of the state" (*Philosophy of Right*, par. 166). The difference between Hegel and Bachofen is that for Hegel the family is conceived in a general way, whereas for Bachofen it is the specific family of maternal law that forms the basis of nature. But no such distinction exists in the way each of them judges feminine law to be an element of the ethical world. Even from his pure, Apollonian point of view, Hegel is able to find that Creon was at least partially wrong vis-à-vis Antigone; that is, he was wrong to the extent that he dishonored and destroyed piety as a terrestrial force of communal life. "With this, revealed spirit (that is, Creon's civil law) transforms itself into its opposite, and it discovers that its highest right is the highest injustice, that its victory is really its own undoing" (*Works*, II, p. 356). That is what Hegel says in the *Phenomenology*, but in the later *Aesthetics*, when speaking of Antigone, Hegel demands the unity of the law of love with the law of the state within a totality whose parts they constitute. "Thus, for example, Antigone lives under the rule of Creon; she is the daughter of the king and the bride of Haemon, so she should be obedient to the orders of the prince. But even Creon, who is a father and husband, must respect the sanctity of blood and must not give commands that run contrary to this piety. Immanent in both of them, this same force alternately rises up in each of them and they are gripped and broken by that which belongs to the circle of their own existence. Antigone suffers death before she can enjoy the wedding dance, but even Creon is punished by his son and wife, who yield to death, the one for the sake of Antigone, the other for Haemon's death" (*Works*, X, 3, p. 556). Thus pre-historic natural law at least appears as a higher order, that is, as the law of interiority in opposition to the law of the day. That for Hegel this interiority increasingly transforms itself into the virtuous life of the model family does not abolish the original music that came from it. For Hegel, this music was rightly a love song—on the basis of the reality that had come to be and the right to power that came with it.

Of course people were not individuals then either, then least of all. Bloodlines united a group, nourished a set of customs, and the inner world was not the least bit individual. Hegel uses this in order to build a bridge from customs to the universal state. With this Hegel ceases to be historical; he restricts himself to the currents of the surrounding world. Although his reason tries to conform only with being conceived as becoming, in the philosophy of right his reason fell more and more into the actuality of his day. For him this actuality was the Prussian state understood as the appearance of objective spirit. Here the individual no longer had any place; indeed the individual as such had already come under suspicion. The right that the individual believes is innate Hegel calls an empty conceit. Only a narrowness of spirit is at work here, even when it is accompanied by a heart beating hard for the well-being of humanity. The people are not sovereign, but are rather an "aggregation of particulars," and consequently they are "that portion of the state which does not know what it wants." Hegel's philosophy of right does grant the people a representative, despite (or on account of) the equation posited in the title of "natural law and the science of the state," which accords no one the right to meddle in the affairs of the government. This representative has the sole task of letting the people know that they are being governed well; it is not the instrument of a will to change for the better, but simply the organ whereby objective spirit is transmitted to subjective consciousness. The representation of estates had its deducible justification solely in the fact that "the moment of subjective formal freedom . . . comes into existence in it" (*Philosophy of Right*, par. 301), that is, in relation to the state. With such an appreciation of the political individual and of the sovereignty of the people, it is not surprising that Hegel never recognizes or admits to a regulative idea, a social contract that is always the fruit of a democratic accord. Nor does "the nature of the state [lie] in contractual relations, even if the state is regarded as a contract of all people or as a contract of the people with princes and the government." Nor "is the defense and security of the life and property of the individual qua particular so unconditionally the substantial essence [of the state]; on the contrary, it is that higher entity which even lays claim to this very life and property and demands its sacrifice" (par. 75, 100). The state cannot be constructed out of individuals, who must already have been members of the state before they could be juridically recognized as persons capable of sealing a contract; and as the "reality of the substantial will" the state cannot be annulled. "This substantial unity is an absolute unmoved end in itself, in which freedom comes into its supreme right, just as this final end has supreme right against the individual, whose supreme duty is to be a member of the state . . . The state is the course of God in the world; its ground is the power of reason realizing itself as will" (par. 258). There obviously remains no place for that natural law which has nourished itself in the private sphere and which, above all, was to have turned away from man as being in a state of oppression. All the postulates become homeless, pulled out of unconcretized concepts like freedom, equality, and "other canonically posited partial determinations of existence." It is particularly with respect to this postulating activity that Hegel says that the present reality, which supposedly already possesses the "identity of the idea and being," is present in the state as the "reality of the substantial will" wherein alone "freedom comes to its supreme right" (par. 258). According to Hegelian doctrine, the postulate confers upon the essence of reason "a distorted position, for it appears here as something that is not self-sufficient, but as having need of an other"; Hegel obstinately holds onto this doctrine, while for the theoreticians of the postulates of natural law, only being appears as needy, not reason. Even the final blow against a natural law that did not want to coincide with the sciences of the state is a physical one. Just as if he were a theoretician of natural law, but in precisely the inverse manner, Hegel establishes a parallel between the laws of jurisprudence and the laws of mathematical physics. Classical natural law had adopted mathematical physics as a model of demonstrability and of a reasonableness that was never, or at least seldom, to be found in the life of positive law. Hegel, who everywhere else is critical of the merely external being of nature and who said of inorganic matter that its truth was to have none, not only accords historical being to the most rigid, physical level of that which has become, but he also vindicates the forms of positive law that have been formed by chance and power—something that Grotius only attributed to his ideal of logical law. This is what is implied by Hegel's remark in the preface to the *Philosophy of Right*: "So far as nature is concerned, people grant that . . . it is inherently rational and that what knowledge has to investigate and grasp in concepts is this actual reason present in it; not in the formations and accidents evident to the superficial observer, but in nature's eternal harmony, its harmony in the sense of the law and essence immanent within it . . . The universe of spirit is supposed rather to be left to the mercy of chance and caprice, to be godforsaken, and the result is that if the ethical world is godless, truth lies outside it, and at the same time, since even reason is supposed to be in it as well, truth becomes nothing but a problem." In this way judicial law is related to the physical law not only etymologically or from the point of view of the history of concepts but also by its real, rational content. This relation constitutes a sort of judicial cosmos. It is characteristic and significant that it is far from the postulated cosmos of the natural law of a nonfalsified nature, one transfigured in its original or matriarchal state. For Hegel posits a basis for the valid laws of the state on the inviolable logos of the Keplerian planetary laws (where the law of the state, as a higher mediation of the idea with itself, represents a rock more concrete than bronze). Thus only rarely, and with reluctance, is Hegel's *antirational law of concrete, far too concrete, reason*, critical of positive legislation, though in exceptional cases Hegel even takes the risk of correcting Prussian conservatism by casting a glance toward the contemporary reality of English conservatism. In making a concord with political givens, Hegel far surpassed the perverse natural law of the Wolffian school with the panlogism of the being of the now. Of course, Hegel extols jury trials, and one even sees connections to Rousseau where they are least expected such as in the attempt to regard crime as a violation of contract. But the fear of the demos, of the visible will that needs to be stabilized, turns dialectic into a movement in a closed house and leaves it standing still in the domain of law. Hegel believes that he has discovered concrete logos at the precise point where classical natural law was at a loss: in the *penal process*. As in Kant, punishment is conceived in the strictest sense as retribution. According to Hegel only from this point of view can the right to penalize be justified, not from the point of view of dissuading or improving the malefactor, nor for the security of society. For retribution is the manifestation and reaffirmation of law, as the law of the universal will in opposition to the nullity of the particular will that raises itself against the order of law. Hegel emphasizes that only retribution "satisfies the criminal in his human dignity"; it alone fulfills his inalienable right to be punished. It is not permitted to conceive punishment as a simple form of constraint, as if punishment were only a matter of constraint and not of sin; for as constraint, punishment falls under the concept of "a form of merchandise for which an other, namely, the crime, is purchased. As a judicial power, the state holds a market with determinations that are called crimes and can only be bought with other determinations, whereas the legal code determines the price that is to be paid" (*Works*, I, p. 371). Punishment should be so little constraint that it even returns to the criminal his freedom by respecting his human dignity; in the restoration of law through punishment, justice (which as a pure nullity is nothing less than freedom) is once again established as a part of the substantial will, and thus of objective freedom. It is a paradox, or a mockery, that Hegel is not embarrassed in calling the death penalty the greatest happiness of freedom: Beheaded, the criminal becomes human again. That is how easily Hegel's judicial conscience regarding punishment conforms to the supreme power of the existing state and social order: Hegel only recognizes justice as penal justice, and this is found in the iron hand of the dominant order.

Not that it would be right to brand a thought that conceives in motion in this way. As if such a justice, which flagrantly opposed the justice of Anselm Feuerbach, did not finally remember the having-been-other, or even the becoming-other. As already noted, in principle Hegel's concept is not a concept of Being that is, but of Being that will be, of Being that places itself in contradiction to all that is fixed.

Then, despite the apotheosis of the Prussian state, as a position that insists upon holding onto that judicial positivity which is fixed, it is methodologically untenable: In opposition to the *non plus ultra* we find *the dialectic of a continuing world process*. Dialectical reason has little to fear from history; insofar as history is fluid, dialectical reason sees in it its own material and thereby finds the cosmos itself to be in ferment. Even the rigid architecture of the law fell to it; the cosmos that had developed in the law was once again ambiguous: Even in Hegel's philosophy of right the frozen music of dialectic as frozen was, in the end, irregular. Having in the past seen a law of Antigone that is absolutely incommensurate with the law of the state, the historical concept ultimately encountered something out of the ancient natural law of the *postulate*. Previously, reason, which was all too concrete, in accommodating itself to the present reality of the state, had refused to admit that it could exceed what had become; but even without finding a more perfect reality, it managed quite well with an "appropriate" one. Nevertheless, Hegel defines *dialectic* itself, in its essential restlessness, as the "effective presence and absence of the more perfect in the imperfect." It is presented in such a way that finitude, the imperfect, "is not the truth, but nothing other than a transition that goes beyond itself" (*Encyclopedia*, par. 386). This renders Hegel's philosophy of right susceptible to sound ideas, despite all of its apologies for that which already exists. But it no longer lacks even the most simple point of contact with natural law, even with the schematism of the older constructions such as those of the Wolffian school. A residue of natural law is already found in the presentation of public law as "abstract law," which was a preamble to the presentation of public law and independent of it. Hegel clearly separates himself from the nonconceptual historicism of the historical school, and in opposition to the mere "historical explanation and justification" he posits the "importance in and for itself of a valid justification from the concept of the subject matter" (*Philosophy of Right*, par. 3). When he explains that as philosophical law, the relation of natural law to positive law is as "institutions to pandects," this means at first only that the relation is a fundamental one according to which natural law must provide the basis for positive law to the same extent that ancient Roman law (about which courses on articles of law were concerned in Hegel's time) provides the basis for contemporary Roman law (which is considered in courses on pandects). This relation sounds like a modest one, but it places the Wolffian, rational character of natural law above abstract or private law. Even more troubling than this is Hegel's critique of judicial positivity on account of its rigidity and the appearance of truth in it (one that is something like the older, oppositional natural law). It is nevertheless true that this critique comes out of the most unlikely region: It certainly does not rise up from below with the immodesty of a political upheaval, but rather from the outside, in the manner of an Alexander or a Napoleon who overturns the state by war. Classical natural law did not number war among its instruments; for Grotius war was too abnormal, for Kant it was incompatible with the rational state and its alliances. But for Hegel, war is the yeast of the public, of the judicial state of affairs itself, insofar as this state of affairs solidifies "finite determinations such as life, property, etc." "In order not," Hegel continues in the *Phenomenology* (at the time of Jena and Auerstedt, the collapse of Prussian feudalism), "in order not to let them get rooted and settled in this isolation and thus break up the whole into fragments and let the common spirit evaporate, government has from time to time to shake them to the very center by war. By this means it confounds the order that has been established and arranged, and violates their right to independence, while the individuals (who, being absorbed therein, get adrift from the whole, striving after inviolable self-existence and personal security) are made, by the task imposed on them by government, to feel the power of the lord and master, death." To be sure, one finds in the law of martial law the most severe constraint, even inhumanity, which is made all the more certain when Hegel unabashedly speaks of wars instituted by the state itself, of deliberate disruptions of the lazy times of peace even in its own land. The state becomes Molech, more for its own subjects than its enemies; and Hegel does not forget to remark "that victorious wars dispatch internal restlessness and solidify the internal powers of the state" (*Philosophy of Right*, par. 324). Despite this robust cynicism, which, even with the beard of the prophet, has nothing oppositional about it, uncertainty is, according to Hegel, installed in property, and "this insecurity finds its effective expression in the form of hussars with shining sabers." Thus, in the final analysis, it is related to the form of the state at the time—Prussia of 1806, Persia and Alexander, Carthage and Rome, Spain and England—and the laws of the state. From this point of view, war, which brings the autonomy of the state into play, contains a criticism of the state—world history is the world tribunal. But according to Hegel's formally optimistic proposition, war is also "the progress in the conscience of freedom" whereby freedom is defined as the being-by-itself of Spirit. As the motive of the becoming-for-itself or the manifestation of the historical subject, there is even something subversive within it, at least if it is looked at *post festum* from whatever advances there have been. Hegel's *Philosophy of History* accentuates this subversive element by focusing upon the disruption that is stronger and more necessary than war, which originates unmistakably from the dialectic of the preceding satiated condition: "Occasionally this Spirit does not appear in a manifest way, but pushes itself about, as the French say, *sous terre*. Hamlet said of Spirit that sometimes it calls from here, other times from elsewhere: 'You are a worthy mole,' for Spirit often burrows under the earth, like a mole, and perfects its work. But wherever the principle of freedom surfaces, disquiet enters the picture, a drive toward the outside, a creation of an object that Spirit has to annul" (*Works*, IX, p. 74). Thus, so-called Spirit—that is, reality as dialectical reason, reason as dialectical reality—corrects the inadequacy of every *fixum*, especially of the political-juridical *fixum*. Hegel measures every empire against the principle of becoming-for-itself; he criticizes Oriental despotism, the Greek slave economy, the cold violence and abstract universality of the Roman Empire, the barbarism and pure transcendence of the interiority of the medieval world (cf. *Philosophy of Right*, par. 355–358). The positing of disruption in the dialectic of the becoming-for-itself is so great that it transforms Hegel's apology for the moment into something inconsequential—indeed, even into nonsense—from the point of view of the Hegelian principle itself. This contradiction makes the beams bend in Hegel's otherwise well-constructed philosophy, as for instance in the assertion that in Germany "everything worldly was improved by the Reformation," or that the monarchy, in connection with Protestantism, was "absolute freedom." It is not always so easy to get the dialectical mole to leave his function of bringing about movement. It is not so simple to bring to a halt the novum of a dialectical rational law, or to reduce it to a simple anatomy of the existing body of law. The concordance of dialectical reason with that reality which emerged for the first time is never stronger than when it is suppressed, because then the repression itself, the supposed concluding wisdoms of the body of existing law, seems comical and paradoxical. It finally appears as an ambiguity, and this ambiguity is the general characteristic of the seemingly reliable Hegelian philosophy of right; ambiguity characterizes the presence of rational law in the clothing of the state in its actual concretion. The sentence with which Hegel opens his philosophy of right, as one would open a portal, the fundamental sentence—"The rational is the real; and the real is rational"—carries his Janus face. Hegel's contemporaries had already reworked the *first* part of the sentence before the semicolon, which is just as *revolutionary* as the *second* part is *reactionary*. Above all, the real, according to the Hegelian definition, is not at all equivalent with that which is somehow existing immediately. There are rather gradations of Being, and that which Hegel calls reality is already one of the highest grades of Being, and for him that means the last determinations of the world according to gradations of value are "Being, appearance, existence, reality." That is why Hegel says in the *History of Philosophy*: "One must differentiate between the world of appearances and reality. The real also has an external existence; that presents arbitrariness, contingency, just as in nature tree, house, plant, encounter one another. Superficiality in the ethical world, the action of men has much bad about it; many things could be better . . . . The temporal, the transitory, does exist, and can even suffice in an emergency; but despite this, it is not a true reality" (*Works*, XIV, pp. 274ff.). Hegel's *Logic* neatly formulates the issue, cramming it into a single unique sentence: "Reality is the unity of essence and existence; in it, formless essence and untenable appearance—or indefinite existence and inconstant multiplicity—have their truth" (*Works*, IV, p. 184). That means, reality is the interior that has become exterior, or essence that has become one with its appearance—it is a question of something completely other than empirical givenness. Consequently, the second part of the sentence, after the semicolon, implies the assertion that "all reality is rational," but does not require recognition of the given. The school of young Hegelians understood both parts of this sentence in a thoroughly postulative sense: Both the rational that is the real and the real that is the rational must prevail. Thus, for the first time revolution is properly situated, namely, in reality, which is the place and last proof of reason. The dialectic of history, where every solution poses a new task, every positive determination contains its negation and thereby the means to a new more positive determination—this true war in Hegel's "truce of reason with reality" has taken rational law out of abstraction and led it ultimately into the possible harmony with the *tendency* of reality. According to a decisive mission to change the world, according to a new pregnancy of right in the social world, it is now called, in Marx, real humanism. The historical school of law had nailed natural law to the cross of history, and history ended. But insofar as the dialectical idea hangs upon this cross, it was inevitable that it not die and, in the end, that it be liberated more than ever before from the grave of the holy alliance.

18

The Death and the Semblance of Life of a Late-Bourgeois Natural Law

The movement of juridical liberalism

From the bourgeois side there was not much left from which to liberate oneself. The times drew to a close where one left home in order to find the right and just way of doing things. Even those who were not related to power restricted themselves to a patchwork activity within the framework of existing laws. One took on the air of not being touched by all of this; one turned to a concern with legal decisions, but did not take any interest in the framework within which these decisions were made. Here we find an expression of the so-called liberal (rather than strict) juridical attitude; this attitude entered the picture as something especially German and as socially well intentioned. According to this attitude, the judge ought not to be bound by the "strict" letter of the law in every case. He ought not to be an automaton into which one throws the pieces of paper with the facts and out of which a verdict is spit with some more or less plausible arguments. English law, which was extremely relaxed and less dogmatic, has always left a considerable margin of play for the free judgment of the judge. In English law the judge is not bound by laws but solely by precedents, that is, by previous decisions of cases. If there is no precedent for a case, then the judge creates a fresh, usable law in the midst of the case itself. Furthermore, even existing precedents, which have been collected in law reports, were open to a much freer application as law, since in some cases the judge is even permitted to omit them from his considerations or to overrule them. At this level "juridical tact" is obviously something conventional and thus something belonging to the middle class; pity the poor devil, the uncommon man, who runs up against liberal prejudices. The German school of juridical liberalism also pushed for creativity in law, but unlike the English school the German school had a predominantly social orientation. It was not simply a matter of discovering the "will of the legislator," the legendary will of a fictional person. It was not any longer a matter of a simple interpretation of an existing law that had gaps in it; and, of course, it is all the same whether this interpretation is made by extrapolation or analogy. Nor was it a matter of the ancient Roman notion of *aequitas*, to the extent that it always only benefited creditor and never the debtor. The school of juridical liberalism, led by Kantorowicz and popularized by Ernst Fuchs, instituted a much more modest tribune of the people, and propagated a more modest, sociologically decorated natural law. To this end paragraph 242 of the Civil Code was invoked; Fuchs saw in it the point from which he could lift and transform the entire juridical world. But this paragraph only defines when a judgment about some action that has already happened (a judgment rendered according to the appropriate law of obligations) is supposed to take into account trust and good faith (*bona fides*) and thereby the other side of the issue as represented by the debtor. On the other hand, in order for such a "free judgment" to be socially responsible, a type of judge is presupposed who is seldom found among the majority of the judges one finds in Germany. In Germany juridical liberalism was marked by progressive intentions, but the existing relations were not at all progressive. And so the Nazi as a judge, servile through and through, but free from juridical nuances, demonstrated what he could do. The wise judge of ancient times, who frequently alluded to juridical liberalism, certainly did not return. In his place we find the look that regards the matter from many angles, and among these are those that are not as good.

Jhering's "purpose in law"

In the bourgeois, knavery, or even coldness, affirms itself with an incontestable complacency. The bourgeois, having become the law, consequently loses all ambitions for new tables of law. He puts himself on the terrain of facts and finishes by accommodating himself flexibly to the given. The fact that every previous given law was instituted by power and its corresponding divisions in the existing social structure was recognized, but did not bear fruit or disrupt matters. Indeed, the successors of Hugo, an adorer of the state, found it laughable that a critical natural law could ever have been conceived. One of these successors to Hugo, the positive jurist Bergbohm, even called natural law corrupt by confusing his conception of it with its pure form, which he did not understand. The clearest and most sympathetic presentation of a positivism that licks the boots of the factitious is to be found in A. Merkel (Introduction in Holtzendorf, *Encyclopedia*, 1890). The bourgeoisie was satisfied with the power of the state that it had conquered, or before which it had advantageously capitulated, as in Germany. Juridical thought itself, cut loose from every movement and every relation that would lead it beyond the given material, thus became increasingly formal. The later Romanist school surpassed itself in the delight it took in distinguishing nuances in the letter of the law; the cleverness involved was great. But the cleverness of this school never pierced the existing state in a critical way, nor did it touch upon the practical affairs of the moment. Juridical material was ordained as never before; it was conceptually purified until every legal judgment rendered appeared as an act of subsumption, but at the price of abstracting pro forma from all juridical content. The result was that the Romanist concept of law, which as a purely formalistic capitalism is alien to the people, became increasingly distant from so-called private life, and thus not even able to be properly used in the capitalistic sense. The schools of Savigny and Puchta had bestowed upon Romanist law an exactitude that it did not possess either in the Roman form or in its modern employment since the sixteenth century; it was without purpose, and it was certainly not the same law that was sung to in its Roman cradle. The recognition accorded the given, absolutely incontestable and finally boring, impeded every effort by the Romanist school to orient a positive juridical content, as well as its efforts to find some such content. Up against this far too empty attitude one sees a movement beginning, a fight over law, one that was not content with picking away at syllables. This battle was begun by Jhering (*The Purpose in Law*, 1877–1883), who at least said that these concepts had a meaning. Conflicting wills were to be arbitrated, rather than subjected to hairsplitting and formulaic exercises that were exhausted in a purely deductive jurisprudence. In fighting against the law of the school of Savigny, a product of itself and subsequently lost in its own subtleties, Jhering touched upon the ancient natural law: Against the obscure error of the belief in a natural development he posited the clearer, less obscure error of a law that was conceived as intentional and made according to a plan; Jhering continued to play with this fiction. But what is more important here is the attempted derivation and evaluation of posited law from a normative purpose of the will. For Jhering, the principles of law are already compelling by virtue of their de facto efficacy, but it is precisely this efficacy, this efficiency at serving a purpose, that must be present. "The goal is the creator of all law": a rational thesis that could equally produce a reactionary fog like the conceptual incestuousness of Savigny's school. This thesis leads of course only to the goal of profit, of private enterprise, and of the liberal state. It leads to places that the inquietude of natural law had long since abandoned; in the liberal good intentions of a parlor reserved only for Sunday, the citizen who never developed is nothing more than a distant reminiscence. He obviously was not the goal in the law of the national liberal Reich. Thus Jhering finds himself on the terrain of facts, and he was proud of that; he adapted the law to a given goal and did not ask questions about it. Even the juridical rules that appeared in Jhering are not entirely distinct from the principle of fixed prices. That was the abundance that fertilized the emptiness and made it human once again.

The state of formal law and Stammler's "right law"; the constitutional state again

But not for a long time, and certainly not everywhere, where the bourgeois worked. Business itself had become too autonomous, too businesslike, too independent of those who make it work. The employees are not the only ones to become the cogs and gears of piecework and machinery. Even the owners of the tools, of the reserves and financial means, were pushed along by the very movement of commerce that they made work; they too are cogs, even if subjectively they looked like the motors. The entrepreneur made a profit, but the economy of profit had already grown over his head since the period of his classical acme. The economy works like a detached and artificial being that runs and stops all by itself. This economy—which is the economy of abstract mechanization—does not work concretely and as a whole abstractly and according to scientific laws. That is why the economic law of the circulation of goods is, as Engels said along with Hegel, a pure law of chance. But this omnipresent chance is simply the other face of an external law that is not concerned with the content of the movement; chance and abstract necessity are two names for the same idea. In the same way, the law that serves this anarchic-formal economic mode cannot help becoming more and more formally

abstract even when it retains the teleological form that Jhering gave
it. Deprived of proper consistency, it obeys the vicissitudes of the
commands of capital; in civil law, as in public law, the law must give
formulas, and in extreme cases it interprets, but never (as in natural
law) provides norms. It interprets the "will of the legislator" of the
moment; that is, of the just mean, which is in the final analysis capitalistic and fixed somehow or other by the large interests competing
for profit. It is to the necessity of this mean, a necessity that never
has more than a purely external character, that formalism is tied in
a complicity of class and method. H. von Kirchmann announced this
long ago: "With one stroke of the pen by the legislator, entire libraries
are thrown into the waste basket" (*The Absence of Value in the Science
of Jurisprudence*, 1848). In any case, it is the concern for the contingent
positive that punches bourgeois law full of holes and simultaneously
transforms it into the form of the most indiscriminate formalism possible—positivistic cynicism. On this score, the complaint put forward
by another liberal, even quasi-materialist jurist is significant, especially
when he clearly opposes the fall from grace and natural law. In 1857
Ludwig Knapp established in his philosophy of law, which was inspired
by Ludwig Feuerbach, that "indifference toward the essence and content of law, an indifference that is opposed to all agitation of the soul
and all seductions of reason, whether satanic or divine, is the trait of
judicial genius"; or more precisely, "the shell of law is the core of
jurisprudence. And just as the essential characteristic of a fortress is
not constituted by the structures that one finds within the outer wall,
but in the ramparts and moats that form the perimeter, the core of
law is indifferent to that jurisprudence which, in subaltern dependency,
continually adopts and abandons institutions according to the will of
an alien, superjuridical power" (L. Knapp, *System of the Philosophy of
Right*, 1857, p. 239). In the meantime, this melancholy satire became
truer and truer; only its melancholy was lost by the more exacting
positivists. The content of law itself was designated as metajuridical,
thrown outside the law, or was at least confined to what was called
sociology. Thus we read in Jellinek, "The juridical position in question
does not want to know what property is, but how it is to be thought"
(*System of Subjective Public Laws*, 1892, p. 16): The juridical question
itself is without content. Yet in the separation that Jellinek makes
between a social doctrine of the state and the doctrine of public law,
he still recognizes the identity of their object, the only difference being

the method by which it is treated. But it cannot be a question of the same object when juridical formalism comes to a reification so that the "purely juridical" is made compatible with injustice itself. F. Somlo, a sort of neo-Kantian jurist who was nevertheless positivistically oriented and a defender of the arbitrary so long as it was formulated, made the following remark without being astonished: "It is a characteristic of the essence of law (!) that a norm, which has appeared in opposition to the law, can also become a norm of law; that in other words conformity to the law as it appears must not be taken into consideration in the concept of law" (*The Fundamental Doctrine of Law*, 1919, p. 117). It is unimaginable that in the times of the "corruption of jurisprudence" by natural law this "essence of law" could have been apparent to a Grotius, or even an Anselm Feuerbach; but the purely abstract formalism devoid of any beastly content already points to the abdication of law, *ab officio*. It is not a question of an abdication that intends to legalize a revolutionary illegality, an illegality that is in opposition to the positive law that has existed hitherto. Such a legalization would rather be an abdication of the higher law, of the guarantor of the human guarantee, such as that which was pushed through with the abolition of obstacles; that would correspond directly or indirectly to the old doctrine of natural law. Instead of this the flexible formalism referred solely to the crude commandment of the legislator, whatever that might be, without concerning itself with its metajuridical character. Throughout the entire nineteenth century, and even beyond, one sees a concept flourishing here that is still completely formal but containing an apparent, even normative, content: the concept of the *constitutional state of the poor and rich*. Liberalism is full of praise for this alliance of words, words that were opposed in part to the police state and in part to the old order of privileges and castes. Formal equality of all before the law of the state is the rallying cry here, for in imposing itself capitalism took an interest in extending universal juridical rules to everybody. Capitalism was obviously equally interested in what could be well formulated and guaranteed as its juridical determination (significantly, it is the law of exchange that is the strictest); calculability demands that it not be interrupted by any rights of privilege whether they be of a feudal or other type. The generality of the law was in fact a claim that was originally revolutionary; it was a progressive bourgeois law, one backed by thoroughly human impulses found in Rousseau and even before him as an essential determination of classical natural law. But in detaching itself from the inequality maintained by property, juridical equality had the function in the bourgeois state of law of dissimulating itself behind the abstract imperfections of the privileges of the ruling class. To this there corresponds another fact: namely, that the bourgeois constitutional state, which often made the effort to hide its apparatus of repression and its class character, in another form had a political exterior that demonstrated an unbridled violence. While juridical equality, the protection of contracts, and so on were tied to the free competition internal to the state, it is the same free competition that leads to another very different generality: total war, which in the relations between states produces judicial anarchy with pure power on one side of the scale. But in the internal politics of capitalism the formalism of general juridical equality served the purpose of concealing the fact that the state carried out the dominant minority, and it did this both long before and after the invention of the so-called market economy. With a vivid light the state of formal law illuminated all of the differences of value that were opposed to the state of declared illegality, the fascist-dictatorial state, which also had a codified law; it is no less clear that at the end of the bourgeois era it could not be maintained even in a simple form except in periods more or less free from crisis. Every time shadows appeared over capitalist prosperity, inner tensions surfaced, even at the edges of this prosperity, where it is reinforced by the production of war and distinguishes itself by a threat of permanent war; in this the formal constitutional state reveals its other nature, by which it can turn into fascism at any moment. Despite the relative juridical security that it gives in period of prosperity, a state that is just for the poor and the rich at once is and must be a masquerade — fascism is thus its permanent disposition, with the amalgam of obvious faults and honest virtues. For the concept of the constitutional state is more qualified than any other concept to confer upon the interested formalism a particular objectivity, that of impartiality and of its justice. This reification, which underlies every capitalist creation, only needs to be elevated to the hypostasis in the formal-general concept of the state in order to give birth to the illusion of an ideal state *per situm*, namely, "above parties." In this sense, Lorenz Stein was the first to argue against the fiction of a state that has surmounted classes to the truth of the class state; it is a fiction that presents itself here as a demand. But the purely juridical theory of the state presented the existing class state as just this objectivity; the formalism that serves the interests of the bourgeoisie, in formulating them abstractly and in being quiet about their content, thus creates a perfect asylum for itself. Once again it was Jellinek who provided the system for the objectivity of the constitutional state as "a power separated from man, torn off from the empire of human arbitrariness" (*Universal Political Science*, 1900, p. 176); proletarian and capitalist, the real movers and contents of the interests of power of the state, do not exist for that which is "purely juridical." And this becomes even more the case when *expressis verbis* the apparent objectivity of the bourgeois state of law decks itself out with the previous glitter of the formal judicial equality of the epochs of natural law. This objectivity looks for a "sense" of law and remains purely formal; it looks for an "ideal" of law and remains nevertheless positive. That is what happens in many idealist thinkers in and around the neo-Kantian camp. They neglected a priori the mission and the social content of the actual state of law. On the other hand they tried to ennoble juridical formalism by putting it into relation with the values of civilization or of a universal cultural conscience. Thus, by starting from a thinly human concept of the end, which he called "a community of men freely exercising their will," Stammler (*The Doctrine of Just Law*, 1902) tried to rejuvenate the tendencies of natural law within the tendencies of late capitalism. Despite his social aims, Stammler considered this obviously only a matter of "dealing with the law that is currently valid"; the only difference between natural law and positive law is a difference of method and not of substance. The first characteristic of the method unique to natural law is that it works primarily with "the lasting definitions of law" or, in neo-Kantian terms, with "the universal forms of thought of the fundamental concepts of law." The pure doctrine of law or the science of "the idea of law in the kingdom of ends" thus "furnished that which could be established with an absolute validity in juridical disputes. . . . That is necessary in order to satisfy the demand of establishing all of the particularities of juridical questions in their own nature as stemming from the idea of law" (R. Stammler, *Theory of the Science of Law*, 1911, p. 3). But if one searches for an essential content for this idea of law ("with which the legislation in every particular situation must agree"), then one does not see anything other than "a community of beings freely exercising their will," that is, the given bourgeois state of law with a social front. The background for the Stammlerian reprise is still grandiose. It is even full of verbal Rousseauism and of hypothetical Kantianism—full of the formalism of the categorical imperative, a formalism of an entirely other nature, especially in the second version, whose "teleology" says, "To act in such a way that the humanity in yourself and others should never be a simple means, but always the supreme end." But while the natural law of the eighteenth century was a revolutionary negation of the feudal social order, its reprise had only an apparent life surrounding the nonnegated law of the capitalistic social order. Thus, in full accord with the school of juridical liberalism Stammler discovered elements of just law already contained in certain notions of the Civil Code (elements such as "appropriate delay," "significant grounds," and "good faith and credit"). Even the act of grace of the sovereign is arranged in this species of natural law; as a part of the "correction of positive law," it is thought to belong to that domain of natural law in which positive law, far from being corrected by monarchs and their grace, quite the contrary had been corrected by monarchomachs and revolutionary tribunals. Thus, natural law in its late-bourgeois reappropriation bore witness to the extent of the modesty and level of display that it had developed; even "creative capital" belongs to natural law then, as it did later in the fascists and in the neo-Thomists. Even the universal norms of civilization, which introduced the Stammlerian program of an "orthosophy" as neo-Kantianism in its ensemble, are nothing more than decorative generalizations of the constitutional state, for they are generalizations with a purely formal and positive criterion, never indicating a content. There is even an appeal to the alpha and omega of the law as soon as the state alone does not suffice, perhaps even because it intervenes too clearly in the administration of justice of the dominant class in class justice. That which is put into the service of the truly just law, a law that is no longer problematic and is no longer open to question, is then the church, which since ancient times has claimed to sit Romanly above the state and its parties. Ultimately, natural law serves here as a decoration; it is an obviously neo-Thomist natural law and no longer neo-Kantian. If this framework of the philosophy of law is itself the making of epigones, it is nonetheless, from the practical-ideological view of capital, a yoke with which one must learn to live and continue to live. Clearly there are methodological differences: Neo-Thomas instead of neo-Kant is not quite so much a formalist, and furthermore this abused natural law is submitted not by the autonomy of reason, but by the heteronomy of the Ten Commandments. But the nonformal element only appears in a methodological form; yet from the point of view of content the nonformal is just as closely tied with the abstract relations of capitalism as to the "end in the law." It is an escape reinforced by the content with which the bourgeois society is pregnant, and which is decorative insofar as it adds itself to the chimera of a precapitalist natural law prior to all capitalist contradictions. It is a natural law that, as already seen (chapter 7), finds its deductive principle, not in the bourgeois reason of beings freely exercising their will, but in the principle of reprisal. It is, however, through this "relative natural law," which is in no way directed toward relaxing authority, that the constitutional state, the state pastorally grown and protected from the dangers of liberty, is recommended to clericalism. That was all the more seductive insofar as the state integrated and protected the most authentic of the capitalistic tendencies, that is, the economic freedom of the person within the limits of the so-called corporate state of the day and its law. The state as "retaliation for the Fall" did not regard private property as sin, but honored it as the dispenser of bread, and even set it up as a juridical model of a capitalism for everybody. The only requirement was that it avoid the "excesses" of exploitation; thus, the papal encyclical *Quadragesimo Anno 1931* puts forward a natural law posited by God wherein the salary of workers should not be too depressed, nor too much, but sufficient to meet the concerns of those who are docile and dependent ("ut salaria opificum nimis deprimatur aut extollantur"). The principal point is still the deification of property (and obviously not only properties of utility) as a natural law that is constructed upon the pathos of the person and subjected directly to God, that is, the pastoral church. This preserves the constitutional state as patriarchal state and, above all, as having to transcend complete injustice (the master and slave) better than liberal formalism.

At least the legal procedures that were established impeded the worst aspects of this relation. The worst happened when the master, having become fascist, was no longer content with stumbling as a consequence of juridical quibblings. When this happened he no longer wanted to be troubled by this species of the bourgeois constitutional state that bore liberal traits (or at least pretended to have them). Even where this happened solely for the sake of naked violence, which is always resentful and impractical, it required a beautiful mask, a mask decorated with traits of natural law, in order to be set in motion;

hypocrisy is then a tribute that vice bestows upon virtue. Nevertheless, compared to the justice of the fascist state, with its complete absence of juridical guarantees and the unlimited flexibility of its law, the justice of the bourgeois constitutional state is a light that shines in the dark by virtue of its relation to values. The bourgeois constitutional state was a motley phenomenon to the extent that it paid heed to relative general legality on the basis of its original efforts to oppose arbitrariness and despotism, even if this original effort had become mere décor. Let us take as our background the description of the juridical situation of the quasi-czaricized Germany that the Danish poet Staffedlt made decades before the Carlsbad Decrees (cf. Brandes, *Writings*, 1902, II, p. 406): "The grim, unholy demon of princely mistrust sits upon the throne everywhere; everywhere one imagines that one hears the whispers of the Jacobean specter and so one has censors and informers lying in wait. A ray of natural law shining upon the rotten edifice of traditional politics is called incendiarism and murder; a modest judgment about the behavior of those in power is treated as a revolt, although the government does not put itself out as infallible as do the priestly powers." The shadows of this state of declared illegality, of the unconstitutional state, repeated and multiplied themselves and were wiped away only in fascism, where the décor of the constitutional state was totally abandoned and the imperialist power, no longer content with perpetuating crimes outside itself and in its colonies, began to attack that which was within its own state. In the place of that juridical formalism which was still rational there was substituted the infamous sham pragmatism that declared that justice is whatever is useful for "the German people," namely, the monopoly of capital or even the monopoly of the state. Jurisprudence was so closely connected with the praxis of a fascist state that not only did the formal democracy of a parliament with opposition parties disappear (under the threat of death), but with it went the last echo of the natural law of the state; civil law, administrative law, penal law, had to be completely leveled into the law of the state, and this law of the state, having become totalitarian, had to put itself at the service of the national socialistic world view, which is represented and defined by the despotism of the Führer and the horizons of that despotism. In his essay "Ideas for Determining the Limits of the Activity of the State," written in 1792 and published posthumously in 1852, Wilhelm von Humboldt—after whom the University of Berlin was named—

reduced the state to the sole function of guaranteeing law in opposition to the totally administrative state: what a light this provided against the background that had become fascist by negating law and values. This must be constantly kept in mind so that the critique of the bourgeois constitutional state, of its hypocrisy and imperfection, can be taken as a reference point for the critique of what is not even hypocritical and imperfect but is unmitigated despotism, characterized by murder pure and simple, not even murder in the name of justice. Furthermore, there is no authentic form of the state, so long as there is a state at all, which ought not democratically to respect the tribute of vice to virtue that the bourgeois constitutional state represented; the issue is obviously the same even when it is a question of an authentic virtue that does not only use the state as a means toward the end of bringing about its own demise. If juridical formalism, which is as dissimulating as it is empty, disappeared, then the content, which no longer needed a veil, goes with it, but not the democratic form of law that no longer has an emptiness or imperfection. The bourgeois constitutional state, which struggled with bourgeois human rights, disappears with the bourgeois state, but bourgeois human rights can so little afford to disappear when the state is constructed socialistically that they accompany it so far as they are not bourgeois. One cannot enter into socialism with a bourgeois constitutional state sitting over the poor and rich as a formal instrument that is ideological and ultimately deceptive. But if one is already within socialism, one of the signs is that it has adopted and cleansed the flag of human rights that were abused in the bourgeois constitutional state and that were completely annihilated in the thoroughly despotic fascist state of illegality.

Reinach and the phenomenological intuition of right; a choice between empty forms

With all that, the late bourgeoisie has accustomed itself to living in emptiness. The formal, having been increasingly reified with greater conviction, almost came to be seen as something stable. This is what happened when the phenomenological method was applied to judicial facts. An intuition presented as an intuition of essence fixed juridical propositions in themselves regardless of whether or not they were found in practice. Stammler, in describing the "juridical will," had already demonstrated traces of phenomenological tendencies. But we have to wait for Husserl's reification of logic before we find a new pride in formalism, and here it even has the fantastic quality of something particularly firm and especially elevated. Formal logic has to research the laws of truths as such and their categorical structure. A "material eidetic" is supposed to investigate the lawfulness of the essence of the specific objects whose relations are the concern of the empirical sciences. But in doing that the very existence, even the empirical relations, are not taken into account; rather they remain bracketed outside the intuition. In this way a new a priori is claimed for expressions of intuitions of essences: It determines the character of all of those propositions that bring their meaningful content to self-givenness purely through categorical intuition, independent of inductive experience. Such essences are therefore conceived apodictically; they exist prior to their conception and therefore exist as original historical phenomena that are not produced by men but discovered by them. For the phenomenologist this seems to be demonstrated not only in the givens of nature but precisely in the material of culture. Pure juridical science, for example, as a part of the pure logic envisioned by Husserl, does not concern itself with producing laws, but only with comprehending them. The act of producing laws is regarded as simply a matter of making selections according to practical-empirical needs, which do not concern pure juridical science. At first glance it seems as if we are only dealing with a dull rational reappropriation of natural law: Here it takes place from a side that is thoroughly formal, but one that is not without relation to a rationally endowed "consciousness in general." Thus Reinach, the first to have practiced juridical phenomenology (*The A Priori Foundations of Civil Law*, 1913), once again takes up the juridical concepts of reason almost like a Voltaire, but Reinach misses the pleasure of finding in them something more authentic that is to be realized. He denies that the fundamental juridical concepts stem from factors produced by law; rather, for Reinach, "they have a being outside positive law, just as numbers possess a being independent of mathematical sciences" (p. 6). Claim, promise, proxy, and relations are just such "intrinsically obvious fundamental concepts"; the juridical propositions whose validity extends beyond time and space are to be deduced from these concepts. Reinach gives an example of such an a priori juridical proposition in the following way: The claim upon a certain action is extinguished in the moment when the action takes place, because what is explained here is "a law that is

necessarily and universally based upon the essence of a claim as such"
(p. 10). Doing this does not require recourse to the law in action, which
would be nothing other than an obscuring of a psychological-historical
application of ahistorical preexistent concerns; the varnished nature
of this vision of law seems above criticism and thus easily agreed
upon. Thus, for Reinach, the proposition *duorum in solidum dominium
esse non posse* "is in no sense a consequence of the definition of the
existing laws," but is rather more solid, more indestructible, "an a priori
truth founded upon the essence of belonging" (p. 67). The absence of
property is inconceivable for this species of intuition: "The relation
between a person and thing that one designates as a relation of belonging or property is an ultimate relation that cannot be further
reduced or dissolved into other elements" (p. 64). One sees that the
superiority over historical-positive law is not so great that it does not
let this law dictate its "essential contents" to it. The blindness of
phenomenology to the economic-historical production and genesis of
"essential contents" has the effect of letting capitalistic patterns of
thought flow unimpeded and uncontrolled into the "intrinsically obvious
nature of the matter." These capitalistic patterns and habits of thought,
this absolutely uncritical abandonment to the historically produced
ideology of capitalism, is precisely that which creates the "evidence"
according to which the relationship of belonging appears as an essential
relationship between persons and things. A subject of a tribal society
of primitive communism or of a future classless society would find it
difficult to find the relation of property "an immediately self-evident
given" as did the phenomenologist of 1913; and this is so, not because
this other subject ignores the phenomenologically irrelevant actual
relation to the essence of property, but because this essence, despite
its supposedly ahistorical quality, is merely a reified abstraction, or
even "ideation" of the class society and its ideology. Thus there is
nothing of a primal given; there is only hasty evidence that is to be
found where the phenomenological doctrine of law finds its supposed
eternalities. In this way the relation that connects the so-called judicial
a priori of phenomenology to the inventories of classical natural law
is not modified (for example, the apodictic treatment of the proposition
pacta sunt servanda). In its attitude and social mission classical natural
law was the perfect inverse of the extreme contemplation of the phenomenology of law. The principles of a Grotius did not clarify the
existing juridical order as an ideology, but as a postulate of better

judicial order; and they were not content with becoming a bookish "self-presence." Natural law was not a formalism; and its juridical a priori did not dwell in widely cast original givennesses, but in an a priori of narrowly conceived freedom prior to the state—and this is what serves as the standard for the state. To be sure, Reinach denies in places "the a priori character of propositions of positive law," but because this denial no longer manifests the least combative character, he defends himself just as strongly as any positivist against being branded as a supporter of natural law. "Positive law can at will do away with essential legalities that are valid for juridical formations" (*The A Priori Foundations of Civil Law*, p. 6)—phenomenology does not make any value judgment about deviations that are "not bound by the sphere of a priori laws." The sublime elevation of the a priori law is so great that it surpasses both positive law and natural law with equal eloquence. "Its proper character lies in being independent of all law, of the 'existing' law no less than a 'valid' law (or one thought to be valid)" (p. 158). Independence from revolutionary legal conscience doubtless exists here, but independence from positive law is always elastic enough to "fill in the gaps of positive law" with its own a priori. In the most extreme point the phenomenology of law leads to a conception of "possible law," which is parallel to the Husserlian "idea of a science of the different possible types (forms) of theories in general." The extent of possible law, according to the formal a priori conditions, appears to be much greater than the extent of positive law; for its propositions include all propositions that can belong to positive law. But once again, the historical positive law only appears as a choice: The legislator of the moment adopts a few propositions from the enormous sphere of law that is possible according to the essence of legality, and he dresses them up with a political validity. But this possible law does not contain any postulates or utopian content that make themselves known in revolutionary tendencies. This possible is in no sense an authentic possible; it is a possible already given as finished a priori. One could not speak in a more contemplative and more inappropriate way of the category of possibility, a category that is open and in the ideal case partially decided even in its content. The phenomenological possible, also the possible of the philosophy of right, remains passively floating in emptiness; only the legislator "chooses the material with which he fills the empty form" (cf. Schreier, who is already close to Kelsen, *Fundamental Concepts and Fundamental Forms of*

Law, 1924, p. 90). The phenomenology of law is related to classical natural law as a panopticon to a manifest, as a play of *de omnibus rebus et de quibusdam aliis* to the seriousness of a *Unum necessarium*.

Kelsen's juridical norm with a simple point of inclusion

Even with intuited emptiness there is no room for amusement, because this emptiness does not tolerate amusement. The formal support does not remain a support, despite its efforts to present itself as concrete and possessing an apparent content. With further escalations, "purity" itself becomes dull and completely senseless. This result was produced by the most perspicacious of all formalists: Kelsen. He came to this point insofar as he pushed *ad absurdum* both the neo-Kantian critical method and the phenomenological method to their consequences. Let us consider the neo-Kantian method first: Perfect "purity" does not, in the final analysis, leave any room for ends. They come from the "empirical intervention" as the founding of the juridical act upon psychological or sociological bases. There only remains a "logic of ought," and it has become so completely formal that it no longer carries, and cannot carry, any empirical determinations whatsoever. The abstract opposition between Being and "ought," which has also made neo-Kantians disinterested concerning Being and has made them into defeatists, becomes the gap between sociology and law in Kelsen. The dualistic "foreign things"—subjective and objective law, even private and public law—disappear in a pure and homogeneous juridical order every time they are posited. Kelsen's rationalism is so extreme that while eliminating the empirical moment in the name of "purity," he ends by eliminating the rational moment as well; thus duty, as juridical duty, cannot be posited and validated in immanent reason, but only from outside reason. That is why it is fundamentally heteronomous; and the outside that he posits (which puts a pure system of order into order) is the legislator of the moment. This legislator is the metajuridical authority who furnishes events with judicial consequences, and who fills a previously empty judicial space with laws. In and for itself, there is no rational compulsion or consequence of any such compulsion that would provide any evidently valid legal propositions. If Kelsen detaches himself, then he equally removes himself from the material a priori of the phenomenological school, that means, from every species of primordial given that might provide the judicial essence of law. The ideal order of the juridical proposition in Kelsen is not at all accompanied by a primordial material given, not even the primordial given of a juridical subject, which seems so evident for phenomenology, or even the primordial given of a juridical relationship. All of that vanished in the formal relationship of the juridical order to itself: "The juridical relation is a relation between legal subjects who oppose themselves to the legal order" (*The Problem of the Sovereignty and the Theory of International Law*, 1920, p. 125). Economic analysis is lacking even more in this doctrine of law, which so distrusts "sociology," than it is lacking in phenomenology; the "purely juridical" is not interested in the fact that legal relations express a reality, a relation between possessors of goods, and that the norm that these relations demand depends upon their interests. In the same way, the legal subject in bourgeois society is a universal-abstract, hypostatized possessor of merchandise; but in Kelsen this material element fades into a normative connection in itself. The juridical subject, as a carrier of rights and duties, is a pure "personification of norms"; even more, the four fundamental juridical concepts—crime, person, deed, sanction—in which the phenomenology of law could have found much obvious "formal material," are obscured in the formal coherence of legal norms. Inasmuch as this formal coherence is a coherence within a juridical-heteronomous duty, it passes hierarchically from one norm to another, and on the highest level there stands the highest authority which posits validity: the act of legislation. And the state is not recognized as being an economic formation, and even less so a formation that can be criticized within law; for the jurist it is not a social reality. It is "the personification of the entire legal order," including all of the juridical propositions that come from a common source, legislation. Legislation itself is the metajuridical par excellence; that is why Kelsen turns to religion more than criticism: "It is the great mystery of the law and the state that is realized in the act of legislation, and it can be justified from the fact that its essence is only illustrated in inadequate images" (*Cardinal Problems of Political Science*, 1911, p. 411). Ultimately, the origin as well as the content of law remains outside the law for Kelsen; its "purity" is limited to being a simple imputation and deduction from a basic metajuridical thesis and norm. If in this way Kelsen's system of deduction becomes a system for the deduction of democracy, that is due to the nature of thetic power of the times when he wrote, to the Germano-Austrian republic that instituted democracy as a norm, and later (*General Theory of Law and State*, 1945) to the incomparable institution of democracy in North America. But in contrast to rational law, no fundamental norm prevents a monarch or dictator from replacing the people as the source of a legal system. Consequently, not only is this source irrational, but according to the variability of sources a great number of legal systems are thinkable, supportable, and realizable. Kelsen explicitly recognizes this *multiversum ex institutione* (the inner unity being preserved in each legal order): "If one asks where the difference between two orders lies, one recognizes that it is the difference of 'sources' from which they have deductively resulted out of different systems of norms. . . . Source in the 'principle' that constitutes the origin of the system of norms. In the unity and particularity of this origin, of this fundamental norm, there lies the *principium individuationis*, the *particularity* of an order as a system of norms" (*The Problem of Sovereignty*, p. 93). That is a remarkable mixture of two methods (applied to law) that are quite different from one another, both from the point of view of history and of content, of non-Euclidean geometry and of medieval Scotism. Non-Euclidean geometry, with the multiplicity of its possible systems (which are always closed), was acquired via the variation of deductive origins (in this case, axioms). Medieval Scotism, the doctrine of a comprehensive primacy of the will over the understanding, has as a point of departure for all of the intellectual determinations and estimations a thesis *ex institutione* thanks to the divine legislator; and this thesis (decision) was not itself bound to the logic of the intellect. In fact, with Kelsen's doctrine of the purely thetic character of the fundamental norm (and consequently the variability of theses) irrationalism is set free; in capsizing itself with an excess of "purity," formalism became ready for this irrationalism from the outset. It even opens a path to the theory of pure sovereignty and to that "decisionism" which turns the juridical chessboard upside down. Kelsen is completely opposed to sovereignty, and to the most violent product of sovereignty — martial law and the state of emergency. To Kelsen, the "subjectivism" of commands seems incompatible with the objectivity of the valid norm. The state here is identical with its constitution as the final point of imputation and the last fundamental norm. Thus Kelsen the democrat says, "The concept of sovereignty must be radically rejected." But Kelsen the formalist finds himself defenseless against the theory of sovereignty, or even of dictatorship, simply because the highest legal norm as well as the highest normative legal power (with regard to the positive law of the moment) is a positional norm. This permitted the leading Nazi jurist, Carl Schmitt, to say that even if Kelsen does not know what to do with the system in a state of emergency, he can easily imagine "a fundamental norm or an imputation point that posits itself." With the little interest that the law has in the origin of its validity, and with the admission of different valid juridical systems (so long as they demonstrate an equally large inner unity), one comes to the point most distant from classical natural law. This distance is all the more certain in that deductive logic, which is adopted from natural law, is perfectly conserved in Kelsen's system; but the deduction is only applied in the framework of interpretation, and the principle that dictates the interpretation is the naked facticity of the legislator of the moment.

Carl Schmitt's "decisionism" or the fascist antinatural law

Thus it is the case that the emptiness of formality and the will that is alien to law, which profits from this emptiness, dovetail one into the other. Before the fact of fascism, which had intervened in the meanwhile, the class deductions of logic ceased functioning. Thus "decisionism" spread unrestrained through right and law; the state of emergency became customary; the mask of the constitutional state was lifted even with respect to judicial means and reasons. The intensification of the class struggle led the bourgeoisie to destroy the *concepts of law* that remained from the long liberal period of free enterprise. Monopolization, on the other hand, transformed or destroyed the *legal institutions* of the long liberal period of free enterprise, and with them went the more or less tattered heritage of 1789. All told it is the "directness" of fascism that was being prepared; the juridical subtleties upon which "decisionism" might stumble were on the way to extinction. The basic rights of the individual disappeared at the same time as the generality of the law (its formally equal application); numerous special laws that bore traits of privilege (or defamation) were promulgated. Contract loses the central position that it once had in the age of free enterprise. Then it played the role of a constitutive element of bourgeois society at the juridical level; even more it belonged to the fiction proper to natural law, which says that a contract lies at the basis of every society. But the contract is only possible even as a fiction to the extent that the dominant class was no longer composed of numerous competing subjects, but of a few monopolistic groups, so that the contract and the promise that guarantees the contract are replaced by the naked relation of power and powerlessness; there has never been any other relation in the employment contract between capitalist and proletariat. The violation of promise, in every sense, did not help suppress the vestiges of the generality of the law, which are signified by the remark that the judge is bound by the text of the law. Even if that law has become a special law, it represents a guaranteed promise on the part of the governmental power in accordance with which decisions are made; instead of this guarantee the interests of the "National Socialist world view" enters into decisions in all of the thorny cases. General clauses permitted the dominant economic-political direction to be validated even in places where positive law contradicted it; thus, as Carl Schmitt says with an unbelievable cynicism, "the juridical abuses committed by means of positive law" are avoided. "Decisionism," that is, the naked power of command of monopolist capital (related to, or in transit to, state capitalism), undertakes a correction of posited law that is reminiscent of natural law itself; but this correction signifies a demolition through monopolistic capitalism. It is by antinatural law that the positive law is broken; because, for the purposes of fascism, it did not adopt too few but rather too many elements of the epoch of the social contract. But even if fascism destroyed the mask of the "constitutional state," including the form of the relativistic formalism that Kelsen had given bourgeois democracy, this does not mean that the perfect cynicism is not capable of finding an even more perfect imposture and mask here. Carl Schmitt, still *ante festum*, had already overtly recognized the "state of emergency" and the suspension of "the sovereignty of the state": "Once this condition has been established it is clear that the state continues to exist while law is effaced. The 'state of emergency' is always something other than anarchy and chaos; it always consists in a juridical order even if it is not a legal order. The existence of the state is confirmed by its undeniable superiority to the validity and value of the legal norm" (*Political Theology*, 1922, p. 13). Consequently, both sovereignty and the politician are conserved; and even more, dictatorship disengages itself for the first time from the concealed dictatorship of a bourgeois constitutional state. In this way the last injury that could affect natural law occurs: fascism, antinatural law *per definitionem*, apparently returns to one of its own positions. Hobbes, isolated and thoroughly falsified,

appeared to be close to "decisionism"; the same happens with Carl
Schmitt. To be sure, Hobbes made the sovereign (whom he had otherwise unmasked as the last wolf) operate under liberal ends, namely,
under the ends of the personal security of the subject and the preservation of peace. Even his starting point was thoroughly individualistic,
that is, the state was founded by individuals for their own well-being;
the Hobbesian concept of the state was exempt from all pathos and
was coldly called Leviathan. But that did not prevent Schmitt from
claiming the rational construction of law for "decisionism," and setting
Hobbes's natural law to work for dictatorship and the absence of law.
Schmitt makes the foolishly simplistic distinction between "scientific
natural law and the natural law of justice" and suddenly discovers in
science a fertile basis for the commandment: "The distinction between
the two directions of natural law is best formulated by saying that
one of the systems takes an interest in certain representations of justice
as its starting point and a *content* of the decision follows from this,
while the only interest of the other system is in making a *decision* in
general" (*The Dictatorship*, 1921, pp. 22 and 118ff.). But with the implacable necessity of imposture the Leviathan itself must be hidden,
the "coldest of all monsters" (as Nietzsche labeled the state); sovereignty
and the person belonging to the state of monopolistic capitalism must
be hidden, and (even in Schmitt) the state must be clothed in folklore.
The Leviathan, or the absolute state, which combats the Behemoth
or the Long Parliament (and thus rebellion), appears as a "failed attempt
at a political symbol." The intersection between the *infamous sham
pragmatism* and the *quasi-natural law of romanticism* increasingly comes
to take the place of the absolute state. This pragmatism declared that
law was what profited the German people, and they know what is
profitable by looking to the large industrial cartels. The quasi-natural
law inherited from romanticism adopts some elements of the "organic
conception of the state" from the time of the Restoration, but only
to make it a matter of general apathy. It latches onto the themes of
blood and earth, that is, to natural qualities of breeding cattle and to
bonds to the soil, as the "eternal life of law and justice of the German
people." This is not romanticism, but conforms to the sense of the
imperialism that arises from the myth of a people who are the strongest
and most noble "by nature"; the same is true about the myth of
eternal war. In Hobbes, on the contrary, the social contract was concluded in order to abolish this state of affairs; for the fascists, it is

renounced with a permanent decision. Thus in this bourgeois variety, natural law ends up as a nonlaw of a natural law that does not exist, and never has existed. The falsification of natural law ends up as its assassination. It ends up as the dictatorship of the perfect crime; but the hope of rescue grows where there is danger—not at all to the side.

19
Aporias and the Heritage of the Tricolor: Liberty, Equality, Fraternity

This was the high point of natural law, but the epoch in which it flourished was an illusion, for out of the *citoyen* there came the bourgeois; it was a foreshadowing, for the bourgeois was judged by the *citoyen*. (Chapter 11)

The undiscovered discovery

No one can escape being some such way; it comes with being. Man is caught in his skin whether or not he feels good about it. In any case, it is his own; within these four walls, if we can put it this way, he is private. But very soon man was decked out with livery, tamed, and only very late was the right to throw away this livery discovered. The free man came out of the ranks a naked man, as he is really found under all costumes. Nevertheless, this deliverance was not simply felt in a negative way; rather it was connected more with a self-satisfied intoxication that felt positive. This intoxication said that life with all of its emptiness and uniformity is worn upon one's own body, or that one could ultimately be a self-propelled wheel. That is how boys and girls feel on the day when they are no longer obligated to attend school: It is a taste of the future that makes one want more. That more, which is to be waited for later in life, was, until this point, just waiting. Three words—liberty, equality, fraternity—point in the direction of a deliverance that ultimately binds men to themselves, to their being in such and such a way that can be developed. With these three words one believes that everything concerning our lives can be made healthy, unconstrained, and harmonious. But one also sees this: that not everything about and between these words is clear; they are full of ambiguity. The bourgeois use and interpretation of these words did not pass over them without leaving behind traces. Their brilliance is marred: It twinkles like the eyes of one who receives stolen goods; it illuminates like the light of 1789. But these three words could not have been misused if everything were clear about them from the start. It is important to see that these words are stratified, and their best attribute had yet to show up. It is that the men to whom the call of the great tricolor appeals are far from having arrived on the scene — they are still on the way.

The core of liberty

To be free means that a person is not imposed upon from the outside. Rather such a person is in the position of doing what he wills, which *appears* to him to be his own free will. The psychological freedom of the will is thus something that presupposes that man has the power to choose between competing and contradictory impulses. It is presupposed as this freedom of choice, not as something like a freedom of making, as if the free will could step out of, or even rip up, causal relationships. The pressures exerted by causal circumstances remain; the human decision is, in varying degrees, determined organically and socially; yet the existing person is a causal pressure too. In this last pressure there lies the sufficient moment for the freedom of choice, namely, when the pressure of subjective factors outweighs the pressures introduced by other circumstances. A man with a completely free will, that is, one who was not restricted by either his previous character or his intelligent considerations, one for whom external circumstances did not even have the force of accessory causes, such a nondetermined man would not be a free man, but a fool and a public danger. He would be one completely irresponsible and full of incalculable blabberings; he would not be a creator, but rather the inverse — he would be the image and model of chaos. Psychological freedom is not presupposed by political-social freedom as arbitrariness, as an anticausal power that permits constant changes of direction, but simply as that pressure of the will, where the pressure comes from the person (or if necessary, from the class consciousness of the person), which outweighs other pressures. There is of course another question that follows the question of the *freedom of choice*, namely, the question of the *freedom of action*, a question that is only properly posed and answered by means of political-social struggle. It is frequently said that freedom is merely a concept of relations, even a mere privation as "freedom from something." But higher than this one speaks of "freedom toward something." Nietzsche's Zarathustra was one of those who praised this freedom as

a true light: "I want to hear the thought that dominates you, and not
that you escaped from a yoke" ("On the Way of the Creator"). But
one does not need to misinterpret the "freedom from" so formally
as did those who were interested detractors of this concept. The object
from which the subject wants to liberate himself was, quite the contrary,
clearly univocal. Liberation always means liberation from a *constraint*
or *oppression*, and to the extent that one avoids being trapped in mere
wordplay, it is never understood in any other way and it was always
understood as having sufficient content. "Freedom from" is always
freedom from oppression, freedom therefore from something that
obstructs and closes the path on which one is able to walk upright;
insofar as oppression disappears, a big question arises concerning *the
ends of maturity*. It was this same maturity that was active when the
yoke was thrown off; it was the opening up of a long self-developing
career. From a political viewpoint the apparently negative activity of
liberation was, in every epoch, connected with a positive activity in
the name of which oppression was erased, namely, the liberation of
productive forces that had become chained to the forms of life and
society. Freedom from the feudal order was not merely the freedom
of a terror or, as Hegel said, a "fury of disappearances" like that which
lopped off the heads of the representatives of the Bastille; it was equally
the freedom to move to the *positivum* of a new, bourgeois-initiated
order of life. In this order the individual will restricted the pressures
and compulsions that opposed its freedom of choice; the individual
conquered a framework wherein the will to profit and—in the construction—the self-determination of the mature person sought self-
confirmation. Even Rousseau formulated this later moment of the
citoyen in the call to freedom of the bourgeois revolution in saying
that "the citizen should not be limited in his freedom except when it
is necessary for the equal freedom of others." A grandiose alliance
then seemed to be constructed between the single individual as a
moral person and the interests of society, which ought to be nothing
other than the interest in this freedom, in the inviolability of the dignity
of the person. It is of course obvious that bourgeois society is just as
far from being a society based on collective planning as it is from
respecting the dignity of the proletariat that it engenders but who is
unable to carry out the bourgeois image of categorical freedom. In a
society composed solely of dependencies, the individual absolutely
cannot be the author of his acts; as Kant foresaw, there could be no

enlightenment upon a bourgeois basis: "the release of man from his self-imposed tutelage." So long as economic dependency remained, freedom of action remained forbidden to most people, and even the masters of the bridge were simply functionaries of an uncontrollable circulation of goods. Even the entrepreneur did not have his own Phrygian cap; there was no democratic polis of Greek freedom and human dignity, and of course the worker had even less chance for these. In *The Holy Family* Marx makes the following observation about this fate of the dream of freedom: "The possessing class and the proletarian class represent one and the same human self-alienation. But the former feels satisfied and affirmed in this self-alienation, experiences the alienation as a sign of its own power, and possesses in it the appearance of a human existence. The latter, however, feels destroyed in this alienation, seeing in it its own impotence and the reality of an inhuman existence. To use Hegel's expression, this class is, within depravity, an indignation against this depravity, an indignation necessarily aroused in this class by the contradiction between its human nature and its life situation, which is a blatant, outright, and all-embracing denial of that very nature." Even the bourgeoisie with its freedom was not converted into the *citoyen*; rather it only became the "appearance of a human existence." By contrast the ideal of the freedom of action continued to live on in the proletariat, which had become revolutionary. This ideal was not only the ideal of self-determination but also—in order that he could be the author of his acts—the ideal of the determination of history. There thus followed an enlargement of the ideal of freedom that said that the domain of unclarified dependencies ought to be abandoned, and that the causes of the self-alienations of the merchant society ought to disappear. For the liberation of productive forces at the end of capitalist society no longer means, in Marx and Engels, that another class appropriates these productive forces and as a result a new mode of alienation and domination arises. Rather the maturity of the productive forces themselves tends toward the socialized form of the administration of government, which had already been carried on collectively for a long time. This entailed the discarding of dependencies and the introduction of human work that creates history, a work that fully enjoys its product and delights in its inalienable rights. This ultimately means that there is a "jump out of necessity to freedom," to that freedom which is born when the necessity of relations has been either conquered or destroyed. Necessity destroyed—that means that the subjective factor in movement and work intervenes so strongly that in history and society no objective relation grows over the heads of men and the so-called power of destiny ceases. After this *freedom of action* it is *ethical freedom* that concerns the final, immanent layer of dependencies. This freedom, which is often oriented toward a pure interiority, appears as the preponderance of "strong and mature men" over all tendencies that do not conform to such men, whether they are disruptive as passions coming from the subject himself, or appear as suggestions that come from outside the subject, compelling or driving him in some way. The ethically free man presents himself as the master of these passions, and believes that this is confirmed when he does not accept any suggestions. In Socrates, like Spinoza, this eminent position is accorded an ethical will and is accompanied by its own form of in-tellectualism: Socrates said that insight into virtue makes one free to practice it; Spinoza teaches that "the will and the intellect are one and the same thing" (*Ethics*, II, 49, proposition 49, corollary). Only adequate ideas liberate man from the slavery of inadequate instincts; but to the extent that these ideas are guarantees of *homo liber* in the ethical sense of the word, they liberate man from inadequate conditions. To this extent one is visibly close—in restricted regions—to quietistic, con-templative behavior; self-mastery changes itself into self-concern. The affective, exterior, real disruptions continue; removing freedom is not only the product of an ignorance that takes the form of an illusion that the hard soul can master. It thus becomes clear that ethical freedom, as really liberating, belongs to the freedom of action; this is perhaps its chief characteristic, but always only as something equally active. Doubtless one finds the attitude of the incorruptible man living at this point, but he still lives only in regions that are beyond pure interiority, in a region far removed from the beautiful soul of a Spinoza, for the recourse to a menacing quietude is lacking. The *homo liber* of Spinoza, the man who was thoroughly theological-political, is the op-posite of such privateness, thanks to public inflexibility (and thus finally thanks to the intellect as will). Ethical freedom, where it appears, is not formed in tranquillity, but precisely as character in the river of the world. And this character forms itself in the world to the degree that it forms the world so that the *homo liber* can necessarily be preserved without constraint.

It is said that man has never been able to hold out for a long time under oppression. That might be so, but the only thing that is certain is that it is difficult to suppress the desire, which is clearly not impious, not to be a dog. Thus, along with the problem of ethical freedom one always finds the problem of *religious freedom*. In part this can be relegated to an even stronger interiority than ethical freedom was, but often it is accompanied by a burning attempt at a countermovement to that higher sphere where man is not found. Primitive Christianity stemmed from a national-revolutionary underground; it ignored servility. It lacked the millions of preachers of humility who were subsequently charged with constructing on Christianity a morality for slaves. Of course even in primitive Christianity there soon appeared the tendency to abolish not only the foreign power of Rome and the Roman Empire itself but also the purely national-revolutionary freedom as something too narrow and too tied to the old world. Society, labor, property, became indifferent matters in the face of the metaworldly order that was anticipated, or already reigning in faith. The decisive point was the sanctity of the soul, that is, the freedom from the drives and works of sins, the freedom to enter the realm of God. Thus immanent ethical freedom came to enter the picture in a more interior and more transparent sensibility: This was the appearance of the ultimatum of *Christian* religious freedom. While Christianity diabolized the creature (whose drives had, for the Stoics, appeared solely as interruptions of independence), it did not on that account divinize the present world. It taught—at the price of transcendence—that there was no joining up with the harmonious course of nature, and pushed toward the sanctity of a better world. No doubt redemption so conceived was also understood as freedom, as an emancipation from subjection to drives and desires, as the entry into a joy without destiny. Thanks to Jesus, those who had been bound were delivered, those who were trampled were able to stand upright—"the spirit is master, there one finds freedom" (2 Cor. 3:17). That this freedom ought not to be applied in a real, objective way is made clear by the warning in the First Epistle of Peter: "Do not use your freedom as a pretext for evil, but live as the servant of God" (1 Peter 2:16); from Saint Paul onward the community follows the path of a fundamental social conservatism. If every species of rebel arrogance was defeated and tossed to the desires of the worst among them, Lucifer and the serpent in Paradise, then the unity with destiny is completely lacking, then the abandonment to God's will is not the abandonment to the course of the world and to those who direct it. The present world, because of the destiny of the planets that govern it, is the world of the devil; that stars, which for the Stoics were the guarantors of order, in Christian gnosis were called tyrants. Because, for the beliefs of the age, they become the issuers of bad luck, they were the "archons" of *ananke*, which had ceased to be loved, the *heimarmene*, which only appeared as a prison. The same Paul, who made peace with Caesar, removed him from this cosmic background, namely, the covering of the sun, the planets, the celestial order; Saint Paul made this order into the order of the devil. In complete accord with later Christian gnosis, the apostle declares war on this reflection of tyranny, which to him looks like its archetype: "For we are not contending against flesh and blood, but against the principalities, against the powers, against the world rulers of this present darkness, against the spiritual hosts of wickedness in heavenly places" (Eph. 6:12). But these masters of the world ("cosmocrats") are none other than the gods of destiny, the celestial powers of old Oriental despotism and astrological faith from whom the Son of God had delivered man. Egypt appeared as the homeland of these beings of destiny; that is the reason that Christian gnosis referred to the Exodus from Egypt with a special allegory, and to the later prophecy announced by Isaiah: "Where then are your wise men, Egypt, your interpreters of the stars? Let them tell you and make known the things which the Lord of Hosts will do" (Isa. 19:12). But these things belonged to the new order of wishes, in which the cosmocrats can no longer turn their heads in such a way that they look at the earth and so harm people. Such a wild accent ended up in a wild flight toward the world, although its wildness, completely fantastic and mythological, did not in the least harm the archons of the real world; but it did remove astrological ideology from their ranks. Even in such a gentle and mild text as the New Testament we find that the worldly fortress is reduced to rubble: The revolution of apocalypse is the most violent of the gifts given from above. It makes religious freedom into a physical-metaphysical phantasmagoria; it disinterests itself in inwardness while it augments otherworldliness. Thus the proposition of Saint Paul: "The Jerusalem above is free, and she is our mother" (Gal. 4:26). It completely destroyed the astrological myth and put in its place a landscape in which *ananke* disappears from the ancient heavens and the ancient earth. "For even creation will be set free from its bondage to decay and obtain the glorious freedom of the children of God" (Rom. 8:21); it is the content of a religion that obviously has very little to do with a morality of slaves, despite the church, despite the inwardness, despite the otherworldliness that was evident in all Christian-revolutionary heretical movements. Of course the church, which would make Christianity into an instrument of oppression, even made the freedom of the children of God into a charlatan; the Protestant church, which consolidated itself in the events of the Counter-Reformation, did this even more extensively than the Catholic church. The theology of both churches concerned itself with the distinction between the freedom from something and the freedom to something in order to underline the purely negative character of the first form. It was noticed that when it is *isolated*, freedom from something can have the effect of something thoroughly negative, as pure being cut loose, as an emptiness without a resting place, which could seem more like hell than light — but only if it is isolated for an interested end in order to make any resting place, any support, look more attractive — that means even old and new forms of dependencies — than the radicalities that were supposedly sterile in the end. To this it is added that freedom, in order not to become a freedom that transforms the world, is quickly reclothed in ecclesiastical robes: Better would be to reduce it to something only interior. Luther's "freedom of the Christian man" limited the freedom of the Christian man (as Luther conceived him) in the most energetic way by means of the simple subjective genitive, "of the Christian man." For Luther's Christian not only lacked the freedom of will and of choice, and not only lived as a slave of sin from the time of his birth, but even the religious freedom, which is put in him by faith in Christ, was not a freedom; rather it was nothing other than a new form of servitude. *Servant of God* is a frequent biblical expression (although it is not contained in the Gospels), and the most authentic Christian champion of freedom, Thomas Münzer, uses it and speaks of himself in such a way: But the servitude to God that Luther posits as religious freedom and even as self-determination is nothing other than earthly servitude transposed into a higher sphere. The nature of this freedom, according to Luther, means that the true Christian should even be ready, for the love of God, to joyfully enter hell if that is the will of God. Luther does not posit this masculine pride before the throne as a paradox, but with direct reference to the "majesty" of God. To be sure, one finds similar attitudes even in medieval mystics, especially in Tauler, as "resignation to damnation," and later still as "disinterested love" in the circle of French quietists surrounding Madame Guyon du Chesnoy. Here, however, it is a question of the irruptions of Christian paradoxes, of tentative attempts to find something exemplary; it is not a question of the extreme subordination of the subject to a master. For Luther, liberation signifies the extreme case of grace "provided by the merciful master who is God"; it means "protecting oneself from the wrath of God under the sheltering wings of Christ." On earth, in the orders of authority, there is nothing for liberation to do; it happens purely in faith, and even in faith it remains a suffering that belongs to the invisible church of inner reflections and not to works, where it is sin. This juxtaposition of world and interiority—even if one abstracts from the corrupted content of the freedom of this interiority—only belongs to Lutheranism, and is foreign to Calvinism. The juxtaposition came to serve the ideology of the political powers of Prussia and the complete encapsulating of freedom in this private sphere, even in pure velleity. Kant himself, whose ethics developed completely as an autonomy of a *human will*, of a *human spontaneity*, posits freedom outside the realm of empirical appearances and its rigorously determined natural necessity. Freedom comes only from the "intelligible character," that is, man as a "citizen of intelligible worlds," and as the condition of moral behavior (as the faculty of conforming to the moral law in all circumstances), it is not an object of empirical knowledge, but a postulate of transcendent faith. Kant transposed freedom to such a realm, into the realm of the unknowable thing-in-itself; it appears solely as idea, not as experience. Freedom is domination of the conscience insofar as it inhabits our supernatural part, and to this extent Kant's concept of intelligible freedom is a religious concept. Of course, this transfer of freedom into the intelligible does not stop Kant from making the idea of freedom into a special type of experience, not only as conscience (from an ethical-subjective point of view), but also as that extension of ethical freedom (from an ethical-objective point of view) which allowed for some progress in history. But above all, Kant's own formula, according to which freedom points to the thing-in-itself, signifies not only a flight from experience (reality) into the intelligible but also a movement toward that source which keeps both theoretical experience and the moral world of the postulate together: the source of spontaneity. Kant's transcendental idealism not only lets that supernatural order (which has no place in nature and can never have one) appear in the power of intelligible freedom, but along with the transcendence of intention (which reminds one of Luther) one also finds the most intensive form, the immanence of freedom, and here, in ethical spontaneity and its actions, that source comes into view which has been alienated in the experience of reality and which, as thing-in-itself, is more real than all that has become in such experience. For Kant of course the "primacy of practical reason" so conceived is only a postulated reason, not a real active reason, because there is in Kant the absence of a concept of history that could have overcome the dualism between experience and postulate, between the "realm of necessity" and the "realm of freedom." Hegel created this concept of history in the *Phenomenology of Spirit*, as dialectically progressive "revelation of depth," of that depth which is spontaneity itself and is not satisfied by its simple externalization or by the reality of dualistic experience. Rather, this externalization appears as a part of history, as the history of the mediation of the self with its content; but the "freedom of the children of God"—the being-for-itself of the self—appears as the goal in becoming. We arrive once again at the question of religious freedom, as the sublation of the alien object of intention (in the framework of a freedom that, of course, remains only contemplative). And it coincides with the homecoming of truth: "Because truth must not relate to objectivities as something alien. Freedom is an expression of the same thing as truth with a determination of negation" (*Works*, XII, p. 167). Being-for-itself thus leads into the principal idea of Christian-religious freedom: God became man. Substance is not an object up on high or something alien that initiates fear and fate; rather substance is the subject. Of course, alienation of all alienation is here only something thought and does not realize itself as the subject of the act of self-liberation, or the content of self-liberation, of the living, real, content that is man—*contra fatum, pro regno hominis*. Freedom—and this is something that was not made explicit in any of the previous concepts of freedom—in all of its levels as freedom of choice and of action, as ethical and religious, is only founded *contra fatum*, thus in a perspective of a still *open* world, one not yet *determined all the way to the end*. This is where the continual revolutionary accent on freedom comes from; this is where the essential irreconcilability of freedom with *closed* determinateness comes from (a determinateness in which there was no possibility of the intervention of the subject that was born of the freedom of choice or action). Only a *partial* determinability of the world, thus an as yet unclosed possibility, makes freedom possible in this world. Enough said here about the first, most vivid color in the tricolor of natural law and its true place; freedom is the mode of human comportment in the face of objective real possibility. Only thus does its purpose have any margin of play on the path that leads to the *content* of freedom: the unalienated *humanum*.

On the multiple forms of equality

Few are satisfied, most hunger their way through life. And the bourgeois life-style is more than ever before constructed so that the great attack the small, strangle them, and feed upon them. These different destinies are distributed by the same society that, in its revolutionary beginnings, spoke not only of freedom but also of equality and fraternity. In contrast to the ambiguous concept of *freedom, equality* and *fraternity* are relatively easily defined in their immediate usage. One cannot limit or obscure equality in itself, as can be done with the "freedom" of the profit motive; at most one can restrict the worth or extent of "equality." Then it appears merely as "equality before the law," or "the equality of all before God": The massive body of remaining inequalities is not covered in this way. The distinction between the poor and the rich cannot be falsified by means of formal juridical or transcendental equality; with fraternity the matter is even simpler: One knows right away that the wolf is not to be counted within the brotherhood of man. That is the advantage of ideals that are quantitatively and qualitatively clear, or which are homogeneous. Sophisms about freedom are possible because of the different spheres in which it is meaningful; but not insignificantly, equality is also a mathematical concept, and what one learns from it one learns clearly. Freedom could be redefined not merely formally but also in part with respect to its content, as a freedom of the individual economic subject; whereas if equality and fraternity take on a content and do not remain formal, then either they are socialistic or they do not appear at all. Neither the danger of the American-mechanical "melting pot" nor even the threat of the fascist "community of the people," both of which undeniably lurk in the formalism of equality, is a match for real equality; these massifications did not disrupt capitalist drives whatsoever—quite the contrary. That is why it was not the ideal of freedom, but the ideal of equality (the *égalité* of Babeuf) before which the incipient bourgeois interests in the French Revolution trembled. The freedom spoken of in this revolution fit quite well with private property (which was still a human right for the French Revolution), and the idea of private property openly contradicted this freedom when it spoke of the freedom of those who did not have any private property and who had to sell themselves; but so long as it was not accompanied by a restriction, equality always implied the equality of assets. Thus it never remained a formal expression of capitalistic interests (as the equality of all owners in the eyes of the law), that is, it never expressed the capitalist need for the most homogeneous calculability possible; rather through itself equality denounced the real inequality of the classes. It was only a matter of practical consequence whether or not the bourgeois demand for equality as the abolition of class privileges is latched onto by the proletarian demand for the abolition of classes. While freedom, as simply individual freedom, sanctioned the entrepreneur, equality, as a reflex of the law of value, disputed his economic necessity. Consequently, the radical, already socialist accent of the French Revolution was placed more on equality than freedom, and Babeuf, the socialist of 1794 who took up the incipient proletarian tendencies in the midst of the bourgeois denouement of the revolution, set himself up as the tribune of *égalité*. He recognized freedom as being dependent upon economic equality, that is, upon the abolition of the distinctions between the poor and the rich. "Private property," said Gracchus Babeuf in his argument to secure freedom by means of equality—"private property is the source of all evil on the earth. In preaching this doctrine, I want to attach to the *republic* those people of Paris who were almost converted *to the monarchy* by the intrigues of the enemies of freedom." So long and so far as freedom is not intimately bound up with equality it remains a chimera; freedom is liberation from oppression, and oppression is brought about by economic inequality and its effects. In its uniquely concrete sense as a freedom from oppression, as a freedom of passing from the self to the we without alienation, freedom is the alpha of revolution, and it furnishes the revolutionary impulse an unprecedented allegory. Delacroix's image of the revolution fixed the memory of 1830: the young woman with the Phrygian bonnet, the sword, and the tricolor, marching to victory through the cannon smoke; this image can only bear the title *Liberty Leads the People*. Freedom is equally an omega of revolution, that is, it opens the door to the identity of men with themselves, an identity in which there is no longer anything alien, no alienation, no reification, no unmediated nature, no destiny. *Equality*, on the other hand, provides neither a suitable allegory of the revolutionary impetus nor an adequate symbol of the content of the revolutionary goal. In exchange *equality* provides *the stable substance of revolution*; it marks the seriousness of that revolution which is distinguished from all previous revolutions by its ultimately classless content. In its material totality, equality is nothing other than the constructive idea, if not the socialistic construction then in the communistic construction that immediately follows it. It was brought into the world in a truncated form by the Stoics and, in the bonds of brotherhood, by Christianity. The Stoics were the first to teach that the context that did not provide "the equality that bore a human face" was not desirable and had nothing obligatory about it: They taught the unity of the human race. The difference between the worth of the Greeks and that of the barbarians disappeared in the Stoics as the difference between Jews and heathens later disappeared in the Christian "Internationale." In the Stoic "realm of reason" all of that stayed literature, but in the formative church an especially intelligible fragment of equality was to be found: The equality of souls before God was transformed into ideology. It was transformed into an ideology of ecclesia—from Christ's parable of the vines on the stalk it was turned into the institution of the clergy, into the ideology of sheep and a shepherd. But the extent to which this equality was fragmentary, that is, the extent to which it only flourishes in an abstract or spiritual consensus, can be made clear by the fact that slavery was not an obstacle to it; indeed, the high functionaries of the ecclesia, and even the church fathers, spoke in favor of this most extreme form of nonequality. It is not surprising, then, that the ideal of fraternity, which has its roots in the doctrine of a common heritage of all as the children of God, did not blossom fully. This ideal of fraternity exacts an especially demanding familial love, one that is not cheaply exhausted in a broad feeling toward a global family, but must manifest itself concretely in love of one's neighbor. But this is particularly difficult to achieve when there are existing class distinctions, or else it deteriorates into that form of brotherly love whose charity takes on a crude form when faced with the nonbrotherly world. Thus equality and fraternity were able to appear in a fragmented form in the class society, and at the time of the French Revolution they could shine like real stars: But property prevented equality from being unrestricted, that is, from being real equality, and it kept fraternity from being without comedy, that is, from being substantial fraternity. From this point of view the Statue of Liberty, which sits at the entrance to the Port of New York, does not completely contradict American capitalism; it would only contradict the American synchronization of capital and labor if it were called the Statue of Equality. The ideal of brotherhood was not removed from the basis of bourgeois society because people no longer believed in a father, but because, under penalty of failure, each competitor must be the enemy of every other; this is a new dimension of *homo homini lupus*, one, as always, directed below. Interested groups have thus cast doubts upon the *solidarity* of the three colors of the tricolor: freedom, equality, fraternity. To the extent that they fully adopted and affirmed freedom in its bourgeois sense as the freedom of the economic individual, as the Manchester principle of this sort of personality and its pleasures, they tried to portray socialistic equality as misunderstanding that had already been refuted. Socialist equality is not supposed to have been ruled out by private property, but by freedom, not by capitalistic interest in amassing wealth, but by the wealth of interests of cultivated personalities. Simmel worked especially hard to cut up the tricolor; thus equality was completely dismissed as a concern of the eighteenth century and was attributed to the insufficient form of individualism found there. Supposedly it is the universal abstraction of man current at the time that is at fault: "And then one understands that freedom and equality were naively conceived as a unitary ideal: If man were only posited in freedom, then his authentic self, his human essence, which historical relations and deformations had concealed and disfigured, would step forward and this self, because it represents the universal person in each of us, must therefore be the same for all" (*Kant*, 1904, pp. 171ff.). But because the abstraction "man" is rejected by Marxism even though it does not lose the guiding idea of the *humanum* in the "ensemble of social relations," which takes the place of abstract man, the rejection of socialism itself—as that which takes this real ideal of equality seriously—is at work here. And just as this rejection coincided with the freedom that had developed under capitalism, with "the individualism of singularity, of being-other, and of hierarchical distance," similarly equality coincided with mere leveling, namely, with what Marx, alluding to Babeuf, had called "a crude and ascetic equalization." Only in this purely mechanical conception, this caricature of equality, is there any contrast to freedom, as that which itself has been caricatured as something personalized; but at bottom there is no such contrast between the expanding members of this pair. In the final analysis only Stirnerism made a travesty of freedom by turning it into radical "mineness," even into something isolated, in order to posit itself as something elite; but the same can be said of the equality of radical communality as it fit into the schema of the superman ideologues. Genuine equality does not measure itself by existing averages, nor after having become classless is it disrupted by canonical personalities; quite the contrary, it raises itself upon these and embraces them as models. The more the form of that to which equality refers (as opposed to averageness and leveling) is not static, the more this happens. Finally, the content of equality is not restricted to the equality of a society that has become classless, but it has in itself a central task and significance that is closest to freedom and even coincides with its inclinations and goals. That is the inclination toward the *human identity* that has yet to arrive; namely, that identity which always threatens, always glimmers, like the harmony of men with the image they have of the *humanum*, a harmony in which they are postulated as one. From this perspective the Stoic thesis of the unity of the human race, which provided first basis for the ideal of equality, can be recognized as one of the more profound figures of equality; Christ's parable of the vines on the stalk is deeper still. The unity of the human race that sounds in the cantus firmus posits equalization least of all; rather as the expression of the wealth of human nature it posits the flowering of distinctions or (another paradox) the unrestricted polyphony of a unison. Its work concerns the identity of ourselves, an identity that, as the community of interests par excellence, is still to come. And the encounter with the "we" on the path of history and society in this identity would have no face if it did not have an abundance of faces and if it were not ordered concentrically.

On the peace of fraternity

The greatest glory is accorded to one who appears here or could appear here. When one looks rigorously for justice socially, then weaker reflections no longer are able to corrupt. The fullness of equality is camaraderie and—*rebus bene commotis*—*fraternity*, the third color of the tricolor. Fraternity, even more than equality, needs a background in order not to be mistaken as a pendant of equalization, namely, as limitless fraternization. Fraternity is the affect of the union of purpose, the affect of the recognition that the communality of all one's worth and all that others value is provided by the communality of purpose. This lineage earlier appeared to be guaranteed by the belief in a common, heavenly father; for according to the immediate meaning of the word, a brother presupposes a father. According to the extended meaning of the word, it presupposes the influence of communality and of the background value out of which this communality flows and on which it is founded. That is why as a sense of value fraternity is never indiscriminate, never an unconditional embrace; quite the contrary, it excluded from its alliance all that was not bound up with it, all enemies of its purpose. That is even true for the Christian alliance (the sects) in which fraternity was not only the form but more importantly the content of its purpose. But there was no indiscriminate embrace here, no "peace with Belial and his empire"; the community is the community of men of goodwill, and there is still no hatred of the children of the world who remain sinners. Divided fraternity rules even the most gentle of the sects, and even more in the sects that are militant, revolutionary, or chase the money-changers out of the temple. The gentle sects withdrew from the bad ones, the revolutionary sects fought them in the name of the empire of brotherhood; it fought with a violent empathy for the poor and in helpful animosity, that is, it fought against the wolves and for the victims and those who had been annulled. Later this exacting and concrete fraternity became the fraternity of the revolutionary class consciousness for the true practical Christianity: "war on the palaces, peace for the shacks." All hatred between the races, nations, and religions is surmounted in this way; an "Internationale" of the oppressed who no longer want to remain objects is raised up. Ultimate accord does not happen without a struggle, but struggle contradicts brotherhood so little that it follows from it *rebus sic stantibus*; struggle only contradicts unconditional fraternization, and it contradicts the imposture of harmony: the community of the people with the assassins of the people. Fraternity does not entail the embrace of beasts, but of brothers; up to this point *fraternitas militans* is the dominant prelude to a *fraternitas triumphans*. Not of course in the sense of the most grotesque alternative, which, according to a saying that can be traced back to holy wars, knows no middle term between embracing brothers and smashing the skulls of those who only appear to be brothers. There is certainly no pardon here for the last incarnation of the beast in fascism. But fraternity, which even in the combative sect of Thomas Münzer introduced the rainbow into the flag, recognized itself especially well in its peaceful fruit, its normal minimum, which is called peace. Peace with shacks and houses everywhere thanks to the "contra" declared against the lords of the manor who push them to war. It was not without cause, then, that in classical theories of natural law peace was set up as a norm of external politics, as the postulated normal state of affairs; Kant's *Perpetual Peace* is only the most grandiose manifestation of this view. And until now there has been no socialism that has abandoned, or could abandon, this heritage; one of the most important functions of the class struggle is to halt the causes of future wars, and in this it is the precise opposite of war, and conducting an unwanted war is its unwanted reprimand. "Brotherly coexisting families of free peoples": On the path to this Rousseauvian effect fraternity loses all sentimentality, which henceforth only attaches to inauthentic, hypocritical fraternity. But even the authentic minimum of fraternity is only something that provides the construction site for the vision of friendship, which is always more positive. The real is still not disentangled from the three words of the tricolor; that is why they actively merit and need to be rescued from a socialistically tested point of view. The struggle for freedom produces equality; equality as the end of exploitation and dependence preserves freedom; fraternity is rewarded with an equality wherein no one is compelled, or in the position, to be a wolf to others.

So the three words are quite compatible with one another, and have a genuine rapport. Under their banner the French and American independence marched. But it never became a real independence, and so these three words retained their validity. They are justified by revolution, they are encapsulated ideals of political and social being. But were the bourgeois revolutions in which these ideals were at work proletarian? That has been recently doubted; but if this doubt were justified, the "Marseillaise" would not be a song of freedom, and revolution in general would become problematic. If that were so, there would at least have to be fundamentally different sorts of revolution, and perhaps the proletarian revolution would not be the best one for the critic who is dissatisfied with Robespierre. Max Horkheimer raised the question of whether or not the habitus of bourgeois revolutions does in fact represent a socialistic habitus ("Egoism and Liberation

Movements," *Zeitschrift für Sozialforschung*, 1936). With this question he obviously went far beyond the insult that Marx in *The Eighteenth Brumaire* hurled at false consciousness, that is, at the historical costumes of a Cromwell and a Robespierre. Going far beyond the distance that Marx posited between the "poetic character" of all previous revolutions and the sobriety of the proletarian revolution, Horkheimer even denies that freedom, and especially equality, as demanded by the most radical representatives of the revolutionary bourgeoisie, could be numbered among the proletarian stars. They are such guiding lights because the struggle for liberation does not accord very well with hedonistic materialism and because the pathos of equality only fits badly with friendly egoism, both of which, for Horkheimer, are of considerable importance for socialism. Bourgeois revolution is thus taken to be resentment against wealth and luxury; its ideal image is always lost altruism. In his analysis of three diverse bourgeois revolutionaries—Cola di Rienzo, Savonarola, Robespierre—Horkheimer tries to show that from its inception even the progressive form of the bourgeoisie has been characterized by traits that "like a bad imitation" repeat themselves in fascism: traits like an interested hostility to pleasure, terror, the rage and anger against immorality, epicurism, materialism, and the aristocratic life; these are, in short, the traits of a "deeply eroticized resentment." In addition to the rationalistic and humanitarian tendencies that have supposedly been overestimated, Horkheimer believes he has found tendencies that are irrationalistic in the worst sense—these he finds under the masks of freedom, equality, fraternity, and even in Robespierre. Indeed Robespierre manifested an especially gloomy ethos, one hostile to happiness: His hatred of theater, dance, play, and of public and private celebrations was on a par with the strictest Puritan; and, in fact, Robespierre was not a bon vivant. In order to be able to prove the antagonism to reason that belonged to the bourgeois revolution, Horkheimer cites the following remark by Robespierre: "Virtue and talent are both necessary qualities, but virtue is the most necessary. Virtue without talent can always be useful, talents without virtue are only a misfortune." On the basis of modified manifestations of the same tendency in Cola di Rienzo (at the start of humanism) and in Savonarola (at the start of the Renaissance), Horkheimer concludes: "The first bourgeois movements manifest an unsteady relation toward, and often a strong rejection of, mind and reason; only later does this antihumanist, barbarizing element, which disparages the

intellectual level of the time, become the clearly predominate element."
Similarly, Horkheimer turns to the ideologists of the bourgeois revolution and the bourgeoisie that it installed (as if these were the same
moment) and finds already there the lie of the communal good that
later prevailed in German fascism under the name of the community
of the people. The purpose of the pathos of altruism is to discredit
the egoism of the poor, and to conceal the existing, extremely effective
egoism of the ruling class; in both cases virtue is an instrument of
domination. This definition is certainly correct insofar as it relates to
the ideology of the bourgeoisie (of the French and English revolutions)
who have come to power and become static; but it is hopeless when
it is applied to the ideal of fraternity of the revolution itself, and it
takes a peculiar form when it speaks of the *citoyen*, as it does for
example in the following passage: "The exalted model of man, the
most sentimental and yet rigorous concept of virtue and self-sacrifice,
and the cult of an abstract heroism all have the same root as do
individualistic egotism and nihilism, with which they are simultaneously
in contradiction and reciprocity." In this way—in the name of a non-
individualistic egoism (a nonegoistic egoism, so to speak)—the bourgeois
revolution is discounted as revolution. Isolated characteristics in the
revolution, only in some of its representatives, even only in a few
moments of its representatives—the inflammatory language of the
envy of the propertyless class often works quite well—are employed
in order ultimately to find some sort of common denominator between
the storming of the Bastille and Hitler's burning of the Reichstag;
between the intentions of human rights and the most ancient form
of tyranny; between the progressive dawn of a class and the night in
which it annuls everything. Even according to the worst form of dog-
matism this seemingly radical representation of the *citoyen* does not
sink into the bourgeoisie; rather the *citoyen* is the seed of the bourgeoisie;
then the "Marseillaise" and the carmagnole logically end up as the
older sisters of the Nazi "Horst Wessel" song. Such a *reductio ad absurdum*
shows the outcome of a theory that denies that the bourgeois revolution
is the root of the proletarian revolution, but which grafts it onto fascism
instead. Such a procedure necessarily turns the proletarian revolution
into something ahistorical and removes it from the historical-mater-
ialistic dialectic, or denies that the proletarian revolution is such a
dialectic even when it occurs and precisely when it puts on the opulent
airs of Figaro's dance. Engels, who was quite hostile toward the "neg-

ative equality" of the Terror and even more hostile toward abstract Jacobin decreeism, never forgot what bound the red flag to the tricolor. It is not necessary to emphasize that from the perspective of their real content, even bourgeois revolutions are revolutions. They begin with an oppressed class, they push for the destruction of an ossified society that has increasingly become an obstacle for progressive, forward-moving social groups and their possibilities of material production. Nevertheless, it is necessary to emphasize that so long as they are revolutionary, even ideologies are elective affinities in the human fight for identity—they are not simply museum pieces. To be sure, there is an enormous quantity of false consciousness in them; they reflect the changes in the society that are not at all radical, namely, those that do not go beyond the history of classes. Nevertheless, they are full of anticipation, are moved by the wish and dream of a classless society, and the enthusiastic revolutionary impulse always goes beyond the simple ends of classes. That is why the socialist revolution, insofar as it surmounts the class society, penetrates to the point where the visions of the bourgeois revolution rest (and where under the penalty of its own unrecognizability it must rest), and it must reappropriate the tradition of what has not yet become. That which was envisioned is expressed by the words *freedom, equality,* and *fraternity,* and by the preconsciousness that these words articulate of a condition in which the class society no longer exists. At the same time as Horkheimer, and in a much more appropriate way, Georg Lukács, a theoretician of the real revolution, examined the achievement of the bourgeois will ("Schiller's Theory of Modern Literature," *Internationale Literatur,* 1937, contained in *Goethe and His Age,* Berlin, 1950). Here the idealistic morality of the bourgeois revolution has a very different look about it, namely, a progressive look. It appears as a legitimate substitute, a serious illusion concerning the contents of the *citoyen,* which are still inaccessible at the existing technical level of production. The role that the ancient ideals of man and polis played—with continual displacement of accent—in bourgeois emancipation is significant in this regard. This is true not only for "Aristides" Robespierre but also in the prereflections and postreflections of revolution found in Winckelmann through Höld-erlin. Significantly the classical ideal moved increasingly from Rome toward Greece during the time in which the bourgeois class became independent by means of the progressive dissolution of its connection to the absolute monarchy: Sophocles took the place of Seneca, Homer

replaced Virgil. The seed of the bourgeoisie renounced itself and Hel-
lenized itself in its illusions in order to become *citoyen*, the citizen of
a polis fulfilled in harmony with democracy and universal interests;
after the victory of the real bourgeoisie, isolated by the division of
labor and its pure special interest, the ideals of the *citoyen* and the
polis continued to exercise an influence. Their influence continued in
nostalgic, sentimental form up to the false tone of a continually unreal,
always abstract idealism; up to the fraudulent classicism of the epigones
of Schiller in the nineteenth century, and to that cult of the true, good,
and beautiful which no longer corresponded to combative, progressive
illusions, to republican altruism, to the *"citoyen* side of the bourgeois
man,"* but simply corresponded to hypocrisy. Conversely, the ascension
of the bourgeoisie and even the postrevolutionary protests against the
bourgeoisie were accompanied by the pathos of that "abstract image
of the model of man" which is so uncomfortable to Horkheimer, and
by that "cult of an abstract heroism" which is so far removed from
the bourgeois type. Obviously there is a rip in the bourgeois consciousness, a division between its phenomenal reality and its original
revolution; the supreme testimony of this is Hölderlin's *Hyperion*, the
incantation and requiem for the fugitive citoyen. But the concerns of the
lofty altruism of idealism, which supposedly accord so well with purely
individualistic firebrands (and with which idealism is even supposed
to be interacting), find a place in its revolution, where it shines and
represents a less lofty humanity, one that has yet to come into being.
The revolt against the debauchery of the nobility, the strict celebration
of human purity, is as a consequence shaped, not by a "resentment,"
but by a pride and by the recollection of the *citoyen*; it is to the *citoyen*
that the bulk of the stylized literature of lofty idealism is dedicated.
Lukács interprets this component as bourgeois, but nevertheless decidedly revolutionary: "From Milton's epics and dramas, from the
time of Addison's 'Cato' up to Alfieri's republican classicism and to
Shelley's revolutionary pathos there necessarily remains just such an—
always changing—idealistic style alongside the great flow of realistic,
social literature" ("Schiller's Theory of Modern Literature," p. 130).
That is the "idealistic stylization of the positive hero as the representative
of the *citoyen* side of the bourgeoisie," as well as the utopian side of
the bourgeois revolution. Even freedom, equality, and fraternity belong
to the side that was never honored and thus, in contrast to Schiller's
pathos, are still unfinished. Thus, with direct reference to the French

Revolution, to human rights, and to bourgeois natural right, Engels said that "the proletariat takes the bourgeois at its word." Without illusion, social revolution fulfills in its task that which the bourgeois revolution promised to the *citoyen* in all of its deceptions and illusions. In most respects the bourgeois revolution was unquestionably more bourgeois than revolution, but as the abolition of class privileges, it instituted a powerful cleansing process; it still contains that promise and that concrete, utopian form of a promise which the real revolution can hold onto. This is the stipend of human rights, and if it has the taste for more, then there is very little of it in history up to this point, which by virtue of its basis was so limited and obstructed, and which by virtue of its postulates was also so anticipatory of humanity. Freedom, equality, fraternity, the orthopedia of the upright carriage, of human pride, and of human dignity point far beyond the horizon of the bourgeois world.

L'homme and citoyen in Marx

The menu often looks different before the meal. When the bourgeoisie had not yet come to power, it was (or appeared to be) more humane than any previous class. It equally represented the free man, the children of the fatherland, and universal humanity. There was something here for the free man to latch onto: The sense of nationalism could become nationalistic, the human sense could become more universal. But what seemed so pure at the outset, and only later on being implemented was abandoned or even reversed, continued to shine later. Frequently, in other instances, the effort is made to begin afresh precisely at the point where everything was still right: as if one only had to reverse or abandon an old course. If everything is only set as a burden for those who come later, then they are the only ones who are put to the test.

But not every menu reads differently before the meal—not even in the present case. That must always be kept in mind for the sake of the image of the heritage that was sought, and for the sake of the image of the *citoyen* too. The same economic and social tendency that was later brought forth by the emancipated bourgeoisie exploited the illusions and anticipations of these images. Thus the essence of the bourgeoisie, still incomparable, and progressive in the wrong sense as speaking of the freedom to profit, necessarily developed along with the image of the *citoyen* — at least in its most important aspects. Indeed, even in 1791, when human rights were still piously affirmed in those dreams of spring that never came to fruition, there was already present a part of the bourgeois spirit that developed later with great force. At the time it was clearly the bourgeoisie, as the egotistic motive of industrial production, but not yet the *citoyen* with real freedom, equality, fraternity, that constituted the economic program of the day. Private property was one of the four essential components of the bourgeois human rights of 1791: "*propriété* " governs the "*sûreté*," the "*résistance*." Above all, private property determines the content of freedom according to the constitution of 1793, article 16: "The right to property is the right of every citizen, at his own will [*à son gré*] he may enjoy his assets, his income, and the fruits of his labor and diligence, and he may dispose of these as he wishes." This undercurrent in the *citoyen* corresponded to the interests of capitalism, even before the Thermidor, insofar as the people had not yet surrendered the ground upon which the flowers of real freedom take root. Or, as Marx said, insofar as the people did not possess the idea of their real interest when they accepted the idea of the interests of the French Revolution. In this way, Marx clearly distinguished the egotistic content of the *droits de l'homme* [rights of man] at that time from the current political, still abstract and idealistic image of the *citoyen*. The special occasion for this peculiarly sharp distinction was the arrogant nonsense of Bruno and Edgar Bauer, who explained that the "pure idea" of the French Revolution had been corrupted by the "uncritical masses." Instead, Marx and Engels pointed to the complete success of this revolution as the emancipation of the bourgeoisie and the profit economy, which was needed by the economy of the time — a reference that could not be made without sharp criticism of the ideology of human rights itself. And in fact even beyond this particular instance, every reception of the socialistic heritage must be critical; none must have a plaster cast crowned with laurel. To the extent that bourgeois freedoms were always more bourgeois than freedoms, the measure of human rights against their ideological content is perfectly understandable; and the first results of such a scrutiny were caution, partial negation, and restriction. Thus, in *On the Jewish Question* (1844), Marx contends: "The so-called human rights, the *droits de l'homme*, in contrast to the *droits du citoyen*, are nothing more than the rights of the member of civil bourgeois society, that is, of egotistic man, separated from his fellow men and from the community. . . . Hence man is not liberated from religion, but merely obtains religious freedom. He is not liberated from property, but only obtains the freedom of property. He is not emancipated from the egotism of commerce, but obtains freedom for commerce" (*Marx-Engels Gesamtausgabe*, I, 1, p. 593). Subsequently, in *The Holy Family* (1845), he wrote: "Even the slavery of civil society appears to be the greatest freedom, because the apparently accomplished independence of the individual fosters the illusion of the limitless motility of the alienated elements of his life (such as property, industry, and religion, which have been freed of general restrictions and are no longer bound by other people) as personal freedom. In truth, however, this limitless motility is to be interpreted as the individual's complete enslavement and dehumanization. . . . What a colossal deception, to have to recognize and sanction under the aegis of human rights the modern bourgeois society, the society of industry and of general competition, of private interest, freely pursuing their goals; of anarchy, of alienated natural and spiritual individuality—and at the same time, within this society, to annul the expressions of life in particular individuals, while simultaneously intending to fashion the political head of this society according to an ancient pattern" (*MEGA*, I, 3, pp. 291ff.). These are the same self-deceptions that Marx later at the beginning of *The Eighteenth Brumaire* (1852) called "a conjuring up of the dead of world history." Still, a significant positive element emerged from this critique, one that did not concern human rights in general, but the "rights of the *citoyen*." At the beginning of the same text Marx refers to the self-deceptions of Robespierre and of Cromwell before him as self-deceptions "that they required in order to conceal from themselves the bourgeois limitations of the content of their struggles, and to maintain their passion at the high level of historical tragedy." It was therefore necessary "to glorify the new struggles . . . to exaggerate the task at hand, to rediscover the spirit of the revolution." It is to the spirit of the revolution that the "rights of the *citoyen*" held fast, and as Marx finally said after all the criticism in *On the Jewish Question*, it is realized "only when the real individual man internalizes the abstract citizen of the state . . . only when man recognizes and organizes his *forces propres* as social forces, and so no longer separates himself from this social power in the form of political power" (*MEGA*, I, 1, p. 599). The abstract citizen of the state, who is wrenched away from "secular man" although still contained in him,

the "true man" brought into relief, is the *citoyen*; but he is also this
as the "political power," the bearer of socialized freedom. And thus
the fellow man no longer represents a barrier to freedom as he does
in the egotism of the *droits de l'homme*; rather he now lives as the
realization of freedom. Nonetheless, even in its bourgeois womb the
image of the *citoyen* was damaged to the extent that it was not originally
recognized, and this damage showed up in the effects that it had later.
But despite the diversity of its source and even its degenerate caretakers,
the healthy image of the *citoyen* continued—even as a slogan—to exert
a critical force against its contrary; indeed, as Hölderlin pointed out,
it always possessed the capacity of self-purification.

From this point on Marx permitted a warmer light to fall even on
human rights. With unsurpassed precision, he demonstrated the bourgeois class content in them, but he also pointed out their futural
content, which at that time still did not have a basis. He discovered
private property as the dominant right among human rights, and as
the reason why these other rights only appeared more disjointed than
before. When Marx rejects private property as the bourgeois barrier
to human rights, does he reject freedom, the resistance of the people
to oppression, and security as other declarations of rights? Absolutely
not. It goes without saying that he concentrated his efforts on the
forward effect of rights, which no private property can impede or
destroy. For Marx, freedom is criticized so little that, quite the contrary,
it is that human right whose radiance and humanity provide the standards for Marx's critique of private property. The Marxist conclusions
follow from this: not freedom of property, but from property, not
freedom of industry, but freedom from the egoism of industry; not
emancipation of the egoistic individual of the merely feudal society,
but emancipation of all men from every type of class society. In such
a thorough way, *liberté* replaced *propriété* as the final dominant right
among the human rights, and as its own actual and real goal, it set
itself against fascism and against dictatorship. Subsequently, the struggle
for rights was directed more than ever to the freedom of assembly,
freedom of association, freedom of the press, security, and the rights
of workers to resist exploitation and oppression. But in the *program*
of socialism, where the exploitation and oppression of workers have
disappeared, the struggle for rights has continued no less critical, but
still positive, as the search for the rights of an uncompromising objective
practical criticism that intervenes in the interests of the goal of socialist

construction within the framework of solidarity. This solidarity of socialism signifies that the "human" in "human rights" no longer represents the egotistic individual, but the socialistic individual who, according to Marx's prophecy, has transformed his *forces propres* into a social and political force. Thus, the *citoyen* is retrieved from the abstract, moralistic other world that he inhabited in the ideology of the French Revolution, and returned to the mundane world of socialized humanity. But it should be the same banner of human rights that exalts the workers of capitalistic lands to their right to resist, and that opens the way for them in socialistic lands by means of the construction of socialism, and the right (and even obligation) to criticize. Otherwise, authoritarian socialism would prevail—*contradictio in adjecto*—even though the Internationale fought for the human right of organized maturity and responsibility.

Something else shone on the old flag that was previously decried by the bourgeoisie. This is nothing less than the passion to go forward, and the prudent faith to serve it. *Liberty Leads the People*: This title of Delacroix's painting unmistakably describes a path leading forward. It depicts a freedom, which, in the same progressive act, tears itself free from the outdated and reaches out to new shores with the day in front and the night behind it. That which is outdated is primarily the relationships of production, which have become chains; thus the new shores of 1791 at first lay in the region of the emancipated egoistic individual, of free competition, of the open market—in short, of the modes of production and exchange that were expanding under capitalism. The bourgeoisie, a class that has so little that is heroic about it, desperately needed a heroic illusion in the style of antiquity. But in the illusions of the Jacobin faith, which claimed to be able to liberate all the oppressed, there was something at work that was radically different from an imitation of antiquity: the work of anticipation with an aura of progress, of an anticipation of an infinitely better "polis," and this first lent the matter that moral radiance which was never had by the emancipation of the third estate (and it alone). It was this human right that prompted Beethoven to put a bust of Brutus in his room, and that in the music for *Fidelio* and the Ninth Symphony is felt as the rescue and arrival of joy; in the novum of the contemporary struggle for freedom lived the ultimatum of total liberation. All of this is referred to by Marx when he spoke of the "spirit of revolution," which, through magnification and imagination, must be rediscovered in opposition to "the restricted bourgeois content" of revolution. And no matter how different the previous revolutions were in their social mission, and no matter how specifically the proletarian-socialist revolution, as the elimination of the class society, differs from all earlier ones, all revolutions are pervaded by that unifying, typical, cohesive tendency which even relates its reminiscences to the tendency to leap into the realm of freedom. The Jacobin movement was at least connected with the anticipation of this leap, and so the French Revolution went far beyond the maturing emancipation of the entrepreneurs by introducing socialist-humanist progressive contents that had compulsory consequences. The same Marx who so penetratingly analyzed the capitalistic factor in human rights announced in *The Holy Family* that which was still only implicit in the Jacobins and their followers: "Secure against this opposition, the French Revolution generated ideas that led beyond those of the whole former condition of the world. The revolutionary movement that began in 1789 in the Cercle Social, featured in midcourse Leclerc and Roux as its chief representatives, and finally succumbed momentarily with Babeuf's conspiracy, had advanced the communistic idea, which Babeuf's friend Buonarotti reintroduced into France after the revolution of 1830. This idea, consistently developed, is the idea of the new condition of the world. . . . Just as Cartesian materialism runs into natural science proper, so the other direction of French materialism culminates directly in socialism and communism" (*MEGA*, I, 3, pp. 294ff., 307). In the old tricolor a strong portion of red already shone, one announced by the fourth estate — the red of an irreducible progress. It was directed against the emasculation of the times, against the alliance with "the archaic powers of life" as seen through the eyes of the nobility and the church, against a nihilism of goals in which the *ça ira* of the French Revolution completely fades. Marx, on the other hand, only criticized the *ça ira* of the contemporary slogans of natural rights; he did this partly in opposition to their immobility, partly against their abstract quality, but always in order to go beyond them by a further process, the socialistic one. *L'homme*, man, was stationary as "egotistic man, as a man separated from other men and the community"; *le citoyen* was abstract and immobile as the merely elevated, idealized image of the neoclassical polis, as an "allegorical, moral person" instead of the bearer of social freedom. And enduring progress is that political element of the *citoyen* — freedom, equality, fraternity — which entered into the *forces propres* of living men; only then, said Marx, "is human emancipation accomplished." Then one's fellow man no longer exists as the barrier to freedom, which he represents in the egoism of the *droits de l'homme*, but then man and his fellows will live together as the community of freedom.

20

The Marxist Distance to Right and Even to Natural Right; the Problem of a Classless Quintessence of "The Upright Path" in Natural Right

Healthy mistrust

Up till now the poor person knows that his situation is out of whack not only from a financial point of view. One who is poorly clothed is well advised to avoid the policeman, for the eye of the law sits in the face of the ruling class. No one who seeks justice from a position of weakness has the prospect of winning against a wealthy party, who is able to procure a better lawyer. Money makes one sexy, money makes one clever, and justice is full of cleverness. Even other brushes with the law are almost always only felt by the little man. The poor are served by the marshal, the prisons; better-placed people are commonly spared legal unpleasantries. A leader of the oppressed classes, who has been politically accused of a crime, has even fewer prospects for success in the courts. He will be shot down, and most certainly upon the so-called basis of law; for this basis of law is laid down by the ruling class and is well prepared with ambushes. This is why the mistrust that the people have toward the court is as old as the court itself. To be sure, a peasant saying holds that "the law finds its slave," but another saying defines the time when this will be the case— namely, "when a cow is worth a penny." And that touches upon the precise reason why the poor have little to hope for from the judge, and much to fear from the judge who guards the coffers. The more the coffers are threatened, the more justice is bent, and allows itself to be bent, in an arbitrary way. It almost always obeys the wishes of the master, and in a quiet war it has implemented those wishes thousands of times over.

Museum of juridical antiquities

That must be remembered, for only then are the enemy and his lie seen through. Another saying ran, "Jurist—angry Christian," and this was not eliminated even by the bourgeois constitutional state, which became increasingly formalized. Nevertheless, this constitutional state could occasionally find itself in a difficult position through its own doing, through its own prescribed, formal rage against arbitrariness, and then it was able to be used for a *j'accuse*. Even if this occasionally succeeds it does not help in the long run, and the man who is forced to steal bread still does not have faith in so-called justice. If the mistrust of the ruling class was equally healthy in other areas, then the masses would have come to power long ago. All law rests upon conflicting wills, and so long as there are classes and people who represent or exploit their class status, the victor will always be the will that is better situated, better armed. This is so clearly the case that the skeptical Sophists already saw through it, and Nietzsche found an expression for it when he said that law is a matter of the will to eternalize a momentary relation of power. In saying this Nietzsche only praised what three generations earlier Hugo, the cynic and historian of law, had already made known: Positive law (neither Hugo nor Nietzsche know any other form of law) is a technique of domination, a particularly transparent ideology of domination. The formal technique of this law was taught by Machiavelli. And the fascists, in an even more affirmative manner than in Nietzsche, deduced the positive law of the times from no other basis than power. Carl Schmitt disclosed the empty power character of most positive law as the subjective and cynical condition of its current pragmatism; but even in Kelsen—this time formally—law becomes a play of conventions. That which neo-Kantianism (without taking account of the difference between one hundred possible and one hundred real talers) leaves outside the philosophy of right, namely, an account of the power through which the positive law was posited or abandoned, becomes the starting point and pivot for Schmitt's "decisionism" (with a fascistic Hobbes). Consequently, it is the state of emergency and dictatorship that, in this "empty legal space," is designated as the most naked, methodologically most favorable place of genesis: "The exception and emergency is more interesting than the normal case . . . in the emergency the power of real life breaks through the crust of a mechanism that is stuck in repetition" (*Political*

Theology, 1934, p. 22). It is not necessary to say that according to its mission this "demythicization" culminates in the most monstrous irrationalism, with the beast as "the supreme judicial authority of the German people." Schmitt's bloody cunning destroyed the liberal fetish for law and above all the current romantic, reactionary theology of the state solely for the sake of giving a free reign to fascistic farce, sadistically enticing, paralyzing like a Medusa. It was the shrewdest caricature of an analysis founded upon interests, and one can easily see where such an analysis can lead when there is the absence of any sort of natural right. Nonetheless, even the threat of the abandon of all masks was nourished, at least on the level of demagoguery, by the popular mistrust of positive law (which continually reappeared from the time of the adoption of Roman law), because it was long known that the law lets the powerful get away while it hangs the weak. Just like "anticapitalistic nostalgia," fascism transformed the penetrating judicial skepticism of the people into its contrary. It even did this when it let the power holders (here, monopoly capital) who posited the law come to power in an open dictatorship while it simultaneously decorated and so covered this action up by projecting sylphs of the Führer upon the eyes of those below.

Nevertheless, the gift of seeing the judge naked existed long before this time, and soon would return. The Marxist light of demystification had an easier task here than it did in the face of good manners and beautiful songs, and it went far beyond the "statute" that had been penetrated by natural law. That is true even in the case of something so enveloped in myth as the contract; Marx had no trouble with this analysis in the first book of *Capital*: "In order to relate things to each other as merchandise the guardians of merchandise must relate to each other as people whose will is housed in those things, so that the one only acquires the merchandise of the other with the will of the other; therefore each only receives the goods of the other through the mediation of an act of will, common to both of them, in which each alienates his own merchandise. They must mutually recognize each other as owners of private property. This legal relation, whose form is the contract, whether it is developed legally or not, is a relation of wills that reflects the economic relation. The content of this relation of law or will is itself given through the existing economic relation itself." Certainly even law, to the extent that it is seen through as a rather immediate reflection of economic relations, is not dissolved into thin air. Marx (and even more, Engels) points to the reifying activity of the professional jurist and to the relative autonomy that the legal sphere acquires in this way (especially in states that have adopted Roman law). In the drive toward calculability found in the modern state, law must express not only the interest of the ruling class but also the interest in a system that is as coherent and noncontradictory as possible; this diminishes the fidelity of the ideological reflex. It must continually be produced anew; this becomes more difficult the more that the economic contradictions are developed, for then they are more incompatible with a "harmonious" system of laws. Nevertheless, this appearance of harmony exists; moreover there is a powerful reification of cunning invested in jurisprudence. This cunning more than anything else has made the law into such a masculine discipline, into something full of definitions, formulas, something so elaborately formed, into a discipline that—looked at from its point of view—is too good for those students who study in order to earn a living, and just perfect for exceptional logicians. But none of this obstructed the positive law from doing the dirty work: protection of the private property of the means of production. And to the extent that private property is the dominant category of jurisprudence, the abolition of private property (of the means of production) automatically deprives jurisprudence of its function and causes it to fade away. Of all the emancipated fractions of ideology it is the only one to die in this way (instead of simply being liberated from its evil ideological character). Morality, art, science, philosophy, and certainly the humanism of religion are emancipated from the ideological superstructure in which they dwell in the class society; they are freed from illusion and establish themselves in reality. For the most part, however, jurisprudence withers away here. All that remains—after the removal of the protection of profit and the governmental apparatus for oppression—is sexual offense and crimes of passion (although even in this instance, the abolition of the category of property completely transforms passions such as envy, ambition, and, most of all, jealousy). With this metamorphosis of causes fraud, theft, embezzlement, trespass, murder, and robbery all become more than outdated, they become as good as prehistoric; the framework and edifice of distinctions, and of judicial nuances, become museum pieces. The precise law of exchange, the law of obligation with its subtleties of performance and satisfaction, is found in the same museum of surpassed sagacities as its strategy; the corpus juris is found next to the machine. Gone is the elegant distinction between agreement and contract, the principal distinction between possession and property; gone the problem of the source of law, the guarantee of law, and the entire nimbus of so-called justice. Thus Marxism has merely a historical interest in positive law, and, *rebus sic fluentibus*, a transition interest. The elaborate and cultivated positive law is alien to interventions and institutions of the classless society; it is foreign to it in a completely spontaneous, nonhypocritical way. Rudolf Sohm began his multivolume *Canon Law* with the hypocritical sentence: "Canonical law is in contradiction with the essence of the church." As a consequence of the sentence, he writes three volumes on the statutes of the message of salvation, because "practically a canonical law produces itself with ironclad necessity." Sohm is of the opinion that the church has to be an ideal establishment that forms itself freely through the Scriptures and rules without constraint—despite this there remains the necessity of harmonizing the actualization of divine purpose with a positive legal order. This necessity no longer remains for a classless society as soon as it is achieved: It would have effectively lost the world (of Caesar). Positive law here is not in contradiction with just any ideal essence; rather it renounces and no longer has need of the hypocritical lamentation of an ideal essence, of an essence still profoundly tied to Caesar.

A completely different museum of judicial postulates

Enough about the law, which is only a yoke and not even a yoke that weighs upon itself. It was imposed by exploitation, with its economy, and only with the economy can it be removed. In this regard is it right to speak of the indifference of Marxism toward the merely juridical superstructure, toward positive law, and also toward the subtly abstract enemy of positive law—*natural law*? Does Marxism accept—as a historical mode of thought—the claim of the historical school of law that from Grotius to Fichte all that we find are the "dreams of the intellect"? Even the positivists regarded natural law at best as the positive law of its time only "garnished with the additions that, according to their authors, were appropriate to ideal social conditions" (Th. Sternberg, *Universal Theory of Law*, 1904, I, p. 26). According to this view, to the extent that natural law is not limited, as it is in Christian von Wolff, to a clarification of given law it is simply an effort to better understand the subject founded upon a few overdrawn and exaggerated partial concepts. That is how the bourgeois positivists of the nineteenth century, and even of the Reformation, speak of natural law; of course one of the most stubborn, K. Bergbohm, had to concede of classical natural law: "It undermines servitude and dependence, and it pushes toward the improvement of property; it unchains the productive forces imprisoned in the calcified corporate structure and the absurd commercial restrictions . . . it secures the freedom of religion as the freedom of a scientific doctrine. It contributes to the elimination of torture and turns the penal process into a regular, ordered legal procedure" (*Jurisprudence and the Philosophy of Right*, 1891, I, p. 215). If such a blind detractor of natural law must praise its merits for the bourgeois juridical order in such a way, then natural law cannot have been the positive law of its time merely garnished with subjective and postulative additions. And how is this leveling of natural law to the current positive law to be adjusted to the other depreciation of natural law where—quite the inverse—it is denounced as something invariant? Certainly, it might appear this way in the false consciousness of its most famous theoreticians, but it is sufficiently evident that there have already been numerous varieties of natural law according to the postulates that vary with the different epochs. Only the *intention* of the upright carriage, of human dignity, was invariant; better yet—these were considered ineluctable, and of course did not only sound abstract to the historical school, which was only interested in the status quo. In fact, some Marxists who are always concrete have a rigid attitude toward natural law, even in its forward-looking, revolutionary form. Few, with the exception of A. Baumgarten, gave natural law—which posited freedom, equality, fraternity—the respect it deserves; the slogan "the will to ameliorate subjectively, abstractly" covered it. Still, it is difficult to reduce classical natural law to a purely subjective and abstract will for improvement, for it shaped the ideology of the French Revolution. And in its illusions, even in its ideals and anticipations (the "noble and proud virility" of Schiller), it was borne along by the thoroughly objective tendency toward another epoch, toward an individualist, democratic epoch. And only toward this? This is precisely the question that lies at the basis of every Marxist theory of judicial principles. The total judicial relativism of Hugo and the historical school (and the cynicism with which Hugo speaks of natural law) is as alien to Marx as is the hereditary or newly revived whip. Marx says (*The Philosophical Manifest of the Historical School of Law, MEGA,* I, 1, pp. 251ff.) that for Hugo "positive law is in one place, the other in another place; the one is as rational as the other; submit yourself to that which is positive within your four walls." And further, with respect to Hugo's complete abdication of classical natural law, even if it is preserved under the mask of a so-called real natural law of the "nature of the issue" as given and so apparently concrete, Marx says: "Hugo's natural law is the German theory of the French *ancien régime* . . . produced by the putrefaction of the contemporary world which enjoys itself. Kant's philosophy, on the other hand, is rightly regarded as the German theory of the French Revolution . . . produced by the self-assurance of a new life which shatters that which lies in ruins and which rejects the rejected." In the cradle of Marxism we find not only economic partiality on behalf of the *exploited* and *oppressed,* but also, in the spirit of natural law, an economic partiality for the humiliated and degraded—a partiality that understands itself in the fight for human dignity, the constitutive heritage of classical natural law, and does not allow any authority (insofar as one is necessary), whether hereditary or recent, to become cocky. Certainly, classical natural law tied its individual, democratic traits closely with the (then progressive) private property of the means of production, and as a consequence with the prevalence of private rights in all areas; and doubtless, this liaison is as transitory as, on the other side, the use of an only abstract genus of man or reason. But when Marx referred to Kant in opposition to the historical school of law à la Hugo, he referred to the humanistic concern from Althaus to Rousseau; and it is this concern, in the sense of a "real humanism," that constitutes the true motive of all the later economically based work. And it is difficult to overlook the fact that man is at the center—a center of classical natural law itself—in the following celebrated sentence in Marx's introduction to the *Critique of the Hegelian Philosophy of Right:* "The critique of religion ended with the doctrine that man is the highest being for man, and thus with the categorical imperative to overthrow all relations in which man is a degraded, enslaved, abandoned, or despised being." Consequently, it would be possible to think, faced with such a *humanum,* that even the individual (the all-too individual as he was defined from the Manchesterian, capitalistic perspective) was only the eggshell of classical natural law and of the natural law that still continues. The transition from free competition to monopoly and to state capitalism, which is frequently camouflaged, put the Manchesterian and even anarchistic edition of freedom and dignity for all in no small danger; the greater danger today lies someplace completely different. Prior to this the hatred that the positive jurisprudence of the nineteenth century felt for the demand of a rational construction (found in the seventeenth and eighteenth centuries) rendered it thoroughly receptive to Marxist esteem. The eggshells and illusions of classical, bourgeois natural law, including those that are not only ideological, do not come under this esteem, but as fascism was able to show in a remarkable way, not everything that is antiperson or antiliberalism necessarily calls itself socialism. It needs to be made clear that, precisely with respect to the humiliated and degraded, Marxism inherits some of this wealth of natural law, and that in places it finds some unsatisfied demands in it. Without question, the illusions and ideologies of that time must never be permitted to mingle with this inheritance; if that were ever to happen there would be a so-called improvement of Marx by a neo-Kantian Kant, and this is completely senseless for the category of the Front and more appropriate for an "idealized realm of the bourgeoisie." Socialism can raise the durable flag of the ancient fundamental rights, which has fallen elsewhere; it does so with illusions that have been seen through, corrected class ideology, perfected seriousness of the matter. "It will be shown that the relation between the past and future concerns more than an enormous dash, but that it has to do with the *accomplishment* of the ideas of the past" (Marx to Ruge, 1843). This sentence, which is so close to all that is creative, should hardly find an exception here. Minus the illusions that, in a critically observed past, are not as tenacious as in others.

Illusions in bourgeois natural law

It is not tenable to hold that man is free and equal from birth. There are no *innate* rights; they are all either acquired or must be acquired in battle. The upright path is inclined to be something that must be won; even the ostrich walks upright and yet sticks its head in the sand. Nor is it tenable to hold that *property* should be numbered among the inalienable rights; for this first arose as a consequence of the division of labor, as a means of disposing of others' capacity for work, and of their products. It was gradually formed in all of its rigor and nuances in the class society; for a long time the private possession of the means of production remained something aberrant. History shows that public property is much more the original form of property; and for a long time this form was retained in communal property (the *allmende*, the Russian constitution of the *mir*). But even in private property there are two clearly distinguishable hues: The more ancient is the possibility of unimpeded ownership and use; the more recent is the possibility of free disposal. This last quality of property ultimately develops into capitalistic private property (with the result that income is not tied to work), because classical natural law was tied by its masculine pride before the royal throne to private property, even to capitalistic private property and not only to "my house—my castle"; and of course it was compelled to be tied to it. Subjective, public rights could only be forcefully announced by the rising entrepreneur, and these rights were his ideological weapon. In this way there were linked to private property, which came to be numbered among the human rights and which played a somber, progressive role, one that rapidly turned hostile to humans. Even if Rousseau did not conceive of property as something excessive and exploitative, but as equally divided and as a shield against servitude, the direction taken by the productive forces of the time eliminated this petit-bourgeois dream. Capitalistic economy, which still had its work to do, was, on this point, an unimpeachable barrier for classical natural law. To be sure, as far as property was concerned, natural law did not even need to crawl out of its egg: Roman law had already taken care of it just as well, if not better. Since its Roman establishment, bourgeois law has been a law of the creditor, one that is fundamentally antagonistic to the debtor—it has been the private law of the owner. To the extent that natural law related its shield of freedom to the camp of private law it became a prisoner of private property and it remained individualistic. To the extent that natural law permitted the trademark of the shop to be imprinted upon its shield, which is certainly the promise of better symbols, it provides manly pride with a full wallet and it thus obstructs, or at least restricts, the very thing that it proclaims. Faced with this, recollections of a golden age, one without mine and yours, have no function. The classless idea rejects these elements of private law as superannuated, and even as having become something hostile.

It is not tenable to hold onto the forms in which men were given their rights. The *social contract* is at the top of the list here, either a beginning or a door, of which no stone remains standing. Individuals, private individuals, are supposed to have come together here in order to found a community by means of a contract, a relatively late judicial means of this same community. This happened as it did to Rutli, or later in a North American general store when the mayor or sheriff was elected by a majority. Though in truth, the social contract was taught by the majority of natural law theorists as a fiction, not as an original fact. But this fiction rested upon the importance that the contract had acquired in the incipient society of free competition. And this importance is transitory; outside the capitalistic society an association constituted for the purpose of uncultivated individuals would not even be thinkable as a fiction. It is true that the contract had an important place in Roman law, and that in the primitive law of almost every people it was accorded a magic inviolability. Even demons, who in all other regards were all-powerful, are tied to the contract and are apparently not in a position to get out of it; one finds an echo of this magic of contract in numerous fairy tales, as for instance in the tale of Rumpelstiltskin, but also in the strange magical force of a pact made with the devil. But the contract consecrated by magic, instituted against all uncertainty and uncanniness that lies outside the domain of the tribe, is obviously not yet a contract in the sense of a well-thought-out unification, for such contracts are magical formulas that are not at all for sale. Even in Roman law, which is so akin to bourgeois law, the *pactum* is not yet the modern contract, but the setting aside, and the satisfaction, of a conflict; even etymologically *pactum* is related to *pax*. Only capitalism, with all relations determined as contractual relations, replaces familial and patriarchal relation with the domination of a rational alliance between possessors of merchandise as the condition of the uninterrupted circulation of value (merchandise—money—merchandise). Thus even the social contract, antedated into primeval times, is completely rational; that is, it is constructed as a legal relation between free competitors. Insofar as the social contract, like every business pact, includes its own termination in the event that one side does not fulfill its terms, it opens the legal path to revolution. But insofar as it makes law into a product of reflection that is logically well grounded, it passes over revolution into the abstract rationalism of the Enlightenment, and forms the narrative introduction to the Enlightenment. It is not tenable to retain and further this introduction, namely, the *a priori construction* founded upon the pure understanding: This is the fiction of a deduction (without holes) of legal norms from a final juridical principle *ante rem* (sociability, security, or the greatest possible individual freedom). The ambition of this a priori construction stems from the new mathematics; its ideal, as we have already seen, was an abstract, rational system of relations, which deduced and calculated all phenomena out of a few fundamental concepts—independent of their concrete material differentiation. This procedure was dictated by the capitalistic need for a world that was abstractly homogeneous and, whenever possible, quantifiable. Kant's critique of reason struck the first blow against this construction; Hegel's dialectic (as the historicism and qualification of the concept) struck the second blow. Marx completely did away with the false relations of deduction, but also with the illusory movements of a world sitting on its head, that is, on the concept. It serves no purpose to pick out partial relations and even partial tendencies in real life and insert them into the head as an arithmetical problem "with a material that had been methodologically purified." It serves no purpose to dissolve intellectually all obstructions and imperfections in order to come up with a logic that formally is like iron, but remains weaker and unreal from the point of view of content. Clearly, the deductions of classical natural law did not, for the most part, want to work with any existing reality (positive legal propositions); nevertheless classical natural law picked its highest concepts from a valid reality (the law that is correct according to nature). But this deduction, which began with final juridical principles *ante rem*, came to lose its object; formal necessity, that is, the absence of contradiction in the deduction and form of a proposition, is hardly a criterion of its truth, of its truth in a dialectical world.

It is furthermore not tenable to hold that from the perspective of justice, men are in agreement. And that they would be in agreement in an immutable way so long as their light was not artificially obscured by princes and priests. Doubtless, men were in agreement in the intention of freeing themselves from oppression and installing human dignity, at least since the time of the Greeks. But only this will is immutable, and not, as we have already seen, "man" and his so-called eternal right. The hypothesis of a natural *consensus gentium* everywhere and always, especially in judicial matters, obviously corresponds to a belief that ultimately lies at the basis of the constructions of natural law. This construction requires a homogeneous substrate, one that is invariant, ahistorical, or, as it implies itself, superhistorical. As such it offered itself an *eternal human nature*; for Hobbes it was one that was originally evil, for Rousseau it was originally good. But the same thing does not exist for Marxism, where static and eternal definitions and determinations are regarded exclusively as reified abstractions. There is no fixed generic essence of man, one with static characteristics upon which a natural law might be grounded; rather the entire course of history is evidence of a progressive transformation of human nature. Furthermore, even the question whether or not this nature should be termed "essentially" evil or good is, for Marxism, a rigidified, reifying question: "Man" is, according to his disposition or basis, an X; according to his historical and moral definition he is a product of the social relations of the moment. The doctrines of the original goodness of human nature have been handed over to the anarchists; for them all evil is a consequence of the church and its derivatives: authority and state. Nevertheless, all such stipulations are just as dogmatic as the church doctrine of Original Sin and the relative natural law (the state as *remedium peccati*), which in the Middle Ages was derived from the Fall. For Marxism, the *humanum* has the function of a historical goal, not the function of an a priori principle of deduction; it is the utopia, which is not present but is anticipated—it is not something that ahistorically lies at the basis of things as the arch-certainty of history. Rousseau himself characterized the task (as possibility) of the legislator as "to change the nature of man." It is not a tenable position that defends the idolization of external correlates, turning them into eternal man, that is, the idolization of a supposed *immutable and normative totality of nature*. In the Cynics, the Stoics, and Rousseauism, nature was constituted in different ways as the category that contrasted with societal relations, and this was powerfully conserved in the genuine and profound persistence of maternal law, and also (and this is important from a critical point of view) as a fetish against social defaults. Accordingly a judicial optimism of nature was formed whose power lay in a peculiarly festive and generous sanction of reformist demands, and whose fallibility was its flight from society and history. Numerous equivocations are gathered in this principle of flight and sanction; it has remained the enduring merit of the phenomenological analysis of meaning to have indicated and dissolved such equivocations (cf. Spiegelberg, *Law and Moral Law*, 1935, pp. 259ff.). According to Spiegelberg one finds three different species of cognitive concepts of natural law, that is, among those that distinguish nature as the *mentor* of justice; they often alternate with each other in one and the same author (in

Cicero for example). First, there is *innate natural* law, which is to be found in everyone and of which everyone may demand satisfaction. Second, there is *obvious natural* law, which, though not innate, can be recognized with natural reason by everyone. Third, there is *revealed natural* law, which, without being innate and without having to be deduced by reason, is communicated to man by nature, which teaches it to him as a voice. As far as the *ontological concepts of natural law* are concerned, those that try to give a definition of essence, we find that there are six different species, and that from the Sophists to Rousseau these are entangled in each other and complete each other. The first sort are described as speaking of the *constant natural* law, in contrast to created, artificial, changing natural law. In the second place we find the *natural condition* of law (found in all theorists of natural law without exception), which was really or imaginatively valid in a real or fictive original condition. Third we find *given natural* law, in contrast to all that was created by God or men. The genitive in *lex naturae* here is a subjective genitive; nature is the legislative subject, naturalness is a sign of originality (at this level nature could under certain conditions, for pantheists, coincide with God again). In the fourth case there is *valid natural* law in the sense of a law that provides the standard for all of nature, a law that is inscribed in nature or constitutes it. Here the genitive in *lex naturae* is an objective genitive; nature is the field of the universal application of laws, or the domain universally governed by laws (in the course of which there is only a difference of domain between the law of falling bodies and the principle of *pacta sunt servanda*, though of course there is a difference in the pleasure of the accomplishment of each). In the fifth place we find the law *founded in nature*, which is not given by nature and is not valid for it, but follows from it and has its concrete ground in nature (and which, from the cognitive point of view, can be deduced from the concept of nature adequate to it). The concept of nature employed here runs from the "essence" or the "nature" of something up to the massiveness of a panlogistic emanation. Deductions from the "nature" of rent, of purchase, of despotism, and of *casus, modus,* and *culpa* are already found in Roman law. Deductions from the logic of the world and its supreme principle are to be found throughout the entire period of the Enlightenment, and most pronounced in the corner giants of rationalism: Spinoza and Hegel. In the sixth place there is law that *conforms to nature*, as that which is neither given by nature nor naturally valid, but which also cannot be inferred from nature. This is the law that is the measure of nature, that takes nature into account and finds itself in accord with the law and the form of the world. This accord (which is comparable to the doctor who follows the indications of nature) is found, as intent, above all in Stoic theories of natural law, but also in the natural law of tolerance. Nature appears here as a model, namely, as the model of equity, of the equilibrium that considers everything, of the avoidance of extremes; it appears as a worldly Solomon. These are the diverse equivocations lumped together under the hat of an apparently unified category of contrast—called nature—and its normative law. The real unity here is only the fixation of the momentary category of contrast into something eternal, and above all into a principle of deduction that is already decided upon and taken as an arch-certainty equal to human nature. The basis for the resemblance between this principle and human nature is that the essence of nature is almost everywhere portrayed as good (otherwise its law would be neither evident nor an invitation to accord). Nevertheless, Marxism is a stranger to such hypostases and such gildings because it does not need an ideology of contrast to relate to history. It believes in history when it is correctly led, and society, the appearance of which it liberates, does not in the end rest in an *already existing matriarchate* of nature that exists as a *standard or homeland* and is statically conceived. Even the relatively happy state of the natural and primitive communistic tribes does not dim the view of the questionable splendor of a law of the natural state, for, as animalistic, this was outside the narrow horde of the clan; it was the right of the mighty, and the law of the fist. In this species of natural law men could be extinguished like insects; that is how one regarded the matter in ancient Rome, that is how one sees things in the new resurfacing of bestial law in the form of fascism. In this realistic declaration Marxism is closer to Hobbes than to Rousseau, and above all it is closer to Hegel than to those who are enemies of history and pantheists of the terrain of nature. On this subject Hegel speaks, in an idealistic fashion, of Plato: "The natural is that which has to be sublated by spirit, and the state of nature and its law can only manifest itself in that it is the absolute negation of the law of spirit" (*Works*, XIV, p. 271). More precisely, this time playing the "ambiguity" of natural law against rational law: "The law of nature is therefore the existence of strength and the empire of violence—and a state of nature is a state of brutality and injustice of which nothing truer may be said than that it must be escaped" (*Encyclopedia*, par. 502). Here, instead of a flight into nature we find a coming-to-terms with history from the moment it develops; this is the same coming-to-terms that—without the idealism of spirit—is proper to Marxism in its most concrete manner. If Marxism speaks of a naturalization of human being then in the same breath it speaks no less of a humanization of nature, which therefore surmounts the sentiment of the perfection of nature, as well as the multiply entangled ambiguities that, even beyond cognitive-ontic equivocations, are contained in the juridical concept of nature. Of course among the optimists of nature it is not animalistic nature or the mathematically perfect laws of nature that are praised, but matriarchal nature; this echo of maternal law in natural law, of Cybele in *physis*, has been noted in an earlier chapter. However, Marxism detaches itself even from this attitude; it does not remove the foundation of the ideology of classes in order to spare a mythology of genders. It is not the case that the naturalization of human being would take place in the house of the mother, and that the abolition of the distinction between city and country should occur as the abolition of the city and return to the mother earth. It is rather only with an optic that looks into the projectable depths of nature that an ancient natural law in the Demetrian sense becomes clear, with another sort of confidence in nature, not static but in process, and in this way utopian.

It is not tenable to defend ahistorical thought that holds itself to be standing upon false heights. The definitions of natural law were developed in such a place, not out of history as something inscribed and developing in it. On the contrary they were brought forth from above, from a fetishly preordained nature, as *ideals*. Doubtless this formation of ideals had a very important psychological origin, which is not immediately variable. It stems from the fact that in all human activity the goal is already in the head before its material realization. In the realm of ideas, where cohabitation is easy, the act of positing a goal necessarily acquires a peculiar autonomy and perfection in the moral sense. This perfection is difficult to attain in the violent collisions of things, but it nevertheless remains spiritually and so furnishes a criterion of what ought to be. That is the psychological formation of the ideal, with all possible eggshells or even fixations in it, such as parents, the superego, and the like; it is a high image that not only completes that which remains behind it, but criticizes and attacks it as well. To this extent the ideal is to be distinguished from mere wish images even where it is connected with them (in ideal conditions and ideal countrysides). But in capitalistic society the psychological root, which *mutatis mutandis* might remain in the classless society, produces thoroughly monstrous flowers and produces an appearance of suprahistorical principles in a rigid opposition to reality. The ideal here appears in particularly sharp contrast to social reality, but simultaneously in a peculiarly powerless distance from it. The origin of this contrast lies in the revolutionary beginnings of bourgeois society itself; its tension is essentially the tension between the rising bourgeoisie and the *citoyen* as that which was intended or hypocritically extolled. In other words, the contradiction between the bourgeois ideal and bourgeois reality, as it was already visible in the eighteenth century and as that which culminated in the nineteenth century, is the contradiction between the heroic self-deception necessary for the production of capitalistic society, and the having come into being to his society itself. It is the contradiction between the humanistic ideals of the revolutionary bourgeoisie and the division of labor, the monotony, the mechanization of capitalistically perfect existence. In Hölderlin this contrast shows itself vitally and as a penetrating truth, sentimental, that is, as world-weariness and romantic pessimism. It appears as well in Byron, Leopardi, and already in Schiller; but in Ibsen it is finally denounced as bourgeois Don Quixotism where, in *The Wild Duck*, Gregers Werle presents "ideal demands" while the cynical realistic Relling translates them with the word *lies*. The ideals of liberalism are best left in the treasure chest; thus we find the Hermann Cohen's reappropriation of his rational law and the jurisprudence of his ethics: The ideal is "the Being of the pure will," "the will is the Being of the ideal," but of an unattainable Being. A Being that never becomes temporal, which therefore stays eternal, a Being not for realists but for idealists, "the look held in suspense between the separation of reality and the eternal ideal" (*Ethics of the Pure Will*, 1907, p. 569). It is characteristic that all previous contents of natural law function as ideals even more than aesthetic contents: "Justice," Cohen said, "is virtue, the realm of God, the ideal of world history." Of course the epigones do not invent anything; they only blabber over the weaknesses of their master, and thus Cohen's recitation (he is the original, so to speak, Stammlerian, and, in the final analysis, social democratic theorist of natural law) isolated and exaggerated the abstract, ahistorical character—the undialectical antithesis of the ideal—in classical natural law. To be sure, this abstract antithesis was already present in the beginnings (as for example in Shaftesbury); the revolutionary idealism, which began on the *citoyen* side of the bourgeoisie, still stands in perceptible tension with feudalism and the feudal absolutism of its time. But even then the ideal expressed essentially more contrasting abstractions than latent tendencies of reality; this is the point where the illusions that ensnare it issue forth, and the source of the surprise about the reality that came to be. The original goodness of human nature is such an illusion, and so is the harmony of private economic interests that appeared to contribute truth, beauty, and goodness to the ideal of fraternity. Marxism, on the other hand, dryly rejected the ideal, but certainly only at first and with respect to an abstract hypostasis of the ideal. In the *German Ideology* Marx speaks against this "ought": "For us, communism is not a condition that ought to be produced, an ideal to which reality would need direct itself. We call communism the *real* movement that surmounts the present condition." And in *The Civil War in France* he speaks even more decisively (almost too decisively): "The working class does not have an ideal to realize; it only has to liberate the elements of the new society that have already developed in the womb of the collapsing bourgeois society." But the ideal looks *entirely different* when it is not immediately introduced into history from above, when rather it is concretely and utopianly extracted from its dialectical mediations. In this regard Hegel is helpful despite himself: The enormity of his achievement consists in making theory and history relative to each other, in order to conceive them as dialectically interpenetrating one another; and with respect to the theory of the authentic ideal, Hegel (at least in his *Aesthetics*) shows the premises of such immanent transcendence. Marxism puts these premises back on their feet; indeed as far as its ideal is concerned (namely, the overthrow of all relations "in which man is a degraded, enslaved, abandoned, or despised being"), it discovers in the social being of the proletariat itself that process whose real dialectic only must be made conscious in order to become the theory of revolutionary praxis, and therefore the praxis of the revolutionary ideal. Here the ideal is posited by the tendency, not the abstraction of a theory, and adjusted by the praxis of the tendency toward always deeper levels of reality, but in such a way that it never backs away, as in Hegel, from the fullness of concretion or even from the strictness and restriction of real possibility (*rebus sic stantibus*). To do so would be to eternalize the pure and simple factical bourgeois concept of reality; the marginal tendencies of reality (*rebus non iam stantibus*) would be denied. For Marxism the problem of the ideal is the problem of appearance and (latent) essence; consequently, it is, as Lukács rightly emphasizes, in no regard merely "an illusory problem restricted to bourgeois class concerns" (cf. "Schiller's Theory of Modern Literature," in *Goethe and His Age*, Berlin, 1950, p. 151). From the bourgeois point of view, the relation between appearance and essence becomes highly abstract, but nevertheless Lukács continues: "The objective reality of this dialectical relation in nature and society does not cease to exist with the cessation of its special form of appearance in capitalistic society." What does disappear is precisely the "insurmountable dilemma that bourgeois consciousness faces between inflated idealism and fawning empiricism": The principle of the ideal that has been rendered *superhistorical* disappears, as does its unmediated opposition not only to the tendency but also to the facts (such as of justice) of reality. Just as little as the revolution consists and exhausts itself in filling the cadres of an abstract social utopia with a little realization, so little does it realize the abstract ideals of a natural law. The more these ideals are abstractly elevated, that is, the more superhistorical it becomes, the more surely another ideal appears in the so-called realization, and this ideal degenerates into hypocrisy or, in the best case, into the rallying point for a questionable and musty nostalgia. Justice is not the virtue, and the empire of God is not the ideal of world history; freedom, equality, and fraternity never range so inflexibly as when they were decreed to be goals independent of history. Not only the ideal that is realizable to some extent, but also the ideal that is already valid must, precisely as valid and as necessary, be historically mediated, and it must be possible to demonstrate that they have their tendency and their possibility in the course of society. Otherwise they only engender the abstract feeling that right is absent, instead of a penetrating, concrete critique of a degenerated and discredited realization, a realization that would be better called a defeat and makes itself known as such. That is what happened in the fall of the *citoyen* into the bourgeoisie, a fall that could not be prevented; other, preventable degenerations are, nevertheless, only immanently criticizable as alien to the thing itself and not transcendent with the frustrated absence of a so-called instant paradise.

The claims of the rights of the people; the origin of an ideal that was ambiguous for so long: Justice, but from below

Does it then seem as if nothing remains at all of the fixed essence? This is unquestionably the case to the extent that it was fixed, but from the thing itself it contained much under its crust that was fluid. This fluidity continues to work, and the ancient motion is pursued with consciousness; there is no absolute, dividing gap between yesterday and tomorrow. The Marxist vision has to understand the past far better than the past understood itself, for only then does it understand why so many excellent intentions miscarried or were perverted. Innate rights are done away with, as well as all those rights that find the pride of man in private property. The social contract is abolished along with the a priori construction, the eternalities of human nature and nature as a whole. But the *ideals* do not rest entirely upon this historical tract; they are not only illusion and an illusory problem. As for the ideals of natural law, they contain (in the classical time) enough revolutionary salt, critical warning, and ingredients sufficient to be a true, appearing essence. Was it not ultimately a legacy of freedom, equality, and fraternity that let Rosa Luxemburg say in a completely contemporary way: "No democracy without socialism, no socialism without democracy." One of the most solid and important determinations of natural law, which rectified the ancient fundamental juridical concepts in the impetus of human rights—the claim of *subjective rights in totality*—still had private property as an infrastructure and, despite itself, even as an auxiliary construction. The next section is dedicated to the investigation of this claim, the regional category proper to human rights. Natural law was the first to have opened this regional category (beyond that of the mere claim of private rights). In positive law the "objective legal order" always retains the primary place; it is the jurisprudence of wishes granted, and even juridical power is regarded as mere permission; fundamental political rights are regarded as mere "exemptions from the sphere of domination." Conversely, classical natural law holds that the fundamental rights are primary; the objective legal order on the other hand is presented as secondary and the burden of proof is placed upon this order. The infrastructure of the private economy does not prevent Fichte from appealing to an "original right to work and subsistence" and from idealizing this claim for every individual in society. Socialism is not so far removed from this incontestable ideal of natural law when it speaks of the working classes instead of the individual; when, in the place of this idealistic original right, it presents a right that is always provisory, Lassallean, but nevertheless material: the right to the products of labor (more precisely, to an equivalent of the quantum of the labor performed). The revolutionary usage of even the rather unsocial ideologies of the masters of the old natural law gives them a remarkably new face. For example, nothing is closer to *patriarchalism* than so-called *justice*; that is why it was denounced in the passages that examine the natural law of the medieval world. In its retributive function, as in its distributive function, justice corresponds to the formula *suum cuique*; it presupposes the father of the family, the father of the people, who dispenses from above to each his portion of punishment or portion of social goods (income, position). This is done according to the criteria of the dominant class, and furthermore upon the basis of the relation of exchange, for it is almost absurd outside this relation. The scales fit in here, which even in the sign of the scales in the zodiac is displaced up high and from there works downward, and this fits in well with allegory of this ideal of justice, which sits upon the throne. The same aged shibboleth shows up here, remarkably detoxified of course, remarkably meaningful (or at least with a suggestive illusion of meaning), as soon as it is used from below in a revolutionary way. Then the only thing that is taken over from the exchange relation is the revolutionary settling of accounts; exploitation and arrogance fall from the tribunal bench. This *real justice*, as a *justice from below*, sets itself in opposition to both retributive and distributive justice, as well as the essential injustice that makes the claim to be practicing justice.

Such a push toward right even begins where tyrannized people have not yet brought it into being, where it is kept awake by a substitute, where, as a substitute practice for such a real justice, it becomes the object of the hopes of men who are still weak. It is, therefore, wherever one imagines a savior coming from the outside, even if this savior is a lord, namely, a Rubezahl of a higher order. That is the case with the homecoming of Odysseus, with the arrival of the minister in Beethoven's *Fidelio*, and with the not unrelated paintings of the Last Judgment. These pictures reveal an especially representative character, a colossal transposition of a substitute-equivalent, mostly upon the basis of human doubt and political impotence; nevertheless, *justice from below* does *not* want to be *suspended* in it. Millions of times the tribunal of

God at the end of time served as a substitute for a revolutionary tribunal that never came to pass in reality. This certainly had the effect of an adjournment, but it also served as a thorn against complete capitulation: The trumpets of the Last Judgment, among others, keep watch for the justice of the "Marseillaise." And the allusions to the Last Judgment, as found in *The Brigands* and in *Cabal and Love*, are in an identifiable connection with the revolutionary situation of the time. The reader so inclined, mindful of the *in tyrannos*, thinks of many things in this regard; Franz Moor had his dream of judgment in the solitude of midnight: "Suddenly an old man bent over by grief, bit in the arm by angry hunger; all timidly turn their eyes away from the man; I recognize the man; he cuts a lock from his silver hair, throws it around—around—and—then I heard a voice resounding from out of the smoke coming from the craggy cliff: Mercy, mercy to all sinners of the earth and of the abyss! You alone are condemned" (*The Brigands*, act 5, scene 1). When the valet in *Cabal and Love* brings the diamonds to Lady Milford from the prince and he is paid by the sale of seven thousand children, who were sold in America like cattle, when he comes before Lady Milford this old father ("Precious stones such as these—I have some sons of my own down there") appeals to the apocalypse in which the omnipotence of the future sleeps, but in a restrained way and with the terrifying serenity of impotence: "Some strong heads left the front and asked the colonel how much the prince would sell the yoke of men for. But our very merciful sovereign had the entire regiment march out on the parade ground and shoot down the gawkers. We heard the rifles pop, saw their brains splatter on the pavement, and the entire army cry out: Hurrah! to America! . . . Still at the city gates they turned around and yelled: God be with you women and children!—Our sovereign lives—we will meet again at the Last Judgment!" (act 2, scene 2). In such a powerful cry religion is reduced to the executioner's ax, to the hope of the executioner's ax; in this way it pushes aside the real tribunal, but it would not be distant from it if it were to appear in Germany. "Heavenly justice" takes on a double life even in its greatest patriarchal poem, the *Divine Comedy*. It is true though that Dante was so profoundly hostile to the rebellion insofar as it concerned the imperial nobility, that he placed Brutus and Cassius, Caesar's assassins, in the depths of hell alongside Judas in the mouth of Lucifer. But it is precisely for this reason that the strictly obedient Ghibelline was an enemy of the papal court; in this case justice was tied to gospels and consequently was a justice directed from below; and this is how the poem came to be understood by the heretics with their seditious justice. He found "the she-wolf of greed" raging most strongly in the church of power; it is corrupt, it woos the giants of power, but Dante's God is the court of cassation for the false justice of this world: The popes can be put in hell, but the prostitute Rahab, because she contributed to the fall of pagan Jericho, enjoys a life in Paradise. Thus the justice of the *Divine Comedy*, which was almost always a justice that *puts things in order*, withstood the test for the criminals among the great and the crimes that only the great could commit. Dante did not learn this justice from a Thomism that is respectful of authority, but from his exile, from a pathos for a prophetic justice instead of a pathos for an administrative and forensic justice. In this case, therefore, justice acted from time to time as a substitutive justice, as if it were opposed to the justice of Ahab and Isabel, as if it held its arm out to the people, as if by the substitution of an otherworldly tribunal it extinguished the injustice rendered upon the people. Even though it is an illusion, it nevertheless produces an agreeable and not unfounded cadence entirely different from the effect produced by the judgment of the class given authority by the grace of God. Nemesis evokes memories of the power of a revolutionary tribunal, Odysseus' bow of the overdue answer. How consonant this real justice was as soon as it was no longer the opportunity for a substitution for elevated mythical figures, as soon as the *revolution* took hold of it and with it set itself to really dismantling the Bastille from the ground up. Without the impulse of justice from below, no human rights would be installed; without the revolutionary tribunal, and without the court of justice that sits over the Nazis who threw the concentration camps and ovens onto the scales of justice, which here are no longer patriarchal, there is no release of humanity. Thus in a justice so constituted, a chapter of natural law, which is not only a chapter of classical natural law, is detoxified. This, especially in its medieval-theological form without its revolutionary redefinition of function, is almost only a patriarchal ideology. Even in its socialistic usage the justice from below cannot be overestimated; there is always still illusion in it even if it is a suggestive illusion. The socialistic revolution certainly has justice from below in its initial moment, but precisely on account of its practiced regard beyond persons, symptoms, and immediacies it renders this justice serious by suppressing social causes and by placing it where no harm can come its way. Beyond this initial impulse and guarantee, which it has at the beginning of the revolution, if it remains a revolution, it concentrates all its time and energy on the main goal of revolutionary justice: socialistic construction. Even justice from below, at least as a revolutionary tribunal, even when measured against the good it brings, is only a necessary evil, only lasting as briefly as possible; the goods of the construction never support the tribunal and they liquidate even better, in a more positive way. Even a completely classless society no longer knows any redefined sense of justice, since the antipatriarch from below has likewise ceased to exist in it. The principle that each produces according to his abilities, each consumes according to his needs, does not contain even the softest echo of the *suum cuique*. It also renders superfluous the right to the fruits of one's labor, but of course only in that it has removed its object, that is, in that it has abolished all relations of equivalence in a life beyond labor, a life that becomes possible for everyone. The inventory of theories of natural law that have existed hitherto do not become museum pieces with the approach of the classless society, as positive law does. For a long while it continues to contain prophetic advertisements and useful instruments even if they must be reassembled if they are to be efficient. This sphere is so little abandoned that for a long while, and occasionally more than ever before, it is sensible of and an instruction against all usurpation from above, all reification of the means of power, and all exercise of uncontrolled power. The ultimate quintessence of classical natural law, without all of the other accessories, remains the postulate of human dignity; man, and not only his class (as Brecht said), is not happy when he finds a boot in his face, and the enduring element of natural law bestowed upon this repugnance, a repugnance that has been revolutionary since Spartacus, a conceptual dimension even if it retained an abstract format. If the social tendency, as truly advancing, is permitted to become more concrete here, then it is all the better for this format. In both outline and detail it was not the format of the anti-Mammon, but of the anti-Nero. To be sure, both are closely related even with the urgent procedure of the anti-Mammon, but they are not simply the same. Thus we find the authentic inheritance of the natural law that was revolutionary: the abolition of all relations that have alienated man from things that have not only been reduced to being merchandise but are even stripped of all their own value. No democracy without socialism, no socialism without democracy—that is the formula of an interaction that will decide the future.

Social utopia and natural law

Ultimately, the free life was believed to be one beyond the life of labor. But what was sought after in this life only appeared as a *dream* on the borders of history. Backward to the epoch that was thus deemed a golden age, forward into the empire of freedom. The right to such a life doubtless sounds utopian, and so natural law as a whole, as free floating, was occasionally called a legal utopia. On the other hand, the positivists claimed that the doctrines of Grotius and Hobbes were nothing other than the positive law of their time with a few subjective, ideal decorations attached. What is the utopian character of natural law in the theories of its great representatives; do these theories have a connection with the genuine *social utopias* of their time? If they do not have such a connection, then natural law (as a mere decoration of positive law) would in large measure fall under the rubric of a historical technique and ideology of economy. If there does exist such a connection, then it would be reasonable to accord natural law the consideration and critical respect brought to social utopias as the more or less awkward precursors of scientific socialism. Nevertheless, there are also essential *differences* and not only relations between natural law—especially classical, rational natural law—and social utopias. The first difference is *temporal*: The apogee of natural law theory was in the seventeenth and eighteenth centuries; the social utopias peaked in the early nineteenth century, in the world of the industrial revolution. To the extent that natural law theorists from Grotius to Pufendorf enter the picture somewhat parallel to the classic theorists of bourgeois political economy, they stand upon the basis of the most progressive bourgeois consciousness and so formulate the demands of the revolutionary bourgeoisie quite openly and logically. There are points of contact, even if only external, between classical natural law and the physiocratic school in the economy; this becomes clearly evident in Quesnay, the founder of this school. There is even a connection with Adam Smith's method: Abstractions such as *homo oeconomicus*, the harmony of interests, and the deductive method of the "correct political economy" (as distinguished from the mistaken feudal economy) all stem from natural law. The rational essence of natural law is also an element common to the leading economists of the age; it corresponds to the general faith in abstraction found in the early stages of bourgeois science, to the faith in constructive powers, at least to the calculative power of the pure intellect. Conversely, the leading social utopian theoretists (Fourier, Saint-Simon, Owen) first surface in an age that had already set aside the bourgeois optimism of the intellect. It set this optimism aside partly as a result of the incipient crises (economic: Sismondi's theory of crises; and ideological: Kant's critique of reason), partly in harmony with the later reactions against the notion of construction and their return to organic growth, ancestry, becoming (the traditionalists in France, and the historical school in Germany). But even the social utopianists did not fully experience their hereditary imagination in all of its shimmering anticipation, even in the direction of the industrial development of the nineteenth century, while the natural law of that time was set aside by the reactionary historical school as an act of construction. This last point, the constructive aspect of natural law, defines a second important difference between the theories of natural law and social utopia, a *methodological* difference: social utopias operate with stories, pictures, and depictions, and with novel-like ways of projecting images of a better future society—none of these procedures is merely an ornamentation. Theorists of natural law, on the other hand, even in the case of Rousseau, operate via deductions from a principle, and with the zeal and rigor of a demonstrative science. This, in turn, is linked to the third, most important difference between natural law and social utopia, the difference between the *objects* of their intentions: Social utopias are primarily directed toward *happiness*, at least toward the abolition of misery and the conditions that preserve or produce such misery. Natural law theories, as is so readily apparent, are primarily directed toward *dignity*, toward human rights, toward juridical guarantees of human security or freedom as categories of human pride. Accordingly, social utopias are oriented above all toward the abolition of human *suffering*; natural law is oriented above all toward the abolition of human *degradation*. Social utopias want to clear away all that stands in the way of the *eudaemonia of everyone*; natural law wants to do away with all that stands in the way of *autonomy* and its *eunomia*. Thus the humanistic resonance in the doctrines of social utopia and in those of natural law is profoundly different; with regard to the most noticeable difference between them one can say that one takes the Phaeacians as its model, the other Brutus.

And yet neither of these dreams of a better social life is even fully disentangled from the other. They intertwine in one another: The doctrines of happiness do not want a garden for irresponsible animals; doctrines of dignity do not want to be contemptuous of fine things, even with the rough outside of a column. That is why it is unavoidable that we notice the real similarities such as methodological affinities, which, in fact, permit us to speak also of legal utopias. These similarities consist in *passing beyond* givenness, in the belief that present existents must be pushed aside in order to liberate and open the way to a better status. In this regard social utopias should not be restricted to the period of their apogee, that is, to the blossoming in the nineteenth century during the period immediately before Marx. They have a long and important history before this period: Plato, the Stoics, and Augustine sketched out the ideal state; Thomas More, Campanella, and Bacon write their *Utopia*, their *Civitas solis*, their *Nova Atlantis* with glances cast throughout to natural law. The Stoics even developed their natural law in close contact with their utopia of a world state; in Stoicism, Grotius and Saint-Simon were not successors, but contemporaries; they were even the same person. But even authentic theories of classical natural law, those of the seventeenth and eighteenth centuries, are tied to social utopian theories by a common denominator: namely, the same sort of *well-intentioned projection*. This is also understood in an equally negative sense: In both cases we find disruptive crisscrossings with the empirical world; that is, they neglect given "bad conditions," and in both cases there is a smooth development, which starts from the "nature of men" and is at the service of this "nature," of a goal with better means than had been employed hitherto. But there is also a positive sense in which this common denominator must be understood: In both cases the corpus politicum is formed anew out of a concept of the end. The social utopian theory of Thomas More lies at the basis of the thought, characteristic of natural law, of the natural freedom of the individual, whereas Grotius's natural law lies at the basis of utopian liberalism (the liberation of individual interests). Likewise, we find connections between Campanella's utopia of radical order and the system of natural law of a radical absolutism in Hobbes. In Kant's project of perpetual peace an object of natural law, namely, the idea of cosmopolitan law and the international state that follows from it, is transferred into the future and *expressis verbis* adjoined to the dream of utopia. Thus the colorful images of the state and the rigorous construction of law are thoroughly united in a project of the ameliorative will. Owen, Fourier, and Saint-Simon clearly attach their constructions to the abolition of misery, to categories of natural law, principally to the ideal of the *citoyen* in the collective, and they set "socialistic reason" against the "unnatural relations of the present." Marxism explodes the abstractness and supposed eternal character of the standards of reason conceived in this fashion; as a transformative act it has even less to do with the supposed eternal natural identity of man. It takes the standards and above all the paths of socialism from dialectical, concrete history instead of the privateness of the will to reform and the ahistorical idea that is introduced from outside real history. In this way social utopia and natural law together became part of the background; what remains, as Engels says of social utopias, are the "ingenious embryonic ideas and thoughts that spring up everywhere under fantastic coverings, and for which the Philistines are blind"; of natural law there only remains a vague recollection. Nevertheless, the movement toward historical, dialectical reality, toward the "freedom, equality, and fraternity of the primitive communist tribe" (at the last stage), would not have been so unambiguously discovered— even in Marx and Engels—if natural law, despite (and even on account of) all of its abstractness, had not so forcefully delineated these "principles of reason." It is not only their social mission that differentiates them; it is also the respect that they accord to the demands outlined in the project of natural law that separates the Marxist seriousness with respect to history from the miserable facticity of the historical school; furthermore, with a nod toward the a priori of the construction of natural law, Marx said once that the historical school of law only "demonstrates that history is its a posteriori." It is not inconsequential that proletarian humanism is close to the tradition of natural law, *mutatis mutandis*, and precisely in its pathos of human dignity. Beginning with this annihilated dignity (even more, man with misery), Marx points to the "class with radical chains," to a sphere that "does not lay claim to any *particular justice* because there is no *special injustice*, but rather *injustice in general*, which is being leveled against it" (Introduction to *Critique of the Hegelian Philosophy of Right*). An absolute, general injustice, as such, can be neither characterized nor measured nor repaired if no absolute, general justice, no legal utopia, is envisioned.

The intended "emancipation of men" takes far less from the philanthropic affect of social utopias than it does from the pride of natural
law. Happiness and dignity, the concerns emphasized on the one hand
by social utopias and on the other by doctrines of natural law, for so
long marched separately and sadly never stuck together with the
priority of human care and support, and the *primat* of human dignity:
It is more than ever necessary that along with the concrete heritage
of social utopian thought, an equally concrete program of the *citoyen*
be recognized. It is more necessary than ever before that even the
differences in the intentional fields finally be recognized as functionally
related and practically surmounted. This thanks to the certainty that
there can be no human dignity without the end of misery and need,
but also no human happiness without the end of old and new forms
of servitude. The spotty respect with which Marxism accords social
utopias as its own forerunner is included as that respect which is *touched*
by natural law. Both belong to the noble power of anticipation of
something "better" than that which has "become"—in the one case
the experimental material of its effort at the *humanum* is made of
colorful, in the other, of more rigid stuff, but both issue from the
empire of hope. The wish of natural law was and is *uprightness as a
right*, so that it might be respected in *persons* and guaranteed in their
collective. And if there were only one person to honor the dignity of
humanity, then even this vast and all-encompassing dignity would be
sufficient to form the quintessence of natural law. This is precisely
what we find in socialism insofar as it simultaneously seeks to come
to grips with the person and the collective, and to the extent that—
far from the normalized masses of men, near to unalienated solidarity—
it seeks to contain the one within the other.

21

Subjective, Objective Right (*Facultas Agendi,* *Norma Agendi*) in Their Bourgeois Opposition and in Their Classless Solution

That which oscillates moves from one side to the other. If it sits down, it does not fail to fall between two stools. A life that is not right also has its division, for the most part an impure and sterile one. The petit bourgeois, who is tossed back and forth and crushed between two classes, best expresses the consciousness and comportment of this confusion. But even bourgeois society in toto, as a disordered society, supports unmediated relations alongside one another. It has a true dead point of "on the one side" and "on the other side," and it supports this point. The double entry bookkeeping of private life and public activity is not at all this contiguity of unmediated relations, for there is a quite common species of doubling that is far removed from being an unhealthy disturbance. The authentic domestic scoundrel and tyrant in public life looks like the hypocritical man of honor, just as, though rarer, the family favorite looks like a rogue or, if he acquires power, a butcher. The incommensurable between the interior and exterior is innumerable, so it is not always necessary that hypocrisy cover it up. A businessman, who, if he could, would take the shirt off the back of each and every one of his fellow citizens, for most of these fellow citizens shines with a patriotic enthusiasm even when expenses begin to rise. Of course even with regard to such double entry book-keeping, bourgeois law has an antecedent that is quite different from hypocrisy; it has two sides that are not found in the private or public worlds without further ado. One of the most strongly marked heritages in bourgeois society is the gap between law as a justification and as a universal order of the state, between subjective and objective law. This issue becomes all the more difficult and complex, since it does not remain within bourgeois society, but is also found in the struggle against that society. The creditor is not the only one who makes a claim or demand to which he has a right; the working class has a claim to raise, and not only in the fight for wages. And this claim is raised, and it is even raised in the name of universality, although not in the name of the present universality, but a future one. What is this confusion, how does it present itself in the bourgeois concept of itself and in bourgeois economic justifications? The issue is at first muddled, but an important discovery is made visible in it.

The person who is too free says that all that pleases is permitted. Juridically speaking the same view appears, not as limited, but as belonging to the capacity to will. The *subjective* right that one has according to this conception is the right one has to something, the claim, the demand, the justification. This is the *facultas agendi*, or juridical faculty, which is not invoked without evoking that faculty which is expressible in monetary value. In fact, private law, which is first of all the law of the creditor and then the law of the owner of merchandise, is the place that forms the nature of claims. Consequently, Jhering remarks that this capacity to will does not suffice as a definition of subjective right. At first he justifies this objection by saying that persons incapable of willing, such as small children or madmen, have rights. In their case, where the will of their guardians in judicial matters represents them, they obviously still do not acquire any participation in right (as, for instance, in the case of property rights). Nevertheless, this objection against the mere capacity to will wants to say even more: Jhering does not only turn against the will because he finds it lacking in minors or those who are incompetent, but because it is without any intrinsic content. What is important is the content of the will, and Jhering defines this, in money matters, as the interest of the will. Thus we find the definition: Subjective rights are "legally protected interests." But because each of these rights must be validated, actively proposed and announced (even if it is through an intermediary), Jellinek was able to expand the definition by saying that subjective right is "that interest protected by the recognition of the human power to will." Obviously this interest can be the economic interest of the weak. But to find a creditor who is in a weak position is a quite abnormal phenomenon. The capacity to will, as the protected power of pleasure, is most easily enacted where it is already customary and freely available, namely, in the matter of money. *Quite the contrary*, as a forceful counterattack, we find the proposition: That which is convenient is permissible. Juridically it opposes the "capacity to will" to the "permission to be able," or subjective right to the objective, the *facultas agendi* to the *norma agendi*. This is what we find in the Roman definition "Publicum jus est, quod ad statum rei romanae spectat; privatum quod ad singulorum utilitatem." Objective civil law is therefore the incarnation of legal propositions and the *judicial order*, which are introduced and differentiated by the legislator. As such it permits and restricts the sphere of free subjective disposition; personality here is not "judicial power," but only "will that is taken into consideration," "guaranteed interest." Even the freedom of having things at one's disposition, and precisely this freedom, must first be permitted, and it is only then that its collective of possible contents is normalized by the state as the guardian of the judicial order. This control and norm were already implicitly contained in Jhering's definition of subjective right as protected interest, for protection presupposes a norm of what is to be protected. That is why Windsheid, in his law of the pandects, had to define law in general as essentially objective, even in the sense of having to be something impartial and universal. He defines it as "a certain content of the will, which expresses itself in a concrete case in the judicial order, which says that it could validly oppose itself to all other wills." If one is given a right, this means that his will is elevated to the level of the general will, and it is this "generality," namely, the state, that bestows value upon it. In other words, law is the will that also has an objective existence for others. In this regard the judicial norm in private law is less compelling than in public law: Among themselves individuals have a wide latitude in making contracts and in the conception of binding obligations, whereas principles of public law can be applied whether or not the parties will it. As the guardian of the judicial order (mostly against the exploited and oppressed, who have no "interest," no general understanding with this order), the state posits judicial commandments and gives them their weight. Economically this weight is felt in the force exerted upon debtors, even when this force is imposed according to standards fixed by the parties involved in a relatively free way, and this weight is felt upon the body in punishment. That the power of juridical norms is limited both in time and space (a new law immediately surpasses an older one that dealt with the same offense; laws are different in almost every land) does not alter their coercive force for the here and now, for the concrete case. It is altered just a little by the fact that not all objective law (for instance, international law) has a force behind it. But it does at least determine the manner in which power is permitted; it posits legal obligations and liabilities. In short, a title of rights is first granted the individual according to the *norma agendi* as the result of what the government demands of other individuals on his behalf. Subjective right presupposes legal subjects, and, armed with these rights, objective right even turns the subject into the object of legislation.

Both forms are profoundly entangled in one another and are, for the moment, insurmountable. The interest that is judicially protected must, as such, be recognized in order to be one. Every judicial relation is characterized by a two-sided caustic elegance: the title of rights for one names the duties of another, and obviously the complaint (*actio*). This decisive manifestation of subjective right (as opposed to the hand in the purse or even the simple lodging of a complaint) presupposes legal order—the *actio* of complaint is *juris actio*. Conversely, the juridical order adopts a right to something, a subjective right to demand. Indeed, the constraint that this order exercises disguises itself straightaway in such a title of rights: The state announces its right to taxation, to military service. It does the first as a juridical person (as exchequer), but the last it does as an imperium. If the carrying out of these demands does not require a judicial path, if there is no recourse needed to a trial, then this straightforwardness is hardly formally distinguishable from the right of exchange (*rigor combialis*), and from the immediate dischargeableness of a demand that presents itself as an exchange. Conversely, Hegel says that a subjective right is the correlate of the penal process; the criminal has his "right to punishment," and in this right he is and remains a legal subject who retains his own right by means of the punishment: In punishment "the criminal is honored as a rational being" (*Philosophy of Right*, par. 100). However that might be, there is no subjective right that does not presuppose an objective right, and no objective right without the presupposition of subjective right. Where one form of right predominates over the other, as in the armed forces or in the Jesuits, the norms are not judicial norms. That is why every dictatorship is a suspension of right; the instantaneous precision of military order replaces the circumspect application of a dictatorial norm. Even if law and right are still spoken of in such cases, they do not resemble juridical law, but a mathematical, physical law, namely, a law that knows no exceptions and tolerates no resistance. By contrast, the normal legal order presupposes persons who actively and willfully raise claims, and who are furnished with rights; this *per definitionem* in the field of private law, *per analogiam* in public law. The interrelation between subjective and objective law does not hinder the continual effort to designate one or the other as primary. The *civilist* conception (particularly in Romanist jurists) in general only admits to subjective right, and to objective right only insofar as it touches upon the process of validating the subjective rights of others. Dernburg, making a historical judgment, remarked in this regard that "rights in the subjective sense historically existed for a long time before a governmental order self-consciously constituted itself. These rights are founded in the personality of the individual and in the respect that they obtain and compel for their person and their goods. Only through abstraction must one gradually escape from the conception that subjective rights were given in the concept of a judicial order. It is therefore an ahistorical and an incorrect conception that holds that rights in the subjective sense are nothing other than emanations of right in the objective sense" (*Pandects*, 1884, I, par. 39). The element of the will, which is hidden in the "obtaining and compelling" and which undeniably characterizes subjective right (the capacity to will), is only related by Dernburg to the "person and his goods," and thus to those rich in feudal power or in capitalistic wealth. But the element of the will is not limited to that, for even the rebel, and surely the tribune, raises a claim under the form of the subjective, juridical will. One easily finds points of contact between the civilist method and classical natural law, and it is even easier to find points of contact with the Manchester principle of laissez-faire, laissez-aller, which (even without a state) has outlasted natural law and which, without any state, has blessed the capitalists by means of "self-regulation of egotistic interests." Along with this there is an occasional tendency to oppose the state in this method, which is not seen in so-called free enterprise, but which is unique to this method and is its own characteristic (though still in brotherly union). Conversely, the *publicist* conception (especially common among German jurists) does not admit any subjective rights, but only subjective duties; the sole source of right is the state, the sole content of right is the collective interest. From the perspective of the administration, police, and criminal justice this collective interest is opposed to the interests of private right; it introduces into civilist logic authoritarian-collective demands that in part are already admitted in the premises and in part are taken into account in the conclusions. Because the oldest and best-formed part of jurisprudence is private right and not public right, the publicist method has most of its difficulties in purely juridical matters; often civilist analogies are applied in order to work against individual demands or subversive class demands by means of a supposed diplomat or ceremonial state god. Accordingly, subjective right is at best a derivative right, a "life that emanates from objective, universal judicial ethicality." A neofeudal reaction mounts here in opposition to capitalistic liberalism; the ideological ties of this reaction with precapitalistic and anticapitalistic "universalism" (cf. Othmar Spann, *The True State*, 1923) can be traced back to German romanticism. There we find the seeds of the "spirit drunken with totality," the first misuse of the Aristotelian truth that the whole is more than the sum of its parts, the first dispossession of subjective rights (with respect to the French Revolution as a revolution and not only as a liberation of capitalism). Accordingly, F. J. Stahl, as the philosopher of right of reactionary romanticism and as the founder of the conservative party, defines subjective right as a "secondary principle." For the publicist method it is not autonomous, but derivative: "Right in the subjective sense is thus the ethical power that a person retains against others in and thanks to the sphere that the judicial order has accorded him" (*Philosophy of Right*, 1878, II, 1, p. 279). It comes as no surprise that even subjective rights external to private right, the subjective-public rights of the publicist method—even without conservatism—can only be assessed as being something derivative. They were forcefully detached from absolutism by the revolutionary bourgeoisie and so became a palladium of natural law. Subjective-public rights such as freedom of movement, freedom of belief, freedom of the press, freedom of association, in short the old fundamental rights of the bourgeois revolution, are certainly no longer denied *in facto* by the publicist method, but are presented thoroughly *de jure* as mere "exemptions from being dominated." Subjective-public rights fulfill the *status libertatis* in the state; this active status must therefore merely be conceded as an exception that is tolerated. The regular condition for the legal subject who is granted subjective rights is thus the *status subjectionis*; only the organs of the legal order have an active status (*status civitatis*), only the guardians of the order and of the state. Consequently, subjective-public rights are certainly still rights, and their content, in the bourgeois constitutional state, is still judicially protected; but they are rights only as reflections of an objective right. According to the publicist definition, there are mere "legal reflexes" (like the interests that the state protects without the violation of the interest giving its titleholder the right to make a claim). To the extent and degree that the state ensures the exercise of the basic rights and other political rights derived from them, it simply protects its own authorization, which it gave to this *status libertatis*. This is as far as the contiguity of subjective and objective groups of rights goes, and likewise with the supposed reduction of the one to the other. In the final analysis this means that despite their relations the person of the bourgeois society and the form of the state that has detached itself from this society do not enter into each other. The match between the *facultas agendi* and the *norma agendi* ends, at least in the bourgeois society of free competition, in a draw. But in the seriousness of praxis, objective right always achieves that victory over the private interests of the individual bourgeois legal subject, which stabilizes the collective interest of the bourgeois class (the interest that it has in maintaining its legal security).

It has already been emphasized that initially a claim could only be made by the creditor. But even the worker demands something for himself and claims the surplus he produces. So subjective right must have two sources even if they are occasionally neighbors; in this way subjective right, as claim, judicial power, demand, and the right to something, takes an ambivalent course: In brief it is that of the creditor within the society, and that of the revolutionary struggle against the existing society as a whole. This ambivalence, on the other hand, is completely lacking in objective right; it does not have such diverse representatives. Here, in the *norma agendi*, there is no path divided among claims as in the *facultas agendi*, where we find the claims of the creditor on one side and those of the rebel on the other. Despite all the other limitations of subjective right, the *sole norm* sharply separates itself from the double sense of the word *claim*. While the place of objective law is always the state of the ruling class, and though its members compete with one another, they remain fundamentally one in their collective interest. For those who are born on the wrong side of the tracks, for those dominated, an illusory universal interest is announced: a formal equality of the law in the bourgeois state, a varnish of homogeneity is put over everything. The apparatus of the modern state was prefigured in the urban communes of the late Middle Ages, in its municipal treasury, bureaucracy, and formal objectivity of the administration of public utilities; it is from this that the absolute monarchy (in an alliance with the bourgeoisie, who were rising against feudal nobility) took its state. Another powerful, though less adequately fitting model was the organization of the Roman church; and this, in turn, had reached back to the class of civil servants of imperial Rome. All of these images of the norm were intrinsically homogeneous and closed; this was a trait that belonged to them as dominate. Capitalistically, competition is only engendered in the *society*, not in the state; the state and its law are never so ambivalent, or antagonistic, as the *facultas agendi* of the creditor and the revolutionary. As the business manager of the dominant, capitalist class the state must present itself as conspicuously above the fray, as standing above the antagonistic interests of its citizens, and especially above the division between capital and labor. It must do so precisely on account of the dissolution of bourgeois society into competing individuals, and especially into antagonistic classes; in so doing the demagogic face of the dominating normative unity often changes—at one time it is the chauvinism of the fatherland, then it is called the social partnership of an economic wonder. This is what Marx is talking about when he speaks of the governmental homophony born of social dissonances: "The formation of the political state and the dissolution of civil society into independent individuals whose relations are regulated by law, as the relations between men in the corporations and guilds were regulated by privilege, are accomplished by one and the same act" (*On the Jewish Question*, *MEGA*, I, 1, p. 598). And as the lictors demonstrated so unequivocally very long ago when they worked with the whip and the ax, in order to have the power to be able to formidably oppose the original domain of classical natural law, that is, subjective-public right, the homogeneity of objective-public right must contain the privilege of punishment up to punishment by death. From the perspective of natural law, the great jurist of the Enlightenment, Beccaria (*Dei delitti e delle pene*, 1764), denied the state the right to issue the death penalty because, since no person had a right over his own life, he could not delegate this right to society by means of the social contract. Precisely at this point the state keeps watch over itself as an undivided power; the number of death penalties, the practice of lengthy imprisonment, and the elimination of cassation all function as a gauge of the unitary omnipotence of the state. When subjective-public right established its duality in the pathos of the claim, then public-objective right establishes its power, which is also called majesty, in consonance in matters of punishment, especially in the death penalty (even beyond that which, going beyond the *jus talionis*, far surpasses the offense). The more state there is, the more there is the prison, the robe, the ax; the more visible the thoroughgoing unity of power of the objective right, which exists for itself. And now to return this monolithic, authoritarian normative right to the ambivalence of the subjective, judicial *claim*: It is initially formed for the creditor, and adopted in a quite different way by the exploited and oppressed, the humiliated and degraded. It is precisely this that appears in its incomparable second sense as the subjective catchword of the revolutionary struggle and actively as the subjective factor of this struggle. Such is the diversity that flows from the two sources of subjective right; it is clearly quite different from the homogeneous power source that characterizes objective right. It has as its sources the private right of Rome and from the revolutionary economy the quality of claims.

Initially, and for quite some time, judicial claims were tied to possession and property: possession as factual power, and property as judicial dominance over something both presuppose that one has invested one's will in that thing. In order to be able to so invest one's will, in order that one be regarded as the possessor of rights in the subjective sense and not as a slave without rights, one must have the potential to be able to appropriate goods. *Property* is the basis of the juridical person; in capitalist society, where the concept of property is most clearly formed, the person appears fully as the possessor of merchandise. Without the support of private interest and its economy there would not be any juridical subjects here; they are posited and multiplied by the unlimited transformation of goods into exchange values. "In order to relate these things," Marx said in *Capital*, I (Dietz, 1947, p. 80), "in order to relate these things to each other as commodities, the guardians of commodities must relate to each other as persons whose will is housed in those things"; this is therefore the immediate function and core of the juridical person. The *private economic freedom* of this person was described by the Romanist Puchta in the following strong words: "Man is the subject of rights because every possibility of determining himself is accorded him, because he has a will" (*Institutions*, 1843–1847, I, p. 5); in agreement with Feuerbach, he even concludes "that the true content of laws is formed by rights" (and not duties). Grotius is not the last in whom this species of subjective right had a progressive effect: The liberation of individual interests and the protection of life and property were essential contents of the purpose of natural law; private right was a presupposition for both public law and international law. But meanwhile the juridical person was so transformed as to be unrecognizable, so much so that it was difficult to take this person any longer as a juridical synonym for human dignity and self-determination. Possession, property, and position in the relations of exchange are not restricted to individuals, for civil law recognizes not only *individual personalities but also so-called personalities of federations*. Even corporations, institutions, and foundations are juridical persons; they are a juridical subject distinct from the sum of persons associated in it, who survive it as legal subjects—quite far from the highest happiness of the children of the earth and autonomous, human personality. Corporations certainly cannot marry, but they can merge; day-care centers certainly cannot falsify a document, but they can exercise judicial power and pass judicial resolutions; municipalities, lacking a soul, certainly cannot practice fraud ("quomodo municipia dolo facere possunt," Ulpian already asked), but they do have enough of a soul to manifest a judicial will. Indeed, even the state has attributed a juridical person to itself, and not only as a treasury or as a subject of international law, but as a corporate power, which even exists spatially as a corporation, that is, as the supreme corporation of the region. In this way even the capitalistic state becomes a juridical person, as the advisory committee for the business of all other capitalistic species of federated personalities and especially as the legal subject of incipient late capitalism with its increasingly anonymous style. In general "juridical person" in this sense implies—in the sense given by the class society—nothing more than a *certification of the aptitude of people or corporations to participate in commercial juridical relations*. Consequently even the power of self-determination, which is accorded to the legal subject, has its limits in the stronger economic power and especially in the stronger political power. This is most evident in the *subjective-public rights* that the bourgeoisie revolutionary conquered from the vantage point of their economic position: Paschukanis appropriately compared the powerful subjective right of a creditor to recover the amount he is owed, with the questionable and fragile right of the voter, or with the equally fragile right of the parliament mandated by such voters to be able to appropriate a budget. Even during the apogee of bourgeois democracy these last rights were made of a significantly less solid material than were the claims of the law of liens; the more time passed, the more the government believed that the task of representing the people included the task (not exactly

characteristic of subjective right) of making the people "aware that it
is being well governed." That is the Hegelian, at that time restorative,
but later fascistic and totalitarian, way of transforming participation
in the government (in the best case) into instruction by means of
propaganda. From this it becomes evident that the subjective juridical
person is increasingly swallowed up by federated personalities and
with this arises the monopolistic deprivation of the subjective-public
and political-legal claims of the smaller property owners, producers,
and proprietors. Indeed, prior to this loss of power—and similarly
mutatis mutandis occasionally after it—the effectively thin "participation
in government," even in countries with parliaments, possession and
property in themselves, and therefore private economic freedom, were
not guaranteed. This is what led Rousseau to announce a democratic
mistrust of a planned parliamentarianism, especially in large countries,
"where only on election day voters are able to exercise the illusion
of participation, and after election day are not even able to partake
even of such an illusion." Furthermore, the claim of the legal subject
is so far from ending with its *first source*, that is, the right of inheritance
including the power to freely dispose of possessions and goods, that
it begins at this point as an *active contradiction*, and ultimately as a
rebellion. The *second origin* of the *facultas agendi* enters here in a thoroughly decisive way, as an origin conforming more than ever before
to the hegemony in men (according to a Stoic expression) that lets
men walk with their heads held high. Every upheaval within previously
existing class societies that has had the goal of making way for a new
ruling class has had as its content simple changes in property relations;
to this extent the factor of private right was not only related to but
also intertwined with the humanistic factor. On the other hand, the
upheaval that leads ultimately to a classless society is to be found
opened up on another page; in other words, this upheaval inscribed
initially in an economic class, indeed even in part in a private economy
that redistributes possessions and property, is indistinguishable from
the protestations of the *humanum* and, in the long run, is intertwined
with it. Previously human pride had animated itself in that which was
subject to it, and often even that which exceeded it; neither the established principle "my house, my castle," which corresponds to the
older form of property, nor the principle of the start, "a free field
belongs to the most efficient," which corresponds to the Manchesterian
form of property, neither principle conceals the second source of

subjective right or makes its material superfluous. In the origin of property in subjective right one finds a species of the cunning of reason, one that is clearly limited to this. In his *Ludwig Feuerbach* Engels cites approvingly the Heglian remark that one believes that one says a great deal when one claims that man is good, but historically it means much more when one recognizes that man is evil, since nothing happens without passion and only the violently active individual pulls the chestnuts out of the fire for the world spirit. Thus, property, as the origin (as the power of the possessive will) of subjective right, is connected with this second origin, whose proper conceptual definition wants to contain, as classical natural law said not only in an idealistic way, the good sense of Hermann and the spirit of Brutus. Whereas the subjective, judicial sources do not endure for long politically outside the sphere of private property and are completely exhausted in political fascism, the source of the Brutus sphere offers up even richer material in fascist times: the material of the revolution (without economism). It offers up *the claim of subjective-public rights in their totality*, and it thus provides the revolution in the revolution or in that radicalism which goes to the roots, namely, to the abused, protesting person. As the slogan of the revolutionary struggle, this second origin of subjective right no longer can be hung up with the concept of private property, that basic concept of all previous economy. But although it lies outside the class economy, the origin (human dignity) is not *therefore outside the economy understood in a Marxist sense.* Marx himself continually returns (and not only in his early writings) to this second origin: to the fundamental right not to be treated as scum. Thus we find the following passage in *The Holy Family* (1845): "The possessing class and the proletarian class represent one and the same human self-alienation. But the former feels so satisfied and affirmed in this self-alienation, experiences the alienation as a sign of its own power, and possesses it in the appearance of a human experience. The latter, however, feels destroyed in this alienation, seeing in it its own impotence and the reality of an inhuman existence. To use Hegel's expression, this class is, within depravity, an indignation against this depravity, an indignation necessarily aroused in this class by the contradiction between its human nature and its life situation, which is a blatant, outright, all-embracing denial of that very nature." The revolution against this self-alienation is here the guiding element of the revolution of the strongest and highest economic force of production: that of the laboring man. It is thus really what is called humanistic, the most profound (with seriousness and not a concealing profundity) humanism. Human health, beauty, dignity: All of these contents of the goal of subjective revolutionary right are themselves therefore categories not only of economy but of the just economy. Thus it is only after having defined the human creator of value that Marx sounds the alarm against tyranny: "In agriculture as in industry the capitalistic transformation of the process of production simultaneously appears as the martyrology of producers, the means of labor as the means of subjugation, of exploitation, and of the impoverishment of workers, and the social combination of the processes of labor as organized oppression of the liveliness, freedom, and autonomy of the individual. . . . Capitalistic production only develops the technique and combination of the social processes of production to the extent that it simultaneously undermines the sources of all wealth: the earth and the worker" (*Capital*, I, pp. 531ff.). Even if the manufacture and development of bones for the factory worker has been alleviated, it has not become unrecognizable and, in any case, there never was such a development for the owners of the factories, but, as before, it is a means of extracting surplus value from another's work, from the always narrow margin of their subjective rights. Subjective-public rights, in their real consequence and plenitude, contain the abolition of all exploitation, that is, of the private property of the means of production, which makes exploitation possible and first made subjective rights known according to their first origin. In a classless society without money markets there are no owners of merchandise, but there are producers of goods who are legal subjects (juridical persons), and not least among their rights is the right not to be compelled to be a producer of goods. Thus the *ultimate subjective right* would be the license *to produce according to one's capabilities, to consume according to one's needs*; this license is guaranteed by means of the *ultimate norm of subjective right: solidarity*. It is only this solidarity— insofar as it thrived socialistically—that could bring to a happy conclusion the requisite liberal predominance of subjective rights (and the individual moral conscience) over objective rights (and their public, their social morality). The radical dualism of the sphere of rights would disappear in a society that was not only nonantagonistic in its interests but would have just as little need of governmental powers and of provisos against the state reserved for individuals, which are especially necessary in a police state. Power alone is not adequate to keep people from being dependent. It takes much time before wages, the state, and classes are surpassed. Rome was not built in a day, anti-Rome or no-longer-Rome is hardly to be expected in less than one or two generations. For the philosophy of right subjective-public rights and objective norms are the two poles. In the socialist society the distance between them diminishes, but it can be emphasized once again when something is lacking. The subjective factor posits a spontaneity which, though frequently highly reasoned, is not oriented beyond itself, whereas the objective all-too objective, side reveals an extreme centralization that is uncontrolled democratically. The extreme form of this case was ultimately able to reproduce the effects of Tiberius, and this, with a wantonness that is not hereditary, in socialism. According to Marx, social revolution that seizes the day uses the means of power of the previous state in order to help give birth to the new society with which the old society is already pregnant. From this perspective the experiences of the Paris Commune are to be seen together, on an entirely new plane, with the traditions that provided classical natural law and tended toward a humanistically limited state. It is interesting to note how, as a consequence, the *objective juridical norm itself* was judged in the course of the revolution. In general, jurisprudence did not have very good press during the first years of the Soviet Union; it seemed as if it were being eliminated as fast as possible. Reissner regarded right as nothing other than a "compromise between the classes," so that he even proposed the following formula: "Right is the opium of the people." The socialist development seemed to be moving rapidly, and did not seem to be in need of any juridical regulation; in fact, it even seemed to be incapable of such regulation, since, as bourgeois, such regulation had been eliminated. Paschukanis, who for a long while was the most respected Soviet jurist until he was written off as a traitor by Vyshinsky, initially did not conceive of judicial norms as a bourgeois inheritance and, in the NEP epoch with the retention of private economy, regarded such norms as still necessary even if already surpassed. It was not until 1934, after the liquidation of the sector of private capitalism, that Paschukanis recognized that one had entered into a zone where new judicial norms could be established, but only to the extent that there was still a society consisting of the exchange of goods; that is, right was a fortiori condemned to being demolished. It is no longer necessary to generalize these purely technical concepts, which, for the most part, belong to the infrastructure:

Therefore "there is no universal doctrine of right in general or as a repository with changing contents; but it once did exist." It does not survive the possessors of merchandise; consequently there is not proletarian right, there should no longer be any socialist right just as "the decline of the categories of value, capital, profit, and so on, during the transition period to socialism should imply the resurrection of new, proletarian categories of value, capital, income, and so forth" (Paschukanis, *The Universal Doctrine of Right and Marxism*, German ed. 1929, pp. 33ff.). All of this obviously depends upon a rather rapid decline of the state "with the unfolding of socialism"; according to this view, objective juridical norms (and of course subjective right as simple norms "of the market upon which individual, independent products encounter each other") are still technically valid and necessary for the transitory bourgeois residues, but are alien to socialism. Nevertheless, long before the hardening of the apparatus of the state, Lenin had already opposed the underestimation of the "narrow horizon of bourgeois right." Lenin's program prolonged the life of right and of the state, of course as vestiges, even in the first stages of communism, up to the time when the market is replaced by an organized coherence, because even then a form of exchange of equivalents persists—but it is no longer between producers themselves, but between them and society. To the extent that each producer receives in return precisely what he gives to society, there does persist the same principle as is found in the exchange of equivalent merchandise, although in a mitigated form, which is essentially civil law. Therefore, "not only bourgeois right but even the bourgeois state persists for a while under communism—but without the bourgeoisie" (Lenin, *The State and Revolution, Selected Works*, Moscow, 1947, II, p. 234). To this extent, once Paschukanis was done away with, Vyshinsky, in speaking of the decline of right and the state, could refer to Lenin's lectures on this decline. But he went far beyond this; far from being an eager prognosticator of the gradual disappearance of norms of the state, he was rather a formulator of omnipotence, which after 1936, under Stalin, was increasingly personified. In opposition to Paschukanis and his school it was emphasized that in the period of transition to the socialist state right was not only able to be created new but the extent of its power could even expand beyond what it had been. But it was Vyshinsky in particular who gave the following definition of right as a whole (administratively including subjective-public rights) in his ground-breaking lecture "The Principal Tasks of the Science of Soviet Socialist Right" (1938): "Right is the ensemble of the rules of behavior, which expresses the will of the ruling class and is fixed in a legislative way just as the customs and rules of communal life that are sanctioned by the governmental powers. The application of these rules is sanctioned by means of the coercive power of the state for the purpose of the security, stabilization, and development of social relations and conditions that are satisfying and advantageous to the ruling class" (cf. *Soviet Contributions to the Theory of the State and Right*, Berlin, 1953, p. 76). Although this formula is related to socialist right, it also concerns any sort of humanistic event insofar as it speaks in a truly universal way of the ruling class and the norms that it imposes without the least trace of the distinction of the proletarian class from previous classes. That is why in 1948 a critic named Stalgewitsch said of this formula first that it was exclusively normative and second that it constituted a despotism without content thanks to which even legal norms "become means in the service of a juridical formalism." One could add to this the patent juridical pragmatism, far removed from all genuine consciousness of right and truly antinatural law: "All consciousness of right is a portion of political consciousness" and nothing else. Vyshinsky does not want to mechanically reduce rights to politics; he does want to view the *individual* forms of right as distinct from the individual forms of politics. In this way he envisages, in a surprising way, even individual forms of subjective-public rights, but solely on the level of private economy and distinct from political forms (almost as exceptions to it). Such an individual form of right would be occupied with the objective safeguard "of personal rights, property rights, family and inheritance rights, as well as their corresponding interest" ("The Principal Tasks," p. 71). But as is the consequence of such predominance of the *norma agendi* from above, not only civil law, the right to a trial, but also the right to work is completely limited and dominated by the objective sphere of right. Yet for Vyshinsky ultimately only public law remains even more formidable than before: "In this way all branches of law can be fundamentally pulled into the circle of public law, if by this one understands the science of all aspects of the development and activity of the state that appear in these judicial forms" ("The Principal Tasks," pp. 82ff.). Obviously Lenin's prognosis of the gradual decline of the state, which was formulated earlier by Engels, is not being discussed here. This is rejected in the name of persistent internal (not only external) threat to the Soviet Union by foreign saboteurs; only in an epoch of global socialism would the Stalinist animation (if one can even use this word) be rendered functionless. Thus this conception itself remains after Vyshinsky's time, though it is put at the forefront less often. In more recent writings on jurisprudence the emphasis is no longer placed upon the repressive role of the state, but upon its indicative and guiding function. Thus, Kerimov, a recent theorist of public right, says "that the path to the withering of the socialist state consists on the one hand in the direct reduction of the repressive function of the state, but on the other hand in the development of economic and *cultural* (educative) functions of the state" (Kerimov, *Political Science and Revisionism*, Berlin, 1959, p. 145). The *norma agendi* is thereby displaced, but simultaneously artificially expanded; Schiller's poem on Pegasus in a harness is positively conceived. But the real law, with which Marxism starts its career and which cannot be overlooked, is abandoned, so that even Vyshinsky must announce in 1938: "We Soviet theorists of international law must assume the responsible and honorable role of propagandists of the real international law that secures freedom between peoples and that guarantees the unity of all who step forth in the name of democracy, progress, and real humanistic culture of men and fight against fascists, brigands, and warmongers" ("The Principal Tasks," p. 88). It is especially in imperialist war that the state arrives at its authentic form, not as an exception or state of emergency, but as rule; but the *jus pacis* knew no governmental omnipotence, and the same is true here in Vyshinsky. In fascism, omnipotence as a religion was not able to be eliminated. Yet it is alien to the very essence of socialism on account of a finality that perpetually impedes but cannot be eliminated, and that—constantly claimed—is called the upright carriage on a habitable earth, one without the tyranny of the factory, without the factory of tyranny.

Providing for this is not a matter of yielding, nor does it come to pass with rigidity. A conducting wire is to be found in the true *norma agendi* itself; one cannot avoid the passages in Engels that speak of it. These well-known phrases in Engels undisguisedly say: "The first act wherein the state really steps forward as representative of the whole society—the seizing of the means of production in the name of society—is simultaneously its final act as a state. . . . In place of the government of persons there enters the administration of things and the direction of the processes of production" (*Anti-Dühring*, Berlin, 1953, pp. 347ff.). This phrase incontestably retains its value as a program in Bebel: "With the disappearance of the state there disappears its representatives, ministers, parliament, standing army, police and gendarmes, courts, defense and prosecuting attorneys, jailers, tax and customs offices, in a word, the entire political apparatus. Tens of thousands of laws, decrees, and ordinances are tossed in the wastebasket, all fundaments of the contemporary 'order' become myth" (*Women and Socialism*, Stuttgart, 1922, p. 508). As we saw, Lenin was calmer to the extent that he permitted the bourgeois state to continue to some degree, without the bourgeoisie, in the first phase of communism. He did, however, continually subtract from it, and this process already began in the *transition* (still not at all communistic, and not yet properly socialistic) from capitalism to socialism: "A special apparatus, a special machine of oppression, a 'state,' is *still* necessary, but it is already a transitional state and no longer a state in the proper sense, because the repression of the minority of exploiters by the majority of the wage slaves *of yesterday* is such a relatively light, simple, and natural matter that it will cost much less blood than the oppression of the insurrections of slaves, serfs, and wage laborers, so that in the end it costs humanity much less" (*The State and Revolution*, p. 227). Of course it should be remembered that Engels and Lenin do not speak of the *abolition* of the state, but of its *withering away*; both from the perspective of time and content the state, according to the anarchistic prescription, is not first to be eliminated, but to be conquered in order to make it increasingly superfluous by means of an economy socialistically directed. This thesis of the perpetual withering of the state was repealed in Vyshinsky's time, and the *justification* for this repeal itself was not counted as having withered away: "Soviet Marxism has arrived at the conclusion that the Engels formula presupposes the victory of socialism in all countries or at least in the majority of countries, and cannot be applied when socialism has been victorious in one country while capitalism dominates in all other countries" (Kerimov, *Political Science and Revisionism*, p. 142). Despite this, Engels's formula—one of the rare (and this is quite interesting) ones that provoked official revision—is so contained at the culminating point of his thought that it is as difficult to hide as a mountain peak in the valley where it sits as a reminder of the goal. "The withering away of the state"—in this there resides not only good conscience for the omnipotence of the state, that is, for the old authentically dominating *norma agendi*. Freedom is freedom from being dominated by other men, ultimately through relations that objectively make this being dominated possible. But socialism, insofar as it is a path taken, already intends upon its path the elimination of precisely these relations. It intends the public order of a *norma agendi* only as the *unreified order of a freedom that has become publicly possible as the* facultas agendi *of all*. That is the limit concept of the classless solution of all previous opposition between these two poles; it is an ideal limit to this opposition, which so often and so far as possible pro rata wants to posit its own realization in freedom, and it is formulated to this end. Vyshinsky's formulation certainly does not move entirely in this direction, but brushes up against a species of fetishized constitutional law and, almost against its wishes, mitigates it. If Anselm Feuerbach's phrase held good in its extreme case, namely, that morals is the science of duties, while law is the science of rights, then fetishistic constitutional law would itself be the supreme form of this morality, because it contains nothing more than duties. Contrarily, it can in fact be established that socialistic legal norms present themselves as codified solidarity pro rata for the production of an economic-political condition wherein, as Lenin said, every cook can rule the state and the state itself would no longer require any codification. As remarked, it is a limit concept, but a concrete one with the state as the means to the process of rendering itself superfluous; objective order is the protector of human dignity, so that it no longer has need of protection. Even that which is regarded as under the empire of freedom does not, according to its sense, have the empire as its content, but freedom, the independence of everyone, which has become possible and whose space represents an empire. It has nothing in common with that which relates to the state, and in this regard one might evoke memories of the otherwise fictive doctrine of the social contract: that there never was a state that was justly intended for its own sake. According to a remarkable phrase of Lenin's, there can be no free state (for where there is freedom there is no state, and where there is a state there is no freedom); likewise a "true state" (true in the sense of value and entelechy) is a contradiction in terms. The true objective figures in this domain are the unities of language, of nations, of cultural and traditional relations, and above all—the ultimate association of all associations, embodied in the state up to the church—of the preparatory relations of the "what for" and "where to." The figure that embraces all of these, which was called the empire of freedom, a figure of an order that has become true and concrete, with freedom as the sole "where to" and content of this order, would be the first polis because it is without *politeia*.

22

Right and Morality in Their Separation (Morality Instead of Natural Law), Classified According to Their Value

Many distant things are still close to one another for what is not yet grown up. The child does not choose his friends by looking at them closely; for him almost everyone of the same age will do just fine. In the primitive sensibility the fur and the oven are related because one, like the other, warms; the weapon and the tool, clothing and jewelry, the city as marketplace and fortress, are still only slightly removed from each other. It is well known that for a long time rules of behavior, such as ethics and law, were almost one. Ethical habits indicated in an unwritten way that which the judge had to discover; he was the most respected guardian of tradition. Then law and ethical customs separated, not least of all through an extraordinary juridical objectification. True, assessors and juries did reintroduce an ethical laity into the exercise of law, but to the degree that a class of professional jurists developed, and with it the consequent complication of relations of conflict; law became its own special domain. Its propositions are related in a different way from those of ethical life and its procedures, which in every case decomposed into assertion, dispute, and counterdispute, and it is distinct from procedures of the refined moralistic sense and especially from that of immediate moralistic judgment. The norms of this law increasingly become those of the technique of business with merely a side glance at morality. Even without this distancing, the connection between law and morality in the modern age would either be denied or a new bridge would have to be built between them. In any event, the judge no longer represents the most virtuous man in the community.

But one must guard against drawing unjust conclusions from this. Occasionally a voice arises out of the private depths of the lawyer, and even of the judge, that interrupts the monotony of the operation. Those who still raise ethical objections through the thousands of holes in the law never place the security of this operation above all else.

Yet above all it is apparent, at least in earlier times, that in the division of labor between law and morality, law was freed from pathos and in this way liberated from morals, though it was not always on that account rendered immoral; one could occasionally say that quite the contrary was true. *In the first place*, this made everything the policeman had to do marvelously easy. He only directs traffic, writes tickets for cars that move too fast, prevents (when he can) things from being stolen, and all is done in the same sober manner. Insofar as all these activities are so soberly useful, the purely ethical idle talk that surrounds law disappears. *In the second place*, the citizen of the state exhaled to the same degree that the magistrate lessened his indignation. That means, to the degree that authority loses the possibility of sticking its nose in pots and in hearts, and of ethically meddling in each and every thing. The old lawbooks blush when they deal with prostitutes, they foam with rage to have to define *mutiny*, they overflow with decency eager for pursuit, a decency that simultaneously unites revenge and moral drumbeating. But one remembers: The distinction of the *justum* and the *honestum*, as it developed in Cicero, Thomasius, Kant, and Fichte, liberated subjective rights. The right over one's body and the private life that is connected with it already prospered only in a conception of law that was moral-free, that was externally held, regarded as practical, technical, and without any moral pretensions. In other words, if juridical rules are not related to private opinion, but only to an action that can harm those nearby, then there is obviously much more permissible juridically than morally; for example, suicide and even polygamy (so long as the civil needs of the child are observed) cannot be forbidden. The space that objective right leaves free is larger than that left open by morality; the space of juridical duties is consequently smaller than that of moral duties. It is in this difference that subjective rights show themselves to be rights of freedom with far fewer obligations inscribed in them than in morality. These are the elements of natural law and they have preserved precisely that portion of freedom which, for the sake of external security, must not be abandoned. At this point another factor enters, as Thomasius demonstrated: Subjective rights employ the separation not only of law and morals but also of morals from law. Subjective right uses the extreme noncompulsory character of moral commandments in order to disguise them as rights; for example, though freedom of conscience cannot be imposed from the outside, when it steps forward and makes its demands it is also not able to be forbidden. From its duty aspect (the duty of conscience) it belongs to morals as the domain of higher demands and autonomous norms; from its unimpossible aspect the freedom of conscience belongs to subjective right and so becomes the model for human rights. Everywhere else it alleviated the law that had been separated as such by not placing so much "ought" against it and surely not so much that was lofty and solemn. Even where talk is of the duty of right, it appears, in opposition to moral duty, not as an inner voice, but as a self-evident or unavoidable public "ought," even if it takes on the solemn airs of the voice of a noble breast or the light of a heart; the more the separation removes from positive right, even that which is well maintained, the more it mildews. In this case, it does not so much liberate subjective right as it removes a certainty from objective right that, even if it were genuine, does not belong here. This is at the root of Kant's falsely maligned definition of marriage as "the union of two persons of different sexes for reciprocal possession into perpetuity of their sexual attributes" (*Doctrine of Law*, par. 24); a juridical relation of the world of goods that have come to be is expressed here in the most extreme and exact moral-free manner. *In the third place*, the separation of legal and moral forms of commandments made the first sort into something external, but also into something that could be instituted only externally. From the purely external character of the juridical order it was not only possible to deduce the great laxity of law (compared to positive, moral zeal) as the mere external imperative not to violate the paragraphs of the law, but also inversely one could deduce its great rigor. Freedom, for example, is, from a juridical point of view, limited purely administratively, therefore heteronomously; but from a moral point of view, it is limited by the will of the subject, and therefore autonomously — at least according to the Kantian interpretation. Consequently, law is a necessity, a must, morals solely an "ought"; law is the authoritarian, alien determination of the will (for the purpose of the coexistence of many wills), morals are autonomous self-determination (and they respect every person as an end, not as a means). Since the separation of bourgeois society from the ideal of the ethicality of the *citoyen*, the disjunction of legality and morality is not the only fundamental ideological trait of the bourgeois condition, but also, on account of the *homo homini lupus* in the bourgeois society of profit, legality is taken as a constraint pure and simple; it is the whip of the animal trainer, not the voice of conscience. To this extent, law—and here this means objective law—becomes a significantly more rigorous bondage than morals; this is true even if the domain in which this strict bondage holds true remains narrower than the domain of morality. Once again the differences between subjective and objective law become evident: Objective law, above all in the gloomy darkness of penal justice, is and remains heteronomous. Whereas morals, even those that speak in the language of objective commandments, can appear to be autonomous in Kant, at least in the way that they internally reproduce inescapable duty and obligation as something apparently self-inflicted. Or, as Schiller explained this path from the authoritarian "must" to the autonomous "ought" (from above to within): "Accept the divinity in your will, and step down from its universal throne." Still, there are—and this shows another difference between law and morals that does not unconditionally favor the latter even if it is supposedly the most inspired—*there are also open, heteronomous morals*, indeed they are the majority and correspond to the domination by the class that reproduces them without any equivocation; these moral systems are equally systems of necessity, of "musts," more systems of "musts" than of "oughts." To this extent these systems are hardly any less imperious, and given from above, than the objective judicial order, and they are certainly significantly more rigid than the subjective rights of freedom. In this way, therefore, there is far more *autonomy* in subjective right than in the majority of moral doctrines, and even more in the expansion of revolutionary freedom, in natural law, to *the right to something*, to the condition of no longer being oppressed. Much oppression is already introduced in the moral pressure that is adopted internally and so profoundly castrates, and that reprimands even more profoundly than objective law, which is always external. Indeed, one could even say quite rightly that even where law as penal law seizes and breaks a thousand times more energetically than the most authoritarian morals, the distinction between law and ethicality has nevertheless interrupted the pathos of the theory of retaliation. In the extreme case there is, even in penal justice, more empty legal space than there is empty space in the norms maintained by morals seen to be the freest morals, and especially in moralistic megalomania.

When an image that is common is torn, the parts do not immediately separate. That which has belonged together for such a long time continues to be overlooked after it has been divided, and whenever possible it tries to find in a concept a proximity that is no longer to be found in reality. Thus, attempts were continually made to build conceptual bridges between law and morals precisely because of the good old times. Through this, an assistance was even recovered that had been removed from the author of the merely external judgment of an act. For in most instances the psychological and moral distinction between actions with and without premeditation (*dolus*) favors the author of an act (the perpetrator). The *dolus* and its extension, which is morally graduated (up to the point of the recognition of the conscientious offender), thoroughly influenced judgment in matters of penal law. All modern law takes into consideration whether or not the violation of a norm protected by penal laws happens because of negligence or premeditation, whether or not the author of the act was completely, partially, or not at all accountable for his deed. Primitive law was barbarous precisely because it lacked the category of *dolus*. But in modern times it is a sign of unadulterated misanthropy to leave the author of the act out of consideration and to simply consider the act alone. Thus, quite logically, Schopenhauer says, "In general the proper standards for penalties laid down by the law are given by the harm that is to be prevented; it is not given by the immorality of the deed that is forbidden. Thus the law can, with justice, hand down a prison sentence to one who lets a flowerpot fall from the window, and one who smokes tobacco in the forest during the summer can be sentenced to the pillory, though the same deed is permitted in the winter" (*Works*, Grisebach, II, p. 704). The separation of law and morals leads to such absurd penalties and to the rationalizations that legitimate them. Conversely, something very surprising becomes evident: Interests close to the heart, up to and including the conspiracy of intentions, which in other respects are sure signs of a police state, are, in this domain, enormous means of defense for the author of the act. Snooping around for this purpose, such sounding-out that gets under the skin, is philanthropic here; the moral analysis of motives is, accordingly, judicial kindness. But all *other* moralizations of law were and are less irreproachable; they reveal themselves as *corresponding with* the positive law of previous moral doctrines with the sole purpose of "refining the law." And this, as we have seen, implies the *elimination* of natural law and a *substitution* of respectable and edifying morals for it; the dominant *jus* should be criticized less, and even with respect to its justification, since it is noble and morally ennobled. To this end, parallels with the history of ethics are supplied, most of which surface only subsequently, in the observations of the nineteenth century. So the sense of justice and a so-called chivalrous sense, which worked by an inner inclination, were brought together. Or erudite law was reclaimed by the ethical understanding because even this understanding judged according to reasons and acted according to principles. A liaison was established between sentiment and reflection, and after this happened they took place both juridically and morally, and they have their advocates in both domains—in the first it is among those more liberal, in the second it is more among the established functionaries. Thus the parallel is drawn: Reflection according to principles can be either a *formal* or a *material* consideration; that is, the law and the ethical equally can be determined either according to an abstract formula or according to a normative content from which it is governed. The *formal* consideration suffices when a proposition of action does not contain any internal contradiction, that is, when it can be proven to be correct; then it can be applied in every case. Nobody, without an inner contradiction against the concept of property and of deposit, can will that theft and embezzlement become universal phenomena. When the law is dealt with exclusively in formulas, then it is easy to raise it to this moral formulism; furthermore, in both cases construction encourages itself with the courage of a moral finesse, the courage of the virtue of being for the law. Hermann Cohen gives the most vivid example of this: Jurisprudence is the "mathematics of ethics," ethics the "idea of jurisprudence." A logic of the will is asserted, a will that is first defined as the pure will, which produces the universally valid will of the community, and this moral manner of positing its object happens by means of the juridical method, by means of the a priori logic of judicial relations. Just as the mathematical natural sciences produce objective experience from the confusion of sensuous givennesses, so too does the law produce the rational image, which is guided by ideas, from that collection of men which is dominated by instincts and affects; in both cases, sensuous impressions, like affects, are not heard, but interrogated. More purely this means that the universally valid will does not realize man as an egoistic being or as a being that is instinctively social, but as a juridical person (among which, or course, corporations are not counted). The legal subject that develops in this way is supposed to be the same as the moral person, and respect for the moral person in each and every man is the guideline of ethical action, the idea of the ethical and social state. This is the theory that, under the flag of the morality of the state, once again tears down the entire separation between *justum* and *honestum*—*Justinianus dat honores, solum Justinianus.* Yet, if law is primarily dealt with, not according to formulas, but according to *normative contents*, then it takes *a material ethics of goods and values* as its headquarters. For formal law, like formal ethicality, an inner homogeneity and absence of logical contradiction are already at work as the criteria of what is right; "realism," on the other hand, measures according to the objective value of the goods that it seeks and the intensity with which they are sought. This is what Max Scheler did when he produced a material a priori of the will in contrast to Cohen's formal a priori, but, once again, he legitimated the law in its currently existing form by what he called a material ethic of values. For the effort of striving and for that which this effort values, a long scale of goods and goals, with a scale of preferences corresponding to them, was laid out. In this arrangement either war was declared in favor of one group of goods (personal images of value) over another group, for instance against the individual in favor of the society (or vice versa), or a harmonious hierarchy of goods and goals was instituted, a climax of individuals, family, people, humanity. It begins with the civilized person, moves to the self-sufficient realm of culture up to what is a predominately theological, crowning *summum bonum*. Even this material justification of the ethical has attached itself to positive law, and in its own way it has withdrawn the glitter from it. For on the detour through the climax, every judicial norm, from the paragraphs on abortion up to the military penal code, can be subordinated to an image of the ethical goal, to a veritable moral cathedral constructed out of norms. Ultimately the opposition between subjective *law* and objective *legal order* is parallel to that between *autonomous and heteronomous morals.* Wherever that possession and nothing else is expressed, subjective law ties itself to the man who wants to determine himself. He adopts the mask of the autonomous man from the ethical perspective so that no one else might try to interfere with his own private economy. To the extent that the juridical subject was a businessman he gladly attached himself to the inner light that is only answerable to his own conscience. Conversely, the objective legal order improved itself through a heteronomous authority, which prescribes, from outside or above, when conscience has to strike. The common element uniting legal norm and ethical norm, between coercion and a commandment imposed, is here subjugation, legislation by something alien. To be sure, coercion does not seem to be in the forefront of every objective law; international law is forced to get along without it, and when it does one tries to define it away as "the binding power of universal conviction," that is, one tries to conceal it. According to this general conviction, the law, in order to be factically valid and executable, only needs to be recognized by this general conviction, and does not have need to be imposed by force, irrespective of the circumstance that the legal order is opposed to the oppressed, who do not contribute to "the binding power of universal conviction," and that it is imposed upon them in a particularly concrete way. If, therefore, coercion is not always in the foreground, then as a result of the content of the dominant juridical class it is always in the background: Authority carries the sword, and the realization of its judgments, from the warrant to the scaffold, is always simultaneously called execution, that is, coercive execution. This has the most elective affinity with heteronomous morals as that given to the subject from outside or from above as the legislation of ethicality. Judicially and ethically the norm here is what the state, church, and God-given commandments demand; the jurist, who interprets "the will of the legislator," works with the same mythology as the moral theologian who finds the will of God exemplified in the Ten Commandments, in the sacrament of marriage, in the imposition of authority. In this connection it was already remarked that an absolute heteronomy of the legal order (ascending to absolute tyranny) does not leave any legal order left at all; even in reactionary cases it must be a heteronomy with standards. Otherwise juridical law is transformed into a mathematical, physical law of nature, that is, into a law that so definitely knows no exceptions that command, an order, a "must," or even an "ought" is no longer possible or necessary. This is so regardless of that which authoritarian regimes recently gladly appealed to as the so-called iron laws of nature, as if the whip came from them, and consequently was not only legitimated by these laws but also showed that they could not be abolished. But water has no compulsion (no "must") to flow downward, and explosive gas has no compulsion to explode when it meets the flame, it simply explodes; mass does not obey the law of gravity, rather this is the form of its motion, the categories of motion of a thoroughly immanent type; whereas the law of jurisprudence and morality, which is still heteronomous, is obliged to admit and leave relatively alone subjects of freedom, so that there is a margin and a tension in relation to the heteronomy and in relation to the authoritarian character that constitutes it. In this margin—as the space wherein freedom can be repressed—the objective legal order has thoroughly reconciled itself with heteronomous morals, sometimes ameliorated as Prussian, sometimes as papal.

Enough then about the efforts to reunite existing law to morals. But how can one explain the great value attributed to this union when it concerns the *existing* law? The bond was sought principally so that the existing, current law would appear as the equally valid, customary *moral obligation*, which is also at work in the order of things. With this there also came the *effort to avoid critical natural law with its postulate of real human dignity*; a substitute was sought for natural law, one that did not attack, one that unlike Grotius and especially Rousseau did not trail the vile odor of revolution behind it. The *corrective expression* for this substitute was *justice*, this safety valve for at least two gases— the juridical and the moral. But was it not also the beacon of that inoffensive relative natural law, which took the natural instead of the divine will as its basis, the social contract instead of the Ten Commandments? The moralists of justice today still extol justice as a Sunday ideal: "Justice from above," the patriarchal *suum cuique*, understands itself as if it were the cardinal virtue par excellence; moreover, as distributive and retributive, it is indissolubly bound to the regime of classes. Morals without master and slave would have other cardinal virtues, and these could not be institutionalized, nor could they be retained by totalitarian constraint even if it were made something lofty by the illusion of autonomy and morality. A moral style that is ideologically free, namely, one intended as ultimately classless, is too good to avoid radical natural law, too central to replace it. *Radical subjective natural law and its claim—each according to his capabilities, each according to his needs—and radical objective natural law, solidarity,* suffice as postulates for steering laws, and they suffice concretely. This is the reason that they are avoided and moral contemplation is set in their place, replete with its ultimate apologistic illusion: *L'Etat c'est nous*. This is supposed to mean that the state, as heteronomous, voluntary, autonomous, and moral, is our best part. In this way the moralistic interior, or even glittering exterior, overwhelmingly becomes an assimilated hypocrisy. Only in the successful administration of a society that is no longer antagonistic, no longer constructed from above downward, can the true saying be accomplished: Socialism, and even communism, is that which one sought for so long and in vain under the name of morals.

The result of all this is that some common places must reasonably be exchanged. Some things that are possible within law move upward, while the ethical falls down the hierarchy *for the moment*. The value relation between law and morals is thus inverted in the critical observation of the class society. According to its subjective aspect, the side of freedom, law is superior to morals, even the morals of autonomy and of heteronomy. Natural law regarded the element of law with such esteem not only because it did not posit any duties, or posited much less restrictive ones than the ethical did, but also because in Grotius one even finds an *objective* esteem, an esteem for law that far surpasses the instructive significance of the moral concerns of a simple inner life, which are often merely the domestication of an outer life. Grotius regards morals chiefly as an individual order, but law he regards as a social, collective order; morals master the first desires (fear and lust), but law governs the coexistence of men. Morals govern by means of the judgment on the true enduring value of goods, which is indicated by desires; law, on the other hand, governs by means of the widespread clarification of the social instinct (cf. *De jure belli et pacis, Proleg.*, par. 9, 19, 41, 44). Consequently, the ethics of the social instinct, if one can speak this way, is a juridical ethics, not an ethics of morality. Law governs only external action; in Kant, as rational law, it creates only the conditions of external, universal freedom; but this external freedom can seem to be more real than internal freedom; indeed it can even be the precondition that moral action is even possible and meaningful in reality. An example of the fact that morals are not right and cannot be right when law, as the external order of social-collective affairs, is not in order is found in the categorical imperative, which is not even thinkable or meaningful without a good social order. Men cannot at all orient the maxims of their action according to the principle of a universal legislation unless the society of this universality is still a purely formal legal democracy, that is, unless it is a class society. In Kant's time, in the year in which the *Critique of Practical Reason* (1788) appeared, not a single instance of this formal legal equality that had abolished classes was to be found on the earth. And when the French Revolution imposed such a society, the universal validity of the law merely covered the class character of

bourgeois universality. A proletarian could not act morally at all if he
oriented the maxims of his action, under current conditions, by the
principle of a universal legislation; for then he would be a traitor to
his brothers. In the solidarity of the strike, according to the sense of
this action, he cannot do right by any universality, including that of
the capitalist; so the morality of the categorical imperative reveals
itself only in connection with the victory of the oppressed classes. Of
course, the substrate of the universal legislation in Kant is not the
society of the moment, and not at all society in the social sense; rather
he posits a "supersensible substrate of man in man." In the end, the
legislation of practical reason relates only to this substrate. Nevertheless,
in praxis the currently existing society is the sole yardstick and standard
of universality. The Kantian moral principle theoretically demands
that the maxims of society themselves be oriented toward the principle
of the humanity in men; but within the existing society this imperative,
very much against its intentions, would simply determine that everything would be demanded that would favor the preservation of the
present society, and everything avoided that would destroy it. All the
same, only in a society that itself was classless, in the real society of
law, or a real external freedom, would the categorical imperative be
liberated from the sympathy that the Prussian general staff has always
nourished for it. But then one would no longer need the categorical
imperative, for the members of the relation, I-universality, are no
longer held in an antagonistic conflictual relation and so are no longer
in need of any corrective, even one that is constantly reflecting upon
the possibility of a universal legislation. Consequently, law—and this
means rational law as the incarnation of the conditions of external
universal freedom—here has primacy over morals. Without the installation of this law the categorical imperative is essentially only a
means of sanctioning the domination of classes for the consciousness
of the oppressed. After the installation of this law, this imperative,
like every other formalistic morality, becomes superfluous; a classless
ethics is certainly not a tautology within the classless society, not at
all, but it is an ethics liberated from antagonistic conflicts. It is therefore
freed from conflicts that belong essentially to the antagonistic structure
of society, yet these conflicts are only ethically dressed up and made
more bearable in an ethical fashion, and they cannot be constitutively
dissolved. There remain enough worries and questions, deep human
inadequacies and lapses—and the conflicts are not always of a non-

antagonistic sort; on the contrary they express the tension between the bad and good will, between the always only approximate accord between the person and society, society and person, even where there is so much solidarity assured. But so long as there is the problem of humanization and our profoundly precarious distance from it, the most serious among these tensions are purified by the addition of obstacles that are purely institutional. The relations between men are definitely purified of institutional shabbiness or weightiness, so that virtues come into their own; virtues like honesty or even fidelity become superfluous; even love of one's fellow man is unadulterated for the first time, and without the conflicts of situations (as in the categorical imperative) no objectively imposed relativizations can be imposed. Morals are not yet morals when they must replace the law of liberation only with the beautiful soul or with virtues that are impregnated with all sorts of ideologies.

Obviously, matters are quite different for an ethics that does not intend to serve as a substitute. Then it does not remain in second place compared with the impressive transformation of the relations of public law. To the extent that the transformations can be given an ideologically free ethical place, this is communicated to that which is transformed as a preparatory element and they do not coincide in their deeds and behaviors. Thus it is not a matter of finding a substitute for morals, such as turning the struggle for a better society itself into a morality and saying that morality is only a tautology for this struggle, or that this struggle is the only authentic one. That is why the sentence, which Paschukanis wrote in his time, is at least exaggerated where it is not dangerous and apologetic as a carte blanche: "When the living bond that binds the individual with the class is in fact so strong that the limits of the ego are virtually wiped away, and the advantage of the class is in fact identical with personal advantage, then there is no longer any sense in speaking of the fulfillment of moral duty, for then the moral phenomenon is entirely absent" (A General Theory of Law and Marxism, German ed., 1929, p. 141). This phenomenon can then disappear, certainly not only as a tautology, but also as a tyranny. To be sure, a heteronomy, which leaves no more moral questions for the individual in the society of this heteronomy than it does for itself, could, as a new style of enlightened absolutism, "wipe out" the person because the "personal advantage" of the person is immediately and only perceived in that person's class. Meanwhile, persons are reduced to mere recipients; the problem of the claims of the individual on society, and vice versa, is not even raised as a moral problem; it is not noted, let alone thought. Those are the symptoms and the consequences of a reduction of morals to an absolute politics; it represents a complete impoverishment of the moral problem of now and even after the goal has been achieved. A later simplification of morality by political scientists is no less monolithic in its effect; for instance, we find in the ideologist Karewa: "The accord between the basic principles and many concrete demands of law and morals can be explained by noting that they are produced and conditioned by the same economic foundation. The societal construction of socialism is, objectively, highly moral, and every legal norm that is demanded by its development and consolidation simultaneously secures communist morals" (*Law and Morals in a Socialist Society*, German ed., 1954, p. 91). The same economic foundation is supposed to unite the two superstructures of law and morals because they both serve the same inviolable lawful necessity. Accordingly, the criteria of all ethicality, incomplete as well as fully developed, must be that an action is objectively right and ethical if it helps further the ultimate success and effectiveness of economic laws when they serve societal progress. It is clear that in this heteronomous procedure one ignores some of the other cardinal ethical questions and questions that are significant for the production of the empire of freedom, such as those concerning the relation of the freedom of the will to necessity, of the person to the society under construction, and of the society to the person to be liberated. Indeed, something remarkable becomes evident: In a different way a *present-day integration of morals and law* pushes radical natural law out of law as that which brings about *the moral elevation of law*. All the same, there can be no realization (production) of morals without a simultaneous transformation in the relation of men to the means of production, therefore without the endeavor to *institutionally* abolish private self-interest, this hereditary enemy of morals. But also, politics, which tries to create precisely these conditions of human purity, will not be able to take one step in this direction unless it sees its human law as in accord with the intentions of human ethicality. All reciprocal substitution of politics and morals is inauthentic; morals, in order not to be hypocritical or ideology, require the construction of public law, and the start of the construction of this law is not only a ceremonial ribbon-cutting, but also serves as the necessary preparatory construction internal to morals itself.

Here we must reconsider the concerns of laws and of the goods to be won. The two coincide completely in their *becoming*, even if what was preached as morals far too frequently holds its breath and far too often tends to conform to tradition. And these morals are far less vigorous, which is why Jean Paul's pertinent remark on morals is so apt: One exhorts the other to good deeds and this one does the same to the first, and so on, and not a single penny is given out in the progress. But no matter how much it is misused and used as a substitute, ethical consciousness has enough elements that belong to tomorrow and the next day. Morals judge the dust and hypocrisy that morals have become; for from where, except from morals, could hypocrisy be judged? This to the extent that it equally neglects refined interiority as well as objective hypocrisy, especially in times when the rocks cry out, in times when fascism is not abolished. This sort of morals has not yet been written, or better, they were almost suffocated by the "accessories" of the doctrine of duties dictated by the interests of the classes of the times, but these morals live in all of their great doctrines as interhuman habitability. They are related to the legal claim of the oppressed, and they surpass this claim in utopian ends as the thoroughly disinterested resolve to mutual aid. Then ethics is not reduced to a sophisticated form of faith in the dominant mores and customs, or to a contemplative butterfly collection of refined problems from life (based on the life of one with private means). But Kant, with his maxim to regard man always as an end and never as a means, with a maxim that explodes the existing universality (which the categorical imperative never contradicted), Kant could sing the most prudent and authentic hymn of the French Revolution on the basis of his morals and not only on the basis of the half measures of his natural law (the denial of resistance against authority); thus in the *Conflict of the Faculties*: "The revolution of a people full of spirit, which we have seen happen in our time, can succeed or not; it can be full of misery and atrocities to the point where an intelligent man, when he could hope, undertaking it a second time, to be able to realize and implement it, would never decide to make the experiment at such a price—this revolution, I say, finds in the hearts of all of the spectators (who are themselves not implicated in this play) a sympathy of aspirations that border on an enthusiasm and the expression of which is itself a danger; consequently, this sympathy cannot have any other cause than a moral disposition in the human race." This shows evidence of relations with authentic subjective law, the law of freedom, natural law, and with the transformation of the external world, and if it could appear in the present-day bourgeoisie, it would be thoroughly unable to replace or obstruct consequences of natural law. The value relation between morals and the just law, which is so unfavorable to morals, pertains only *for the moment*, in the critical consideration of *class society*, and above all in the bourgeois, and late-bourgeois *class morals*. But from a socialist perspective this relation no longer pertains, that is, it no longer pertains vis-à-vis the profound dawn of the human experiment of all great moral doctrines. Indeed from this point of view great moralities surpass natural law, but only in this end with its utopian content, and they are even integrated with radical natural law, to which they are superior in utopian content. In this sense, the continuing transformation in the value relation of law and morals can subside: Radical natural law posits human freedom in the solidarity that has become possible, while authentic morals are on the path to the production of such solidarity in the attainment of the classless condition, in the clearing of that species of human alienation and lostness which does not only stem, or no longer stems, from the class society. Positive, existing law is primarily "corrected," that is, judged in a revolutionary way, by radical natural law; genuine morals say yes to this and leave their amen open.

23

Penal Law, Tragedy, and the Real Negation of Crime

The paternal judge

The child is struck with a peculiar ease. The adult, who otherwise does not know how to help, practices on the child. Relations with minors are often difficult, the blow shortens the path. The less talented a teacher is, the sooner he reaches for the rod, and the less this is capable of straightening matters out. The pain of being beaten already counts as punishment. It appeases the one who does the punishing; it is supposed to connect the forbidden deed with pain, and so work against the repetition of that deed. Perhaps vengeance does not yet intervene in all of this, but severity does and it is a severity that does not even want to know if the child is responsible for his actions. The rod is supposed to improve insofar as it frightens; it is supposed to lead to breeding; punishing (*züchtigen*) is the verb corresponding to breeding (*Zucht*). Whereas the father is the earliest judge, the judge becomes the strictest father for those who stand before him as fully responsible minors. For many, childhood and then school were times of that trembling, that abandon to vengeance, which later is only the lot of the difficult life of the criminal. Punishment is practiced on children; the judge is rooted in very early feelings and times. The youth is struck less as things become less gruesome behind bars.

The job market and imprisonment

If one lashes out at you, you respond in kind—that is easy to understand. Punishment is vengeance; that is how it begins, everything else comes later or is nothing but an excuse. Eye for eye, tooth for tooth, and better still with a premium: A poor wretch gets his twice over. Of course this still biological phenomenon of vengeance is strongly influenced, and sometimes even tempered, by economic considerations. It is certainly not reduced to formulas of exchange so that the punishment can be regarded as the price one pays for the crime. But even when one abides by retaliation as the form of punishment, it is clear that the *measure of the penalty* and its *execution* vary with the relations in the job market. Thus the High Middle Ages did not demand an eye for an eye, a tooth for a tooth, but the equivalent reduction. One needed the eye and the tooth, the countryside was sparsely populated, the penalties were reduced to fines. The trial only began after the injured party pressed charges not prosecuted by the court. Theft, robbery, homicide, nonpayment of a debt, were indiscriminately regarded as the basis upon which the individual could receive reparation in the form of a fine. The lord of the manor obstructed the private war of his wards, from whom he received a delegation; even when his wards were reduced to being serfs, the fine prevented the work forces from being unnecessarily annihilated by physical punishment. To the extent that a part of the sum paid out was remitted to the feudal lord, this sort of penalty recommended itself as a supplement to the subsidy that the lord exacted. Such an abnormal image modified itself in the later Middle Ages; the power of the vengeance of punishment entered with a monumental force, and it did so to the same degree that natural science declined and the job market lost its capacity to absorb people. Fleeing before the efforts of the lords of the manors (who themselves were declining with the rise of the businessman and princely capital) to press them into service and squeeze everything out of them, impoverished farmers traveled around the countryside as beggars, vagabonds, and highway robbers; but social unrest was dangerous for the authorities. Nothing could be made out of these criminals; penal law was fiscally uninterested in coming to justice by means of a fine. That is why the triple effect of vengeance, intimidation, and annihilation was all the more obviously indicated. Henry VIII of England alone had seventy-two thousand vagabonds hanged. This is when the police and investigative services first came into being; the rack has existed since the thirteenth century. According to official principles, the penal process, now raised from the court itself, handed the completely defenseless defendant over to an official who was both the investigatory judge and sentencing judge, two responsibilities in one and the same profoundly partial person. The accused was merely an object of the proceedings; his only right was to produce evidence against himself, and if he refused to speak or attempted to defend himself, he could become the object of torture. The penal process was conducted completely closed to the outer world, in shadows, secretive, full of horrible abuse, with the result being mutilation or death, with acquittal regarded as a miracle; that is why the determination and definition of punishments found in the Carolina of 1532 is not only a legal document but an instruction manual of sadism. Until the recovery of the job market in the seventeenth century, the death penalty appeared to be quite unprofitable. That began in the seventeenth century: Epidemics and wars, especially the Thirty Years' War, the expansion of commerce, the ratio of the mercantile system, all had as a consequence an increased need for labor forces, and this reinforced the tendency to keep the criminal alive and put him to use. It was in this epoch that the prison sentence was introduced; the condemned served his sentence in a reform house as a slave in chains, as forced labor. There were, of course, jails in antiquity and the Middle Ages, but the prisoner was not held for a prescribed length of time; he was held until his death or until he bought his way out. It was only with the debut of capitalist prosperity (without the introduction of black slaves) that the prison became more profitable than the gallows, and no longer was every small offense punished with corporal punishment. It is only then that justice becomes human, with standards; even the abolition of punishment as pure vengeance finds an audience in a rejuvenated anomaly, even the complete abolition of the death penalty. But under this human impulse, which accompanies the economy of every revolution and which was briefly immobilized during the French Revolution, we find especially the relation between the job market and the execution of punishment. And the humanity of this relation had its limits: The rack and gruesome executions persisted in capital crimes, and, in part, remained until the beginning of the nineteenth century. That the will to vengeance and annihilation was not able to be pushed back everywhere by the economy is evident in the two milder epochs of penal enforcement. This will is evident in the early Middle Ages and in modern times for one who believes that he is not faced with a worldly, temporal injustice (*injuria*), but with a magic, religious injustice (*nefas*). Murder could be expiated by a monetary fine, but the penalty for defacing a tree was that the body of the offender was opened up, his entrails pulled out, one end was nailed to the tree, and then the offender was chased around the tree until his intestines unraveled, forming a new bark for the tree. And if modern times no longer have their share of such old Germanic *nefas*, they have still had the witch trials; neither the job market nor natural law nor the mathematical natural sciences rose up in opposition to them. Unimaginable are the Spanish boots and the racks of torture, the iron chair upon which the poor woman accused of sorcery was made to sit, exhausted by a terrible imprisonment, deadened by the darkness and hunger in stinking dungeons, weighed down with chains, emaciated and half dead. Unthinkable are the extremes of torture and the death by fire that they, and heretics, suffered—in the time when Grotius lived, but also in the time of Newton and Leibniz. Thus the rack and murder as punishment triumphed as retaliation even in relatively refined times; they triumphed especially where this riposte-murder did not even need to be called forth by a previous murder.

Original guilt and history as penance

All of this goes deeper than the simple urge toward retaliation. Otherwise it could not divide man even in himself, producing self-hatred, namely, the hatred of the one who partakes of vengeance, because he is damned by a conscience perpetually burdened and never in order. Conscience is the language of the superego, of the superego that makes itself into the chief judge, and is the ideal image that man has of himself; this is the image that adapts and accommodates ethical demands in the conscience of man. But insofar as this superego judges, insofar as it is a constant pressure extorting confessions, always producing a new feeling of having atoned and thereby forming a sort of internal instrument of torture under an ideal mask, insofar as this is the case, its demands must be viewed with suspicion. In all cases of reproach these demands stem from that which man is not, to the extent that the superego comes to man from a heteronomous past and that it holds him prisoner by the fascination that it exercises. As Freud was the first to determine, this fascination distinguishes the superego from all images of satisfaction that liberate and introduce an uplifting utopian element. Individually it is the parents, especially the father, who live in the superego; phylogenetically, according to the history of the race, which is repeated in the individual, it is the despot and his taboos. All conscience of obligation has its archaic roots in this superego; the fundamental obligation shrinks before it. And it is none other than its aura that appears in the *external* institutions of vengeance, in the tribunal and its trials. It is not insignificant that court trials in all ages have been adorned with ceremonies: the disguising of the judge, the supcrego in the form of the state, and even the participation of the crucifix (irrespective of the fact that it represents one of the most famous legal assassinations of all times). All of this contributes to, and is supposed to contribute to, the impression that a special, juridical being exists alongside the matter-of-fact world, a being of punishment. In this way it is not simply the abstraction "state" that concretizes itself sensibly, for in the court the power of vengeance also reaches that threatening basis and background which not only coincides with the simple relation of equivalence between guilt and sin but also does not end with it. In this respect it does not matter whether or not the procedure is liberal or forceful, whether or not the advocates and the jury do not abandon the accused. The court itself is so demonic and unsuppressable that even a well-intended correction like opening trials to the public, in the age of the press, has been practically transformed into an additional punishment, into a new species of pillory, a pillory in print. Thus the punishing superego is amplified in the court and powerfully tied to the backgrounds that, as heteronomous, constantly accuse the human will, the free human will. Only the subjective law urges that the law be defined as the science of rights, morals as the science of morals; but the objective law, as well as the order of punishment, is bound not only to the most heteronomous doctrines of moral obligations but also with a general *mythology of culpability*. This species of servitude is evident in all of the great haters of the self, in Kafka as well as in Kierkegaard, in Dostoyevsky as well as in Luther. Kafka gave it its final and fundamental form: that of naked violence, which is the most veiled, yet open and perfidious violence—only in the monstrosity that is the court is the punishment that hunts men down rendered visible, while the crime is never disclosed. Kafka wrote his novel *The Trial* about the never-ending process that he waged against himself, and that raged in both light and night in the mythical loft. Kierkegaard, or the trembling at the thought that God was so infinitely easy to fool; Dostoyevsky, or the complicity in the guilt of all that is evil, the consciousness that every injustice had been done to the Son of God—both of these people are the speaking, confessing, worn-out objects of punishment, on the one side of divine wrath, on the other of divine innocence. Kierkegaard said, "In the consciousness of sin" (which is an exacerbated sense of culpability) "the individual becomes conscious of his difference from that which is universally human, the individual, who only becomes conscious of himself through himself, which is what it means to exist qua man." And here, criminal despair is a reflection of Luther's despair: to be damned de facto, *de jure* in his own work. Luther's faith necessarily included in itself the unconditional self-condemnation as the recognition of the divine tribunal. In this tribunal—from the perspective of the nullity of all men before God—there was no acquittal; the accused, who was accused in his essence, could only hope for grace, that is, for pardon. Luther's seriousness leads back to the *source* of the mythology of culpability, to the myth of the fall into sin and the corresponding legend of an original guilt found in all higher religions. The feeling that life is punishment and penance runs through the Vedas, the Greek mysteries, and the Bible (though with differing interpretations). This feeling is a subterranean feeling everywhere—and with it goes the "memory" of a prehistorical injustice, which one had committed oneself or which one had committed in one's "parents." Where life is not regarded as punishment, death is; Anaximander summarized in a single phrase the entire missing mythical complex when he said that all things must return to the primal stuff from which they have arisen "in order to give reparation and pay penalty for their injustices according to the order of time." Even the definition of an individual protestation, of an individual being, is contained in a remarkable phrase that also already contains the idea that arrogance and defiance merit punishment, because the death sentence for the "injustice," the *adikia* (even insult, affront, and illegal possession), is levied against the already intrinsically criminal being of being-separate. Death is the wage of sin; even in the myth of the Fall it happens literally as an execution: Adam and his children are sentenced to death, and the angel of death carries out the sentence. It is the sentence that God himself has handed down, and God has transferred the authority to prematurely carry out and increase this sentence. From this perspective, all penalties given by Christian authority are nothing other than the enactment of the primal penal code born of the wrath of the Lord—*et poenae et remedia peccati*, according to the Church Fathers, according to Thomas, according to Luther. Hell burned in the innermost place of God's wrath; criminal justice even gives its victims a foretaste of this hell. Death by fire for heretics, sorcerers, and witches is directly borrowed from ancient images of hell; their screams and gnashing of teeth were preparations for other, greater pains. The monstrosity of an eternal damnation quickly eliminated every proportion between guilt and atonement. With all of that, punishment as vengeance and punishment as equivalence were mythically far surpassed by inherited sin and inherited punishment: Just as the fall into sin formed the metaphysical root of crime, so the curse of God formed the metaphysical justification of punishment. Even F. J. Stahl, the latest reactionary ideologue at the service of this *remedium peccati*, following Luther, gave this definition: "Law is the ethical transformed by the Fall into the external coercive force." Even the latest mythology of ideas, which was developed under the influence of Baader and subsequently reinterpreted by Schelling and by E. von Hartmann in Gnostic terms, even this still has the sentence of Anaximander as its principle: The world is a process of penance and healing, and its basis is the primal guilt of an unimaginable crime. Something terrible happened at the beginning; thus the trial as a penal process is simultaneously mixed with the process of healing an original wound; only later was the concept of development added to this. In Schelling the original guilt decisively becomes that of the being-separate, of the radical evil that is called freedom or the break with the universal will. Decline, decadence, is the ground of existence; the fall into sin precedes history as well as the entire world. Historical process is nothing other than the repression or dissolution of the particular will to rule, order, and rational form. World history in this new sense is a world court: "But the unruly lies always in depths as though it might again break through, and order and form nowhere appear to have been original, but it seems as though what had initially been unruly had been put in order" (Schelling, *On the Essence of Human Freedom*, 1809, *Works*, VII, p. 259). This quotation of Lucifer came as a consequence of the French Revolution; the breakthrough of the economically free individual in it, a break through class orders, was regarded by reactionaries as the work of the devil. Schelling also had a friendly word for the "inflamed egoity" (which had its impulse in God himself and which engendered motion); nevertheless, it hardened itself into arrogance, and thus is and remains original guilt. Criminals are clearly the exaggerated manifestations of it; obviously the Restoration included the Jacobins, the "eternal troops of Corah" of the revolution, in this original guilt. In the end, the remote speculations of Schelling characterized that which the dominant class of every age has felt itself close to: Under the world there is a fire, there is a snake. The authority crushes its head, posits

metaretaliation in the place of retaliation as the effect of the mythology
of guilt.

The rupture of original guilt, tragic light

Only a few freed themselves somewhat from the fascination, mostly
imaginatively. On the stage where they were, guilt and sin had a quite
different allure. Tragedy portrays people who were both culpable and
declining, but it equally portrays them as victorious. The empathy of
the spectator here corresponds to a paradox of the matter: The tragic
hero is simultaneously confirmed in his actions by his condemnation
to destruction. Guilt, which is the violation of order, implies destruction
as a sin; this element of guilt persists, but guilt is usually a pretext,
at best an exterior element. This is quite clear in ancient tragedy:
Aeschylus heaps every sort of reproach upon Agamemnon, but Agamemnon does not die on account of these reproaches. Sophocles gives
Oedipus a surplus of hardness, but this does not form the basis of the
destiny of the hero. In more recent tragedies, "tragedies of character,"
the destiny of the hero depends to a much more definite degree upon
his guilt or fault; indeed the guilt that can, or does, lead to defeat can
even be defined juridically (insubordination in *The Prince of Hamburg*,
high treason in *Wallenstein*). But this coordination between guilt and
defeat does not mean what the schoolmasters of tragedy, the moralists
of the Promethean play, have made it out to mean. Behind this aesthetic
fault attributed to the heroes of ancient tragedy, behind the psychological faults of modern heroes, the sole fault from the point of view
of order is the person who *rises up* against this order and who is broken
in this uprising. Nothing could be more wrong than seeing involuntary
suffering in the ancient hero simply because his fate is not mitigated
psychologically and is encountered without any mediation; this is in
opposition to the heroes of modern drama, who are culpable by virtue
of their convictions. In Sophocles even Oedipus, whose fate seems
mostly to come from outside, seems to accommodate himself to this
fate; he is at least predestined in a personal union with it. Whether
consciously or not, a modern distinction is at work here; it is simultaneously moving and telling that Oedipus believed that it was necessary
to discover the murderer of Laius at any price "as if Laius had been
his father." Ceaselessly, the lamentation rises above the suffering, and
the accusation rises over the lamentation; it is ultimately stilled in

Oedipus, turns into a cursing of the gods in Philocrete, and remains without measure and vaster than even the world in Prometheus. "You see," the chained Titan cries to the ether in the last verse of the tragedy by Aeschylus, "you see what injustice I endure"—that is the expression of suffering, but it is also the expression of indestructible, dangerous arrogance. It is the lamentation of death at the close of the Dionysian celebration, which continues to echo through tragedy, but only in this lamentation is there something indestructible; Prometheus is and remains the fundamental tragic hero, and he is a rebel. Prometheus's arrogance even in patience is found behind Oedipus and Agamemnon, and it makes them into bearers of a tragedy, but not of a drama of sadness or martyrdom. The ancient hero is also such a character, although only a contributor who acts more as a rigid and obstinate individual against the existing order (this is evident in Lear, Hamlet, or even Julius Caesar). If the dramatic personage is the supporter of an ancient order, such as was the case for Antigone, then this person fights to the end the conflict that results with the dominant order, as if this person exercised to the end the métier of the character of the person. In modern tragedy, the tragic individual, according to Hegel's phrase, picks the only fruits of his own deeds, and these fruits are those of the most sublime destruction and death. In sum: out of the destructions of destiny tragedy paves the constancy of a great person who is victorious even in defeat. The death sentence of the tribunal becomes the scene of an irrefutable glory, the glory of the guilt itself. This is the source of the empathy on the part of the spectator of the tragic event, the feeling that the end is necessary, even from the point of view of the hero, but that it is not necessary, since the order that reinstates itself is out of order. The ambivalent edifying elevation of the end is, or was, also true of the rule of so-called eternal justice; it is even more profoundly true of the person whose greatness and silence, whose exemplary defeat, is judged by the tribunal itself. This can be expressed in the following aristocratic way: Only great natures can be guilty in the tragic sense; they have the privilege of being guilty. The democratic interpretation goes more to the fundamental element of the issue: Tragic guilt, even in its most visible human deficit, is still related to that which is legitimated in the fateful action, that is, that which is better than the existing order of things with which it has collided. To the extent that tragedy shows this, it breaks through for the first time—even if in a poetic manner—

the chains of guilt and atonement by means of arrogance and hope; it raises its superiority to the God of punishment.

For this an external, and even more than external, condition was presupposed, one that the cutting word practiced. Even when the hero was silent at the end, he nevertheless worked in dialogue and replied earlier. It has long been noticed that drama never developed from mimicry, but had its origin unilaterally in the sacred, in the alternating chants of the Dionysian chorus. In fact, it would have remained with this if an actor had not been added to it, if conversation and dialogue had not been formed elsewhere, namely, in the assembly of the people and in the *court*—it was the court appearance that first opened the way for tragedy; it began at the bar, and not only in the mysteries. And this in the following way: When the ancient judicial procedure deprived the injured party of their vengeance in the name of something higher—atonement—this happened according to a rigid formula under the pressure of magic. It was not only the contract that was accorded such ceremony and owed its sanctity to this ceremony; in ancient Rome the magic of the word had an even more profound effect: The plaintiff who failed to make his accusation according to the traditional formula lost his case. But then from the sixth century onward there appeared a rupture in the Athenian trial, especially in the penal process, a rupture in the restricted wording of the juridical ceremony, a rupture that was clearly related to Dionysus. It happened in such a way that freely flowing speech, even the ecstatic defiance of the accused who was combative, invoked a new, higher justice than the justice consigned to the archaic ceremony. *This image of a new penal procedure penetrated tragedy*; it reappropriated myth—and by way of exception, the myths of guilt and atonement—as a sort of judicial proceeding. Contemporary events were rarely dramatized, whereas on the other hand, the curse that weighed upon Tantalus and his race brought Agamemnon, Orestes, Electra, and Iphigenia one after another in a dramatic trial of atonement, and the curse upon Oedipus brought proceedings against his sons, Eteocles and Polyneices, and his daughter Antigone. But if the myth becomes a trial, it is, in Benjamin's subtle remark, "simultaneously a revision of the trial in its poetic reproduction." Furthermore, the celebrated doctrine of the three unities (which, even if they were not formulated in Athens, were always thoroughly observed in Athens) is itself a consequence of this image of the tribunal. Corresponding to the forensic origin of tragedy we find "the unity of the place (the place of the tribunal itself), the unity of time—which has always been limited by the course of the sun or in some other way—and the unity of action (the action of the trial)" (Benjamin, *The Origin of German Tragedy*, 1928, p. 111). Only after uncovering this neoforensic origin of tragedy does its other origin in the Dionysian mysteries acquire its true value. The theater was built in the vicinity of the temple to Dionysus; the performances took place on the first day of the Festival of Dionysus and were viewed as a part of the worship of the god. And it was these lamentations on the death of the god that would bring death to the tragic hero and that removed from atonement its ancient resonance and its piety toward Olympus. It was not the decision (the death sentence) itself, but the satisfaction that was revised in the decision pronounced in the myth. The tragic hero is still a victim of atonement, and with his defeat he pays tribute to Prometheus-Lucifer for his own guilt, the essential guilt, but he is the final victim of atonement. He exhausts the right of the Olympians to demand atonement; thus there appears for the first time the arrogance of an individual against an order that had been rendered sacred. But most importantly with this individual there appears a concern that is always social, or outlasts the individual, and expands to all of humanity. This extends far beyond the simple strong-headed character of a heroic individual, beyond that hubris which only remains formal insofar as it is a mere proclamation of itself that lacks any significant content. To the true tragic hero there belongs a sense of protest, which has the sense of being objectively right; this is what first makes the phenomenon of tragic defeat great, and leaves the hero unconquered in the defeat (if not dialectically on account of the defeat). The power and the dignity of the tragic assault always enter the picture (in terms of their content) in *another order* which the hero represents and brings into the midst of the existing order; this entry is directed partially or centrally against the existing order, which has been judged to be unjust. This is so even if it is the case, as in *Antigone*, that the order is one that has sunk away, that of "piety" and therefore of the maternal law; but the warmth of this old order is still lacking in the new order, and in its own way, it is better than Zeus the master. This is so even when it is the case that the tragic individual, even in a unilateral and exaggerated way, represents an order that is not yet realized such as is the case par excellence in Prometheus's defiance and the hope it expresses. Such a claim is even recognizable where the transgression of limits takes place within the same society of which the tragic hero continues to be a member; in this case, there is a double rupture and an unsuccessful rebellion for something that has already come due. This is the case in *Wallenstein* (the establishment of a unified empire under a new leader), just as it is the case in all of the tragedies where the heroes really touch that which Hebel naively called the great sleep of the world. But the representatives of a *future society* primarily belong here, essentially opposing themselves to the depraved existing society that engulfs them, tragic in a sense that in its most bitter form, comes to resemble Prometheus. It is quite evident that these tragic individuals do not pick the fruits of their individual deeds, but—like Spartacus and Münzer—simply the fruits of a premature objective, historical anti-Olympian condition; it is only this "guilt" that constitutes their tragedy. There is a surprising, yet illuminating correspondence between such figures dedicated body and soul to a future, all too futural, world and the position of Antigone; namely, one is the inversion of the other, changing twilight into dawn. In *Antigone* the problem of an unfinished past with its relative law was announced; here it is the obstructed human future with the absolute law. The inadequacies of the means of arriving there were mostly objective, not individual, obstacles: the still supremely powerful "Zeus" and the prematurity of the occasion at the moment defined by the tendency and situation. Of course, with Spartacus and Münzer one leaves poetry, since, despite the inversion of the Antigone motif, no Sophocles came to their cause; nevertheless, both of them are an incarnation of tragedy. But the idea that man might be better than his gods was first portrayed in the tragedies of antiquity and its effect and influence was felt from this point. According to Schiller, tragic destiny has not only elevated man, insofar as it crushes him, but also lets the questionable sinister majesty of the court appear, the court before which Prometheus formed his image. The tragedy of antiquity viewed the gods as inferior to their human victims, who, precisely in their defeat, always become more instructive and monumental. This is so even when the tragic hero radiates an extreme isolation, where the space of the poem is not restricted to a real cassation court. Despite everything, the stage went far, and the great tragic individual, even in his apparent isolation, succeeded in giving birth to the very public insight into the injustice that had been committed against him. The effect of this idea is more substantial, since that which was characteristic of Zeus could be reproduced more easily than that which was Promethean. The relations are already at birth, where Prometheus appears without Zeus and thereby achieves a new meaning within the completely new (despite *Oedipus at Colonus* and *Egmont*) space of an optimistic tragedy.

Up to this point tragedy could not cease to teach an entirely different optimism; namely, *in tyrannos*, such as was written by one of the clearest poets of the tragic, Alfieri, apropos of his dramas *Virginia*, *Filippo*, and *Saul*. Therefore it was the entry of the objection, the retort, that brought tragedy, the entry of retort before a culpable court in the Dionysian, and especially Promethean, figures of the archaic myths. Its actor (and here we are speaking, not of drama, but of tragedy) is, as a criminal and as destructive, the true believer in law.

Theft, murder, and burglary; counterfeiting; relative and absolute penal theory

Of course most common criminals have nothing in common with this. They would sooner fall under the wheel than drive a heroic chariot. The noble brigand, if he ever existed, and even the avenger have long since disappeared. Among common, nonheroic criminals one customarily distinguished two or two and a half types. This distinction is made from a perspective that is psychological (so to speak): It distinguishes the occasional criminal from the recidivist. It is therefore (without being false) an *external* classification that only separates the offender who is more or less honest (bourgeoisly speaking), the occasional delinquent, from the inveterate delinquent. Among the occasional criminals one finds counterfeiters; among the inveterate criminals one finds those who repeatedly steal bread. More telling then is a social distinction, namely, crime arising from *need and neglect* (nine-tenths of all criminals come from profoundly oppressed social strata) and crime arising from a *bankrupt citizenry*. Both have economic causes, but the causes of need (even in chronic offenders) are almost obligatory, whereas those related to bourgeois difficulties are only an invitation. The crimes of the neglected are certainly especially barbarous, and are not limited to stealing food for immediate consumption because of an immediate, nagging hunger. They increase to theft, breaking and entering, assault up to murder; they quickly take on very assertive qualities. The criminals of means, on the other hand—concerned with counterfeiting documents, insurance fraud, and the like—are no match for them, even though arson for an insurance claim and poisoning for an inheritance have forms that tend to be in this line. Bad and grievous qualities are not lacking here, even if they usually hide behind carefully nursed concerns: the great American wealth or the huge profits of the East India Company are born in the ways of Nero. The Pitaval of distinguished persons, the criminals who have been decorated with medals, even the provocations of the police, and the burning of the Reichstags of every age have yet to be brought to account. Of course the true perpetrators of these crimes seldom dirty their own hands; no letter of a Uriah is sullied with blood. Nevertheless, even if one does grant the great cruelty and barbarity of the criminals of the slums, and especially the frequency of these cruelties, then it is always the society that produces these slums that is being accused. This society demands of the criminals from the slums an enormous capacity to resist the well-lit shop windows and displays, the wealthy villas and their inhabitants, while the bourgeois criminal belongs to society itself and, at the level of international swindling, is even indistinguishable from the most shining examples of this society. A thief who has come from a background of neglect and need does not relate to property in the same way as a member of the bourgeoisie; consequently, the defense of property against the first does not make the same claim to such emphasis as it does against the second. "For no one," rightly said the suspicious yet honest theorist of natural law Jacob Fries, "for no one can be obliged to respect the property of another if, in the general division of property he did not receive his share, and if he is abandoned to helplessness and distress on account of the opulence and surplus of others" (*Philosophical Doctrine of Right*, 1803, p. 135). The refined thief recognizes property straightaway precisely when he injures it in order to legitimate his own; embezzlement is an affair internal to the bourgeoisie, it is not situated at the margins of the power of society. The counterfeiter does not call the society to the witness stand as something that has opposed him, for he belongs to it even if in a bankrupt manner. For his falsified papers he demands public belief, which he himself has upset by his forgery; he is in complicity with the world he deceives. Even the criminal acting out of the need from a background of neglect can follow suit with the more refined, so to speak socially immanent, infractions of the law. But only a minority arrive at this level; the majority remain the proletarians of crime at the service of an indistinguishable gangster boss. And the one succeeds in raising himself into the region where the physical risk of an entry or robbery is replaced by the forms of a crime that presuppose a widespread entanglement in capitalistic interests and development of business concerns. One belongs to the world of stocks and bonds, not of lock picks. Both types are of course only concerned with their personal advantage, with a geometry in which it is not the straightest line, but the crooked one, that is the shortest route between two points. The criminal is never a revolutionary, and so even in his form shaped by slums he would, if given the opportunity, end up as a profiteer and man of private means. The criminal still sees himself as cunning, not heroic; he is untragic: Instead of disturbing the deep sleep of the world (according to Hebbel's basically false definition of the tragic actor), the criminal has only disturbed the small sleep of the property owners, and afterward they fall right back to sleep. Nevertheless, there are transitions from a certain type of slum criminal (and only from this type) to the semblance, and even beginnings, of rebellious acts; these transitions are, from time to time, made by the brigand, not in the sense that the propertied class has always called its respective revolutionaries brigands, and has effectively treated them as such. But letters from the French Revolution report that the property owners in Paris barricaded their doors with extra bolts in expectation of the famous brigands; months before the outbreak of the revolution a panic of this sort spread over the land: "les brigands arrivent." What is decisive here is that the great brigands were regarded as the avengers of the poor, even if that was only a side effect of their actions and they were celebrated as such in folk songs, where they were portrayed not without sympathy. This is the case with Stenka Rasin in Russia, Jacob Szela in Poland, and even Schinderhannes and the Bavarian Hiesl in Germany; it is also significant that Schiller's drama about brigands bore the motto *in tyrannos*, and that it could carry such a motto. But soon the poetry on brigands declined, and only continued to thrive among the anarchists. It was always possible apropos of the sort of crime committed out of need and cultural abandonment but not called a legitimate defense. The difference between this sort of criminal and the crook at the desk, who in general is related to the cultural monopoly, is illuminating. Fraudulent bankruptcy, extortion, poisoning—the entire collection of offenses internal to society has sometimes enjoyed an attenuated comprehension and understanding, but it has never inspired a folk song.

In revenge the judge, who no longer wanted to be an exacting judge, propagated himself. This feeble type grew to the same degree that he came to be regarded with suspicion and as threatening by the good citizens even in other social strata. The fascist state presumptuously assumed, as no state before, the right to punish as total elimination. Liberal penal theory on the other hand had become relative; it not only distinguished between occasional offenders and recidivists, but it looked for a way of punishing both, in a hierarchical manner, which was anaesthetic. The goal of punishment here was the *protection* of society, not *retaliation* as in absolute penal theory. But retaliation was always adapted to liberal times insofar as it passed itself off as clever. Practically, retaliation as punishment was sanctioned as the surest means of intimidation and the most unrelenting extirpation. Theoretically the old *jus talionis*, which, in attenuated form, still constituted the basis of the construction of penal law in Binding, permitted a particularly impenetrable and compact consistency: No psychological disturbances enter into it. If penal law as such represents the *norma agendi* par excellence, then compared to it, private law is only "a rip in the net of norms," as Binding somewhat disapprovingly said (*Norms and Their Transgression*, 1872). Penal law on the other hand encloses the prohibitions of its domain in a perfectly explicit and uninterrupted fashion; it only knows infractions and nothing else; all psychologizing as an effort to tear a hole in the Draconian curtain of law itself does not concern it. Even the objection that the theory of retaliation necessarily presupposes the freedom of the will and that "modern science" no longer recognizes this does not have the validity that it seems to have. This is because all nuances of *dolus* and of accountability, which even absolute penal theory now recognize, only concern the degree of punishment, not the right to punishment itself, which retaliates with evil for evil. In this way punishment remains intimidating, even in cases of severely diminished accountability; the pedagogical rod, which worked on small children and primarily served the ends of intimidation, was not troubled by the problem of an infantile freedom of the will. Punishment remained retribution even if the culprit was so determined, for atonement primarily concerned the quality of guilt itself, and only secondarily concerned the perpetrator. This conception reaches from the magically precise "correspondence" between the types of crime and the type of punishment up to the rigor of a penal law in and for itself. The *jus talionis* of a higher order extends from the Code of

Hammurabi, the oldest code of laws known, which reprimands the crime by repeating it negatively in the punishment, up to Hegel's definition of punishment as the "negation of a negation" and the restoration of law that this produces. In short, in its pathos for punishment (not in its manner of punishment or its tangential purpose, intimidation) the theory of retribution, which is both mythological as well as dialectically idealistic, sets itself against the guilty act itself, and only secondarily against the psychological personal union of this guilt. Nevertheless, the *defensive theory* defeated the theory of retribution precisely from this psychological side. This was unavoidable as soon as the relation between guilt and atonement lost its mythological background, so that consequently there was no guilt that intrinsically could be regarded as demonic. Thus along with and during the liberal period of the bourgeoisie the theory of punishment as protection began, the theory of relative punishment that is a psychological, and thus sociological, expansion of the concept of *dolus*. The concept of *dolus* itself, although absent in primitive law, is equally old; the differences that it posits in the degree of punishment are already observed in the Code of Hammurabi and in the Bible (2 Moses 21:12–14). But only from this point of view did the myth of punishment as guilt reprimanded correct itself by research into motives, a research that was not only interested in psychological motives. It pays attention to the motivations of the criminal that are not free, the organic, social causes from predisposition, education, milieu, based upon the hypothesis of determinism and intended for the abolition of atonement. Feuerbach provided such a theory of relative punishment (*Revision of the Principles and Basic Concepts of Positive Penal Law*, 1799–1800) and in this he represents a final echo of natural law. As already noted, penal justice was an embarrassment for all of natural law (with the exception of Kant); Grotius had already fought against punishment as retaliation. This embarrassment corresponds, at the ideological level, to the reduction of corporal punishment, which, in modern times, followed the reestablishment of the job market. It corresponds equally to the precaution with which a more advanced, but already economically unsettled, society guarded itself from an all too clear brutalization. This happened in the nineteenth century, when the job situation deteriorated and when compulsory labor in penitentiaries no longer proved to be profitable. Nevertheless, in this time so-called prisoner welfare work proliferated as a reflection of the sense of clemency and even of the tendency to treat the offender as sick. In the wake of different crises, nothing would be more conceivable, economically speaking, than to discard as worthless the human material of criminals; but only fascism practiced such a complete extermination, even turning imprisonment into the promissory note of the guillotine. But up until then Feuerbach's influence was felt, one that recognized not only the principle *nulla poena sine lege* but also the principle *nullum crimen sine lege* and one that measured the value of the punishment exclusively against its effect as a warning. Feuerbach's influence throughout the entire nineteenth century made it difficult for the theory of retribution to regress to the mythological theory of a superretribution. Feuerbach respected criminal law only "as a political institution without any sort of ideal principle of right," and all extremism was attributed to this ideal moral mythology. The persistent influence of Feuerbach's liberalism in penal law protected not only the state from the criminal but also the criminal from the state (that is, from emotional judgments, the seething rage of a lynch mob, or lynching by higher-ups). At the turn of the twentieth century a liberal penal theory was still possible; indeed it culminated then in the epoch of criminal anthropology (Lombroso), criminal sociology (Ferri, Garofalo), and other "auxiliary sciences" of bourgeois penal reform. The real reason for this effort at reform was also found at the basis of the social legislation of that time: fear of widespread demands, philanthropic cleverness that simultaneously preserved the existing order, reformism, *ut aliquid fieri videatur*. Nevertheless, an attempted installment payment is unmistakable; all the more reason that insofar as Feuerbach still thrived there, certain principles of the theory that punishment is a defense are not without influence later, occasionally or in passing, in the Soviet Union. Liberal penal theory in Germany culminated in the eclecticism of Franz von Liszt, who added to punishment as defense the functions of intimidation, improvement, and even neutralizing. Punishment was supposed to intimidate the occasional offender (and other "latent scoundrels"), to improve the repeat offenders who had not yet become calloused, and to render harmless those who were incorrigible. Those are the three categories of offenders that Liszt wanted to turn into the Magna Carta of a graduated and modified penal code, and that he envisaged as punishment without retaliation—punishment as protection of society against lawbreakers, with the right that the supposed "society as a whole" has to its protection. Punishment is no longer posited as delegated divine wrath, nor as any sort of quantitative reparation of guilt; here punishment is posited as coming from the supposed interest of the majority, even the homogeneity of interests of a "society as a whole." Security in the face of crime is the purpose of punishment; it is a forward look that is prophylactic, not a judgment that looks back revengefully; all criminal justice is only a part of the "systematic struggle against crime." But these aftereffects of natural law do not go beyond the bourgeois limit—especially not these consequences—the limit that essentially is reformism and its eventual weakness. The defensive theory considers all possible determinations at work on the criminal: predisposition, education, milieu, and it draws its principal argument against the (nonpsychologically based) theory of retaliation from the unfreedom of the will. But it is precisely the superabundance of determinations considered that impoverished the look and so blocks the sole decisive direction, the sole radical direction. Even the equalization of the so-called criminal disposition and milieu, if not the privileging of the criminal disposition, is a means to relegate the causes of crime to the pathological. If, according to Lombroso, there are born criminals, then the struggle against crime has a natural limit in this fact; education and milieu no longer need to be changed even in the fight against crime. Criminal anthropology thus serves the theory of retaliation just as well: Against the "born criminal," against his unsurpassable constitution and mass of inheritances, genocide is almost as obvious as neutralization by means of punishment as a security measure. Lifelong imprisonment of one who is not in the least insane, as the theory of security requires, is connected with the most extreme corporal suffering; even when, according to a definition that itself runs about freely, this suffering has nothing in common with atonement. But the entire doctrine of the "born criminal" is little more than an ideology in order to sidestep the trial of the real culprit: capitalistic society. Even research into environment, as practiced by bourgeois criminal sociology, works with a chisel made of soap; for bourgeois sociology as a whole has the task of using one-quarter of Marxist methods to stamp out or chase away Marxist theories and insights. Penal reform based upon anthropology and sociology only results in a graduated improvement of the prison beds (in the course of which the penal institution, in order not to incite and be an invitation to crime, must still be more unpleasant than the most miserable slum). Liberal penal reform cannot *eo ipso* overcome the society that first produced the conditions for crime. Punishment as protection also applies to men from whom an abnormal "capacity for social-ethical resistance" is demanded, which, on account of the abnormality of this demand, cannot be required. In this sense, the majority of the offenders are not abnormal enough, that is, they only possess a normal measure of the capacity to resist the seductions that appear from the surrounding world of wealth and its display by others. The forger of documents, the bourgeois criminal, might sooner muster up such a measure, for even in times of crisis he does not face such difficult problems as the lumpen proletariat and the reserve industrial army. But the very existence of the slum criminal, against whose dangerousness punishment as protection appears especially designed, is an accusation against the same society that, in its liberal theoreticians, renounces making an accusation of guilt, but does not renounce intimidation, improvement, neutralization. The relative theory of punishment is also intrinsically still relative, not radical. On the route from Feuerbach to Liszt it was difficult to hold onto a spark of Prometheus, even in its modest form. The defensive theory, with its reappropriation of elements of natural law, had intended a revenge-free punishment as an instrument in the war against crime. This instrument and this fight do not easily find a place in a world that lets the poor be culpable, that must condemn them for infractions that the rich normally are not led to commit.

Neutralization of society as the truly radical penal theory

The blow that is helpful here is itself considered forbidden. For it fights crime by taking it to the rich people themselves. The revolution takes the slaves away from the rich, who have squirreled away so much in villas and banks that a burglary is worthwhile. It dries out the places of corruption and levels the slums, which necessarily engender crime. It even takes the countryside (gained by deception) away from the incriminated bourgeoisie who prefer the most crooked path to the path of common crookedness. Cleverly, the order of society, acting in complicity, had surrounded the real fighters against the causes of crime with all of the horrors of the underworld. All real revolution handles plundering as harshly as the army treats those who rob corpses; but this advice is ignored: The petite bourgeoisie were nevertheless inclined to see in the revolutionary worker the mob, the horde, crime let loose, and something from which only evil could be expected. The revolt of the masses was considered the outbreak of chaos (in the face of which the ruling class was to save the day "in the last hour"); the commune and the underworld are ranked as identical; all the archetypes of below, of the opening of the prisons to the opening of hell, were applied to the social revolution and were mobilized by the ruling class. Thus the rescue from crime appears itself as the highest crime, the fulfilled Enlightenment as the praxis of the night. The truth, that only fascism needs and organizes mobs and masses, does nothing to help counter this view: Just as little help comes from the spectacle of bands of gangsters who play at legalized government mandated by the old order. Indeed, when the image of an infernal cesspool does not suffice, it is the archetype of the realm of heaven, employed ironically, which defends the incoherent consciousness of the petite bourgeoisie (which is a reflection of its contradictory and effaced class situation) from the revolution. On the one hand, the communists are seen as born murderers, the menagerie of the Antichrist; on the other hand they are laughable idealists who believe that man can become an angel and that the earth can be turned into a paradise. Both images hang together—the rat and the angel—and against both there works the community of the people, the "society as a whole," which, already in liberal times, has legitimated the state in its oppressive measures, which in full or partial fascism put politics in a greater danger than criminals ever did. The revolution is thus forbidden, because the monopoly held by a small, recently formed social group on the means of production, which support this class as well as obstructing the true society as a whole, is sacrosanct. Therefore the only radical penal theory, the theory that is not only systematic but above all a fight against the causes of crime, namely, true socialism without the monopoly of a caste, is punished as fascistic. In fascism the entire anomaly of a relative penal theory stemming from natural law also disappeared, and the brutal, yet well-ordered equivalences of the theory of retaliation disappeared as well. Punishment merely as the mask of murder has become the criminal form of this anti-Marxism; Prometheus, who brought fire to mankind, no longer has Zeus against him, but Caliban and Nero (with Zeus's lightning bolt). But from the outset social revolution is, among other things, a fight against crime; it attacks the causes themselves, it is not content with bumbling around with symptoms and reproducing the causes. In his reactionary theory of retribution, Hegel posits the justification of punishment by saying that only through it, as the negation of a negation, is the existence of the criminal elevated. But the existence of the criminal is never more concretely elevated than in the elimination of the conditions under which he arose, and which will continually engender him anew. A Marxism that was what it was supposed to be would be a radical penal theory, indeed the most radical and at the same time most amiable: It kills the social mother of injustice.

24

The Origin of the State, Public Law, *Arcana Dominationis*, and Its Opposite

Marriage under supervision

For the primitive man everything was innate. He found the tribe already given, just as today one finds one's parents. No one felt like an isolated individual; but after anarchistic sexual relations ceased in farming tribes, which had become sedentary, the women soon became the object of a special search, and were abducted, or even raped. If something was founded, then it was marriage that always sealed it. It was different from the tribe, because man and woman always had to be brought together first; it was always something newly made, and an act of foundation. This aspect of the self-bonding of individuals is essential to marriage, since it is a unification. As something that does not at all remain private, it easily returns to the group, and later to the state. The founding of a household turns the originally seemingly private event of love into a contract that is not merely a matter of private law. This does not change at all in childless marriages; even then the household acts as a cell of the state. The contract by which two become one body seems to be as much a matter of civil law as possible, and it is so from the inside out; but afterward (and this is true not only of a couple with children, but even of a childless couple with their own affairs) it is no less the establishment of an institution, which is at least half a matter of public law: Here we find the difficulties that accompany the dissolution of the contract (whereas in civil law all contracts can be immediately dissolved by means of the agreement of the partners), the prohibition against a second marriage contract while the first is still in force, the difficulties of adopting children under the age of five, and so on. Marriage as procreation is not only partially but also fully a matter of public law, for procreation is directly incorporated in the state. In growing up children increasingly have their parents behind them, but the state in front of them, awaiting them and ready to make them dependent in a new way. It enters into the marriage through the children, who are the garden from which it takes its citizens; it imposes the obligation to support and educate the children so that the future citizenry (even subjects) shall be as normal as feasible. Thus marriage, which is not there in order to be able to enjoy itself, passes from the private domain of choice, of pleasure, and of habit into the control and supervision of public law. Lovers close the abyss of the sexes as well as of the family, that is true, but in forming a young couple they constitute the cell of an order that is not and cannot be theirs alone. The relation of love, of marriage, an apparently purely private event, can and does participate in the forms of public relations. Jealousy is old, but it is only intensified feelings of possession, which exacerbate it; according to this feeling, one can be "deceived" or "led astray," as in a business. These expressions and at least a portion of the feelings connected with them do not at all require that a public, legal marriage be sealed; nevertheless, it is the state that primarily introduces the twofold illumination. It introduces the most beautiful and richest of all possible relations (excluding its role, which is ultimately a reflex of its patronizing nature). Up to today bourgeois marriage contains residues of the patriarchal, patronizing power over the woman and, even more, over children. The sovereign, as the father of his people, who has disappeared from public law (insofar as worse does not surface there), continues to live in the family, and most schools when they replace nurseries are the old police state in miniature. Only when no spouse, and especially no child, "belongs" to another can a house be unquestionably, namely freely, happy. The family remains a cell of an extended society, but is mildew and pressure for another cell—cells then do not find a subsidy. Love is the best thing that can happen between two people; it succeeds or not according to its own, completely unclouded measure and law. When external woes and worries of marriage are publicly diminished, then it is not necessary that they overburden it.

Origin of the state, *arcana dominationis*

Visible powers are feared less than invisible ones. The state is among the latter, especially since ghosts have disappeared. It shows itself in supreme clarity in police, prisons, and soldiers, but none of these is the state; they only represent it. They lend weight to the state; behind them a committee of the ruling class is at work, one that portrays itself as a universal representative. Its extent is equal to the height with which it seems to overshadow its highest point, and not much is said against it when it is explained as an ideological fetish. But the mystery of every phenomenon is solved in its history; this principle is incontestably true for the phenomenon of the state, which is so very real. One thing is certain: The class state is not an "extended" family, and does not come from one. The ancient original familial association of production recognized servants, children, woman, and the master, but property was held in common; they had a division of labor, but one still natural, not formed by classes. There were the beginnings of classes; exploitation is as old as the division of labor, but the cohesion of the large family still held everything at least halfway in accord with primitive communism. At this stage, community is still real, no caste has risen to a level that is separate from the collective interest, dominating all others. The slaves of the south and west have long preserved the communality of the family and the community of families. The members of the community are immediately socialized in the act of production; work is divided according to tradition and need, and the products of labor, insofar as they are consumed, are treated according to the same principle. The surplus of the products of labor beyond the operating costs of production, the formulation of a social fund of products and reserves from this surplus, had not yet become the property of a privileged class that was thereby accorded political dominance.

How then did the jump finally occur from the most ancient and—in familial and market associations—progressive primitive commune to well-formed relations of domination? How was the jump made to ancient Oriental despotism, to the ancient slaveholder state, to the medieval feudal nobility, to the modern bourgeoisie? The pure form of the *theory of violence* (put forth by Gumplowicz, Dühring, and especially by Franz Oppenheimer, but also, in the end, by the older Kautsky) denies that the class state could have arisen from the widespread division of labor and of the exchange economy. Consequently it was not formed from factors internal to the primitive community itself, by means that the old gentlemanly constitution disintegrated. Instead of these factors an "attack from outside" is said to be responsible for the production of the state: Hunter tribes, but especially growing tribes (among whom the division of labor and private property had already begun), were attacked and subjugated by warring nomadic, cattle-breeding tribes. It is in this clash, when the agricultural tribes became Helots, that the formation of classes, class oppression, and state violence have their origin; war and nothing else lays the cornerstone. The state arises out of the war of conquest, through the unification of two communities from which the victorious become the exploiters while the vanquished become the exploited class; the coercive state is imposed from outside. The political purpose of this theory of violence is avowedly not only an apology for democracy and occasionally, with an anarchistic twist, the introduction of violence, but not by means of the economy; rather (and this is completely incompatible with anarchism) it wants most of all to be an apology for *capitalistic* democracy: A wage laborer is not a slave. Because—at least this is how Kautsky continues with this theory—the *capitalistic modes of production* do not rest upon the supremacy of the military as do the modes of production of slavery and of feudal serfdom. Capitalism is the first pure economic formation, even if it is incorporated in the heritage of the coercive state. It is only the coercive state, taken in isolation with its feudal configuration, which is only partially overcome, that might be combated, not industrial capitalism, because this, by its very nature, is not restricted to a state and is without coercion. If exploitation in the slaveholder state and in the feudal state is the result of naked armed violence, then the coercive state, as having arisen purely from power, can be completely isolated from economy with the consequence that exploitation becomes a militantly alien element in capitalism. As a result exploitation can be eliminated; and once it has been liberated from this militant alien body, capitalistic democracy is not only possible but ordained, as evolving peacefully into socialism. All of this rests upon the view that the pure theory of violence is the primary means for understanding the rise of the state and the equally pure exception that the capitalistic state constitutes in this theory. Nevertheless, even the extremely suspect later purposes (the apology for capitalism) do not totally refute a theory of the state that is originally purely historical, and not consciously ideological. The relation of conquest that existed between the Spartans and the Helots, perhaps even between the Roman patricians (often of Etruscan origin) and the native plebeians, between the Anglo-Saxons and the Britons, and between the Normans and the Anglo-Saxons, all of these relations could be used to support the theory of violence. The same is true of the Brandenburg-Prussian state; it arose as a military colony in a slave region and for a long while was "a sadomasochistic amalgam" (Mehring, *The Legend of Lessing*). But these events could not be hypostatized, much less projected backward into the dark nights of time; for in them the first state was not effectively formed, but possession was taken of an already existing state, which was then transformed. There is no historical evidence that the power of the conqueror everywhere and always was the first form of a domination of a majority by a minority, and that class divisions and the formation of the state had not already begun in the subjugated peoples out of immanent economic causes. That is why the only other theory, the *economic theory*, of the origin of the state correctly posits the genetic accents—with the precise result that it can really work against the causes of the persistence of power, a persistence that is overextended. The economic theory of the origin of the state (put forth in its classical form by Engels) does not deny the complicity of violence and robbery in the division of the classes and the formation of the state, but it does not separate politics from economy; it regards the wars of conquest as the result, not the causes, of organizations of exploitation and violence. The primitive commune of hunter tribes did not need to be attacked by herding tribes in order to become a society of classes. Quite the contrary, the progressive, immanent division of labor itself formed the dominant class, which was ultimately made into something formidable by the state; all progress in the division of labor entailed the transformation of the state into an instrument of domination, but this process was not in the least imposed from without. *Inequality in the ownership of the means of production*, and nothing else, led, in an economically immanent way, to the destruction of tribal solidarity and to the formation of a political class violence. Consequent to this one can say that rather than being alien to the state, capitalism must be viewed as its culmination. All the same, it is only then that it fulfills its most important ideological function: to serve not only as the instrument of class domination but also as its *disguise*. It presents itself then as a universal power, which apparently stands above the society and equalizes what takes place there. It complements the bourgeois society to the same extent that a faded universal interest (the interest of the citizen of the state) complements atomistic private property. This power of the state, with its "objective" hauteur, constitutes itself as the mutual assurance of the bourgeois class for its individual members and against the exploited class, "an assurance," said Marx in 1850, "that only becomes increasingly costly, and apparently more autonomous vis-à-vis the bourgeois society, because the oppression of the exploited classes always becomes more difficult"; fascism at least has proven this to be more than true.

But the bourgeois state presented itself as being a neutral power above classes and parties, as economically free, indeed as a living transcendent power whose objectivity and disinterestedness is always ordered toward the well-being of the whole. The origin and main-tenance of this power as the power of the dominant class demystifies its objectivity even where it is continually established as *res publica*. The most frequent manifestation, up to this point, of this image of community was in the political interior of the police state and the political exterior of war; in an antagonistic society this community was never really a constitutional state, and even less—*contradictio in adjecto*—a civilized state, and it could never be these. The superstructure of the state, although it will sooner or later disappear, is revolutionized more slowly than the basis, and even more slowly than the super-structures of art, of religion, of philosophy, although these do not disappear.

It is precisely in modern times that the essence of the state acquires a sharp contour. Never before were bullets and father so close, so defensively united. Instead of being a legacy of the past, which is imposed upon it, the state is the true product of the bourgeois economy. The growing internal and external oppositions have polished the state; they have become ways of serving the dominant class. As the most general form of capitalistic enterprise, the state destroys and impreg-nates its early, so to speak organic, loosely stratified forms: the for-mations of dependencies according to classes. It sets aside the church, takes that which is mundane away from it, as well as the relative beyond of ethics and education. In almost total opposition to the splendor of the court, the absolute monarchy becomes the first form of the capitalistic state; it thus smashed the power of the feudal orders, and established itself as autonomous with respect to the church. Bodin (*The Six Books of the Republic*, 1577) is the first to give this definition: The state, which is the most reasonable government and is provided with supreme power, is a sum of families and of that which is common to them. Sovereignty is a constant and unconditional violence done to the subjects, with the right to give laws but without having to be bound by them. "Absolute and perpetual power" was already estab-lished in the French state of that epoch; for Bodin, the first to disdain natural law from a perspective of positive law, legislation should be directed according to the condition of the society at any given moment. But in *The Prince* (1532) Machiavelli had already announced a technological realism well adapted to such power. More Attic than Roman, nourished by the image of the polis, he nevertheless described what the ruling criminals of every age did and must do. Machiavelli, who was not very original theoretically (he never produced any genuine theory of the state), did not differentiate between forms of government here. Even in his *Discourses*, which are a commentary on Livy, he was a republican in order to be an adviser to the absolute sovereign in *The Prince*, with a cynicism of a grand style that is interested only in its goal. The sole goal is the stabilization of the national state, which is free of churches, amoral, and areligious; and the mass of the people only experience and understand the state as dominating. For their bourgeois and monarchistic detractors, the mass of the people are simply vile, a heap of something thoroughly evil, which is the eternally same human nature; consequently, the hoi polloi must be kept in check by all means, and for them Machiavelli first formed the secret recipe for domination. On their side, one finds the secret recipe in relations with foreign powers; the apology of the clever struggle of interests is multiplied and made more elastic by means of the acknowledgment that it is happening. The success of *The Prince* in the sixteenth and seventeenth centuries rests not only upon the fact that it is the basic book of princely absolutism. Its success rests just as much upon the fact that it is the basic book of public conspiracy, of overt cabinet politics, of the counterpoint of exquisite intrigues. The success (in the governmental domain of serene highnesses) is tied to the counterthrust to natural law, to the elasticity of the rationale of the state in opposition to the subversive rigor of the argumentation of natural law. Fascism did not invent anything here; it only enforced and totalized the praxis of the white terror that already functioned perfectly in all revolutionary times from the peasant work to the Paris Commune. In addition, fascism, as the most perfect form of the oppressive state, developed its final touches: the *criminal secrets of the conquest and consolidation of power*—in other words, the secret plans and practices, of a technological sort, by means of which domination is set to work and preserved internally and externally. In the seventeenth century there is a well-used literature on this secret formula, and it is almost exclusively related to Machiavelli's catalogue. The leading jurist of the National Socialists, Carl Schmitt, was the first to reestablish theoretical contact with the complex of "state secrets," and the resounding silence of an awesome trickery. This has nothing to do with recesses and the like, nor with the "unethical dealings of the courts" about which the petite bourgeoisie, since the Enlightenment, have been enviously indignant. The dramatic figure of the "intriguer" is given a better image; from the time of the baroque theater up to Schiller, he is usually a courtier, and certainly a master of objectionable providence. Up to the present he is associated, on the left, with well-practiced servility, with dogs nourished on despotism, with trembling alleyways. Tacitus's phrase holds true for brute power: "Socordiam eorum irridere licet qui praesenti potentia aevi temporis memoriam extinqui posse credunt." Cunning power was beyond this sentence for a long while. In this domain the authoritative text was the best collection of secret formulas of all the ministers of propaganda, by the jurist of the crosier and the crooked state, Arnold Clapmar: *De arcanis rerum publicarum* (1605). Clapmar made the premonitory observation that trade also has its recesses, its tricks, which not everyone knows, its form of cunning and deception in order to reach its goal. Even medicine, the art of war, even painting, have secret means, but the only domain where they are unavoidable is the leading of the state, because the net of subjugation has to be as brutal as it is sublime. Without fanfare this disciple of Machiavelli differentiated two aspects here: *Arcana dominationis*, that is, the doctrine of how one does away with the people who rebel, and *arcana imperii*, which is the doctrine of how one keeps peace among the people in normal times, how one protects sovereignty, forms alliances for oneself, and how one gathers soldiers and money. Both of these aspects continually merge with each other, just as shrewdness and tactics of violence merge, or at least complement each other in a well-governed state. The principal tricks of *arcana* are certain organizations that give the appearance of freedom in order to pacify the people, "simulacra libertatis," decorative institutions that give class orders a noisy, but politically insignificant role to play. Instructive for the latent fascism in that political wisdom is this advice: Promise everything to people who are revolting, "nam postea sedato populo retractari posunt." Again, that which is promised can be presented with "rhetorica pro realitate," with pretty glosses, as if it would be fulfilled. Dictatorship from above is appointed a specific *arcanum dominationis*: It intimidates the people by creating an authority against which there can be no provocation. This is the most extreme antipode to classical natural law, which was being formed at the same time, and it is the truth of the "positive law." The Bible of *arcanis* itself gives the following enormous climax: "Jus naturae corrigitur a jure gentium, jus gentium a jure militari, jus militari a jure legationis, jus legationis a jure Regni sive dominationis"—here, in this "correction" by an increasingly narrower and stricter power, is the reality of public law, even where the *jus Regni* is, by chance, absent. To apply concepts of private law, such as *aequitas* or *justitia*, to public law seems naive in the eyes of this *arcana* power. Where "eventus solum judicabit," the categories of law and injustice are valid only as paraphrases that designate conformity to the goal, or they are included in the calculus as expressions of ideas that are dominant among men. Incipient classical natural law, which has its debut among the monarchical powers, saw in the "pestifera doctrina" in this Machiavelli-inspired literature the spirit of Saint Bartholomew's Night; but it is more than that. The identity of power and law belongs to formation of class domination in the state; according to this, the law of the people itself and the natural law of peace, which it contains, can be made into an affair of the general staff. When what Jakob Burckhardt said is true, that states are maintained by the same principle according to which they were founded, then the institution of the state as such is maintained thanks to the economic division of men, which was established right after the primitive commune. According to this law, Caesar enters the picture and is vital to the end—from Nimrod up to fascism, up to the difficult beginnings of a society that is becoming classless, where, according to Engels's phrase the "government of persons" can give way to the "administration of things." Until then, and to this end, the socialist state would be, according to the instruction given by Marx and Engels, in a *completely inverted form* and without comparison with any previous state. Its sole function would be to serve its own decline, a provisional structure and supporting beam in the construction of the nonstate that is to be erected. Thus, in *Anti-Dühring* we find the following definition: "Political authority is appeased to the degree that anarchy disappears from social production." Without the reification of power in the construction of its opposite in the non–*arcanum liberationis*, and all the more so without the use of means that profane the goal. This characterizes class societies up to today: The stooped shoulder is adjoined to need, and these stay together, with economic dependency as primary, so that neither one can be eliminated without the other. This means, exploitation does not disappear by means of a powerless freedom; it is only the case that white-collar workers, proletarians with shirt collars, proliferate; the condition of administration is not at all impeded by the mere participation in property that is being socialized. The pride of the upright carrige, natural law, whether consciously or not, is the element that resists, the insurgent element in all revolution. Spartacus did not only rebel for economic reasons, any more than the French Revolution is thinkable without the spark of human rights; they were directly opposed to the "discomfort" of Gessler's hat, as Schiller called it. "In place of the old bourgeois society with their classes and class oppositions there arises an association wherein the free development of each person is the condition for the free development of everyone" (*Communist Manifesto*, 1848); Beethoven could have endorsed this. And because no constitutional state in prosperity can in the long run conceal the true catastrophic essence of capitalism, nor can any Stalin, with very modifiable causes, conceal the most humane of all victories: socialism. These words of Marx are true *ante rem*, even *in re*, *post rem*: Their truth is the index of both itself and its opposite. The basic tenor of radical natural law against the state is the classless society, the realm of freedom; it only grows insofar as it is a prelude.

25

The Nationalized God and the Right to Community

Even when something has completely ceased to be, it does not immediately disappear. A gap remains, one that retains the form of the previous fullness. The house that has been torn down and has become a thing of the past still clearly occupies the place in which it once stood. This is also the case with the state, where another power, standing in a quite dissimilar place, gladly fills whatever gaps may be left by it. This power is the church, whose demise along with that of property and classes at least is not as manageable or necessary as the state's. A future world management, which fits well with the needs of productive processes, does not undertake any kind of state business, though it is quite conceivable that something like a centralized advisory bureau remains, something like an administration for the meaning of things, something that orders feelings and instructs the mind and spirit in order, like the church, to live in preparation and with a sense of direction. This is why in the same society where the processes of production and distribution take place at the margins of the society, the essential human concerns move to the center, to the end, into the final questions of "where to" and "what for." Instead of the shabbiest of all concerns, the concern for profit, which used to shroud and preoccupy the final places of the lives of most people—instead of this, the genuine, worthwhile, proper concerns stand out in sharper relief than ever before: the question of what is not right in life. A society that is no longer antagonistic will of course hold all worldly fates in its hand; its members are not in economic, political situations, they have no economic, political destiny, but it is precisely this that sensitizes them to the indignities of existence, from the jaws of death down to such ebb tides of life as boredom and weariness. The heralds of nothingness have lost the weight that they had in the class society; they wear a new face, largely inconceivable as yet, but the train of purposes they break apart has an equally new way of gnawing away. The church has tied such things to the allegedly ineradicable earthly vale of tears, justifying this by the destiny that men have merely brought upon themselves. To the metaphysical need, which is bound up with so much, the church has advanced mythological answers in which the masters of earthly powers occurred once again, so that the state existing on earth was reinforced by a heavenly state. And yet, no matter how transparent its ideology has become, the real metaphysical question will outlast the mythological, transcendent answers that are handed out by the churches of the masters. This question will not go away with those churches; in its own way it even lives in the adventures and obscurities of unadulterated immanence, in the objective, real obscurities of this immanence, and precisely in them. If culture has a strategy against the seclusion of existence, then it is not completely unthinkable to have a general staff for this campaign, even long after the five-year plans of the socialist construction are completed, even after all possible insights have been won into the *Écrasez l'infame* concerning the church, its funeral pyres, its stultifying effects, and the blessing that it never accidentally bestows on all the white guards. Because this is not the whole story, the natural law of the revolutionary sects has never damned the church in the same total sense that it damned the state power. The natural law of these sects condemned the state because, *a limine*, there is too much of Nimrod, of Ahab, of Nero, connected with it; but they condemn the church because, having allied itself with the Neros, it has too little of anything, of Christ and of his community. And because of this metaphysical (not mythological) need, which is difficult to satisfy socially, that which is connected with the church is not going to become quite so rootless as the state, once the society of property and classes is abolished. Instead of the "government of persons," we shall be "administering things," managing processes of production and exchange. But where does one find a place for the *organism* of persons, for the *apse*, and, above all, *apse window of solidarity*, which casts a transcending light without transcendence? The gates of hell will not overpower the church; it has opened them itself far too often. It is one thing when the power church, the church of superstitions, passes away, and it is something different when a power-free force is on guard and stands guard in teaching conscience the "where to" and "what for." Bebel said that in the "future state" it will not be the officer but the teacher who will be the first among men; and the same would be true in a church en route and without superstition. It would be thoroughly religious, but not as *religio*, or the reunion with domination and its mythologies, but as the forward reunion of a whole dream with our deficient fragments.

Now to return to the given church; it lives almost completely chaste and pious toward money. It zealously speaks against the harm done to Joseph and the sheep, but it has made arrangements with the masters and it defends them spiritedly. It bristles at see-through blouses, but not at slums in which half-naked children starve, and, above all, not at the relations that hold three-quarters of mankind in misery. It damns desperate girls who abort a fetus, but it sanctifies war, which aborts millions. It has nationalized its God, nationalized him into an ecclesiastic organization, and it has inherited the Roman Empire under the mask of the crucified. It preserves misery and injustice insofar as it tolerates, then approves, the class violence that causes them; it obstructs the seriousness of liberation by postponing it to a St. Never-Ever Day, by shifting it into the beyond. As a means of mollifying the proletarians of antiquity, the church has been victorious; as a feudal, and then capitalistic, often openly fascist, world power it has splendidly prepared "the coming of the kingdom of Christ." The entanglement with the interests of the bourgeois state, a new Constantinian state of affairs, has ultimately united the Catholic and Protestant churches in anticommunism; after all, the anti-Ghibelline tension between the church and state was profoundly conspiratorial. It only concerned the competitive portion of the profit and domination, not a negation of both on the basis of the Gospel. In Spain, and even more in the France of the *ancien régime*, where the church was the largest landowner and received tithes, the state had no trouble with the church, and the laws of both were as inseparable as Castor and Pollux. Similarly, the church became the patron of the fascist attempts to form a so-called corporate state; Leo XIII's prescription for this was not the first, but it was the first to have a goal that was antisocialistic. Under the given, highly developed capitalistic relations, the clerical idea of a corporate state has nothing in common with medieval reality; rather it is the modern ideology of the class struggle from above. It fantasizes a vertical "occupational link" between the worker and the owner of a shoe factory; this verticalism is supposed, by means of a plant community and an edifice of such communities, to overcome the horizontal chasm between capital and labor; and in this the church sees an element of the idea of the *corpus Christi*. Gone are the competitive anomalies that led Jesuits like Bellarmine and Mariana to teach the

right to resist an evil authority, even to the point of tyrannicide: What
the Vatican advertises to the capitalist states now is the cure for the
souls of its obedient citizens. It only consecrates a decidedly capitalistic
authority, not the legal authority of Spain, which fought against the
fascists, and of course not the Bolshevist authority. But here no transitions are possible at all for all the "honorable past" of papism (the
most decisive form of the organized church); too much of this past,
not to mention the present, is not worthy of honor. It is without a
doubt an excessive simplification and journalistic sloganeering to call
the church a Roman branch of Wall Street, but it always was a structure
of compromise and its elasticity only broke down when confronted
with socialism. A separation of church Christianity from capitalism is
therefore hard to envision, although the young clergy was, and never
is, quite like the old clergy, although even socialism no longer has to
speak of religious matters in terms of the dregs of a sham Enlightenment. Nevertheless, the authoritarian administration of the vine and
its branches has almost always been more in line with Caesar than
Christ, just as is the case in any clericalism, even one that shrinks
from bureaucratizing, centralizing, and dogmatizing itself; we find in
the church of the past an example that is instructive not only for
Catholicism. After its Hispanization, the intellectual life of Italy died
down; after Galileo's trial important segments of the Lutheran intelligentsia, who had begun to vacillate, became immune again and were
as embittered or indifferent toward the ideas of Mariana as if they
were an armistice in chains. An encyclical issued by Gregory XVI in
1832, a prelude to the proclamation of infallibility of 1870, made
reference to the "madness that every person is entitled to the freedom
of conscience." "Ergo vestigia terrent, aut Caesar aut Christus" applies
in every respect, and discredits that which belongs to Caesar. And
yet—so far as one can see into the lingering grayness of dawn—
catholicity, without any parallels to the reified institutional church with
its absolutized role as a shepherd, might well be implied in *solidarity*.
The new ecumenism belongs to a society that is not essentially antagonistic; it belongs to a community that can grow undisturbedly.
And the ecumenism, in order to live not just for a day but beyond
the day, belongs to an institution that does more than administer
things, an institution that takes seriously the friendship that runs deep
and the fraternity that is so difficult. Socialism is the path to this; it
is the finally realizable inheritance of what was meant by an inner

emancipation and an outer peace. The red faith was always more than a private matter; there is a basic right to community, to humanism, that is equally political and in the goal. This is what the demanding right was en route to: the *eunomia* of the upright carriage in community. Art is not alone in holding the dignity of humanity in its hands.

26

Appendix: Christian Thomasius, a German Scholar without Misery

That there is only truth. That this consists in the living knowledge of the true Good.—Thomasius, *Summary outline of the basic doctrines that a law student needs to know and which must be taught in the universities*, pt. I, chap. I, 1.

It is time to commemorate an upright man. He was justly uncomfortable in his sleepy and servile surroundings. If they had had their way, then they would have destroyed this annoying innovator. But this did not happen; instead once again an honorable spirit, one who is both honorable and spirited, and who speaks of progress, makes himself unavoidable in the long run. In what follows we will meet a powerful and suggestive figure of that "doing right" characteristic of the ascending bourgeoisie. This educator was German and he acted German, in the best sense of the word. There was nothing rigid or inflexible about him, except that he would not bow down before anyone.

Such a truthful man was Christian Thomasius. Jurist with philanthropy, philosophy, and, not least among his merits, one of the first German journalists. He was born in Leipzig in 1655, he died in Halle in 1728, still full of powerful ideas for the public welfare. His father before him was already a renowned scholar; the young Leibniz numbered among his disciples. Thomasius studied law in Leipzig after he became a professor of philosophy; in 1697 he was accorded the title Dr. Juris, and soon after he gave lectures in Frankfurt-on-the-Oder, and then in Leipzig. These lectures were permeated with the warmth of a love of natural law, with a love of the rights that are born with us, as one said at that time, and that are the inalienable rights. Thomasius was led to the study of law by this faith in the human dignity that is expressed in natural law. His lectures on natural law drew much attention, though of course it was not always a pleasant, sympathetic attention. But the stumbling block and scandal came from another side.

The lecture

It is well known that Thomasius was the first to speak German in German lecture halls. In 1687, he posted a notice on the bulletin board, which had never been "profaned" by any such thing, that announced a lecture in the language of the people. This lecture was to be on the book by the famous Spaniard Gracián, *Oráculo manual, y arte de prudencia*, the title of which Thomasius vividly translated as *Basic Rules for a Reasonable, Clever, and Civil Life*. Even the choice of such a book, one so full of ruses and double standards and polytonal, was uncommon; but even this was not so uncommon as the study that Thomasius wrote in Latin two years earlier, *De crimine bigamiae*, in which he taught that on the basis of natural law monogamy could not be logically deduced as an obligation. But this book stayed far removed from the world of public opinion; it was taken more as a scholastic study of logical consequences. Nevertheless, the astonishment and indignation that the respectable citizens of Leipzig felt in the face of such an unusual study is quite easy to imagine. But soon these and other sorts of impertinent provocations ceased, and then Thomasius created a sensation in the double, and best, sense of the word. With the novelty of a lecture held in German, the young professor taught the precise opposite of bigamy, namely, fidelity to the German language, a call for that which had been repudiated in the highest institutions of learning and science. The lecture course began, ironically, with a eulogy on the Goths and "the forms in which one should imitate the French," namely, not as it happens among all of us where even diseases are supposed to be French, à la mode, and only one thing is not imitated: the profound respect that the French have for their native tongue. It is this aspect of France that, above all others, must be introduced among us, even as concerns scholarly lectures and the writing of scholarly works. With the Thirty Years' War and the ruin of the German cities, with the decline of the bourgeoisie of early capitalism, with the victory of the "princely liberality" in Germany, with all of this, it is a great irony and rare patriotism—and a century and a half after Luther's translation of the Bible, this was an unprecedented audacity—that the German language was introduced into the world of scholars, this language so full of images and vigor in Walter and Wolfram, so full of nuance and depth in Meister Eckehart and Tauler. The merit of Thomasius is even greater because he began with language what could only be finished today by opening the doors of the institutions of higher learning to the people. Insofar as only Latin was accepted in German institutions of learning, insofar as the student was restricted to hearing only Latin, was obliged to think in Latin and then to express and write what he thought and learned in Latin, he only had foreign words for all that he knew, and his native tongue became completely helpless for such higher employment. Above all the already unbridgeable division between the class orders was amplified anew by a new barrier: the barrier of the academic language. The monopoly of culture, aggravated by Latin, further divided the citizenry into the lettered and illiterate; and a fortiori it preserved the distance between science and the people. In one fell swoop Thomasius introduced the possibility of the entry of the Enlightenment into the general populace. In teaching science by speaking German and insisting upon the importance of this, long before the philosopher of the Enlightenment, the "praeceptor Germaniae," Christian von Wolff, he developed in Germany a national linguistic form with a content that was both bourgeois and European. And in the midst of the empire divided by a hundred territorial principalities, he bestowed upon his domain, the highest domain of knowledge and of science, the unity of a fatherland, at least as something spoken.

The journal

But Thomasius even outside of the lecture hall made his German quite accessible and public. This he did, alongside his teaching, as a journalist, as a man of the world and simultaneously as magisterial in the best sense of the word. This enterprising man did nothing less than publish (from 1688 onward) the first cultural journal of his country, the *Teutsche Monate* [Monthly German Chronicle] (though he frequently changed the title). For two years, until Thomasius left Leipzig, the journal was published monthly; for this representative of the Enlightenment it was important that it reach bourgeois women and that it put them in touch with the intellectual spirit. In many ways the first German journal took the *Journal des Savants* [Scholars' Journal] as its model, a journal that, founded in 1665, was already some twenty years old. But—and this is certainly worthy of note—it also appeared some twenty years before Defoe's *Review*, and before Steele and Addison's journal *The Tatler* (1709) and its continuation (*The Spectator*, *The Guardian*), and almost forty years before Gottsched's *Vernünftigen Tadlerinnen* [Reasonable Criticisms], which appeared in 1725. Thomasius's journal was quickly imitated in many German cities and in Anglicized Hamburg. In the charms of its language, its witticism, and in the wealth of its scenes, dialogues, and themes *The Tatler* is far superior to Thomasius's effort, as well as all others. But there is something extremely surprising that has yet to be adequately emphasized: In the dialogical form as well as in the narrative form, which served as its framework with its invented persons and situations and its alteration between caricature and genre, Thomasius was obviously the forerunner. On this point consequently there is little of the German misery and distress that characterizes other important moments of German literature, and least of all is any exalted misery found here. Rather, the style of the *Teutsche Monate* is very definitely of this earth; it is even an almost unique style, blended of different earths, from the crude style of Abraham a Santa Clara to the concise irony that almost anticipated Lichtenberg. One of the most important masters of form was Pierre Bayle, who wrote the *Nouvelles de la république des lettres* (1684), but Erasmus of Rotterdam was one of the most decisive figures in this regard, the most independent mind of his age, whom Bayle and Thomasius both claimed as a predecessor. Doubtless some of the "vocabulum eleganter sonans," as Thomasius said, could not yet be adapted to the German of that time; nevertheless, the predominant style of the journal is, in Thomasius's own words, "joyous and ingenious." It was joyful as a result of the faith in reason expressed by the ascending bourgeois class; it was ingenious as a result of the well-aimed and well-proportioned satire. This satire was not overly general, directed toward abstractions such as drunkenness, coquetry, or foppishness in general, as was often done in Germany where there was seldom a concrete target of satire from its beginning in the Middle Ages up to efforts of this sort in the young Jean Paul. Rather, the *Teutsche Monate* made its targets clearly visible; in Thomasius the work of the "vinegar factory" (as Jean Paul called satire) had a concrete task and object. Here the object was the Leipzig of his time (with clearly identifiable figures) looked at as the mirror of a world: Its object was the hypocrisy of the orthodox, the pedantry of an outdated university reduced to Scholasticism, and, at least secretly, the impertinence of the princely police state. A man who was self-taught, learned in law and the philosophy of right, and who enriched these domains showed himself to be the absolute enemy of the Whigs.

Even the material of Hans Sachs, such as the love story of Aristotle
(with which Thomasius wanted to attack the practice of Scholasticism),
are repeated in an almost Offenbachian way.

It is now necessary to take a look at this earliest, fine German
journal. From its first volume it developed its critical content as a
conversation among four people. More precisely, these four people
are drawn into this conversation during a journey on a postal car.
They are Christopher, a salesman who knows how to live well; Augustin,
a cavalier who is well acquainted with society and the larger world;
Benedict, a learned and fastidious scholar; and David, a pedant held
captive by his prejudices. The discussion covers the sermons of Abraham
a Santa Clara, then, in a leap, moves to recent French novels, which
the unprejudiced scholar appreciates for their worldly and national
quality, while the pedant degrades them for the same reason. Instead
this pedant praises Scholastic logic, rhetoric, and metaphysics, and
from this wonderful problems are raised that he wanted to see discussed. This narrow mind suggests—and real academic science only
is manifested in him at this point—that history should be examined
to see "whether or not David had already drunk coffee because among
other gifts Abigail brought him dehydrated beans." In physics, according to the doctrine that says that air and not water is the wettest
element, it must be proven *per deductionem* that there could be water
that was not wet. Medicine must refute *per inductionem* the troubling
discovery of the circulation of the blood, "because anatomy shows
that in its object there can be no circulation." And now the argument
that seals the fate of all the praiseworthy doctors: Calculus must be
a Christian mathematics with uniquely religious examples and it must
be proven "that proof by addition, which operates with the cross, is
more Christian and more correct than proof by subtraction." Here
Thomasius's sarcasm anticipates Lichtenberg, and even Lessing's satire
The Young Scholar. Thus Lichtenberg spoke of a skull that looked so
natural that one could believe it was alive; and before a discussion on
women, Lessing's young Whig wanted to know if the *status controversiae*
is in the syllogism in Barbara or Celarent. Thus, almost two centuries
later, Dostoyevsky invented a German dissertation on the importance
of the city of Hanau as a Hanseatic city and on the peculiar circumstances that explain why Hanau is absolutely not a Hanseatic city.
And that is why Swift had a typically English, compromise-minded
person say that the soul is neither mortal nor immortal, but that the

truth of the matter, as in all things, is found in the middle between the two. With his scorn Thomasius takes up the authentic tradition of humanism and of the Renaissance against extravagant arguments and worthless pedantry. And even more so against that subalterity that makes progress itself into a formal spider's web and transforms the fruits of a learning in bloom into a spiritual desert. The conversation continues on the same subject; Thomasius caricatures science with the illustrative thesis that one can find more reason and right in soldiers and women who are unprejudiced than in an ivory tower scholar. This caricature undoubtedly struck home, as the reaction to it clearly demonstrates, especially among those who were typical manifestations of Protestant neo-Scholasticism—in other words, among that swarm of emaciated epigones who, since Melanchthon, were well installed everywhere, and who had set up a remarkable sterility and bigotry everywhere (and perhaps especially in Leipzig). In the end the discussion turns to political books, and they are rejected à la Chveik. They are called useless because the private individual is not as clever as the prince, "who knows all of the secret agreements"; and these books are dangerous "because high heads have long arms, and if one wants to be sincere one cannot always speak of them in the best light, since princes and lords are also subjugated to human weakness." One of them then looks at Benedict, the scholar because he pulls out a notebook of *Acta Eruditorum*, and then he asks what is really in this *Actis*. But Benedict immediately begins his tale and has no sooner mentioned Mr. Mencke, the editor of the famous scholarly journal of Leipzig (on which Thomasius himself collaborated) than the car turns over, and "their discussion comes to an abrupt end." This end simultaneously marks the end of the first issue of the first month of the journal, and it does so in an unquestionably charming manner. But even this sort of conclusion caused the Whigs to be greatly irritated with Thomasius; they contended, with a singular lack of humor, that he was predicting, in an allegorical manner, an ignominious end to the *Acta Eruditorum*. Thomasius retorted with perfect seriousness, and even angelically, that he would have to have been mad as a hatter if, as a young man without any counsel and authority, he were to arrive at such an idea. Besides, he only took recourse to the snow, and had from this decided to come to the end because otherwise the month would have become too dull for him. That the fall in the snow, besides being a literary device, had another consequence is evident in the next issue of the journal: David, the pedant, injured his head in this unhappy fall. That is why he must give himself over to the care of the barber in the next city; meanwhile, the conversation of the three remaining travelers continues all the more freely. It would be too much to sketch out the content of this and the following issues, but what is common to them all is the explicit goal "of revealing to the human race, who are largely blinded by pedantry and bigotry, the teachings of true virtue and of honest learnedness." In the midst of these critiques, the dialogue on excise taxes and on the injustice of taxes is quite conspicuous. Insofar as the authorities, "who have a great debt to pay to the poor," nevertheless extort taxes from them, the nobility and the church can live tax-free in Christ. Christopher, the worldly-wise businessman, suggests than instead every amorous rendezvous should be taxed; henceforth, all the clerics would be in a good position to make their contribution. A contribution that would be equally pleasing to God, because, as it is reported, all taxes only serve to bolster the funds that the prince of Saxony needs in order to fight the war with the Turks. Therefore this money contributes to the war against the owners of the harems and the repudiators of the doctrine that no one who is rich can pass through the gates of heaven. The story continues in this tone, constantly playing the "contra," in the early employ of the German Enlightenment.

A particularly successful rebuff must be alluded to for its uniqueness and instructiveness. This one is not directed against antiquated traditions, but against a real thinker. Even the tone is different, sympathetic, but without suffering from a loss of critical wit or the force of argument. Quite the contrary, one sees here an elegant nastiness, and besides this, an extremely important this-worldly profession of faith that is nevertheless not a materialistic faith. The adversary in this case, or the one who was set up as an adversary, was the important contemporary philosopher, mathematician, and physicist, Tschirnhaus, the author of the text *Medicina mentis*, which sought to point out evidence of immediate certainties in self-consciousness. Tschirnhaus, who followed the tradition of Descartes and was acquainted with Spinoza and Leibniz, had claimed that in the *Monate* Thomasius had called into question the purity of his Christianity. This was related to the way in which Tschirnhaus had founded morals in his *Medicina mentis*, where he says that the immediate certainty that forms the basis of morals is simply the unpleasant and pleasant affections of consciousness. This is the only certitude from which Tschirnhaus derived his moral philosophy, which was to investigate the well-being and happiness of man. This last aspect was completely in the sense of Thomasius, but Tschirnhaus charged that Thomasius said that the *Medicina mentis* recommended Lucretius, the infamous poet who was even more infamous as an atheist and materialist. Tschirnhaus, obviously vexed and disturbed, demanded reparation for this incongruity. And then the June issue of the *Monate* appeared with the splendid riposte that, by means of an ironic correction, turned the intended insult into an even greater praise. Without making much mention of Tschirnhaus, Thomasius defused the objection of Epicureanism by coming to the defense of Epicurus. In the first place he placed an engraving on the issue, in which Epicurus lay sound asleep with his head on the breast of Cupid (which the historian Luden almost blushingly recounts in his book *Christian Thomasius* (1805), a book that is still quite worth reading); Plato shoos the mosquitoes away from him (an allusion to the Ideas that had become otherworldly), and Aristotle catches the noisy crickets (an allusion to the Colleqium logicum, which had become crude, and to the entire new Scholasticism). As for the rehabilitation of Epicurus, Thomasius does not defend his atomic theory, since he lacks the interest and knowledge of physics for this. But unlike Tschirnhaus, he does accord a great honor to Epicurus the moralist, the teacher of a worldly happiness that is not terrorized by the fear of God. The pleasure in which Epicurus found the purpose of human life is thus as perfect as the word itself is sweet and lovely, as the harmony of man with himself and his world. In saying this Thomasius already affirms here something that he will affirm again later with respect to happiness, which he characterizes in his philosophy of right as a human honor; on this point he is genuinely a materialist. No lasciviousness is in this, no vulgar, that is, isolated, pleasure is found here, but we do find the morality of pleasure here, and it is this that Thomasius liberates from the ill repute into which it had been bought by so many centuries of false otherworldliness. Indeed, he said that the intoxication of an otherworldly, transcendent God, which is found in the sciences, where it does not belong, is often nothing other than "the effect of a glass of wine or brandy." Epicurus himself had, of course, already been discovered by Gassendi, and Thomasius made use of his ground-breaking work *De vita, moribus et doctrina Epicuri* of 1647. But even if the philosopher Gassendi had a much greater knowledge of Epicurus's atomism than Thomasius did, Gassendi the canon (which he also was) withdrew all the more anxiously from the "Epicurean" Epicurus. But Thomasius had especially glorified the infamous philosopher at precisely the point where he was accused of indecency. And he made this profession of moral faith in the public light of a journal, instead of concealing it in the distant and guarded observations of the Latinized republic of scholars.

Halle, Pietists, remarkable backgrounds

Now the measure was full, the cup overflowed. The rebellious man only seemed to have friends among the persecuted whom he helped. He could not help himself as persecuted, for he had made enemies and struck far too many respected people. Add to this foreign quarrels with servile Lutherans, and the clerical orders trembled; those in academic gowns, especially the jurists, demanded retribution. At the instigation of the clergy, and assisted by furious colleagues, Thomasius was expelled from Leipzig in 1690. The formal reason was that Thomasius had profaned the true faith insofar as he had stated in an affidavit that there was nothing objectionable about the mixed marriage between reformed and orthodox Lutherans when it conerned the royalty. The more important reason was obviously this man without misery, the natural light, the impetuous journal, and a natural law that was not covered with an ointment that made it easier to live with. Those who were attacked by the journal did not like the Epicurus, but then liked even less the multiformed image of themselves in the journal and they found no resemblance to themselves in these images. "Because," Thomasius already said in the second issue of the journal with a marvelous knowledge of men that evokes the memory of Lichtenberg, "we like to look at the shape of our bodies in the mirror, but as far as the portrait of our souls, which we should recognize best of all, we usually prefer to scrutinize others." The Privatdozent, now dismissed, left the city and the University of Leipzig in 1690 without knowing that an order for his arrest had already been issued in Dresden. He found a position at the academy at Halle, which, thanks to his collaboration (and here his brilliant teaching in German was particularly important), soon became the court university of Brandenburg, and was then transformed into one of the central universities of the new Prussian kingdom. As Mehring indicated (*The Legend of Lessing*, 1920, p. 233), at that time Prussia was interested in having a university that

was not a nursery for an old Lutheran orthodoxy, and, regardless of
its own profession of reformed faith, took in the industrious Huguenots,
who augmented their revenues. Prussia tried to erect a special public
law, one that was constructed upon particularities and that did not
bring to mind the law of the empire or of the kaiser professed and
taught in other universities. If such a special law was expected from
Thomasius, then he would certainly disappoint them; very soon he
lost his good standing with the court, and only the increasing fame
of the partisan professor protected him; it was ultimately this fame
that led to the title that was bestowed upon him by the court. Thomasius
taught in Halle until his death in 1728; when it was proposed that he
make a triumphant return to a repenting and transformed Leipzig,
he refused even though he clearly would have reveled in such a triumph.
In Halle he concerned himself primarily with the science with which
had made his entry in Leipzig: with the doctrine of natural law. In
this discipline and beyond it, he became the pioneer of both the
Enlightenment and practical Christianity. But both directions only
served to further distance him from the bickerings of the church, and
made him into an ally of the scattered Christian sects who lived without
dogma. After a while he became close to the Pietists, the preacher
Spener, and the educator Francke, who were branded as heretics and
who, after Thomasius had already defended them in Leipzig, sought
refuge in Halle.

It was without a doubt the love of the persecuted that led this man
of the Enlightenment to the side of the Pietists. He did not stay among
the sanctimonious, but his remarkable contact with the Pietists, especially its relatively long duration (until 1707), cannot be entirely
explained by reference to their common enemy: the Lutheran pastor.
Pietism came from a cringing, or at least spiritually overcompromised,
petite bourgeoisie, and so it rejected the ideology of domination as
well as the dogmatic venalities and rigidities of the Lutheran church.
It especially opposed the intolerance of the church, all the more pro-
testingly as the church yielded to, and often surpassed, papist intolerance. In its beginnings, which were influenced by Dutch Calvinism
and even English Puritanism, Pietism soon abandoned male political
pride and ideologized cowardice into a species of proud humility, and
turned defeatism into a privilege of the spiritually chosen. Even the
constant contact with medieval mystical baptism of the Middle Ages,
which was so opposed to regimentation (a contact that Pietism shared

with a movement in Catholicism with which it corresponded in many respects, namely, French Jansenism), only led in Germany to an interiority that was consumed without flames—up to and including the "beautiful soul." In the end, Pietism in Halle lost itself completely in an attitude that was monkishly hostile to life. "Market days and days for music are holidays for the devil" (a view that later led to Pietist attacks on Bach's music): such were the slogans of Spener and Francke, bound up with a haughty and presumptuous attitude of hostility. But this is what Thomasius was unable to bear; and so, for the same reason that first attracted him to them, Thomasius finally turned away from them, from the neoclerical church, and from moralistic surliness. Even during the time of his friendship with Pietism, Thomasius never regarded morality as a melancholy matter, not as the administration or effect of a potion of repentance or penitence; and yet, the book that is intended to rehabilitate Epicurus, where even common pleasure is numbered along with stinginess and ambition as one of the three cardinal vices, is still entitled *On the Art of Loving Reasonably and Virtuously as the Only Means of Living a Life That Is Happy, Gallant, and Pleasant; or, An Introduction to the Science of Ethics.* This text appeared in 1692, during the first part of his time in Halle, and it gets along quite well without religion in the first two parts. Only the third part looks to God, but not as the supreme executor of the ethical law, nor as a gloomy, somber, barbaric force, as God appears in Francke's *Padagogium Halle,* but the look is to a God who is the dispenser of human happiness. Nevertheless—and here the problem begins of why Thomasius only returned to rationalism some twenty years later (1707) under the influence of Locke—nevertheless, it would be one-sided to consider the original relation of Thomasius to the Pietists only externally and to disregard an ancient *heretical Christian* content, which is precisely what attracted the "natural light" in Thomasius. In other words, Thomasius turned away from the Pietists on account of the squabbles among the clerics, which he quickly encountered, but the intention of practical Christianity, which he nevertheless saw in Pietism, provided the basis for a long relation that was not excessively tumultuous. We have already made mention of the rather tame and perverted contact between incipient Pietism and the lay movement of the old German mystics and the Baptists. Spener had said that one should diligently read Tauler and Süsre, Sebastian Franck (an admirer of Münzer), and

Valentin Weigel, so that one could entertain hopes for better times where practical Christianity would finally govern. In connecting general human reform and the Christian realm much more closely, Thomasius brings to mind his contemporary, the great pedagogue Comenius, who came from the community of the Moravian Brothers. In his *Pansophia* Comenius imagined that Christ's communism of love could become public and replace the compliments addressed to Christ and, a fortiori, to the princely tyrants. In this way, Comenius did not so much apply the wisdom of Solomon to the tyrants, where all is vanity, as he did the parable of the eye of the needle and the kingdom of heaven. Close to Comenius as well as to the Pietists, one finds Gottfried Arnold, the defender of heretics who was the first in Germany to introduce the Enlightenment formula—priestly artifice, pastoral lies— and whose *Impartial History of the Church and Heresies*, 1699–1715, even Thomasius called the best book after the Bible. There are echoes everywhere here of that "mystical democracy" whose intentions ultimately stem from Joachim of Fiore, the Isaiah of the thirteenth century. It was Joachim of Fiore who first instituted the doctrine that the New Testament, like the Old Testament, is transitory, and that a society of free spirits, of spirituals, of brothers in the pure spirit, a society full of spirit and free from domination would come to be. In this "mystical democracy" the real was made utopian, with a religious shell, but also with an enormous background that alarmed all mankind. And yet, transitions to the Enlightenment are not lacking here; Comenius and Gottfried Arnold, who was admired by Thomasius, represent such a transition. Thomasius was well versed in all of the earlier figures of the anticlergy from his copy of Gottfried Arnold's history of heresies, and for a long while this gave him a better image of the Pietists; it even made them seem like elective affinities to him. To the extent that Thomasius was originally attracted to Pietism not only out of solidarity with the persecuted but also from the perspective of heretical Christianity, the early German Enlightenment demonstrates a polytonism that, till now, is often overlooked and clearly distinguishes the German Enlightenment from the Enlightenment of Western Europe, which is more clearly, and increasingly, capitalistic. This difference rests upon social and ideological backwardness, but at the same time upon counterpoint remembrances that are, at least occasionally, more colorful, remembrances according to which some degree of connection with the early German Enlightenment is not lacking, but which, by the same token, tie it to a certain dimension, which is still mystified yet full of imagination. The same connection with this dimension is recognizable in Lessing, in the last part (par. 86–89) of his *Education of the Human Race*, where he speaks of "certain visionaries of the thirteenth and fourteenth centuries" and where he holds open the possibility of a "third epoch" (that of a humanity without masters). In Thomasius, and even more so in Lessing, one never finds any high-blown exaltedness; but this philanthropist, and friend of the laity, originally found in Pietism the reason of the heart and most of all the faith in the possibility of a world that would be a fraternal community.

Eggshells in natural philosophy

Something else that comes from Spener and Francke makes the enlightened image virtually Teutonic. Even too Teutonic at the point where it blinds Thomasius to the achievements of the mechanical insights of his time. As we have already said, Thomasius, who only had a passing knowledge of physics, lacked an understanding of Epicurus's atomic theory. What he defended in the materialists of antiquity against Tschirnhaus was their fearless *hedone*, their doctrine of the pleasure of life. Then in 1709 this member of the Enlightenment, Thomasius, produced a remarkable work of natural philosophy, with a curious title rich in speculative eggshells: *An Attempt on* [sic] *the Essence of Spirit or Fundamental Doctrines of Natural Science as well as Ethics. In which it will be shown That Light and Air Are Spiritual Essence and That All Bodies Consist of Material and Spirit and That in All of Nature There Is Only One Force of Attraction But That in Man There Is a Double Spirit, Good and Evil.* The text is not very coherent, and wherever Leibniz, despite his admiration for Thomasius, spoke of his "wildly expanding philosophizing" he referred to it. But above all the text is directed against the mechanical explanation of nature, against atomism and the corpuscular theory. How then could Thomasius, fully participating in the legal assassination of his epoch, attack Spinoza in other places because Spinoza had divinized created beings? On the contrary, Thomasius posited a primacy of the spirit even in nature, and this included an objective idealism that did not sit very well with the rehabilitation of Epicurus. To Thomasius the "philosophia corpuscularis et mechanica" seemed incompatible with morality, the same morality whose immanence he had defended in Epicurus. But what is the essence of the spirit that Thomasius, the natural philosopher, considers primary in the world? It is, as the fourth part of the book announces in its first thesis, the active essence of materiality; whereas materiality is passive, spirit is the agent of division, tension, motion, and the attraction of bodies but most importantly it only works through matter and only through matter does it become a visible reality. In the thesis 166 Thomasius goes so far as to say that "the activity of the intellect only works in the brain, for thoughts do not exist outside the brain." And so little remains behind of the transcendence of the spirit that it largely becomes a world spirit that eternally forms itself in the same way and eternally forms itself in all things that have been and that are, in metals as well as in plants, in animals and in men. So that the detractor of Spinozism himself becomes a thinly veiled pantheist, of course not in the sense of a mechanical pantheist, but in the sense of a qualitative pantheist with a "gushing" fullness of "qualities," according to Jakob Böhme's etymology, a nature that was physically and spiritually gushing. In Thomasius, whose strength certainly did not lie in natural philosophy, all of this is quite insufficient, and the exposition is often particularly prosaic and eclectic. Above all the extraordinary progressive force of the mechanical explanation of nature at that time (Thomasius wholesalely called it Cartesian philosophy) is not at all comprehended. Nonetheless Thomasius recognized that the Cartesians had "straightened out half of the science of nature, namely, that which concerned visible things, and saved it from the whims and vagaries of the philosophy of the schools" (Preface). Moreover Thomasius's battle against mechanism, as the search for the "spiritual bond" that is retained in death ("chemistry gives it the name *encheiresis naturae*"), is completely useless for the theists and their school philosophy. This because the influences of heretics, transmitted via Pietism, are still actively present in this case in the form of a relation with pantheistic mysticism. There is much from Paracelsus in the "sympathia et antipathia rerum" of which Thomasius speaks; Thomasius explicitly cites the Paracelsian Fludd (*Essay on the Essence of Spirit*, 1709, p. 100n) as well as Comenius (ibid., p. 87n). The book abounds with allusions to Jakob Böhme, who remains unnamed, as well as to Sebastian Franck, who taught that God is in all things as an essential qualitative force, in metal as shine, in the bird as flight and song, in man as will. Once again we see the remarkable difference between the mathematically, scientifically developed French and English Enlightenment and the slower, not so thoroughly capitalistic German Enlightenment. It is this distinction that makes the conception of the world found in Leibniz, the greatest mathematician of his time, something that is not mechanistic, but qualitative and architectonic, though albeit monistic, and it is this that ties him more closely to Nicholas of Cusa and to Giordano Bruno than to Cartesianism. Of course, as far as knowledge, coherence, and creative power are concerned, Thomasius's occasionally completely mystical efforts should not be mentioned in the same breath with Leibniz. And yet in both we find a residue of the Italian and Geman Renaissance natural philosophy, which was not yet mechanistic—this much at least is common to both of them. And this element runs so deeply in Germany that even Goethe's theory of color could be in strong agreement with Thomasius's principle that light was a spiritual being and, as Thomasius said, its "more or less active doses" produce light or darkness. Goethe's *History of the Theory of Color* omits this passage, but it fits well with the remarkable succession of anti-Newtons in Germany, with the "actions and passions of light." Or, as Thomasius wrote in a text that was almost a romantic philosophy of nature: "But because the doses of this proportion are innumerable, there arises from out of the discrepancy the so-called meterorum. In some things there is too much light, as in foolish flightiness, in some things there is too little light, as in rain" (*Essay on the Essence of Spirit*, p. 92). But the Enlightenment—in its imaginative, extremely imaginative side—was even to be found in Thomasius's curious attempts at understanding nature. In it the Enlightenment sought that which corresponded to it externally; it looked for the same vigorous free spirit in things; it sought, in other words, the overwhelming doses of light and pure air in the material mixture of the world. All of this appeared in Thomasius, despite his claims to the contrary, in physical matter. It is impossible to overlook this heritage of Paracelsus, who, along with Descartes, still lives in this pregnant German Enlightenment—an Enlightenment that is unevenly developed, with Gothic but also colorful clothes.

The rules of happiness and peace

But the import of the upright man for what follows is based on something else. It was law and right that he always held close to his heart, not diverse mixtures of air and light far away or high above. The intelligible good was the basis upon which he was at home; his task was not to alarm others or to cast spotlights on foolishness. The supreme concern for this representative of the Enlightenment was reason, the common good of bourgeois reason; and this public good could not be realized by the Pietists of the heart or by the animation of nature. In Halle Thomasius's influence was above all as a man of *recta ratio* in *law* and *ethicality*, and this influence extended throughout Germany and into the future. He shook the Philistines out of their hollowness, and he did this a generation before Christian von Wolff and the horrifying cultural decadence that survived the Thirty Years' War. He did more than the theorists of natural law Pufendorf and Christian von Wolff to destroy at least the ideology of renewed and older forms of feudalism (the destruction of which the German bourgeoisie was not yet prepared for). "Jurist—angry Christian" runs an old proverb: It was precisely this experience that clearly turned around the professor of the beginnings of human rights. In the land of Thomasius there is now opening up—after and during so many sidetracks—the enduring perspective of his heritage: the philosophy of right. He had already written a three-volume work on natural law, *Institutionum jurisprudentiae divinae libri tres* (1687), while still in Leipzig; it was of course still housed in the framework of the Ten Commandments, in the style of the relative natural law of the Scholastics. To the astonishment of his readers, however, the content of this work, which had already established a school," was radically modified in 1705 when religious associations were removed: in the *Fundamenta juris naturae et gentium*. This most mature work of the jurist and philosopher of right, which is directed toward a pure social ethics, omits God from the domain of law. Even in the first, milder conception of the book Thomasius was in clear opposition to the theologizing philosophers of right. This opposition rested upon the difference between the independence of the natural light in natural law from the supernatural, churchly light. Insofar as Thomasius only recognizes a natural light and not a divine light (which issues forth from the Ten Commandments) in matters of jurisprudence, the possibility of a religious sanction of law is completely removed. Grotius had said that the law of reason was valid even when—though this is impossible—there was no God; Thomasius intensified this principle by saying that one could not speak of natural law at all if there was a God above men. Thomasius presented law, and consequently morality, as not only without any religious origin but equally without any religious goal or direction; among the traditional obligations to God only those that are valid according to reason remain valid, namely those that manifest themselves in the fulfillment of obligations toward one's self and others. In this way the philosophy of right is removed from the vicinity of theology, a vicinity that the otherwise extremely methodical theoretician of natural law in Germany, Pufendorf, who was Thomasius's predecessor, largely remained within. According to Pufendorf only the judgments, and not the contents, of true law have their source exclusively in reason; for Pufendorf the juridical "entitities" on the other hand stem from the "impositio Dei," the divine injunction expressed in the Ten Commandments. At this point Thomasius produces in Germany a purely liberal natural law (on the model of Grotius), this ideological instrument of the ascending bourgeoisie, and he even radicalizes Grotius himself. In place of a proximity to religion there is only the proximity to morality, whose content is earthly, but earthly in the best sense of the word. And Thomasius characterizes this content with a formula that has never ceased, today least of all, to possess the highest actuality and humanity at once: He characterized the "ought" of the social ensemble as *happiness and peace.*

These are what make it right to further a just ethics by means of the ethical law. In doing this Thomasius makes a distinction that today seems strange to us, the distinction between external and internal peace. He does this in the three rules of happiness and peace as the rules of *justum,* of *decorum,* and of *honestum (Fundamenta juris naturae et gentium,* I, chap. 5). *External* peace is achieved by means of law as something that is compulsory, by means of the *justum* or *that which is right.* It is further advanced by means of the more perfect and complete, morally transmitted (and so not compulsory) law that is called *decorum,* or *that which is proper.* The rule of *justum* runs: "Do not do to others that which you do not want to happen to you." Or in short, harm no one, neither your neighbor as an individual person nor your neighbor as a people. The rule of *decorum,* which as Thomasius said is more noble and refined (and more positive), runs: "Do to others what you want to happen to yourself." External peace is supposed to be promoted by all of this, by means of the guidance and improvement of the individuals including those who, according to the bourgeois natural law theory of the social contract, have founded the state and, in the aggregate as the people, constitute the state. The promotion of external peace therefore already contains *in nuce* the drive and framework of inner peace as the peace of the *ethical person* and of the people as the aggregate of ethical persons; peace is founded upon the pure *positivum* of intention. Thus the first two rules, those of external peace, are followed by the third, the most positive, that of the *honestum*, or the ethicality that is related to *inner* peace. The observance of this rule, in contrast to that of the first two (especially *justum*), cannot be compelled; ethicality is only produced by personal conviction, not by violence. Of course, love runs through all of the rules, even through the *justum*, but as soon as the *justum* must be compelled, love no longer has any place in it. Thus Thomasius teaches, with the antithesis that stems from Paul and Luther: "From the start you easily recognize the general difference between justice and love. Justice is that portion of love which gives man the capacity of compelling others to do what he should willingly do; that is why love can be without justice, but never justice without love. Indeed, justice loses the name of love when one really uses constraint. And this makes it very easy to understand why the other part of love keeps its name for itself, namely, that part of love in which there is no possibility or faculty by which another can be compelled" (*On the Art of Loving Reaonably and Virtuously*, part 5, par. 104). For Thomasius the commandment of the *honestum*, of ethicality, dwells in the *positivum* of intention, in the *forum internum*, and it runs: "Do to yourself that which you want the other to do to himself." Or, according to the commentary that Thomasius appends to it: "Do not be a hypocrite, apply to yourself the perfection that you demand of others." A remark that sounds strongly like the Kantian rule, that man should not seek happiness for himself and perfection from others but the inverse: He should strive for his own perfection and the happiness of others. Enough said about Thomasius's three rules, especially about their *main point*: the epoch-making juridical *distinction between compulsory* justum *and noncompulsory* honestum. This criterion, which distinguishes between that which is and is not compulsory, divided the spheres of law and morality decisive for a long while. The bourgeois science of right has retained this division, including its criterion; that is why for this science international law, lacking executive force, appears to be something quite irregular when compared with other legal institutions. After Thomasius did this, Kant only had to put the finishing touches on the limitations of the juridical domain, and on the distinction between compulsory law and noncompulsory morals. But something else is clear as well: This distinction is directly tailored for the bourgeois society and its state. It loses its essence in the socialist society and especially in the communistic society: It loses its meaning where men do not need to live according to the antagonisms that make peace impossible without a vast edifice of compulsory laws, and where between the individual and society there is no longer that separation which requires a noncompulsory, even oppositional individual ethics of intention. But the distinction between law and morality in Thomasius must be understood in the thoroughly progressive meaning it had in his time. It does not express the self-love of the bourgeois individual against the police state that surrounds him everywhere; it gave to human dignity—as an element of the person and of a humanity that was not merely bourgeois—a peace that did not yet exist for it in the society of the time. Of course, the private and public law Thomasius demonstrated on the basis of his first two rules did not immediately result in the police state, but it has, obviously, not yet resulted in anything other than the bourgeois class society. This to the degree that, as Thomasius clearly indicated, positive morality is absent from the exclusively negative injunctions of law. All the same, morality, which Thomasius places against or even above legal relations, is essentially a morality of intentions that are not only general and bourgeois but also a species of Lutheranism; and yet it is clearly and fundamentally distinguished from Lutheran morality because, to the extent that it cannot be compelled and cannot be regulated, it wants to (and can) manifest itself in external work. It does this by emancipating the conviction that resists the police state by rising above the nonethicality of all bourgeois law, which is only demonstrable. In this way, therefore, moral conviction in Thomasius is not there as an asylum for cowardice, or even only as an asylum for an inwardly stooped over, eternally interior, subjectivity. On the contrary, as Thomasius himself showed in a series of frontal attacks against patronizing foreign legislation, this moral conviction becomes a weapon in the arsenal used in the struggle for freedom of thought, for the humanization of public life. Actually, in this way rather than being distinguished from law, morals are reattached to the direction in which law moves; in Thomasius, morality is and remains the highest among the three rules of his natural law. That is why in his *Summary Outline of Basic Doctrines* (1699) Thomasius announces this rule in the following way: "That no one is a good *politicus* who is not in fact a good *ethicus.*" This is comparable to another Kantian principle in *Perpetual Peace*: True politics could not do anything without first paying homage to morals. And the goal in all of this is and remains peace; for Thomasius, far more than for Grotius before him, it is the normal condition of just, moral existence, inwardly as well as outwardly. *Justum, decorum, honestum*, the three ideological stars of a bourgeoisie which, unaware of its basis and still believing that it was headed on the path of total prosperity, render humanity inevitable.

Natural law and the morals of happiness

Many elements in Thomasius's well-intended directions, when taken in isolation, are not especially new. Even the first rule presents a commonplace that was already rather current at that time. What you do not want one to do to you—this sentence with its consequence is clearly audible at the base of the first rule. Even the abbreviated form, the "harm no one," already appears as a general prescription ("alterum non laedere") in the articles of law, therefore in the basic book of corpus juris. But bourgeois natural law did not want anything innovative in such rules. It only wanted to reassert and repeat what was in the heart of all peoples at all times. That is what Cicero handed down to Grotius as an ancient Stoic heritage: There are common ideas, *communes notiones*, that are absolutely innate in human nature. Among these is the rational path to what is just, the *recta ratio*, of which man is well aware in his dark impulses. Moreover, the hypothesis of a consciousness of law that is identical in all times and all peoples only resulted in an empirical derivation of natural law, not a rigorous deduction. That is why besides the empirical justification Grotius described a second, less popular, but apparently more scientific justification: that based on the original "human nature." This provided the "principle" from which natural law would appear to be rigorously deducible; the same spirit of logical consequence is found in Hobbes. But "human nature" itself, this "principle" out of which natural law was deduced, in Grotius had as an essential distinguishing feature the *appetitus socialis*, or social instinct; in Hobbes on the other hand, who knew capitalism well (which he antedated to the origin of the state), it is the ruthless egotistical power instinct with the *bellum omnium contra omnes*, the war, which is not at all social, of all against all. Consequently, in accord with the different definitions of "human nature" the state has different characters in Grotius and Hobbes. In Grotius it arose in accord with the *appetitus socialis* through a contract of association with mutual assistance as its goal; it thus had a liberal allure. In Hobbes it was born in disaccord with the wolf character of men and their *bellum omnium contra omnes*, by means of a contract of subjugation with mutual security as its goal; it thus had an authoritarian allure. Pufendorf—who was otherwise not independent and showed himself inclined to compromise insofar as he made a synthesis of Grotius and Hobbes by positing at the base of small communities the instinct of sociability and its satisfaction, and at the base of large communities egoism and its training— thus adjoined a new element when he implemented, in a concise and really orthodox manner, the rigorous deduction of natural law that Grotius had announced and that Hobbes had introduced. Thus natural law, following mathematics, which was the model of all sciences at the time, appeared to be a fully demonstrable science. The principles from which it was deduced are supposed to be created purely out of reason and contain no other content than the essential characteristics of "human nature." And it is from this point that Thomasius begins afresh, not in his rules of natural law, but in its "principle." With an almost grandiose turn, one that is as natural as it is optimistic, Thomasius replaced Grotius's *appetitus socialis* and Hobbes's *bellum omnium contra omnes* with the *search for happiness* as the basic feature of "human nature" and the *impeded search for happiness* (fear and neediness) as indicating the motive for the social contract. The institution of the state itself, after it has arisen, does not need to be anything other than the suppression of this impediment, nothing other than the observance of the human determination to constantly search for an always more perfect joy. Thus the worth of the state for its inhabitants is the measure, as the deducible law, of every institution of the state. Once again one finds traces of Epicurus here, at the center, the same Epicurus Thomasius had defended against Tschirnhaus, the hedonism of Epicurus augmented by both internal and external peace and the happiness of all manifesting itself in the appearance of humanity. Thomasius thus introduced a radically new tone into natural law, all the more so because of the way in which he joined *human happiness* to *human dignity* in *natural law*. With this he lovingly bridged an essential difference that existed between the attitudes toward the image of man in social utopias and natural law theories. For previously it was only from the perspective of social utopias that one was directed toward human happiness, whereas modern theories of natural law—in part on account of their actively antifeudal mission, in part because of the rediscovery so beloved of this misson of masculine Stoicism—had essentially envisioned the dignity of men. But Thomasius, who was not far removed from the social utopias and took both into account, sought a unity of happiness and dignity. This manly sermon on happiness, directed against the discouragement of the bowed head as well as against a virtue become monstrous in its hardness, profoundly stimulated the passion for life in the bourgeoisie, who were just beginning their gradual ascension in Germany; a later preacher for "the awakening of the body and spirit of humanity" was Herder. Kant proved to be a setback in this movement during the late Enlightenment by means of his separation, which was as much Prussianly sparing as it was Pietistically monkish, between inclination and duty, and therefore between eudaemonistic morals (which only give "the counsels of prudence") and the absolute ethical law (which in all circumstances gives orders that are not hypothetical, but categorical). But in the end one even finds in Kant a carefully attempted synthesis between happiness and dignity; nevertheless happiness cannot be based upon virtue, and cannot be seduced, but virtue "makes one worthy of happiness." In any case Thomasius himself gave a simple sign of the equality between happiness and dignity expressed by a materialistic reality par excellence. If impeded happiness does not form a "principle for the deduction" of the formation of law and the state, then the "principle" of society— the elimination of impeded happiness—does nevertheless contain an excellent criterion for judging the existing law and the existing morality. The institution of the right to happiness, as a basic right, does not fit well with the old structure of injustice: This sort of natural law was not yet a Samson who could destroy the pillars, but it rises up as a pride against degrading suffering and authority, and it stood up as the hatred against the barbarism of authority, and as the love of the victims of this barbarism.

The throne, the fight against torture and witch trials

Thus the upright man became visible as one always on the offensive. In his candor and frankness he surpassed all of his German contemporaries; if some of his statements seem milder that is only because of their floweriness. Thomasius himself was a swordsman of words; on this score one of his petitions to the sovereign affords an astonishing example. Thomasius wrote to the prince elector on the occasion of a debate on the conditions for the flowering of science: "It is freedom that gives the true life to all spirit and without freedom the human intellect seems to be dead and without soul. The intellect recognizes no authority except God, that is why the yoke, which is imposed upon it when a human *auctoritas* is prescribed as a guideline, is intolerable; if it is tolerated the intellect becomes unfit for the sciences. . . . It is only freedom that has given so many learned people to the Dutch and English, yes even the French (before the persecutions of the reformers); on the other hand it is the lack of this freedom that has so severely suppressed the cleverness and intelligence of the Italians and the finer spirits of Spain." In this declaration, which has nothing servile about it, there is a notable, almost sociological, perspicacity in the progressive distinction between the Dutch and the English on the one hand and the Italians and Spaniards on the other. The unimpeded early capitalistic, liberal development of England is indicated, a development that was not hindered or interrupted by any neofeudal hesitations. But Thomasius also points to the horrifying effect of the neofeudal reaction: in Italy with the first victories of early capitalism with which the Renaissance commenced and with the suffocation and domination of the people by means of their Hispanization; and even more strongly in Spain, which was totally oppressed by despotism and the Inquisition. It was this Hispanization of Italy that extinguished the flame of creative natural science there, since after Galileo's trial intellectuals were no longer willing to dedicate themselves to it. In foreign countries the effect of Galileo's trial was such that important parts of the Protestant intelligentsia, who had been disgusted by the increasing spiritual desert of Lutheranism, began to sympathize with Catholicism while Lutheranism completely declined. During Thomasius's lifetime there was another theorist of public law living in Germany named Spattenbach; in his *Political Philosophy* (1688) Spattenbach announced that after God created the earth he thought it good to choose an especially precious and appropriate "material" in order to bring together all of the traits and traces of his divine image in it (namely, the kings); accordingly one could recognize this divine image immediately on the forehead of the king. This is unquestionably an astounding supplement to the story of Creation: a porcelain basis for the body of the princes instead of the lump of mortal clay from which the common Adam was created. But it is in this sort of sentence, which was not extreme in the Germany of that day, that the arrogance and defiance of Thomasius's relations to absolutism must be gauged. Before his petition to the prince elector of Brandenburg, Thomasius had endured some nasty quarrels on account of a book called *On the Advantage That True Religion Confers upon Princes* written by a man named Masius, who was a preacher in the Danish court. The thrashing given this book in the December issue of the *Teutsche Monate* of 1688 also contained a severe criticism leveled against the pretension of princes to be accorded divine grace. It was not entirely groundless when Thomasius's enemies in Leipzig at that time said that his criticism had compared majesty to a slap in the face. Thomasius had initially said of this divine right of princes (and of religion when it supports this view) "that it is not easy to find a more absurd idea than this and one further from all reason and all that has been written." He then refers to the approbation of the people, for this is the ineluctable condition of all princely power; the people can bestow princely majesty even if it does not possess any majesty itself, just as—and this is the real Thomasian analogy—"as if it had a slap in the face in a beggar's wallet." This was strong language, democratic, and reformatory in a way that was no longer heard in Germany; it almost echoed the German of the peasants and Baptists, a language that had long since disappeared. Even when he was dealing with absolutism, which had nothing sacred about it in Thomasius's eyes, Thomasius spoke in the most uncommon ways (often quite rhetorically flowery); nevertheless, he only conceived of it as an evil from which the best could be extracted and put to work for the bourgeois Enlightenment. But for Germany this was an illusion; it was a fallacy deduced from the completely different example of absolutism found in France, where there was a relative alliance between the monarchy and the bourgeoisie that was developed by capitalism, a bourgeoisie that was in fact progressive. All the same, unlike the German theorist of natural law, Althaus, a century before him, Thomasius was not moving toward the termination of the relations of subjugation, that is, up to the revolutionary doctrine according to which all the power of those who are accorded the power of government can *de jure* be revoked in the event that they have not fulfilled their mandate. And yet, even in his petition to the sovereign, the sole principle for Thomasius is political backbone. No people has the right to let itself be ethically and spiritually destroyed; this above all resounds in the exemplary warning to the throne. And, as will be seen, this exemplary character continues to be affirmed in Thomasius in the true actions of the early Enlightenment—against barbarism, stupidity, and madness. In this point, despite all of the changed circumstances, one finds striking similarities to Anselm Feuerbach, the great liberal, humanitarian jurist of the still-enlightened nineteenth century. It is the similarity of law that has been purged of all demons, of the passion for law that wants to have man at its center and not a feudal terror and all of its idols; in short, it is the similarity to that which, against its wishes, agrees to penal law. In Germany it was Thomasius who gave the signal for this—against method with madness, against madness with method.

Thus, he was one of the first to call for the abolition of torture. None of the very noble souls of his time had raised any objections to it. And one would have difficulty finding another area in which the ingenuity of the human wit had been so active and so fertile as in the invention of instruments of human suffering and unbearable pain. In order to be compassionate or cruel one must be able to be both: thus the highly developed compassion of Christianity was especially successful when it came to be schooled in cruelty. The incarnation of agony by means of burning, stretching, hanging, cutting, and breaking limbs in order to prove something for the penal question is called imperial law. It was a law that was totally different from the civil process; it was distinguished by the fact that it was not applied to the relations of property as it was in the prescriptions of Roman law, but essentially to those who were propertyless, those who had completely gone astray: peasants uprooted from the soil, soldiers who had been dismissed, and others who since the sixteenth century had been forced to be vagabonds, compelled to crime. But Thomasius fought to make the ways of gaining evidence in the penal process the same as those in the civil process; the principle of *confessio regina probationis* should at least be supplemented by a thorough investigation. Because even this principle, the only one remaining in penal law—when it was not possible to find two witnesses who could testify for either innocence or guilt—made evidence obtained by torture necessary (often very false evidence). In 1705, in a disputation, Thomasius characterized torture as a disgrace to Christian states; in 1708 he let one of his students publish a text for him: *On Banishing Torture from Christian Courts.* This proclamation began as follows: "In torture the extremely unlucky and still not yet convicted accused is punished in a way that exceeds in cruelty the punishment that would be imposed if there were perfect proof for the crime. . . . Oh, such criminal absurdity in the application of the power of punishment! What is more unjust, what can be thought more alien to justice than to tear away the flesh of the poor mortal who has not yet been convicted, what else can so make the heart shudder in one who still has even the slightest sense of humanity left?" Torture was only eliminated in Prussia a half century later; in other states it remained for a full century. Even in 1769 the criminal code of Maria Theresa depicted in forty-five large engravings for the instruction of judges the three most atrocious degrees of torture. And in 1805 a professor of law in Giessen named Koch defended torture in the preface to the ordinance of high penal justice of Charles V, and only complained about "rash and passionate judges" who occasionally applied them falsely. Despite this, legalized torture disappeared just as Thomasius demanded; in this sense the nineteenth century was an enlightened century. Until fascism wrote a new page in the book of torture; with it the bourgeoisie repudiated its Thomasius.

But Thomasius was also among the first to fight for an end to the witch hunts. In this matter he was preceded, in 1631, by the Jesuit Spee; but Spee did not attack the belief in witches, only the hasty trials against them. Balthasar Bekker, the courageous Hollander of the Cartesian school, was the first to come to the heart of the matter in *The Bewitched World* (1690). The belief in witches was represented here as a product of stupidity and madness; but above all it was the pillar of this entire view that was eliminated: the devil. In Protestant countries the devil had almost become stronger than in Catholic countries; Luther had removed Mary, the gentle one, but had reinforced Lucifer's ability to terrorize all who might rebel. Thus the festivities of Walpurgis Night blossomed more happily than ever, and with them grew the general danger of being a woman, that is, a potential witch even if not a probable witch. Women were not any better off where women themselves ruled: In the Abbey of Quedlinburg, which was right in the heart of the empire, one hundred and thirty-three witches were burned at the stake in one day in 1589; out of Christian charity they attached sacks of powder from nearby Blocksberg to the breasts of the witches. The excesses of the panic and deranged imagination of the search for witches raged everywhere; never before did the world witness such a lengthy and wild mass psychosis. In 1702 Thomasius published the text *De crimine magiae*, which appeared in German as *Brief Propositions on the Vice of Sorcery*. This was long after he had already published (in

Leipzig in 1687) a disputation entitled *Whether Heresy Is a Punishable Crime*. There he clearly denied the authorities the right to punish heretics, and instead had opposed the delirium of the devil and all forms of fanaticism. After Thomasius was made full professor of the law faculty in Halle, he had access to the testimony of the witch trials and he could give decisive affidavits on the subject. Thus he saw another face of madness with method, one different from the one he saw in torture—murderous desire with theology—and he sounded the alarm. Bekker had done away with the belief in the devil, but Thomasius completed Bekker's demystification in a way especially appropriate to the witch hunt: He added to Bekker's work the conscience of the jurist before what one might call the unreal material of the accusation. What sort of trials were these: In every other there was an objective deed and evidence, in the witch trials there was neither at all, it was only a mass psychosis and its victims. And what an atrocious absurdity: In normal court cases the judges determines the facts, in the witch trial it is the facts that determine the judge and, because everything is possible for the devil, the protection of the alibi disappeared, since it concerned a blood brotherhood, the Blocksberg, and the covens of witches. Thomasius pressed hard on the devil in a historical and satirical way; he made the devil ridiculous by his extraordinary youth. For as Thomasius noted, though the belief in the influence of evil spirits is ancient, the Christian devil to which the abominable league of Blocksberg related could hardly even be five hundred years old. The Old Testament does certainly recognize a witch of Endor, but without a devil; the New Testament does, of course, refer to Satan, but knows nothing of Master Urian [the devil] or of his abysmal court. The Roman Empire did not recognize any devil of sorcerers, nor did the emperor Charlemagne and his champions; even the ancient popes are silent on this matter and nothing demonic is reported of any Walpurgis Night. All of this changed in the thirteenth century with the antisatanic papal bull of Gregory IX; it was the first godparent of Master Urian. Thomasius thus made the theological phenomenon of Satan into a very historical phenomenon: The principal property of the witch trials is thus inserted into an awkward time of five hundred years earlier and so made questionable. The more Gregory's papal bull ruled the insanity, the more its terrible jurisdiction blossomed, and blossomed as the saying goes *ad maiorem Dei gloriam et confusionem Satanae*, in other words, to hold the people not only in a fear but also in a paralyzing horror of the authorities, even when there was no threat of political revolt. With the preaching of this insanity the church, which was intimately bound to this authority (both the Protestant and Catholic churches), brought to earth, not paradise, but the terrifying hell that was useful to its purposes. In Protestant countries the fires of joy of the witch replaced the Spanish auto-da-fé, for without the pyre neo-feudalism would never have fit in well. The strangeness of the ideas that were offered on this subject, even among the highly placed intelligentsia, is evidenced in a book that appeared in Berlin as late as 1750, a book of a "sage" named Meier, member of the Prussian Academy: *On the Actions of the Devil on the Earth's Surface*, which appeared almost simultaneously with Kant's *Universal History and Theory of the Heavens*. But Thomasius did not restrict himself to drowning the devil of the witches in history; he combated all sorts of superstitions in and around this intoxication with witches: exorcisms, fear of comets, miraculous signs, amulets, and astrology. Indeed, by 1692 in his *Introduction to the Doctrine of Ethics*, he had announced the following result at the conclusion of the third part (pp. 151ff.): "And consequently the superstitious or idolatrous man is more than an atheist ... because not only is the atheist usually not unreasonable in his conduct and in his external life, but also often reasons subtly apropos of God. . . . You must not be shocked that atheists are fought and detracted, but seldom does idolatrous and irrational superstition provoke the same response. Almost the entire world is plunged up to the ears in superstition, and everyone strives to depict this superstition to the poor ignoramuses as the true fear of God. . . . And to be sure, if one looks at the history of this superstition, then one sees that it is an old trick that an honest philosopher, indeed almost every one of them, is denounced as an atheist. Thus reasonable men are accustomed to the observation that most of the time, even in our age, one who is denounced as an atheist by one of those irrational beasts is usually an honest and virtuous man." Once again we find a greeting from Epicurus here, obviously not the Epicurus of atomism and the corpuscular theory who as we have seen Thomasius later rejected in his work in natural philosophy, *Essay on the Essence of Spirit*, in favor of a "spiritual bond." That which is at work here, which even governs the work, is the memory of the philosopher of the demystified earthly garden, the happy morality without fear, superstition, and mythology. It was this that joined the arsenal of weapons in the struggle against the worst of all forms of practical superstition: the belief in witches. Under the influence of Thomasius the witch trials diminished in Prussia and in Saxony, but after an apparent death, they were vigorously renewed, *suo genere*, by fascism. With different victims, a modified superstition, without the God of the church, with the "myth of the twentieth century" — it was nevertheless a retrieval. The last witch was not burned in Germany in 1775 in Kempten; rather, thousands of similar victims, called Jews by the Nazis, went along with so many others, even in 1945, into the gas chambers and crematoria of Auschwitz and Meidanek. Something genuinely diabolic had reappeared, and its consequences are not limited to Germany. But the German lights, which appeared with Thomasius, illuminated the best of every Enlightenment, as Kant later remarked: "Enlightenment is man's release from his self-imposed tutelage." This is what happened in Thomasius's *Exercise of the Doctrine of Reason*; it happened in the philanthropic art of serving the intellect — socialism docs not repudiate this, its own, Thomasius.

Once again the German lecture

A last look to the praiseworthy man who taught in German. This was a patriotic act in a grand style, one that was overdue and rapidly had an effect. Logan, Opitz, Fleming, Lohenstein, and Hofmannswaldau were thus models for Thomasius, because in his eyes they worked poetically in their mother tongue. Previously Paracelsus and Böhme showed what German could do when it tried. Thomasius was so partial in this regard that he went so far as to contend that Lohenstein and Hofmannswaldau, the current lights of the German "language of courts and heroes," "could take the place of six Virgils." Thomasius himself, on a celebratory occasion, could fall into the superlative of baroque German, as on the occasion of a death in the faculty at Halle: "The greatest part of the new university gathered here would weep bloody tears for this cruel event if this loss of their most noble mind had not also robbed them of their eyes and the justice of God's wrath had not once again reduced them to a mutilated body." The fact that Thomasius, as we have seen in his *Teutsche Monate*, but also in aspects of his popular philosophy, already occasionally evoked the German of the later eighteenth century is all the more remarkable. The philosophic activity, not as it was practiced in the philosophy of the schools, but universally, had a favorable influence on the German language, and obviously prevented the language of jurisprudence and philosophy from merely being a translation of the Latin of the school philosophers. The Latin of the schools gives way to the warmth and vitality that can only come from a native language, and this joins forces with the vitality of Thomasius himself, his inventive style of speaking, his pedagogical force. Doubtless, with the abolition of Latin as the language of scholarship, something irreplaceable was lost: the Internationale of expression. An Internationale that would permit one to lecture easily from Leipzig to Kraków, Paris to Oxford, thanks to a similar terminology, and that would make scholarly books available everywhere without the dangers of translation. Louis XIV performed a similar service for French, but it was much more limited than the service to Latin, because English scientific literature hardly took part, just as little as Italian did. Scholarly Latin did in fact afford some advantage, and as a universal it was a good inheritance from the Middle Ages—but the development of bourgeois philosophy, which became national and dynamic, accrued significant restraints and disadvantages. Above all the dynamism of bourgeois thought, in contrast to the class-ordered, hierarchical thought of the feudal society, found no expression in impoverished medieval Latin. To be sure, medieval Latin permitted the most subtle of distinctions to be made, but because of the instantaneous substantivation of these distinctions as well as the dialectical representations in it, they became fixed, static, hard. Much later, Goethe lamented the substantivation of the world even in humanistic scholarly Latin; after having freely and movingly glorified Greek in the *History of the Theory of Color* he made the following remark apropos of Julius Caesar: "The Latin language, on the other hand, because of its use of substantives is preemptive and imperious. The concept is set forth as finished in the word; it is rigidified in the word, which is treated as a real being." German, which in its verbs, infinitives, and participles is so flexible, exercises a less substantivizing charm. Thomasius's action not only made German national literature possible even in the sciences, it also led to an increasingly elastic form of expression in relation to the closed bourgeois dialectic and its process. There is no better witness for this than Leibniz, who used Latin and a standardized French; on this score he said (in his *Thoughts Concerning the Exercise and Improvement of the German Language*, par. 57): "Wealth is the first and most important quality requisite for a language; this must never be lacking; on the contrary, there must be an excess of fitting and energetic words to serve all eventualities, so that one can forcefully and genuinely represent everything and simultaneously paint them with living colors." Leibniz wrote this text in 1697, stimulated by Schottelius, the first Germanist, who in 1641 had already published a German grammar; but this text by Leibniz was stimulated in practice by Thomasius, ten years after his epoch-making German lecture and the *Teutsche Monate*, with the thoroughly "living colors" of their language. Through Thomasius's action, the linguistic unity of culture and science could henceforth come to stand alongside awakening German poetry and alongside the linguistic unity created so long ago in Luther's Bible, a unity that miscarried. A unity that extended beyond hundreds of internal frontiers, and beyond the separation of confessionals, which divided one single European nation: Germany. Language itself does not belong to the superstructure, but to the installation of the mother tongue for the purpose of a national literature that also encompasses scientific culture. The consciousness of the nation was itself won with language; it was won against all of the tollbooths, petty kings, and small-town markets of the empire. Thomasius, by the most popular of his actions, decisively contributed to that superstructure which made both separatism and xenophilia equally harmless. Thomasius is the birth of the German university, and one of the first and most expressive consciences of German freedom and unity. Since then, Minerva has not forgotten to speak German, and to speak it with a special vigor, but the effort on the bulletin board in Leipzig, which pushed toward a popular basis of science, is still not yet at its end.

True community

We have paid tribute to a bourgeois man without fear and generally without reproach. He was far from being a rebel, but he never bent a knee and he represented the strongest that was able to be represented in the German citizenry. So he put himself in the middle of all German misery and took a stand against it. With a spontaneity full of character he inaugurated the public German Enlightenment, and he related the scholar's study to the world, intervening in the world as no one before. Even Thomasius's common sense has nothing mediocre about it as is claimed by philosophical reactionaries and romantics and almost every late-bourgeois history of philosophy as soon as they come to speak of this representative of the Enlightenment in whom it has no interest.

But this same history, at least since the imperialist age, only treats the entire Enlightenment disparagingly and with categories such as superficial, flat, trivial, banal, and so on, and—so that there can be no doubt about the denigration of the social task—all of this applies equally to materialism. It is true that Thomasius was not a creative thinker in the grand style, but if he had been a reactionary like Halle or Adam Müller or Stahl or other jurists of the age of Restoration, who were even less capable of representing Promethean genius, then he never would have been reproached for this supposed mediocrity. Nor is it a matter of judging the entire German Enlightenment—as the reaction did—following, for instance, Friedrich Nicolai's shabby model; that is like trying to evaluate romanticism according to Vulpius and *Rinaldo Rinaldini*. In Thomasius concepts breathe fresh air: the powerful, joyful, critically laden popular delight in science. This delight in Thomasius, which is connected to a progressive praxis quite rare in Germany, is a vigorous and certainly not superficial opponent of that emasculation of knowledge into the connoisseurship of however many and whatever species of spiritual tastes one wants; it is an opponent of the bloated platitude sitting on its high horse with a "view" of everything except Thomasius's principle: "That there is only one truth. That this truth consists in the living knowledge of the true good." A philosophizing that seriously searches for truth and the true good will never find Thomasius an alien element, and it never mistakenly regards the light of the Enlightenment as a light that falls from the outside or even as light that falls at all, as is the case in a shrewd obscurantism and, with it, the dogmatic clericalism that unquestionably knows everything. So Thomasius always has his worth, including the Thomasius who once really was—after a point, the difficulties in what is philosophically powerful are obvious. But Thomasius's unforced spontaneity belongs to this and should never be abandoned, because in the end nothing in the world does as well as this double signature: proximity to the people and the best at the frontiers—from which Thomasius was certainly distant, but not barred—at the frontiers of humanity.

Much about this highly respected man is doubtless outdated. The class restrictions remain clear, especially with regard to the far too private rules recommended for happiness and peace. They are not self-conscious of the economic basis and social relations they rest upon. Thomasius's distinction between a compulsory external law and a noncompulsory morality of intentions has become untenable. Even if this distinction had, as was shown, a certain progressive sense against the police state and against a natural law that was demonstrably bourgeois, it nevertheless disappears within a socialistic solidarity. But at the same time the general limits that Thomasius's natural law shares with every modern bourgeois natural law are evident: the assumption of a static human nature, an unmediated human ideal, whose "universal good" is impossible in antagonistic class society. In this respect, Thomasius seems just as abstract and only concerned with the pure consequence of the ideal as every liberal, harmonizing theory of natural law, and all such morality up to its crowning achievement in the categorical imperative. But—and this is the last surprise offered up by this supposedly so transparent member of the Enlightenment— then one finds a way out in Thomasius that has absolutely nothing liberal about it. And it relates to nothing less than the *socialistic consequence* of human rights—therefore from the point of view of the economy, which is not referred to in the three rules of happiness. Thomasius makes a declaration in which he names the real table at which morals can sit. This declaration is found in the sixth part (pp. 300ff.) of the text *On the Art of Loving Reasonably and Virtuously . . . or, An Introduction to the Science of Ethics*; it reads as follows: "Now there follows the indissoluble community of all goods, and similarly all reasonable conduct and behavior, as the complete testimony, that henceforth reasonable love has arrived at its perfection. . . . And therefore all property must disappear and everything must be held in common, because all forms of property are born of a lack of love and of disunion. We have detailed this elsewhere and shown that from the beginning of the world there has been a community of goods . . . and that even at the beginning of Christianity, when Christian love still retained the ardor that belongs to it, all goods were held in common among the first Christians. . . . God wanted that no person be poor or rich." Thomasius continues against all of those who have misgivings about such a communal morality: "Surely, property is so intertwined in every level and stage of the public world that at first one would not be able to envision what sort of shape this world would take if there were no property. But a clever and insightful mind has already spared us the trouble of overcoming this scruple; he did this insofar as, under the deception of having discovered a new people whom he called Severambes, he artfully and intelligently described the sort of government and the form of the republic where all goods were held in common, so that there could not be even a residue of the least doubt of its possibility if only the hearts of men were not so conceited." Thomasius is referring to the social utopian book by Vayrasse, *The History of Severambes* (1672), but in the content of this and many other passages he goes beyond bourgeois natural law by means of the natural law of the revolutionary sects, with which Thomasius was well acquainted, and by means of the primitive communist goal they contained. And Thomasius does not describe the society of communal property in a utopian novel, but in his doctrine of ethics, a scholarly work that demonstrated the seriousness of the deduction current at that time. This was an act of great audacity, especially in Germany, the land where the peasant wars had hardly been forgotten; it was an audacity even if one recognized that it was Christian love that opened the way, and not revolt as in Münzer. "Bring love to the people first, and then the questions of property or of the community of goods will resolve themselves" (*On the Art of Loving Reasonably and Virtuously*, p. 310)—that is naive, but is it not true that this naiveté reaches up to Ludwig Feuerbach? Today the same type of person as Thomasius, in such a fundamentally altered situation, would no longer have recourse to the fiction of the Severambes. He would have an answer in the real attempts at the socialism of communal property; he would have half of the world as a model and as an answer to the question that refers to the public world—"what sort of shape would it have if there were no property?" Besides, for the man who drew the conclusion of real humanity from natural law this would not be a question; this is only a question, what Thomasius called a scruple, for those who "have been entangled in property" until their will and intellect have been enchained. For Thomasius, the innate fundamental right is the right to happiness; a true community should bring with it the whole of happiness without hindrance, and the basic means to this end is the abolition of property. But at the same time the images of happiness are discovered with those of virility, without the one ever being able to replace the other. Enough now on the Thomasian humanity, since it can be seen even in its bluntly lucid eclecticism and totality, in its lived basic right. In the German Enlightenment the career of happiness begins its run in Thomasius; it allies itself equally, as the examples have shown, with human pride and human worth.

Supplement

I

Advice that is perhaps not limited to the law students of that time

It is not to be denied that the study of law, as it is commonly taught at the universities, does not speak or teach of many things that it is quite necessary to know, and with much trouble and diligence teaches much about many other things that subsequently have little or no use in everyday life.

> *Summary outline of the basic doctrines that a law student needs to know and must learn at universities and according to which, God willing, Dr. Christian Thomasius is prepared to conduct his private lectures at Halle in four different colleges.*

II

A special selection from among all of the dying dedications given in the deep devotion with which seventeenth- and eighteenth-century authors had to present their works to princes or other persons in high places

Noble Baron, Gracious Lord.

I should indeed be hesitant to come to the court with my Socrates, in which there is no doubt that if he were still alive, he would probably serve as court jester because his *mores* are not in accord with the gallantry of the court. He certainly did have two virtues very necessary at the court, namely, that he tolerated with great patience insults that were leveled against him and that he was *interested* very little or not at all. Simply that he was so patient and on the one hand endured the abuses of his Xanthippe and other cross people without any ir-ritability, but on the other hand never once accepted the gifts that were spontaneously offered to him by his good friends or even sent them back without speaking of other circumstances. These are such things that are held to be very contrary to form and deemed laughable by the contemporary world.

And how should Socrates find *approbation* at the court, since he never was able to attract attention in the *universities?* I am especially sure that if he should be resurrected, his manner of teaching and living would be laughed at by everyone in the higher institutions of learning. He would find many Aristophaneses among us who in public spectacles would treat him as the worst possible *pedant.* Indeed he would have to condescend yet again as an *atheist* and disrupter of the common peace to drink the vial of poison, and it remains to be seen whether or not he would still find a faithful Plato or Xenophon who would have the audacity, as they once did, to defend his innocence.

However all this might be, a closer investigation of the circumstances would reveal the fault as not so much on the side of Socrates as on the side of the general degradation of the customs of our times. I do not want to touch this sore too harshly in part because such would cause more bitterness than improvement, and in part because such work on my part elsewhere has met with so little pleasure on the part of those who are so afflicted. This much is established, that Socrates was no *pedant* and that he was revered in his time by the most virtuous people of the state as a father and by the most famous sages of all sects as a leader. He did not hold regular hours in his teaching: He did not assign any seats to any listeners; rather he taught in public places, in archways and shacks, in which the people frequently gathered, and yet he did more damage to the Sophists of his time, and he led many more young people away from the detours of a hasty, illusory wisdom back to the path of true virtue as far as these can be attained by reason left to itself. He did this more than Plato, Zeno, Epicurus, Aristotle, or any of our contemporary sages have done. According to the praises of antiquity, he is the first to have brought down from the heavens the science of ethics, which was not respected at the time, but must be the basis of all honest philosophizing; he was therefore an intelligent *politician* and he instructed those who wanted to preside over the public affairs of Athens in what was most useful; indeed, he even gave useful counsel to *generals* on how to lead a war, as is sufficiently testified to by the memorable things that Xenophon has written of him.

> At the beginning of the difficult dedication "very humbly and obediently" given to his "most gracious Lord," Lord Dodo, Baron of Inn and Knyphausen, Lord at Lutzburg, Gennelt, and Helffte, Secret Counselor and President of the Court of His Excellency and Grace the Elector Prince of Brandenburg, on the occasion of the translation by Thomasius of Charpentier's Life of Socrates (1693). In accord with Tacitus's oft-quoted remark: "Socordiam eorum irridere licet qui praesenti potentia aevi temporis memoriam extinqui posse credunt" ("One can only laugh at the narrowness of spirit of those who believe that the power of the present can extinguish the memory of future times").

Index